PC Tools Deluxe™

Other Wiley Titles by Ruth Ashley and Judi Fernandez

PC DOS: A Self-Teaching Guide, 3rd Edition

PC DOS 4: A Self-Teaching Guide

Advanced Excel™

WordStar® *Professional Release 5*

Job Control Language, 2nd Edition

JCL for IBM® *VSE Systems*

PC Tools Deluxe™

An Essential Guide

Ruth Ashley
Judi N. Fernandez

John Wiley & Sons

New York • Chichester • Brisbane • Toronto • Singapore

Publisher: Therese A. Zak
Editor: Katherine Schowalter
Managing Editor: Ruth Greif
Design and Production: DuoTech, Inc.

This publication is designed to provide accurate and authoritative information in regard to the subject matter covered. It is sold with the understanding that the publisher is not engaged in rendering legal, accounting, or other professional service. If legal advice or other expert assistance is required, the services of a competent professional person should be sought. FROM A DECLARATION OF PRINCIPLES JOINTLY ADOPTED BY A COMMITTEE OF THE AMERICAN BAR ASSOCIATION AND A COMMITTEE OF PUBLISHERS.

Copyright © 1990 by John Wiley & Sons, Inc.

All rights reserved. Published simultaneously in Canada.

Reproduction or translation of any part of this work beyond that permitted by section 107 or 108 of the 1976 United States Copyright Act without the permission of the copyright owner is unlawful. Requests for permission or further information should be addressed to the Permission Department, John Wiley & Sons, Inc.

Library of Congress Cataloging-in-Publication Data

Ashley, Ruth.
    PC tools deluxe : an essential guide / Ruth Ashley and Judi N. Fernandez.
        p.   cm.
Includes bibliographical references.
ISBN 0-471-52476-X
    1. Utilities (Computer programs)   2. PC Tools (Computer program)
  I. Fernandez, Judi N., 1941– . II. Title.
QA76.76.U84A84 1990
005.369--dc20   90-31397
                                                                                      CIP

Printed in the United States of America
90 91 10 9 8 7 6 5 4 3 2 1

Trademarks

1-2-3 and Lotus are registered trademarks of Lotus Development Coporation.

CompuServe is a registered trademark of CompuServe Information Service.

Connection CoProcessor is a trademark of Intel Corporation.

dBASE is a registered trademark of Ashton Tate Corporation.

EasyLink is a registered trademark of Western Union Telegraph Corporation.

Epson is a registered trademark of Epson Corporation.

Hayes is a registered trademark of Hayes Microcomputer Products, Inc.

Hercules InColor is a trademark of Hercules Computer Technology.

IBM and Proprinter are registered trademarks of International Business Machines Corporation.

LapLink is a registered trademark of Traveling Software, Inc.

Laserjet is a trademark of the Hewlitt-Packard Corporation.

Microsoft Word and Excel are registered trademarks of Microsoft Corporation.

PC Tools, PC Tools Deluxe, PC Shell, Desktop, PC Backup, PC Cache, PC Secure, and Diskfix are all trademarks of Central Point Software, Inc.

SpectraFax is a registered trademark of SpectraFax Corporation.

WordPerfect is a registered trademark of WordPerfect Corporation.

WordStar is a registered trademark of MicroPro International Corporation.

Preface

PC Tools Deluxe™ is a powerful set of programs that give you mastery over your personal computer. They include PC Shell, which lets you control your directories and files, PC Tools Desktop Manager, which lets you create and edit files, databases, and macros as well as other features, and a set of utilities to protect and recover your disk data and manage file space more efficiently. Not only does PC Tools do more than DOS, it does it better, avoiding many of the pitfalls that DOS encounters. And PC Tools is easier to use than DOS, providing a full-screen graphic interface with mouse capability.

This book shows you how to use PC Tools to your best advantage. It goes beyond the documentation that comes with the package to show you not only what to do, but also what *not* to do and how to recover from problem situations. Numerous examples and exercises give you practical tips and experience for using the various programs included in the package.

The book is divided into four sections. Section I introduces PC Tools and shows you how to use the basic functions to manipulate PC Shell. Section II shows you how to use PC Shell to manage your files, directories, disks, and programs. In Section III, you will learn to use Desktop's word processing, database, calculators, appointment scheduler, macro editor, telecommunications, and utility programs. Section IV covers a variety of PC Tools programs that help you format, back up, restore, compress, secure, and rebuild disks. The utilities covered in Section IV help you make your computer system more efficient, as well as perform such routines tasks as format disks and back up files. You should read all of Sections I and II in order. You might want to skip some of the information in Sections III and IV. For example, if you do not plan to use Desktop's database facility, then you should skip Chapter 10.

Once you have used PC Tools to handle your day-to-day computer functions, you'll never be satisfied with DOS commands again.

Contents

Section I: Basic PC Shell Usage   1

Chapter 1: Introduction to PC Tools   3

Overview of PC Tools   3
Starting PC Shell   4
   Locating PC Shell Files   5
   PC Shell as a Stand-Alone Program   5
   PC Shell as a Resident Program   5
   Getting Out of PC Shell   6
PC Shell Startup Options   6
   Resident and Memory Options   7
   Monitor Control Options   8
   Resident Loading Options   9
   Mouse Control Options   9
The Main Shell Screen   10
   Upper Part   11
   Screen Windows   11
   Lower Part   12
   Using the Keyboard Keys   13
   Using the Mouse   14
   Getting Out of Trouble   14
Exiting PC Shell   15
Help Information   16
   Help Index   17
   Leaving Help   17
Scrolling   18
   Keyboard Scrolling   18
   Mouse Scrolling   18
Selecting Files   19
   Selecting with the Keyboard   20
   Selecting with the Mouse   20
   Selecting with a Global Filename   20
   Unselecting   22
File Size vs. Disk Space   22
Viewing the Rest of the Directory Entry   23

Chapter 2: Basic Menu Options and Dialog Boxes 25

Menu Overview 25
Using File Menu Options 27
    Viewing Files 28
    Rename a File 30
    Copy a File 31
    Moving Files 34
Deleting Files 35
    Clearing Files 36
Using Directory Maintenance Options 37
    Adding Directories 37
    Renaming a Directory 38
    Deleting a Directory 38
Undeleting Files and Subdirectories 39
    Using Delete Tracking 41
    Using the DOS Directory 42

Chapter 3: PC Shell Screen Management 45

Using Basic Options 45
    Displaying Windows 46
    Zooming a Window 47
Sizing and Moving Windows 47
    Using the Mouse 47
    Using the Menus 48
    Saving the New Configuration 48
    Forcing a Directory Re-Read 48
    Quick Run 49
Using the Setup Configuration Pop-Up Menu 49
    Controlling Screen Layout 50
    Setting Viewer Defaults 51
    User Levels 52
    Modifying the Screen Colors 52
    Changing the System Date and Time 53
Using the Modify Display Pop-Up Menu 53
    Selecting and Unselecting Files 54
    Displaying a Limited File List 54
    Displaying More File Information 55
    Rearranging the Directory List 56
    The Directory Sort Option 57
    List Displays 59

Section II: Using PC Tools Utilities   63

Chapter 4: File and Directory Utilities   65

Editing a File   65
    Editing an Existing File   66
    Creating a New File   66
    File Editor Screen   66
    Moving the Cursor   68
    Exiting the Editor   68
    Saving an Edited File   68
    Cut and Paste Operations   69
    Search and Replace Operations   71
Printing   73
    Printing a File   73
    Printing a Directory List   76
Locating Files   77
    Locating across Directories   77
    Modifying the File Locate Pop-Up Menu   79
    Finding Information in a File   80
Checking File Integrity   81
    Verifying Files   81
    Comparing Files   82
Attributes   83
    Examining File Attributes   84
    Changing File Attributes   84
    Changing Directory Attributes   85
Additional File Information   86
Directory Maintenance   87
    Pruning and Grafting   87
    Moving a Directory   88

Chapter 5: Disk and System Utilities   89

Rename Volume   89
Complete Disk Information   90
Copying a Diskette   91
    Disk Copy Principles   91
    Copy Disk Process   92
Comparing Two Diskettes   94
    Compare Disk Background   94
    Compare Disk Process   94

Verifying the Disk 95
    Verify Disk Process 95
Searching a Disk 96
    Search Disk Process 97
Parking the Disk 97
Complete Computer System Information 98
Mapping Disks and Files 99
    Disk Map 100
    File Map 101
Memory Information 101
    Memory Map 102
    The Memory Information Command 103

Chapter 6: Running Programs and Hexadecimal Processing   105

PC Shell as a Program Launcher 105
Running Programs under PC Shell 106
    From the Applications Menu 106
    From the DOS Command Line 106
    From the File List Window 107
    From the View Window 108
Modifying the Applications Menu 108
    Moving an Application 108
    Deleting an Application 108
    Adding or Editing an Application 109
Hexadecimal Manipulation 113
    Background Concepts 113
    Viewing The Hexadecimal Display 114
    Editing a Hexadecimal Screen 115
    Changing the Sector 116
    Editing and Viewing Files 117
    Undeletion Using Clusters 119

Section III: PC Tools Desktop Manager   125

Chapter 7: Notepads   127

Introduction to Desktop 127
Installing Desktop 129
Starting Desktop 129
    Starting Desktop in Stand-Alone Mode 129
    Starting Desktop in Residence Mode 129
    Startup Options 130

Manipulating Windows   131
    The Active Window   131
        Moving and Resizing Windows   132
        Changing Window Colors   132
Function Key Reminders   132
Notepads   133
    Starting Notepads   133
    The Notepad Window   134
    Printing   135
    Saving the File   136
    Autosave   137
    Exiting Notepads   138
    Cursor Movement and Scrolling   139
    Search and Replace   139
    Spell Checking   140
    Formatting the Screen and Printed Documents   142
    File Manipulation   146

Chapter 8: Outlines and Clipboard   *147*

Outlines   147
    Starting Outlines   148
    Creating a New Outline   149
    Editing an Outline   149
    Manipulating the Outline   150
Clipboard   153
    Using the Clipboard with Desktop Applications   153
    Viewing the Clipboard   155
    Editing the Clipboard Text   155
    Using the Clipboard with Non-Desktop Applications   156

Chapter 9: Appointment Scheduler   *159*

Introduction to Appointment Scheduler   159
    Starting Appointment Scheduler   160
Manipulating the Window   161
    System Date/Time vs. Current Date/Time   162
The To-Do List   162
    Adding a New To-Do Entry   163
    Attaching Notes to To-Do Entries   164
    Repeating Entries Yearly   164
    Editing or Deleting a To-Do Entry   164
Daily Appointment Schedule   165

Making an Appointment 166
Using the Alarm 168
Viewing an Attached Note 168
Editing and Deleting Appointments 168
Setting Automatic Actions 168
Running a Program 169
Loading a Notepad 169
Finding Appointments 170
Finding Free Time 171
Examining Your Time Usage 173
Personalizing Appointment Scheduler 173
Manipulating Schedule Files 175
Printing Your Schedule 175

Chapter 10: Databases   *177*

Database Structure 177
Creating a Database 178
Defining Fields 178
Edit vs. Browse Mode 179
Entering Data into the Database 180
Viewing Records 182
Handling an Existing Database 182
Adding Records 182
Deleting Records 182
Modifying the Database Structure 183
Formatting the Database 184
Creating a Column Format 184
Typical Row Format 186
Sample Form Letter 186
Applying the Format 187
Printing the Database 188
Working with a Subset 189
Hiding Records 189
Selecting Records 189
Searching for Records 191
Sorting Records 193
Copying Records to Another Database 193
Transferring Records 194
Appending Records 194
Interface with dBASE 194

Chapter 11: Telecommunications and Autodialer 197

Telecommunications 197
Modem Telecommunications 198
    Telecommunications Phone Directory 199
    Modem Setup 200
    The Telephone Directory File 200
    Placing a Straightforward Call 202
    Manual Dialing 203
    Using a Connected Service 203
    Terminating Connections 203
    Using the Central Point Software BBS 204
    Script Files 205
    Sending and Receiving Files 208
    ASCII Protocol 208
    XMODEM Protocol 209
    Telecommunications in the Background 210
Fax Telecommunications 211
    Configuring Fax Telecommunications 212
    Sending a Fax 212
    The FAX Log 213
Autodialer 214
    Number Criteria 214
    Configuring Autodialer 215
    Using Autodialer 216

Chapter 12: Utilities, Calculators, and Macros 219

Utilities 219
    Hotkey Selection 220
    ASCII Table 220
    System Menu/Window Colors 222
    Unload PCTOOLS Desktop 222
Calculators 223
    Algebraic Calculator 223
    Financial Calculator 227
    Programmer's Calculator 229
    Scientific Calculator 231
Macro Editor 233
    Working with the Macro Editor 233
    Macro Format 234
    Typing Key Names 235

Creating a Text-Only Macro 235
Activating Macro Files 236
Using Macros 237
Action Macros 237
Sample Macros 239
Special Macro Functions 240
Invoking Macros from Appointment Scheduler 245
Printer Macros 245
Nested Macros 246

Section IV: Disk Management and Recovery 247

Chapter 13: Formatting and Rebuilding Disks 249

Background Information 249
Formatting Disks 250
    During PC Shell Installation 250
Methods of Formatting Disks through PCFORMAT 251
    Making a Data Diskette from the Disk Menu 251
    Making a System Diskette 253
    Recovering from Format 253
    Formatting from the Applications Menu 253
    Formatting from the File List 255
    Formatting from the Command Prompt 255
The MIRROR Program 258
    Copying the System Area 259
    Establishing Delete Tracking 259
    Saving Partition Information 260
    Running Mirror Other Times 260
The REBUILD Program 261
    Rebuilding a Disk after Mirror 261
    Rebuilding a Disk with No Mirror Files 262
    REBUILD Parameters 262
Repairing a Disk 263
    Starting Diskfix 263
    Handling Errors 263
    The Diskfix Main Menu 264
    Fixing a Disk 264
    Media Surface Scan 266
    Revitalizing a Floppy Disk 266

Chapter 14: Backing up Files — 269

- Backing Up Files 269
  - Backup Decisions 270
  - Result of Backup 270
- Starting PC Backup 271
  - Configuring PC Backup 271
  - The PC Backup Screen 272
  - Changing the Configuration 273
  - Startup Parameters 275
- Backup Selection Decisions 276
  - Archive Attribute Methods 276
  - Limiting Files Selected for Backup 277
- PC Backup Options 278
  - Backup Method 278
  - Compress Options 279
  - Formatting during Backup 280
  - Error Correction during Backup 280
  - Verifying Data 280
  - Backup Reporting 281
  - Subdirectory Inclusion 281
  - Attribute Exclusion 282
  - Inclusion by Date Range 282
  - Saving the History File 282
  - Overwrite Warning 283
  - Time Display 283
- The Backup Procedure 284
  - Partial Backup 284
- Selecting Files 284
  - Choosing Directories on the Screen 285
  - Starting the Backup 285
- Permanent File Selection 286
  - Saving Your Backup Setup 287
  - Using a Saved Setup 287
- Comparing and Restoring Files 288
  - Comparing Backed Up Files 288
  - Full Restoration 290
  - Restoring the Files 290
  - Partial Restore 291
  - Restoration Problems 292
- Tape Backup Considerations 293

Chapter 15: Compressing Disks 295

Efficiency of File Access 295
    Fragmentation 296
    Identifying Fragmentation Outside of Compress 296
Running Compress 297
    Starting Compress 297
    The Analysis Menu 298
    The Sort Menu 302
    The Compress Menu 303
    Analyze Disk Organization 304
    Print Report 304
    Begin Compress 305
    COMPRESS Command Parameters 307

Chapter 16: File Security 311

PC Secure 311
    Outside the United States 312
    Types of Security 312
    General PC Secure Operation 313
    Key Considerations 313
Using PC Secure 314
    Start Up 315
    Using the Options Menu 316
    Encrypting a File 317
    Encrypting a Subdirectory 319
    Decrypting a File 320
    Decrypting a Subdirectory 321
    Additional Information 321
    Security without the Menus 321

Appendix: Installation Tips 325

Index 329

Section I

Basic PC Shell™ Usage

Chapter 1 | *Introduction to PC Tools*™

PC Tools Deluxe Version 6.0 includes many functions. This chapter will overview them and get you started using PC Shell. You will learn to:

- Start PC Shell in resident or stand-alone mode
- Exit PC Shell in resident or stand-alone mode
- Interpret the main PC Shell screen
- Use the keyboard with PC Tools
- Use a mouse with PC Tools
- Use the onscreen help system
- Scroll in PC Tools windows and boxes
- Select files
- Unselect files

Overview of PC Tools

PC Tools provides a comprehensive collection of services to help you manage your computer hardware, software, and data. It includes all the same facilities as DOS, your standard operating system, plus much, much, more. While some people use PC Tools as an extension of DOS, most rely primarily on PC Tools, relegating DOS to the back burner. Version 6.0 provides access to the DOS prompt while it is running.

PC Tools is made up of four sets of programs: DOS Utilities, Data Recovery Utilities, Desktop Manager, and Hard Disk Backup. All except Desktop

Manager are accessed through the PC Shell program. All use a similar screen interface; you control it with a mouse or the keyboard, making menu selections as needed.

DOS Utilities: These programs let you manipulate files, directories, and programs. They include all the standard DOS functions, such as copying files and making new directories, as well as many functions DOS never heard of, such as verifying the readability of all the files on a disk and searching through all the subdirectories on a disk to find a particular filename.

Data Recovery Utilities: Going way beyond DOS capabilities, PC Shell includes a set of programs that protect you against accidental loss of data on the hard disk, speed up disk access, correct file fragmentation, and protect sensitive files from prying eyes. Also included in this group is the PC Tools version of FORMAT, which works differently from the DOS formatting program; it allows you to recover data from a formatted disk.

Desktop Manager: These programs include a word processor, a database manager, an outliner, an appointment scheduler, a telecommunications system, a clipboard editor, several calculators, and more.

Hard Disk Backup: The standard DOS backup and restore facilities have many problems. PC Tools includes a hard disk backup facility that is faster, more reliable, and more powerful than the DOS one.

If PC Tools is not yet installed on your computer, refer to Appendix A for some helpful hints, then follow the instructions in the documentation and on the screen.

Starting PC Shell

PC Shell can run as a stand-alone program or as a resident program. As a stand-alone program, you start it by typing a command at the DOS command prompt, use it as needed to accomplish your current tasks, then terminate it and return to the command prompt where you can start up some other program. As a resident program, it stays in memory and is available to you at all times, even when you are using some other program such as your spreadsheet system or desktop publisher. To use resident PC Shell, you press a special hotkey to switch to PC Shell, accomplish the necessary tasks, then press the same hotkey to exit PC Shell and return to your previous function. PC Shell works and looks the same in both modes, and all of its features are available.

Locating PC Shell Files

All the PC Shell files and DOS files must be available when you start up and use PC Shell. If the files are in the current directory, the system will find them. If not, then you must tell PC Shell where they are by including the correct directory names in the system's search path. (The search path is a list of directories where the system looks to find files it needs.) If you followed the installation instructions in the documentation, the search path has been set up to include the directory that contains the PC Tools programs. To check, type PATH at the DOS prompt and see if the name of the directory containing the PC Tools programs (usually PCTOOLS or PCT6-0) appears in the response. If not, enter CD \PCTOOLS (use the appropriate directory name) at the command prompt before starting the PC Tools program.

PC Shell as a Stand-Alone Program

A stand-alone program must be started with a command at the DOS prompt. The DOS and Data Recovery Utilities portions of PC Tools are included in the program referred to as PC Shell. Start it with the command PCSHELL at the DOS prompt. If DOS can find the program, it will start.

PC Shell as a Resident Program

If you want to be able to use the PC Tools utilities from within another program, such as your word processor, spreadsheet, or accounting package, you need to make PC Shell resident. If you specified this option when you installed PC Tools, it is already set up for you. During your boot procedure, while processing the AUTOEXEC.BAT file, DOS executes the command to make PC Shell resident. When you make a program resident, DOS runs it briefly and terminates it, and the program stays in memory. Such programs are often called TSR programs for "Terminate and Stay Resident".

You can make PC Shell resident from the keyboard. Just type PCSHELL /R at the DOS prompt. You'll see a message telling you how to access PC Shell, then the DOS command prompt returns. Once the program is established as resident, you can start it at the DOS prompt or within any running program by pressing a special key; this is referred to as hotkeying into PC Shell. When you press the hotkey, DOS saves the current status of memory and the screen, then brings up PC Shell just as it was the last time you left it.

The default hotkey for starting the resident PC Shell is Ctrl-Esc; you hold down the Control key and press Escape, then release both. If the application software you use has some other function for the Ctrl-Esc key combination, you can use a special option in the PCSHELL command to set some other hotkey. While you are using PC Shell as a resident program, you use the same hotkey to exit it and return to the previous screen.

Resident PC Shell takes up memory space that you might need for some other applications. If you want to remove all PC Tools programs from memory, canceling the resident qualities, enter the KILL command at the DOS prompt. This frees up all the memory associated with the PC Shell. After you enter the KILL command, the hotkey no longer works. If you want to use PC Shell again, you have to enter either the PCSHELL or PCSHELL /R command.

Getting Out of PC Shell

If you can't hotkey out of the shell, you can exit it and return to the DOS prompt by pressing the Esc key. When you see a box asking if you really want to exit, type X and the shell is terminated.

✧ Try It Out

Throughout this book you will encounter "Try It Out" sections, which encourage you to use your computer to try the techniques you have just read about. Take the time to go to your computer and follow the suggestions given to you. You will learn a lot more about PC Tools by working with them at the computer than by just reading about them. If you follow the guidelines in sequence, your introduction to PC Tools will be fairly easy. If you wait until you finish a chapter or even longer, you may find that you have too much to try out at once.

1. If PC Shell is currently on the screen, exit it.
2. Enter the KILL command to kill the shell if it is resident.
3. Start up PC Shell as a stand-alone program.
4. Exit the shell.
5. Start up PC Shell as a resident program.
6. Exit the shell and kill it.

If you had any trouble in this exercise, the options in the next section might help.

PC Shell Startup Options

If you have any problems starting up or using PC Shell, you may be able to benefit from one or more of the startup options. The PC Shell options can be used in any combination. Be sure to use only options that are appropriate to your hardware configuration. If you want to try a different option with a resident PC Shell, enter KILL at the command prompt to eliminate the current residency, then start it again with the desired option. If the PCSHELL command is included in your AUTOEXEC.BAT file, you can edit it to include additional options.

Normally, the first time you start up PC Shell, it reads the directory for the current drive and stores it in a special file (PCSHELLC.TRE for drive C). When you start up again, it saves time by reading from that file instead of the drive. If you want PC Shell to make a different drive current at startup, include the drivename in the command, as in PCSHELL A:.

If you want to force PC Shell to re-read the directory from the disk more often, you can use the /TR*n* option. The command PCSHELL /TR0 causes it to be read every time PC Shell is started. The parameter /TR2 causes it to be read every two days, or as soon thereafter as PC Shell is started again. You'll need to use this option in your AUTOEXEC.BAT file if you perform many operations outside of PC Shell that affect the directory.

Resident and Memory Options

When you make PC Shell resident, you can tell it how much memory to occupy when not in use. The more space you give to the inactive shell, the quicker it can start up and terminate, but it might be robbing memory space from other applications, slowing them down or even immobilizing them. If you find this to be the case in your system, cut down on the amount of space you give to the inactive PC Shell.

Table 1.1 shows the resident memory options and the approximate amount of space each requires when it is not active. Options that appear on the same line are synonyms. For example, to put PC Shell in residence and assign 117K of resident memory to it, you would enter PCSHELL /RS or PCSHELL /RSMALL at the DOS command prompt.

Table 1.1   Resident Memory Requirements

Command	Short form	Approximate memory
/RTINY	/RT or /R	10K
/RSMALL	/RS	117K
/RMEDIUM	/RM	155K
/RLARGE	/RL	235K

In most cases, start out with the smallest size by specifying /R, and increase it only if you have problems. If you have expanded memory, you can safely use the maximum amount, represented by /RL. PC Shell will use expanded memory for much of its storage rather than conventional memory.

When the resident shell is active, it uses about 200K of memory. You can use the /A*n* option to use less memory (down to 180K) or more memory (up to your total memory minus about 200K, depending on what other memory requirements your system has). If the shell has more memory available, it can perform certain operations, in particular single-drive disk copies, more efficiently. Unless you do a lot of single-drive disk copies, the default memory allocation is just fine. Suppose you want to give the shell 440K. You would start it up with the following command:

```
PCSHELL /R /A440
```

Disk space is crucial in both stand-alone and resident operation. PC Shell uses various existing files and creates others; it must have a place to store and manipulate these files. It normally uses the default drive for file storage. If you have expanded memory, one file may be loaded into it automatically, saving some disk space. You can speed up operation by telling PC Shell to use a RAM drive instead, if you have one large enough.

The file sizes depend on several factors, including where you hotkey from, the type of monitor, and the inactive resident memory space. If you don't have enough space for the necessary files on the designated drive, whether real or imaginary, the shell won't run. In general, you need more disk storage space if less of PC Shell is in memory. If you use the smallest amount of memory (/R) for the inactive program, have a VGA monitor, and hotkey into it from within other programs, you would need at least 600K of disk space to store all the files.

You can use the /O*d* option to specify a nondefault drive to hold the PC Shell files. The command PCSHELL /R /OF tells DOS to make PC Shell resident, occupying the smallest amount of memory while not in use, and to store its files on drive F (which is probably a RAM drive).

Monitor Control Options

PC Shell offers several options that may improve monitor performance. If you have a color card and a monochrome monitor, try loading PC Shell with the /BW option. To make PC Shell resident, enter PCSHELL /R /BW. You can decide if the display is better with or without the /BW option.

If screen response is very slow on your CGA monitor and the snow isn't too bad, you might try the /FF (flicker free) option. This disables snow suppression features that are built into PC Shell. It speeds up screen response and scrolling but may result in an unacceptable amount of snow and an increased amount of flickering. If you have a CGA monitor, you can try PC Shell with and without the /FF option to see which you prefer.

If your system has a Hercules InColor™ card and a color monitor, PC Shell as a stand-alone program uses color just fine. If you use it resident, however, the shell will come up in black and white. To force PC Shell to use colors in resident mode, you have to use the /IN option. The command PCSHELL /R /IN makes PC Shell resident and requests color from the InColor card.

If your system has a VGA monitor that can handle 350-line resolution, you can use the /350 option. This makes some of the background and features of the screen clearer, but it may make the entire screen a bit smaller. You'll have to experiment to see if you like the effect.

If your system has an LCD screen, as many laptop computers do, use the /LCD parameter so that it can handle colors.

Resident Loading Options

When you hotkey into PC Shell, DOS saves the status of the current program in a disk file. This is essential when you hotkey from an application program so that you can return to that application at the point you left it. Since the status of the DOS prompt isn't important, PC Tools saves time when hotkeying from the prompt by not saving its status. However, you can use the /DQ option to disable the quickload process, causing the status of the DOS prompt to be saved. This causes the shell to load more slowly. Try this option only if you are having trouble hotkeying back and forth between PC Shell and the DOS prompt.

If any of your application programs use the designated hotkey (Ctrl-Esc) for some other purpose, you can change the hotkey combination in the PCSHELL command. The option /Fn sets up the specified function key (from F1 to F10) to work in place of the Escape key. If you use PCSHELL /R /F9, you would use Ctrl-F9 as the hotkey into and out of the shell.

Mouse Control Options

If your mouse works with other software, it will probably work with PC Shell. A mouse with older software, however, may not work in resident mode. Call the technical support people at Central Point Software if you have problems. They may advise you to upgrade the mouse driver. In any event, the mouse should work just fine when PC Shell is used as a stand-alone program.

In some situations, the mouse works fine in the hotkeyed shell but not when you return to the application program. While upgrading the mouse driver can solve this problem, you can also just cancel the mouse in the shell so that it will work in the application. The /IM command leaves the mouse functional in the application software but disabled in the resident shell.

If you use your mouse with the right hand, the left button (under your index finger) is the primary button. If you use the mouse with your left hand, you can use the /LE option to exchange the button effects so that the right button (under the left index finger) has the same functions. For two-button operations, both buttons are reversed if you started the shell with the /LE option.

If your mouse does not reappear when you reenter the shell from an application, use /PS2 to reset the mouse when you start PCSHELL again.

The Main Shell Screen

The main shell screen appears on your monitor when you enter PC Shell. Exactly which components are present depends on how it has been set up. Figure 1.1 shows how the screen appears immediately following installation.

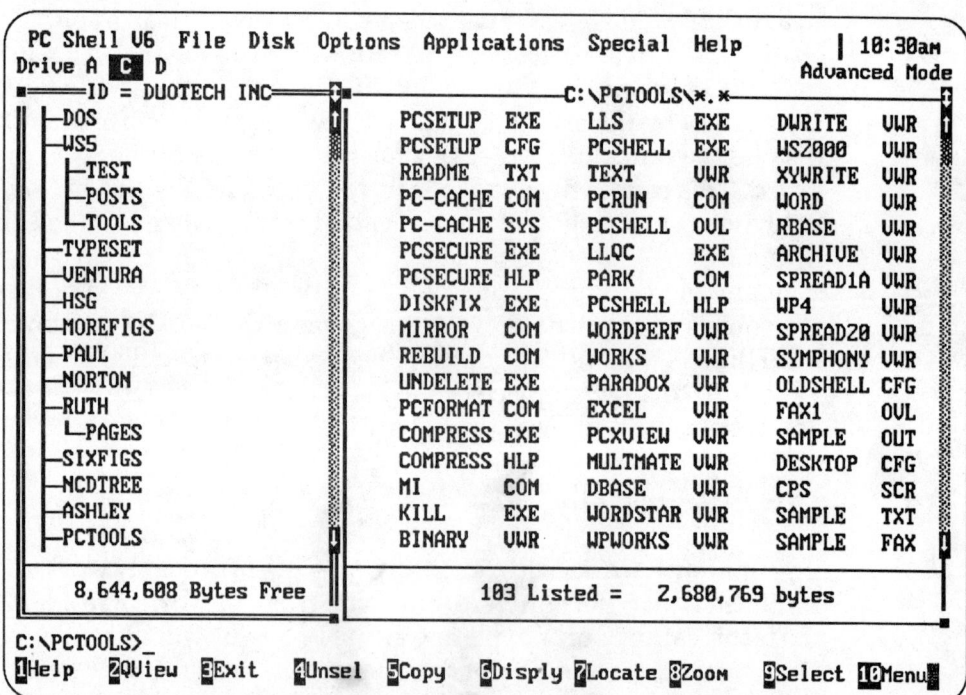

Figure 1.1   PC Shell Main Screen

Your screen might look somewhat different. It may be set up to show only the applications that are available. It could include a view window. It might have a line of shortcut keys instead of the DOS command prompt. This section covers the details of the screen and shows how you can move from one part to another using both the keyboard and the mouse.

Upper Part

The top line is the menu bar. At the very left is the program name (**PC Shell**) followed by the names of menus. On this screen, **File, Disk, Options, Applications,** and **Special** represent menus that you can select. **Help** gives you immediate information. If the menu bar is active, one of the menu names will be highlighted. Each can be pulled down to a full menu from which you can select options. The menu bar shows the current time on the right.

The next line of the screen shows the valid drive names in your system. In the example, drives A, C, and D are available. The current drive is always highlighted in this line. On the right you can see the current user mode: Advanced, Intermediate, or Beginner.

All PC Shell options are available in Advanced Mode, fewer in Intermediate Mode, and only the basic options in Beginner Mode. This book deals with Advanced Mode in order to cover all the options. If your setup uses a lower level, you can change it later.

PC Shell can also be set up for use primarily in running programs. In that case, it comes up with the **Applications** menu pulled down, ready for you to select a program and run it. Pressing F10 switches to a standard mode.

Screen Windows

The bulk of the screen is occupied by windows. A tree window shows the directory structure of the current drive and a file list window lists the files in that directory. It may also include a view window that shows the current file, depending on the display configuration. Only one of the windows is active at a time. The active window is surrounded by a double border, like the tree window in the figure.

Each window has the same general layout. A small box in the upper left is called the close box. Clicking on this box with the mouse closes the window. The small box in the lower right can be used for resizing the window. The double headed arrow in the upper right lets you zoom the window so it fills most of the screen; clicking on it again restores the former size. All these functions can also be achieved through menu selections with the keyboard; you'll learn to use them, and the scroll bars on the right of each window, later.

Tree Window. The tree window contains a tree diagram showing the directory structure of the current drive. The volume label is shown in the top border. On networks, the tree shows only the directories to which you have at least read access. The current directory is highlighted when you start up PC Shell. Below the tree window, the amount of free space on the drive is shown.

File List Window. The file list window lists the files in the current directory. The top border shows the directory path and current list criteria; *.* means that all files in the directory are listed. One file is highlighted at a time. The file list window always shows the files contained in the directory highlighted in the tree window. Below the filenames, you can see how many files are listed and how much space they occupy.

View Window. The main screen can also include a view window, which shows the contents of the highlighted file. The view window can appear below the tree and file list windows, in which case they are shortened. Or it can appear on the right, occupying two-thirds of the screen; in that case, the tree and file list windows are on the left, one above the other. The view window is covered later.

Lower Part

The line below the windows can be blank, or it can contain either a DOS prompt for use in typing DOS commands from within the shell or a line showing shortcut keys that you can use. If your screen shows the DOS prompt, you can type any DOS command there. The screen clears, your command is executed, you are prompted to press a key or click a mouse button, and then the PC Shell screen returns. When the DOS prompt is present, any characters you type appear there.

If the shortcut keys appear, they replace the DOS command line; these predefined keys are shown in Figure 1.2. They let you use a single keystroke to achieve an effect instead of going through the menus from the top of the screen. One letter in each word is highlighted; you can just click on it or press that letter to cause the command to take effect. Most of these commands operate on the selected file. We won't cover the shortcuts separately, but you'll see how to use all the commands from menus.

Copy **M**ove Dele**t**e **R**ename **V**iew He**X**Edit F**i**nd **P**rint **L**ocate File**E**dit **U**ndelete **Z**oom

Figure 1.2   Shortcut Keys Line

The bottom screen line displays either function key numbers and their effects for the current screen or a message to you from PC Shell. When a menu is highlighted or a command selected, you'll see a message. Normally, you'll see the function key values. You can click on the value or press the function key to get the effect. On all screens, F1 gets help, F3 exits the system, and F10 activates the menu bar. You can change the other key settings to meet your needs. The function keys are effective even when the reminders are replaced by a message.

Using the Keyboard Keys

You can use keyboard keys to activate any part of the PC Shell screen. The Tab key causes the active window to switch among the tree and file list windows; it also includes the view window if present.

When a window is active (has a double border), pressing the up or down arrow key highlights the previous or next item in the list. The PageUp and PageDown keys move the highlight a larger amount, depending on the window. Home selects the first line of the contents, whether it is a directory, a filename, or a line of a file. End similarly selects the last line.

If the tree window is active, changing the highlighted directory causes the File List to change to show files in the highlighted directory; the contents of a view window change as well. If the file list window is active, moving the highlight does not select files; you have to press Enter when the file name is highlighted to select the file. A number appears next to a file name when it is selected.

You can press F10 (from the bottom line) to make the menu bar active, then use the right and left arrows to highlight the menu name you want; press Enter when the one you want is highlighted. If the DOS command line is present, you can press the Alt key and the first letter of the menu you want; that menu is automatically pulled down on the screen. If the shortcut keys are displayed, just pressing the first letter of the menu name pulls it down. You can change the displayed menu by pressing the right or left arrow key. You can remove a menu without making a selection by pressing Escape.

To change the current drive, press the Control key and the drive letter. To make drive A current, for example, press Ctrl-A. The contents of all the displayed windows change to reflect the new current drive.

To select a command from the shortcut line when it is displayed, press the highlighted letter. You may have to select a file first, however. To enter a command at the DOS prompt, just type it. Any characters you type appear there; they are processed when you press Enter. To use one of the function keys displayed on the message line, just press it.

Using the Mouse

You can use the mouse to activate any part of the PC Shell screen even more easily. When you bring up the shell, you'll see the mouse cursor in the middle of the screen. It takes the form of a rectangle. Move the mouse; you'll notice that the mouse cursor moves with it. Common mouse terms have the same meaning in PC Shell as in other mouse-oriented software. Pointing means positioning the mouse cursor on the screen item you want to affect. Clicking means pressing and releasing the button under your index finger. Dragging means moving the mouse cursor while holding down the button. PC Shell relies mostly on the left button, with just a few operations where the right button has an effect. You can switch the button effects with the /LE parameter when you start PC Shell.

You can change the selected directory by pointing to a different one and clicking; it will be highlighted and the file list will change to match the selected directory. You can select a file by pointing to it and clicking. A number appears next to a file name when it is selected. When using the mouse to select files or a directory, it doesn't matter which window is active. You can use the window scroll bar by clicking on the up or down arrow at the end for single line moves or by dragging the highlight for larger ones.

To pull down a menu, point to it and click. The menu will appear immediately. You can click on another menu to change menus. You can remove a menu without making a selection by clicking outside the menu. To change the current drive, simply click on the one you want. The displayed windows change to reflect the new drive.

Similarly, you can use any of the displayed commands or function keys in the bottom row by pointing and clicking. You'll have to use the keyboard to enter DOS commands, of course.

Getting Out of Trouble

When you are using a new program such as PC Tools, you may get a box, a message, or a menu onscreen that you don't particularly want. If it includes a choice of EXIT, make that choice by pressing the highlighted letter or clicking on it. If not, try pressing the Escape key. If you press Escape and nothing happens, check the message line. If you don't see an explanation, press it again. If you are using the mouse, click on the close box (upper left corner) to eliminate the box without causing anything else to happen. If you can't get rid of a box, try pressing F1 to see if the help text gives you any clues. In virtually all cases, the EXIT option, the close box, or the Escape key gets you out of trouble without doing any damage.

Exiting PC Shell

Getting out of PC Shell is easy. If you hotkeyed in, you can hotkey out or select an exit option. You can also exit it with Esc or F3. If you entered PC Tools as a stand-alone program, just select the command to exit. If you have a mouse, you can click on **3Exit** in the bottom line. If you didn't hotkey in, the result of trying to exit is a dialog box like the one shown in Figure 1.3. This is a message dialog box; it doesn't ask you do anything except make a selection.

You treat all message dialog boxes you'll encounter the same way. Just read the information and select the button that represents your choice. In this box, you have a choice. When you select EXIT by typing X or clicking on it, PC Tools is terminated and you are returned to the command prompt. If you select CONTINUE by clicking on it or typing C, the dialog box disappears and you continue in PC Shell as before. If you press Escape or click on the close box, it has the same effect as selecting CONTINUE; you'll remain in the shell. Certain changes you may have made cause the choice of saving to be included in the dialog box. If you want to save any changes, select SAVE when the exit dialog box appears.

✧ Try It Out

1. Start up the shell in either mode.
2. Examine the screen layout. If your screen shows a view window remove it by following these instructions: Press Alt-O to pull down the **Options** menu; press V to turn off the view window; the menu and the view window disappear. If the screen shows only a pulled down **Applications** menu, press F10.
3. Use either the mouse or the Tab key to change the active window.
4. Change the highlighted directory and watch the file list change.
5. Change the drive and watch both the file list and the tree window change. If you see a message box indicating that the drive isn't ready, insert a diskette and select RETRY.

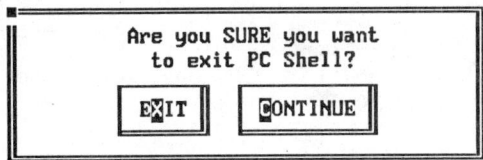

Figure 1.3   Message Dialog Box—Exit

6. Pull down and release various menus. Notice the messages that appear on the message line when a menu is pulled down.
7. Exit the shell. If a dialog box asks if you want to save the changes, select SAVE so your changes aren't lost.

If any strange dialog boxes appear during this exercise, get rid of them by selecting the EXIT option, pressing Escape, or clicking on the close box.

Help Information

PC Tools has an extensive online help system, accessed through **Help** on the menu bar, by pressing F1, or by selecting **1Help** on the bottom line.

You can get help from the menu bar by clicking on **Help** or by pressing Alt-H. It has the same effect as pressing F1; both give you a **Help** dialog box. This help is context sensitive; that means it is related to whatever area or command is active at the time. Figure 1.4 shows the result of selecting **Help** or pressing F1 when the tree window is active. The dialog box shows the title **Tree Window Help**. When you're finished reading the information, select EXIT to remove the help box. Alternatively, you can press Esc or click on the close box to remove it.

Help information appears in message dialog boxes that may hold more text than appears on the screen. The scroll bar on the right includes a highlight that indicates where the displayed text appears in the complete set of information. You can see later text by pressing up and down arrow keys to move one line at a time or PageUp and PageDown to move one boxful at a time. With the mouse you can scroll by clicking on the arrows at the top and bottom of the scroll bar or by dragging the highlight in the bar.

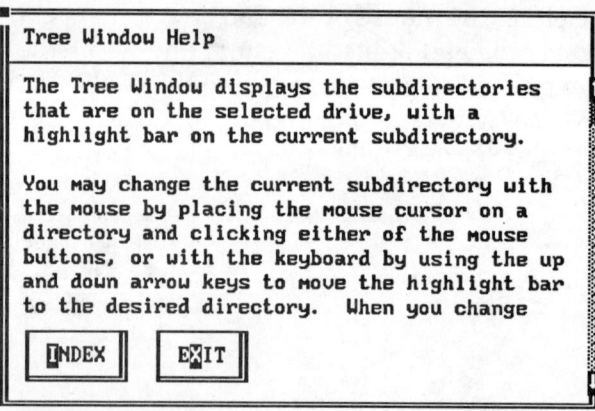

Figure 1.4   Help Dialog Box

Help Index

You can access the Help Index from the **Help** menu or by selecting INDEX in any help dialog box. The result is a dialog box like the one shown in Figure 1.5. The Help Index includes at least 50 items, each of which takes you directly to a Help dialog box for the topic specified. The topics are not in alphabetical order; they are sequenced by screens or menus from which you might want to access that information.

You can scroll or page through the index to see the contents. To select an item and see its Help box, you highlight it and press Enter or click on it. From the resulting dialog box, you can either exit to the main screen or return to the Help Index.

Leaving Help

You can leave Help from the keyboard by selecting EXIT, by clicking on the close box, by pressing F3, or by pressing Escape. If you have a mouse, you select the EXIT button by clicking on it; if you use the keyboard, just type the highlighted letter.

✧ Try It Out

1. Start PC Shell and get help from the opening screen. You should see help information about the main screen.
2. Check out the Help Index. A list of topics should appear. Scroll or page through the entire list.

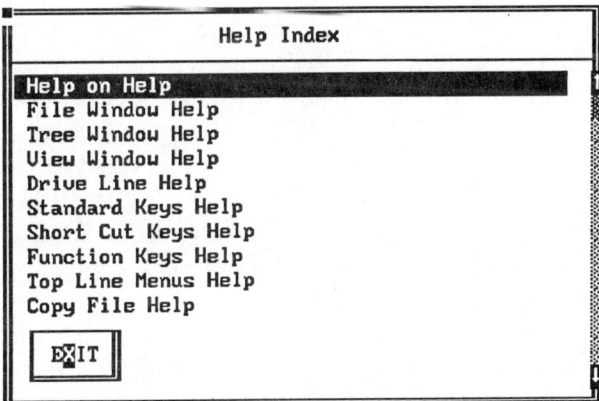

Figure 1.5   Help Index

3. Select "Help on Help" and read the resulting information.
4. Remove the Help box.

Scrolling

You can scroll in any dialog box or window that contains more text than shows at one time, as in Help dialog boxes. Many directories contain more files than will display at once so you will need to scroll to see all the filenames. The PC Tools directory, for one, contains more files than can be shown on the screen.

Keyboard Scrolling

With the keyboard, you can scroll by using the arrow keys. The highlight moves one filename in the direction of the arrow. When it is positioned on the lower right filename, pressing down arrow scrolls down, displaying the next filename. When the highlight is at the upper left filename, pressing the up arrow reveals the previous filename, if there is one.

You can use PageUp and PageDown to scroll in larger increments in the indicated direction; it's about a half page in the tree window and to the next column in the file list window. The End key scrolls to the end of the text, displaying it in the window and highlighting the last filename in the file list window. The Home key scrolls to the beginning of the text, displaying it in the window and highlighting the first filename in the file list window.

Mouse Scrolling

The scroll bar on the right of a window helps you to perform scrolling quickly and easily with a mouse. To scroll the display one line at a time, click on the top or bottom arrow, depending on which way you want to scroll. To cause a continuous scroll, keep the button depressed after clicking on a scroll arrow. To scroll in larger increments, you can point the mouse at the highlight on the scroll bar and drag it in the direction you want the scroll to occur. If you drag it to the top or bottom of the bar, you'll see the first or last part of the file list. You can also click on any position in the scroll bar. The highlight will jump to that position. If a horizontal scroll bar is present, it works the same way.

You can also scroll within a window by using the opposite mouse button. Point the mouse anywhere in the window. Then press the right button (if you haven't reversed them with /LE) and drag the mouse toward the top or bottom of the window. When you reach the border, the text will begin to scroll. Release the button to stop the scroll.

Selecting Files

If no files are selected and a single file is highlighted, PC Shell often considers that file selected. Usually, however, you must select files from the File List before you can operate on them with any commands. You can select one or more files for most operations. For example, suppose you want to copy three files to a diskette. You first select the three files, then use the **Copy File** option. If you want to view the contents of a file when the view window isn't displayed, you first select it, then use the **Quick File View** option. If you want to delete a group of files, you select them in the file list window, then use the **Delete File** option. The next chapter covers these functions.

A highlighted filename is considered selected only if no other file is selected. When a filename is selected, a number appears to its left. The numbers are sequential. If one file is selected, it is numbered 1. If three are selected, as in Figure 1.6, they are numbered 1, 2, and 3 in the order in which they are selected. They will be processed by PC Shell in that sequence.

The number of files selected appears at the bottom of the file list window, replacing the number of files listed. PC Shell adjusts this every time you select or unselect a file. Selection is a toggle function; the same process that selects a file unselects it if repeated.

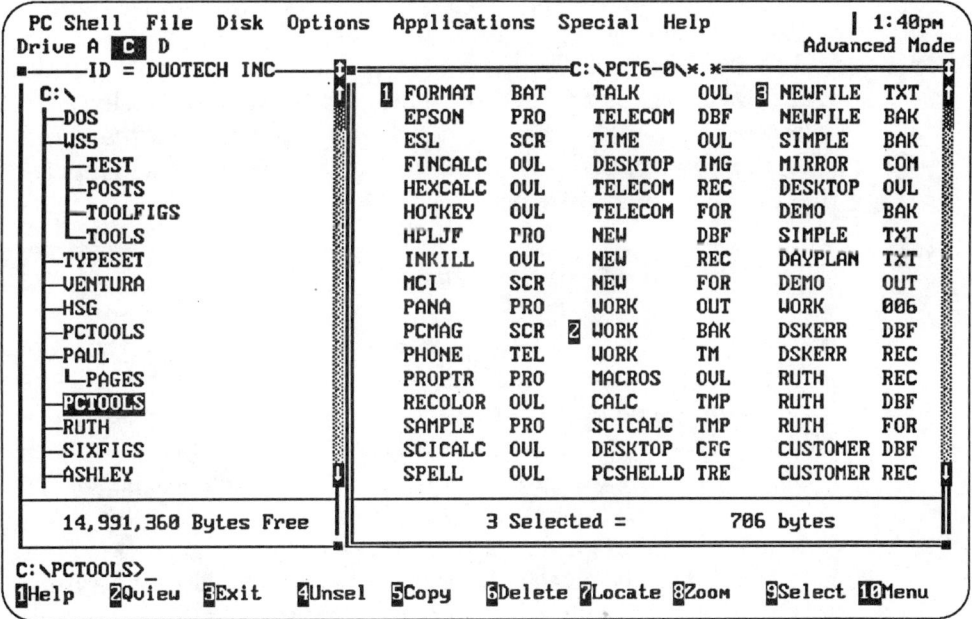

Figure 1.6   Individually Selected Files

Selecting with the Keyboard

To select a file from the keyboard, move the highlight to the filename with the arrow keys, then press Enter. The selection number appears in front of that filename and the highlight moves to the next name. You can then move the highlight to the next file you want to select and press Enter. If you highlight a selected file and press Enter, it is unselected; the number disappears. Other selection numbers are adjusted as necessary.

Selecting with the Mouse

You can select a file with the mouse by pointing to the filename and clicking. The selection number appears immediately. You can continue to select other files as needed. To unselect a file, point to it again and click. The number disappears.

You can select multiple filenames that are displayed in sequence by using two mouse buttons. Point to the first file you want to select, then press and hold the right button down. Then press the left button and drag the mouse over the adjacent files you want to select. When they are all selected, release both buttons. Use the opposite buttons if you reversed the effects with /LE. (If you press the left button first or both buttons together, you will trigger the copy function instead of the group selection function. Simply release the buttons to clear the copy function.)

You can unselect files by dragging in the same way. If the filenames over which the mouse is dragged are selected, they will be unselected. If they aren't selected, they will be. If you drag over a mixture of selected and unselected files, the status of the first file in the group determines whether the remaining files are selected or unselected.

Selecting with a Global Filename

Just as you can use a global filename in DOS, you can indicate a group of files to be selected by specifying a global filename. To do this, click on **9Select** in the bottom screen line or press F9. You'll see the dialog box shown in Figure 1.7. The dialog box shows the current global filename and allows you to change it. The default global filename is *.*, which selects all files. Close the box without choosing SELECT to prevent selection.

The cursor starts in the **Name=** field. You can type up to eight characters here to correspond to the eight-character name field. The symbol * matches any filename. The value ???????? also matches any filename. A value such as PC* matches any filename beginning with PC. A value such as P? matches any

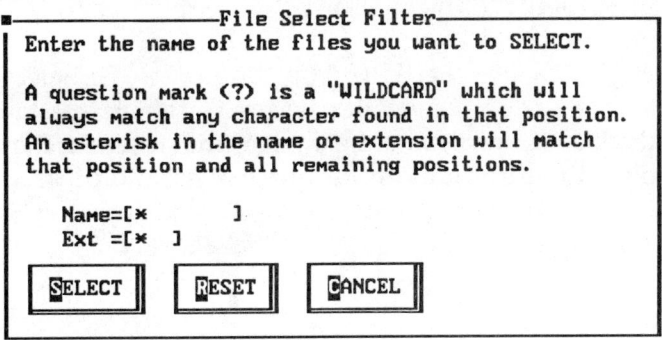

Figure 1.7   File Select Filter Dialog Box

two-character filename beginning with P. A value such as TO??4 matches any five-character filename beginning with TO and ending with 4.

After you type a period (.) or press Enter, you can type a global extension indicator in the **EXT=** field. The default * matches any extension. If you press Delete to erase the * and leave this field blank, you will get only filenames that have no extension. If you want to select files with extension BAT, you would type BAT in this field.

Once both fields are correct, the SELECT button will select files based on your values. Figure 1.8 shows the result of selecting when **Name=PC*** and **Ext=***. Every file that matches the global filename is selected. The number of

```
===============C:\PCT6-0\*.*===============
     ARCHIVE  VWR    SHEETZ0   VWR    CPS       SCR
     INSTALL  BAT    SYMPHONY  VWR    CSMAIL    SCR
     KILL     EXE    TEXT      VWR    DBMS      OVL
     ASCII    OVL    WORD      VWR    DESKTOP   EXE
  1  PCSHELLC TRE    WORDPERF  VWR    DESKTOP   HLP
  2  PCRUN    COM    WORDSTAR  VWR    DICT      SPL
  3  PCSHELL  CFG    WORKS     VWR    FORMAT    BAT
  4  PCSHELL  EXE    WP4       VWR    EPSON     PRO
  5  PCSHELL  OVL    WPWORKS   VWR    ESL       SCR
     BINARY   VWR    WS2000    VWR    FINCALC   OVL
     DBASE    VWR    XYWRITE   VWR    HEXCALC   OVL
     DWRITE   VWR    LLQC      EXE    HOTKEY    OVL
     EXCEL    VWR    LLQCSERV  EXE    HPLJF     PRO
     MULTMATE VWR    MI        COM    INKILL    OVL
     PARADOX  VWR    BACKTALK  EXE    MCI       SCR
     RBASE    VWR    CALC      OVL    PANA      PRO
     SHEET1A  VWR    CIS       SCR  6 PCMAG     SCR
     ──────────────────────────────────────────
             7 Selected =    373,254 bytes
```

Figure 1.8   Result of Selection of PC*.*

files selected and the amount of space they occupy on disk are shown at the bottom of the window.

If you choose the RESET button in the File Select Filter dialog box, the default filter of *.*, which selects all files, is reestablished. If you choose CANCEL, click on the close box, or press Escape, the dialog box is removed and no file selection is performed.

Unselecting

As you've seen, you can unselect any selected filename by repeating the selection of that file. You can also click on **4Unsel** in the bottom line or press F4 to unselect all selected files.

✧ Try It Out

1. Display the file list for the PC Tools directory.
2. If you have a mouse, scroll down line by line. Then scroll down by dragging the highlight. Scroll up by clicking on the scroll bar. Scroll up and down using the opposite button.
3. Scroll down line by line using the arrow keys. Scroll by page. Use the Home key to jump back to the beginning.
4. Select any five files, not in sequence. Unselect three of them.
5. If you have a mouse, select a column of files by dragging. Unselect them again.
6. Select all the files with the EXE extension.
7. Unselect all files using F4.

File Size vs. Disk Space

As you select files, the number of bytes they contain is displayed on the status line. The amount displayed is usually smaller than the amount of space they take up on disk. Disk space is allotted to files in chunks, called allocation units. If a file takes up less than an allocation unit, the whole unit is still reserved for the file. Thus, a one-byte file might occupy 2048 bytes on a hard disk or 512 bytes on a diskette. Therefore, you cannot be guided solely by the value on the status line when trying to figure out the impact of a deletion or copy operation.

Viewing the Rest of the Directory Entry

A directory contains more information about each file than just the filename. A complete directory entry includes the file size, the date and time it was last modified, and several attributes, which you'll learn more about in Chapter 4. If you have a mouse, you can view this information by highlighting the filename and pressing the opposite mouse button. The status line changes to show the file's directory entry for as long as you hold down the mouse button. Suppose you want to find out how many bytes are in a file (remembering that it probably occupies more space than that on the disk). Highlight the filename and press the opposite mouse button. Hold it down as long as necessary to read the information you need, then release it.

Now that you can work your way around the main PC Shell screen, you're ready to begin using the shell to manipulate files, directories, and so on. The next chapter introduces you to some of the most basic functions of the **File** and **Disk** menus.

Chapter 2
Basic Menu Options and Dialog Boxes

This chapter will help you start using PC Shell's menus and options. You will learn to:

- Manipulate menus using the mouse and keyboard
- View files
- Rename files and directories
- Copy files
- Move files
- Delete files and directories
- Undelete files and directories
- Add new directories

Menu Overview

The menu bar contains the names of the menus available from the screen. When you pull down a menu by clicking on it with the mouse or pressing Alt plus the first letter, you can select any of the displayed options.

Figure 2.1 shows the **File** menu. Most of these options act on a file or group of files that you have already selected. If no file is selected, PC Shell assumes

26 Basic PC Shell Usage

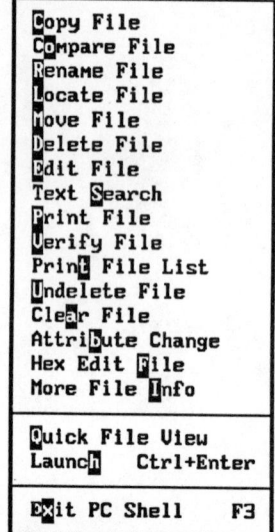

Figure 2.1   File Menu

you want the highlighted file. The resulting dialog box names the file (or files) to be operated on. If any other information is required, you will have a chance to enter it in the dialog box.

The **Disk** menu, shown in Figure 2.2, contains options that affect an entire disk. Some options act on the current disk, while others affect a diskette or a directory. One option, **Directory Maint,** is followed by an arrowhead; if you select this option you get the pop-up menu shown in the figure.

The **Options** menu, shown in Figure 2.3, lets you control many factors of PC Shell. The upper section lets you change additional features of the configuration and display. The next section lets you turn windows on and off. The bottom section lets you manipulate the current window, force PC Shell to

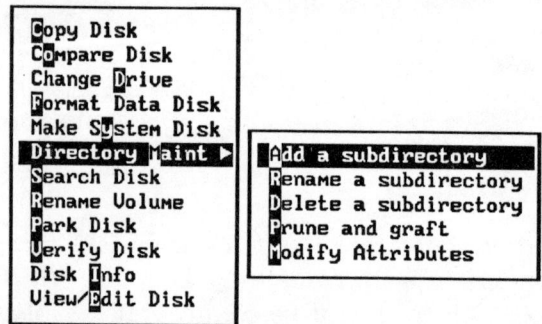

Figure 2.2   Disk Menu with Pop-up Menu

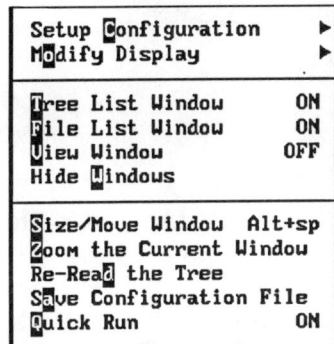

Figure 2.3   Options Menu

re-read the tree to take account of actions you might have performed that aren't automatically recognized by PC Shell, and save changes.

The **Applications** menu is unique to each installation. It includes various applications that are available in your system. Some of the applications are part of the PC Tools package. Others, such as WordStar® and Lotus 1-2-3®, may be identified during the installation procedure. You can add applications to this menu as needed. You can start up any application that appears in the menu by selecting it.

The **Special** menu, shown in Figure 2.4, includes several options you may need at various times. The most useful one is **Undelete Files**, which lets you retrieve files and directories you have deleted from a disk.

Using File Menu Options

Some of the options you'll use most often appear on the **File** menu. Whenever you want to copy a file, move it to another directory, rename it, or delete it, you'll use the **File** menu. You can affect more than one file with a single menu selection.

Before pulling down the **File** menu to choose an option, select the file or files to be affected. If none are selected, PC Shell assumes you want to operate on the highlighted file. If any files are selected, PC Shell ignores the highlighted file unless it is also selected. You'll always see the name of any file to be affected

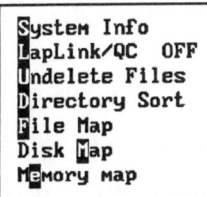

Figure 2.4   Special Menu

by an operation in a dialog box before the operation is performed. You'll have a chance to cancel the operation if you wish.

Viewing Files

You can view a single file or a series of them using the **Quick File View** option of the **File** menu; you can also use **2Qview** from the function key line. The result is a view window that covers the entire screen. Exactly what you see in the view window depends on several factors. A file with extension TXT or BAT is viewed as text. A file with extension COM, EXE, OBJ, BIN, or SYS is shown in the binary viewer. Files that PC Shell recognizes as being associated with various word processors, spreadsheets, databases, and other programs are shown via specialized viewers so they appear much like they do in their native programs. For example, a file with extension XLS is shown in the Microsoft Excel™ viewer and one with extension WK1 is shown in the Lotus 1-2-3 viewer. PC Shell can identify the source of many files, so files created under WordStar, WordPerfect®, and Microsoft® Word files, among others, are automatically shown in the appropriate form. If PC Shell can't tell which viewer to use, it uses the default.

If you view most highlighted files, you'll want to have the view window included on your screen. If you view files only occasionally, or want to have larger tree and file list windows, you'll want to use **Quick File View**.

Standard Viewers. If PC Shell can't identify a particular viewer for use with a file, it uses the default viewer, which is either Text or Binary. You can't switch from one viewer to another. The only control you have is to change the default viewer. To do this, pull down the **Options** menu, then select the **Setup Configuration** option; select **Default Viewer** on the resulting pop-up menu.

To view a file in PC Shell, first select it. Then select the **Quick File View** option. Figure 2.5 shows a file in the text viewer. Notice that the viewer takes up most of the screen. You can use the menus while a viewer is displayed; the file being viewed is selected.

You can page through the file using the keyboard or scroll bar. You can remove the window by clicking on the close box or pressing Esc. If you want to view several files, select them all before you choose the **Quick File View** option. Then the **9NextF** option causes the shell to end viewing of the current file and start on the next selected file.

The binary viewer is formatted differently. Details on this viewer and on editing binary files is covered in Chapter 6.

You are already familiar with most of the function key values for the view screen; they're the same on most screens. Selecting **4Launch** starts a program;

Basic Menu Options and Dialog Boxes 29

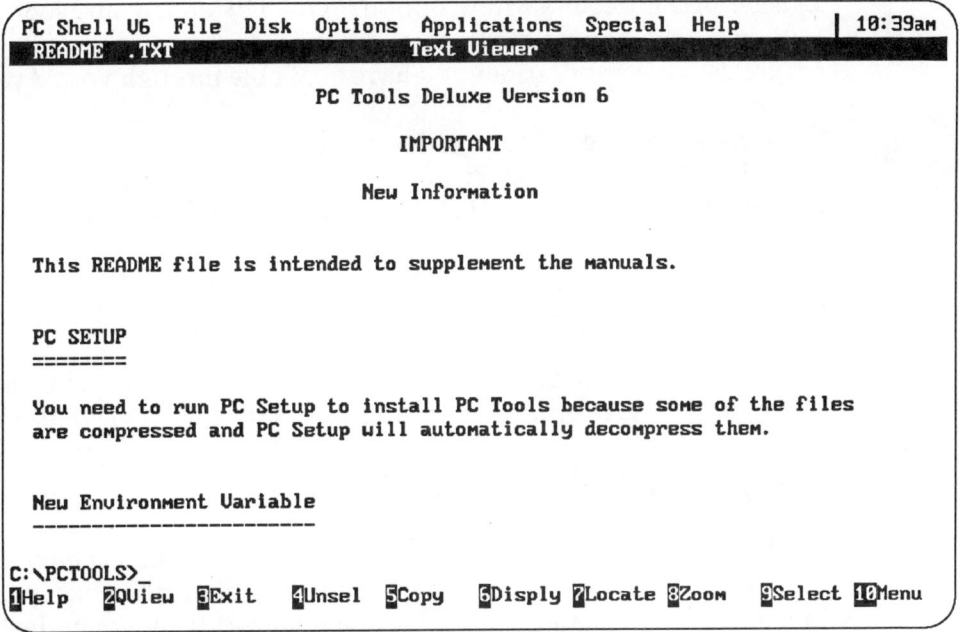

Figure 2.5   Text Viewer

if the displayed file does not have extension BAT, COM, or EXE, PC Shell checks to see if the file's extension is associated with an installed application. If so, it runs that application. If not, you will be notified that the program can't be run. Selecting **7Search** lets you enter a character string to search for; this is useful in longer files. Selecting **8Unzoom** reduces the zoomed window to standard view window size; F8 again restores the zoom.

Specialized Viewers. If you view a file that PC Shell recognizes as using one of the specialized viewers, you'll see the file contents in the format of its native program. In most cases, you have the same choices available for paging through the file. Selecting **4Launch** when a WordPerfect file is being viewed, for example, starts up the WordPerfect program (if it is set up as an application) so you can edit that file. Some viewers, especially those for spreadsheet and database programs, include an option (**5GoTo**) for locating a particular record or cell as well.

✧ Try It Out

1. Bring up the shell and examine all the menus.
2. Find the **View, Copy,** and **Delete** options on the **File** menu.

3. Select the **Directory Maint** option on the **Disk** menu and look at the options on the pop-up menu.
4. Notice what applications you have available through your **Applications** menu.
5. Find the **Undelete** option on the **Special** menu.
6. Make the root directory current and view AUTOEXEC.BAT.
7. Select CONFIG.SYS, AUTOEXEC.BAT, and two files with extension COM or EXE. View them all.
8. Make the directory containing the PC Tools files current. View DSKERR.DBF and notice what viewer is used. Try the GoTo option to find record 80.
9. If you have them, view some files created by a well-known word processor, database, or spreadsheet program. Notice what viewers are used.

Rename a File

To change a file's name, first select the file in the file list. Then pull down the **File** menu and select **Rename File**. You'll see a dialog box like the one shown in Figure 2.6. The name of the file to be renamed is shown in the top portion of the box. You type changes in the input fields.

If the file named in the box isn't the one you want to rename, just select CANCEL or otherwise remove the box. If it is correct, type the new name. Notice that you have to type the two parts of the name in different fields. Type or edit the first part of the name, then press Enter or type a period to get to the **Ext** field. Type or edit the extension. When the desired new name is typed, press Enter or select RENAME. The dialog box disappears, and you'll see the new name in your file list. It is still selected, since it is still the same file.

If you want to rename several files, select them all before selecting **Rename File**. You'll next see a dialog box like the one in Figure 2.7. Here you choose

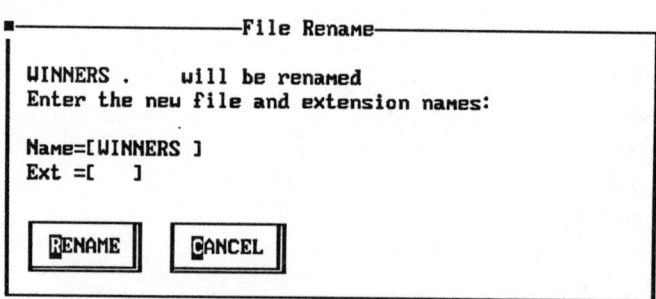

Figure 2.6   File Rename Dialog Box

Basic Menu Options and Dialog Boxes 31

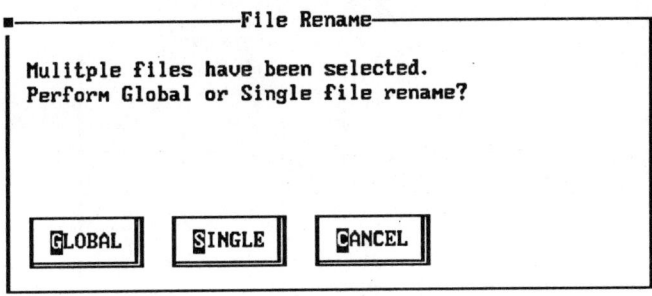

Figure 2.7   Multiple File Rename Dialog Box

whether you want to rename each individually (SINGLE) or using a pattern (GLOBAL). If you choose SINGLE, you'll get a separate dialog box for each file, much like the one in Figure 2.6. If you choose GLOBAL, you'll get a dialog box like the one in Figure 2.8. You must enter a global filename here, using appropriate characters and the * and ? symbols as explained in the dialog box.

If you want all the renamed files to have extension REN, for example, use * as the **Name** field and REN in the **Ext** field. LISTER.DOT will become LISTER.REN, FORM3 will become FORM3.REN, and so forth. If you want to change just the first character of the **Name** field to X, use X* in the **Name** field and leave * in the **Ext** field. Then LISTER.DOT will become XISTER.DOT, FORM3 will become XORM3, and so forth.

Copy a File

A copy operation results in two identical copies of the same file. If you copy a file to the same directory that contains the original, PC Shell forces you to give it a new name to avoid duplicate filenames. If you copy it to a different drive or directory, PC Shell doesn't change the basic filename and extension.

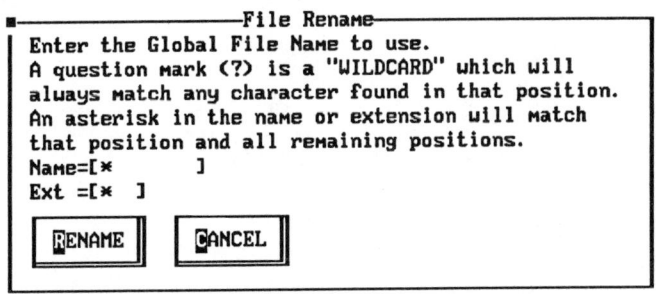

Figure 2.8   Specifying a Global Rename

Figure 2.9   File Copy Target Drive Selection

If you want the copy in a different disk or directory to have a different name, you can rename it later.

The first step in creating a copy is to select the file to be copied; then pull down the **File** menu and select the **Copy File** option. Next you'll see a dialog box like the one in Figure 2.9. Here you select the drive that will hold the target copy. You can interrupt the operation by removing the dialog box.

If you select a drive that contains only a root directory, the copy is made immediately. If the drive contains subdirectories, you'll next see a box like the

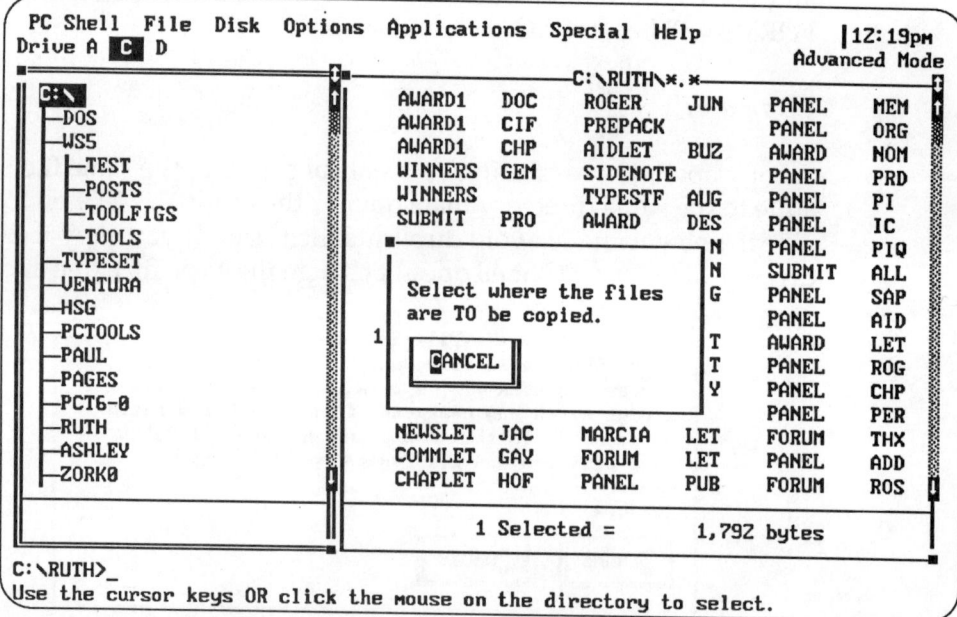

Figure 2.10   File Copy Target Directory Selection

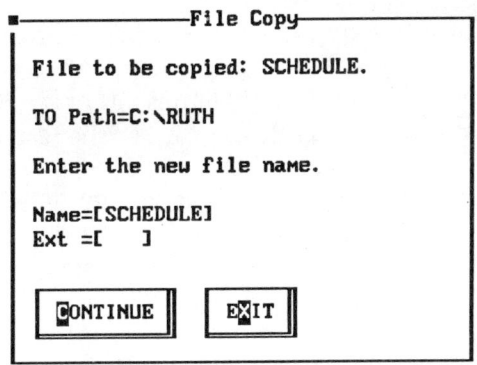

Figure 2.11   File Copy New Name Specification

one in Figure 2.10, which tells you to select a directory to hold the target copy. The directory tree of the drive you selected is shown and made active, so you can select the target directory just as you select any directory. When you press Enter or click on the desired target directory, the copy operation continues.

If you select the same directory that contains the file being copied, you'll next have to enter the new filename in a dialog box like the one in Figure 2.11. The name of the file being copied is shown in the upper part of the box. The target path is shown as well. The original name is shown in the input fields, but you must change it to another valid name before the copy can take place.

Once you've provided the target filename and extension, press Enter or select CONTINUE. You'll get one last chance to confirm the copy or interrupt it in a dialog box like the one shown in Figure 2.12. When you select COPY, the file is immediately copied to the target location. Once the copy is completed, you'll be able to see the filename in the file list for the target directory.

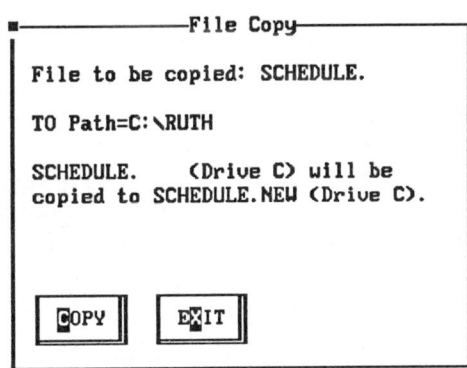

Figure 2.12   File Copy Confirmation

A multiple copy requires that the files all be copied from one directory to the same target directory. If they are copied to their original directory, you'll have a chance to provide new names either singly or globally. The process is very similar to providing the names for the **Rename File** option.

File Already Exists Message. When you copy a file, you may see a dialog box containing a filename with a message that the file already exists. This occurs when a file of the same name is in the target directory. You will be offered a choice of several actions here; just click on the button that represents your desired action.

REPLACE ALL replaces all files with matching names; this destroys the existing files and replaces each with a file copy. REPLACE FILE replaces only the file named in the dialog box; you'll be notified if another filename duplication occurs. NEXT FILE abandons the current file copy and continues to the next one, if there is one. SKIP ALL skips the rest of the selected files and doesn't copy them. EXIT cancels the box and returns you to the main shell screen.

Copying with Mouse Drag. A mouse gives you a convenient way to copy a file from one directory or disk to another. First display the file list containing the file(s) to be copied and select them using any method. Then point to any selected file, click and hold the button down. Drag the mouse pointer to the Tree window; you'll notice a small box that tells you how many files are being copied. When the pointer is on the desired subdirectory name, release it, and the copy is accomplished. If any filename duplication arises, you'll see the same dialog box as with a standard menu copy; the same choices are available.

Moving Files

Moving files is much like copying them, except the files are removed from their original locations. Functionally, it is similar to a copy followed by a deletion of the original file. You can't move a file to the directory it is originally on; you can achieve the same effect by renaming the file, however.

To move files to another directory, first select them, then pull down the **File** menu and select **Move File**. You'll see a dialog box that reminds you that the source files will be deleted; you can select CONTINUE or EXIT to complete or cancel the operation. If you continue, the next dialog box you see is much like the one for copying in Figure 2.9. After you select the drive, you see a dialog box much like the one in Figure 2.10. After you select the directory, you'll see an error box if you selected the one that contains the source files. If you selected a different directory, the file(s) are moved to it and deleted from the original directory. You won't have a chance to provide new names. If you want to provide new names in the new locations, you can rename the files later. If any filename duplication would occur as a result of the move, you'll have the same choices as with a file copy.

Moving with Mouse Drag. You can move files with a mouse much as you copy them by dragging. After selecting the file(s) to be moved, hold down the Control key, then point to any selected file, click and hold the button down. Drag the mouse pointer to the Tree window; this time the box tells you how many files are being moved. When the pointer is on the desired subdirectory name, release it, and the move is accomplished. If any filename duplication arises, you'll see the same dialog box as with a standard menu copy or move; the same choices are available.

✧ Try It Out

1. In your root directory, make a copy of AUTOEXEC.BAT named AUTOPLAY.XXX and a copy of CONFIG.SYS named CONPLAY.XXX.
2. Copy AUTOPLAY.XXX and AUTOEXEC.BAT to the directory that holds your PC Tools files using the menu or command.
3. Use a mouse to drag a copy of CONPLAY.XXX to the PC Tools directory.
4. In the root directory, rename AUTOPLAY.XXX as MYFILE.ZZZ.
5. Move MYFILE.ZZZ to the PC Tools directory.
6. Move AUTOPLAY.XXX from its current location to the root directory.
7. Move CONPLAY.XXX to the root directory; replace the existing file of that name.

Deleting Files

To delete a single file, select it in the file list, then pull down the **File** menu and select the **Delete File** option. You'll see a dialog box like the one in Figure 2.13. The name of the selected file is shown. To delete the file, select DELETE. To cancel the deletion, select CANCEL.

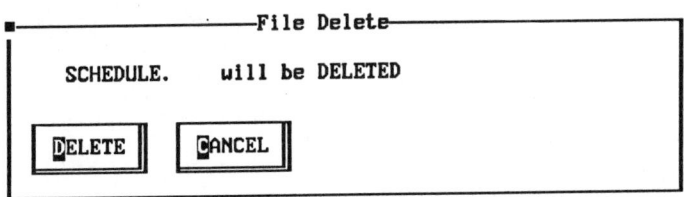

Figure 2.13   File Deletion Dialog Box

36 Basic PC Shell Usage

The deleted file no longer appears in the file list. If you see a message that the file can't be deleted, you'll have to deal with the file's attributes, which are covered in Chapter 4.

If you want to delete a group of files, select them all before choosing **Delete File** from the **File** menu. You'll see a dialog box with two additional options, as shown in Figure 2.14. You can still select CANCEL to interrupt the complete operation or DELETE to delete the listed file.

If you select NEXT FILE, the currently named file is not deleted, but the next selected filename is shown and you have the same four choices. Any files you choose to bypass in this way remain selected when you finally return to the screen. If you choose DELETE ALL, every remaining selected file is deleted immediately; you won't have a chance to examine or bypass any. On the other hand, you won't have to sit at the desk making choices while PC Shell deletes the files.

Clearing Files

Normally deleted files actually remain on disk; they just aren't accessible by standard means. Another user, or yourself, can recover them using an undeletion operation. If you want to make sure a file is completely removed from the disk, you can use the **Clear File** command instead of **Delete File**. PC Shell can then delete the file and overwrite the space it occupied so the file can't be recovered. When you pull down the **File** menu and select **Clear File**, PC Shell lets you specify a special value to be written to each byte the file currently occupies. If you prefer, you can use the default, hex F6. You can also let PC Shell write the value once to each byte or repeat it as often as needed or to U.S. government standards.

After you specify the values to use, you'll get one more chance to confirm the operation; when you select CLEAR, the file is totally removed. It can't be recovered at all. Multiple files are handled just as in the file deletion process; all are removed in the same way.

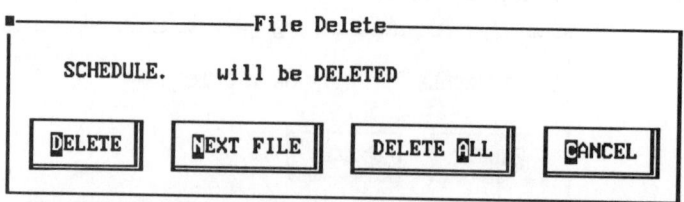

Figure 2.14   Deleting Multiple Files

❖ Try It Out

1. Copy CONPLAY.ZZZ and AUTOPLAY.XXX to the PC Tools directory.
2. Delete CONPLAY.ZZZ from the root directory.
3. Delete both CONPLAY.ZZZ and AUTOPLAY.XXX from the PC Tools directory.
4. Make the PCTOOLS directory current again and make a copy of README.TXT named INFO.OLD. View, then delete, INFO.OLD.

Using Directory Maintenance Options

As you use DOS, you frequently have to manipulate directories. When you enter PC Tools, the current directory is the one that was current under DOS when you entered. When you change the highlight in the tree window, the current directory changes.

Some operations always affect the current directory. Files to be copied or renamed must be in the current directory, for example, in most cases. If you want a particular directory to be current when you leave the shell, you must make it current first.

Adding Directories

You can use the **Disk** menu to create new directories, rename existing ones, and delete directories you no longer need. The first step in any of these operations is to pull down the **Disk** menu and select the **Directory Maint** option. You don't have to select the appropriate directory first.

To add a new directory, select the **Add a subdirectory** option on the pop-up menu. Next you'll see the dialog box shown in Figure 2.15. The tree window is made active and you can select a parent for the new directory. Whatever directory you select, the new directory will be added beneath it. To cancel the operation at this point, select EXIT.

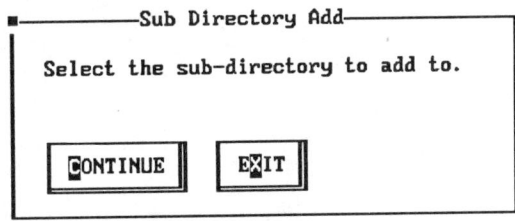

Figure 2.15 Sub Directory Add Selection Box

If the intended parent directory was selected before you pulled down the menu, you can just press Enter or click here. If not, select the appropriate parent directory next. When you click on it or highlight it and press Enter or select CONTINUE, you'll see the dialog box in Figure 2.16.

You type the name of the new subdirectory at the cursor. After you press Enter, you can type an extension if you want one; many users prefer not to use extensions on directory names. Just press Enter again to bypass this field. When you select CONTINUE, the subdirectory is added and appears in your directory tree. If you select the new subdirectory, you'll see that it contains no files at this point.

Renaming a Directory

You can rename any directory using the **Directory Maint** pop-up menu. Renaming a directory through PC Shell works much like renaming a file. The only difference is that you are prompted to select the directory after you select the **Rename a subdirectory** option. While you can rename directories almost at will, you have to be careful. If you rename a directory that appears in your system's search path, be sure to change the name in the search path command as well; it won't be found if you don't. Renaming directories used by your applications can also be dangerous. Take care to rename only directories you have created unless you are sure you understand the implications of the change.

Deleting a Directory

You cannot delete the root directory on any drive. You can't delete a directory that contains any files. And you can't delete the current directory. If you try any of these invalid deletions, you'll get an error message, and nothing is deleted. To delete any other directory, select **Delete a subdirectory** from the **Directory Maint** pop-up menu. You'll be prompted to select the directory you want to delete. When you're ready, select CONTINUE. If the directory you

Figure 2.16   Sub Directory Add New Name Box

selected can't be deleted, you'll see a dialog box with an explanation. If it can be deleted, you'll see a confirmation dialog box. You can select DELETE or EXIT to accomplish or cancel the deletion.

✧ *Try It Out*

1. Add two directories named PRACTICE and SAMPLE under the PC Tools directory.
2. Rename PRACTICE as TRYOUT.
3. Copy AUTOEXEC.BAT and CONFIG.SYS from the root directory to both SAMPLE and TRYOUT. Examine the file lists.
4. Try to delete TRYOUT. Notice the message, then cancel the operation.
5. Try to delete the current directory. Notice the message, then cancel the operation.
6. Delete all files from the SAMPLE directory. Then delete the directory.

Undeleting Files and Subdirectories

PC Shell lets you recover a file that you deleted and have it appear in the directory and file list once more. You can also recover a subdirectory that has been deleted, then restore its files. The undelete feature is a great advance over DOS, which offers no method of recovering deleted files or directories. You can't recover a file removed with **Clear File** under any circumstances.

PC Tools includes a program called UNDELETE.EXE that you can use at the DOS prompt. Most choices you make in the shell can be specified as parameters. Undeletion is more convenient through PC Shell, however.

Undeletion is easier if PC Tools is installed with the MIRROR option; then information on every file and directory you delete through PC Shell is tracked and recorded in a special file. You won't be able to restore subdirectories at all if they aren't tracked by MIRROR. (More information about MIRROR is included in Appendix A.) You can also undelete files deleted at the DOS command prompt or on other drives, even from diskettes that may never have been used with PC Tools, although these undeletions are done differently and require an extra step.

The first step in recovering a deleted file is to select its former drive and directory in the tree window. Then pull down the **File** or **Special** menu and select the **Undelete File** option; both work the same. You'll see the dialog box in Figure 2.17. If the directory is correct, select CONTINUE. Otherwise select EXIT and highlight the directory that formerly contained the file.

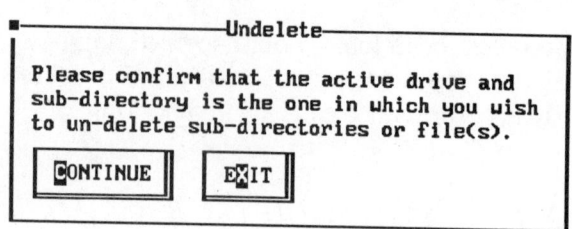

Figure 2.17   Undelete Drive and Directory Confirmation

If you select CONTINUE, you'll next see the dialog box in Figure 2.18. Notice that the dialog box refers to subdirectories as well. Undeleting a subdirectory works exactly like undeleting a file. You specify whether you are dealing with a FILE or a SUB-DIR. Select CANCEL to stop the operation. You'll choose CREATE only if you are trying to recreate a file from specific clusters; Chapter 6 covers details of processing clusters. If you don't know a cluster from a hex byte, you probably won't want to try this option.

If you select FILE or SUB-DIR, you'll next have to decide which method of undeletion to use. Basically, there are two types, one that uses MIRROR output and one that doesn't.

Through MIRROR, PC Tools maintains *Delete Tracking* records of all deletions you do on the drives it covers. To recover a file deleted recently under PC Tools with MIRROR in effect, use this method. In fact, any time you are offered the choice, try the delete tracking method first. If no files in the selected directory can be undeleted through delete tracking, PC Shell won't offer you this dialog box.

Whenever a file is deleted using any method, DOS overwrites the first character of the filename in the directory slot; by this special delete character, DOS knows that a file has been deleted and won't show it in a listing. The space and directory slot can be given to another file. When the file wasn't tracked by MIRROR, undeleting lets you look at the names of deleted files in the directory and put the original first character back in, so that DOS doesn't realize the file is deleted and, in effect, restores it. While this method is a bit

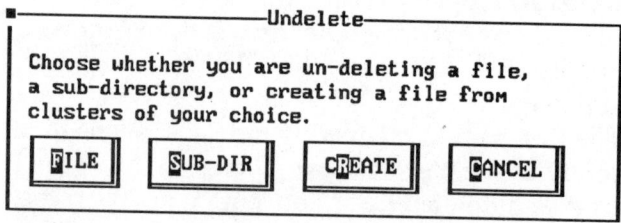

Figure 2.18   Undelete Type Selection

more complex, it can be used to restore files on disks and diskettes that haven't been used with MIRROR.

When you see a dialog box like the one in Figure 2.19, you can select DEL TRACK or DOS DIR to specify the type of recovery you want. Try DEL TRACK first if you are offered the choice.

Whenever you add data to a disk, either by creating a new file or by extending an existing file, DOS uses up deleted file space first. New file entries overlay deleted ones in the file directory. Therefore, if you delete a file, then immediately create a new one, you might destroy the deleted entry or part or all of its data. If this has happened to a file, it can't be easily undeleted. If the directory entry slot or part of the space the file occupied has been overlaid with another file, you won't be able to get at them. If the directory entry and the file space are intact, PC Shell often knows the file can be recovered automatically. If you are offered a choice between MANUAL and AUTOMATIC undeletion, select AUTOMATIC unless you know it won't work. With AUTOMATIC undeletion, you'll have to make a number of selections to keep the process going, but PC Shell does all the work. MANUAL undeletion involves specialized decisions; the process is covered in Chapter 6.

Using Delete Tracking

Figure 2.20 shows the result of selecting DEL TRACK. All files recorded in the delete tracking process are listed. The symbol @ following the extension indicates that none of the file's clusters have been destroyed by other data; delete tracking can undelete these files automatically. The symbol * means that some of the clusters are available, but not all of them. You might have to use the manual recovery method for these files. If neither symbol appears, the file is most likely not recoverable. Each file has one line, with the filename, extension, size, date, time, and attributes as they were at the time of deletion. If files with the same name were deleted, you might see several files listed with

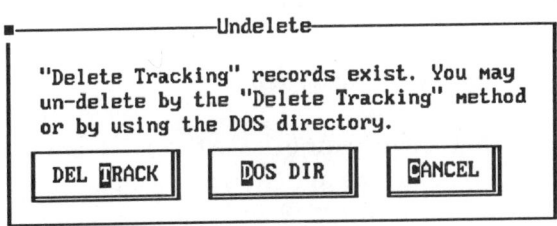

Figure 2.19 Undelete Method Selection

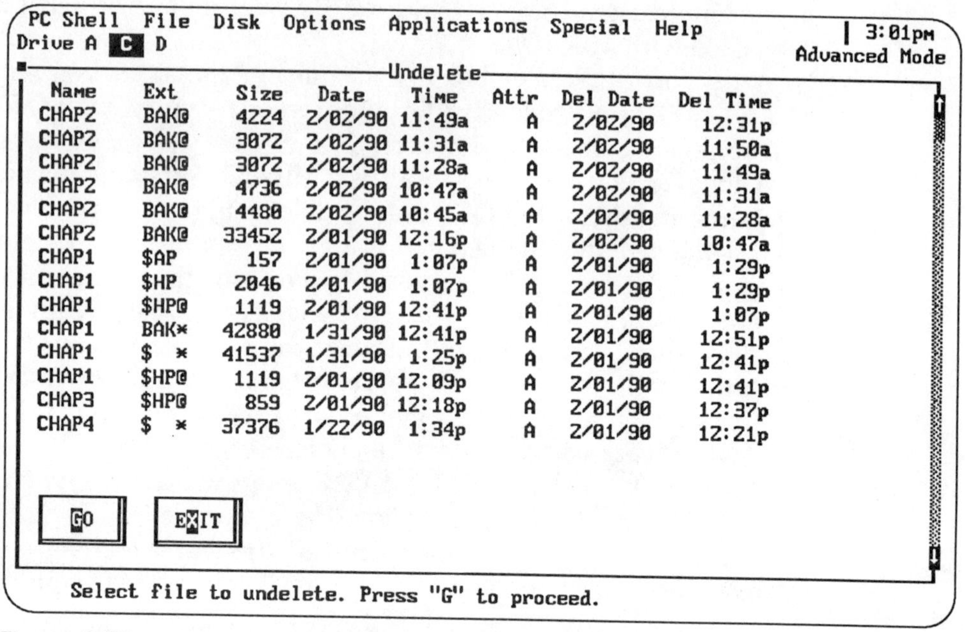

```
PC Shell  File  Disk  Options  Applications  Special  Help        | 3:01pm
Drive A  C  D                                                     Advanced Mode
■─────────────────────────────Undelete─────────────────────────────
  Name   Ext    Size    Date     Time   Attr  Del Date   Del Time
  CHAP2  BAK@   4224  2/02/90  11:49a    A    2/02/90    12:31p
  CHAP2  BAK@   3072  2/02/90  11:31a    A    2/02/90    11:50a
  CHAP2  BAK@   3072  2/02/90  11:28a    A    2/02/90    11:49a
  CHAP2  BAK@   4736  2/02/90  10:47a    A    2/02/90    11:31a
  CHAP2  BAK@   4480  2/02/90  10:45a    A    2/02/90    11:28a
  CHAP2  BAK@  33452  2/01/90  12:16p    A    2/02/90    10:47a
  CHAP1  $AP     157  2/01/90   1:07p    A    2/01/90     1:29p
  CHAP1  $HP    2046  2/01/90   1:07p    A    2/01/90     1:29p
  CHAP1  $HP@   1119  2/01/90  12:41p    A    2/01/90     1:07p
  CHAP1  BAK*  42880  1/31/90  12:41p    A    2/01/90    12:51p
  CHAP1  $  *  41537  1/31/90   1:25p    A    2/01/90    12:41p
  CHAP1  $HP@   1119  2/01/90  12:09p    A    2/01/90    12:41p
  CHAP3  $HP@    859  2/01/90  12:18p    A    2/01/90    12:37p
  CHAP4  $  *  37376  1/22/90   1:34p    A    2/01/90    12:21p

    [ GO ]     [ EXIT ]

    Select file to undelete. Press "G" to proceed.
```

Figure 2.20   Undelete by Delete Tracking Method

the same name. The deletion date and time are given on the right end of the line; you can find the latest deletion of a file by referring to this field.

If the file you want to undelete appears with the symbol @, select it (with Enter or the mouse). If you want to undelete several files, select them all. Select GO when you are ready. All the selected files marked with @ will be restored and you'll see a message that the files were successfully undeleted. When you select CONTINUE, you'll return to the PC Shell main screen.

If you select files marked with * or with no mark, you'll be offered manual recovery. If you reject the manual method, you'll see a message that the file was NOT undeleted. The manual recovery method involves examining and selecting clusters; it is covered in Chapter 6.

Using the DOS Directory

If you don't see the name of the file you want to restore under delete tracking, select EXIT. Start the undelete process again and select DOS DIR in the dialog box shown in Figure 2.19. This time you'll see a list of deleted files to undelete similar to the standard file list, as shown in Figure 2.21. Notice that the first character of each is replaced by a question mark; the DOS delete character is not printable. The codes @ and * have the same meaning as before. Just select

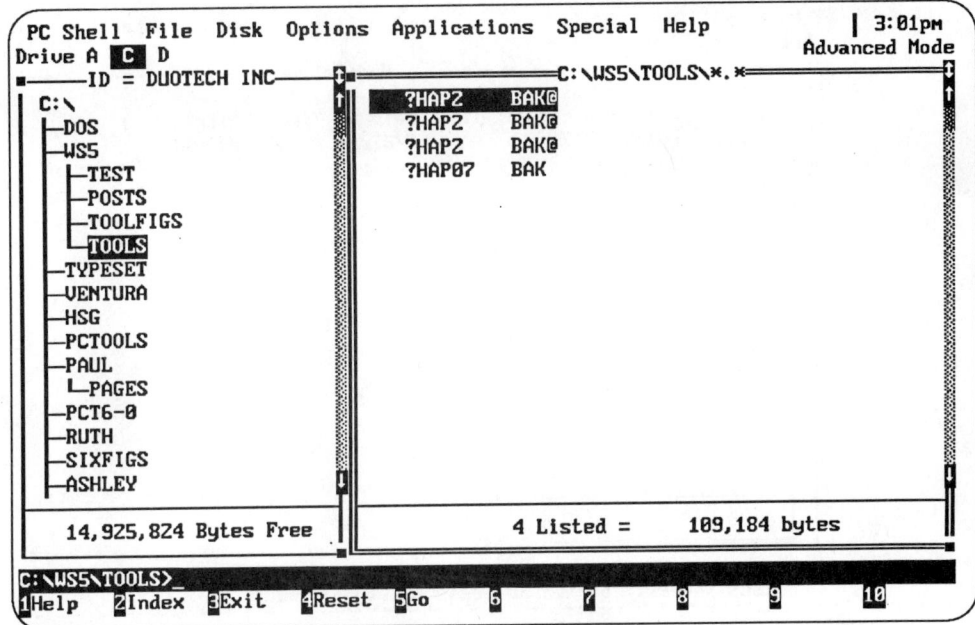

Figure 2.21   Undelete by DOS Directory Method

the file or files you want to undelete and press F5 (**5Go**) as indicated on the screen. You will be offered a choice between MANUAL and AUTOMATIC undeletion for some files. For other files, you'll be informed that automatic undeletion is impossible.

When you select AUTOMATIC, you'll see a screen like the one in Figure 2.22. The screen shows the first filename and prompts you to enter the first character. In this case, you'd type C; actually, any character will do since DOS doesn't know or care what you named the file originally. If another file with the same name exists in the directory, use a different first character. If you duplicate an existing filename, PC Shell might just end up with two identical file names; it may display both, but since it can't process them, you'll end up losing one file or the other. You have to be aware of what files are in the directory so you can create a unique name. After you type a first character, select UNDELETE to continue to the next step.

If the file was marked with @, the file is restored to the file list and you can process it as before. If the file requires manual undeletion, you'll be prompted to use that method. If the file can't be recovered, you'll be notified.

44   Basic PC Shell Usage

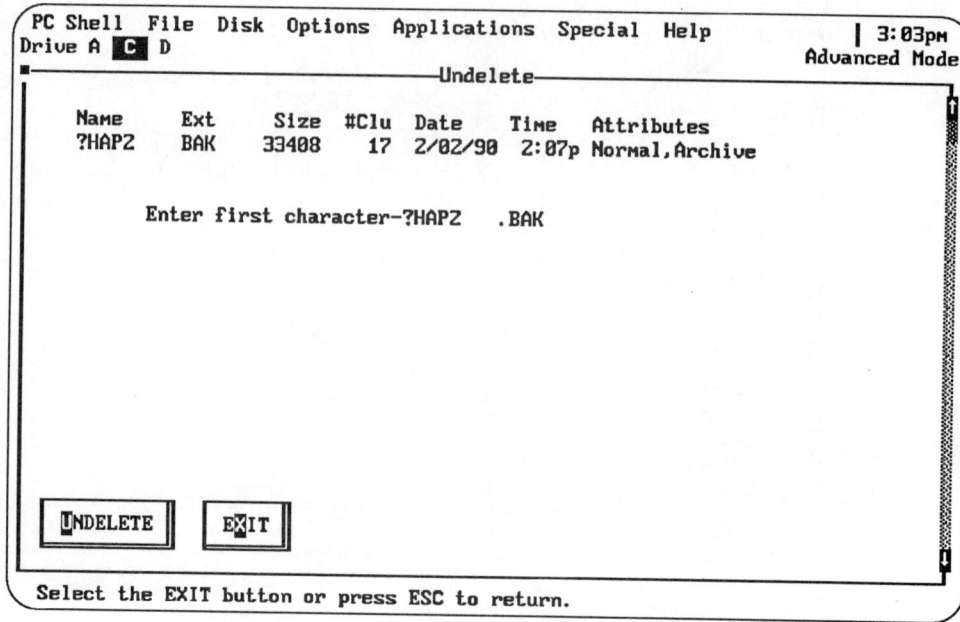

Figure 2.22   Supplying the First Character of the Filename

✧ *Try It Out*

1. Copy AUTOEXEC.BAT in TRYOUT as MYFILE.OUT, then delete the copied file.
2. Undelete MYFILE.OUT from TRYOUT. If you get a choice, use delete tracking. Otherwise use the DOS directory method.
3. Undelete the SAMPLE directory (from within the PC Tools directory). Then restore the two files in it if it can be done automatically.
4. Examine the files available for undeletion in the PC Tools directory. Undelete one marked with @; use INFO.OLD if it is present. Try undeleting one marked with *. Cancel the undeletion or exit it if you get into the manual undeletion mode.
5. Copy any two files to a diskette. Delete one and clean the other. Try to undelete them.

✧ ✧ ✧

Now you can use basic commands to process files and directories through PC Shell, using its default mode and arrangement. You're ready to learn to control the screen and displays and apply what you have already learned to the new arrangements in the next chapter.

Chapter 3 | PC Shell Screen Management

In this chapter, you'll learn to control windows and other components of the PC Shell screen. Specifically, you'll learn to use these features:

- Turn windows on and off
- Zoom, size, and move windows
- Change screen colors
- Size and move windows
- Rearrange screen configuration
- Specify global filenames
- Display detailed file information
- Sort directory lists
- Limit and expand directory lists
- Work with single- and multiple-list displays

Using Basic Options

The **Options** menu (shown in Figure 2.3) lets you manipulate what appears on the PC Shell screen. You have already learned to use several options from the keyboard. We'll cover all the menu options here. You'll see how to use the basic **Options** menu to turn the tree, file list, or view window on or off, move or size the active window, re-read the tree from the current hard drive, and save any configuration changes you have made.

Displaying Windows

When you select **Tree List Window**, **File List Window**, or **View Window** on the **Options** menu, the associated value toggles between ON and OFF. When the value is ON, the window is displayed. When the tree or file list window is OFF, you'll see either a shaded background called a mat or the DOS screen that underlies the shell. When the view window is OFF, the other windows are enlarged to occupy the space on screen. The screens you have seen so far show the view window OFF and the others ON. When all the windows are turned off, the menu bar disappears as well. You can also suppress the windows by selecting **Hide Windows**; this entry is replaced with **Show Windows** while the windows are hidden. You can restore the menu bar by selecting **10Menu** or by clicking on the top line of the screen; then you can use all the menu options, including those to restore windows.

The view window shows the contents of the highlighted file in the same format as Quick File View, but not at a full screen size. It can appear in either

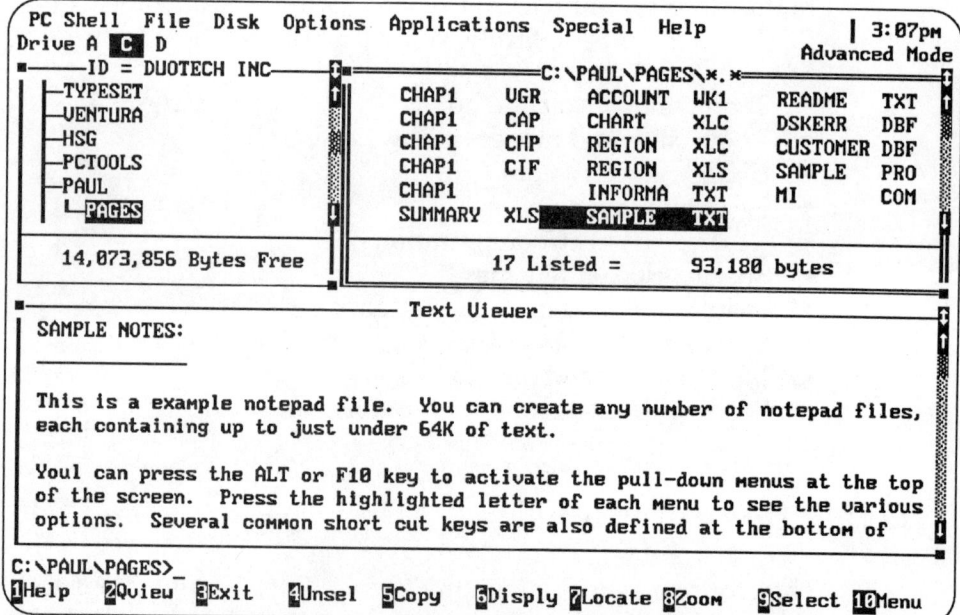

Figure 3.1   Horizontal View Window

of two positions, horizontal or vertical. Figure 3.1 shows how it looks horizontally. The two other windows are shortened. You can change the position of the view window on the **Setup Configuration** pop-up menu. The function key line remains standard, rather than changing as with **Quick File View**.

Tabbing rotates the active window (remember the double border) among the displayed windows; Shift-Tab rotates in the opposite direction. Clicking in a window makes it active as well.

Zooming a Window

You can enlarge the active window by clicking on the zoom icon in the upper right, by selecting **8Zoom** from the bottom line, or by selecting **Zoom the Current Window** on the **Options** menu. That window then overlays any other displayed windows. If you press Tab while the active window is zoomed, the next window overlays it. You can have more than one window zoomed at a time; switching among them brings the active window to the front. When you select **8Unzoom** while a zoomed window is active, the window returns to its previous size.

Sizing and Moving Windows

Windows on your screen appear in a default size and location. For example, the standard display has a tree window and a file list window, both the same height and arranged side by side on the screen. You can change the size and position of any window, including the view window. You can't change the size or position of dialog boxes or message boxes, however.

Using the Mouse

A window that can be sized has a small box in the lower right corner; this is the size box. When you click on this box, you can drag the mouse pointer to change the window size. Sizing changes always occur in relation to the lower right corner; if the window is positioned in the lower right of the usable part of the screen, you won't be able to make it larger unless you move the window away from the corner first.

To move the window, click on the top window border, but not in the close box or zoom icon. Then drag the window to place it where you want. Once you have moved a window away from the lower right corner of the screen, you'll be able to resize it as needed.

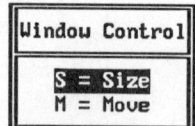 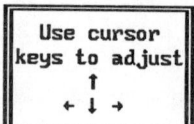

Figure 3.2   Window Control Boxes

Using the Menus

With the menus, you can move or resize the active window by pressing Alt-Spacebar or using **Size/Move Window** from the **Options** menu. You'll see a small box like the one shown on the left in Figure 3.2. You press S to change the active window's size or M to move it to another location on the screen. You cannot select an option in this box with the mouse; you must type a letter on the keyboard.

Next you'll see a small box like the one on the right in Figure 3.2. Just use the cursor keys to move the window or to change its size. As with mouse adjustments, the upper left corner of the window remains in the same position when you change the window's size.

Saving the New Configuration

If you want changes to apply to later PC Shell sessions, you can save the configuration. Pull down the **Options** menu and select **Save Configuration File**. The current status of various options is saved and will be used every time you bring up PC Shell, including such features as screen colors and window sizes. You can cancel the effect by resetting the changes you made and saving the configuration again. You can reset all the defaults at once by erasing the file called PCSHELL.CFG, but this may remove more than you bargained for, such as applications added during installation.

Forcing a Directory Re-Read

If hard disk files or subdirectories have been deleted or added under DOS, they may not be listed correctly in the file list window. When the active directory tree isn't displaying correctly, you can force PC Shell to re-read it from the disk by selecting **Re-Read the Tree** on the **Options** menu. Re-reading affects only the current hard drive, so make sure it is current first. You can use the /TR*n* parameter when you start up PC Shell to force the tree to be re-read from the disk at least *n* days.

PC Shell Screen Management   49

Quick Run

The **Quick Run** option is available only when PC Shell is being run as a stand-alone program. When it is ON, PC Shell doesn't free up memory until PC Shell is terminated. If it is OFF, any DOS command causes memory to be freed, resulting in more available memory but taking more time. Applications can override the **Quick Run** setting individually. Memory is always freed when DOS commands are run under a resident PC Shell.

✧ Try It Out

1. Turn on the view window. Tab and click to select different windows.
2. Make the PC Tools directory active and view several different files.
3. Remove the tree window and notice the background. Hide, then restore, all the windows.
4. Resize the file list window so it covers the former locations of both it and the tree window.
5. Zoom the view window. Then make the file list window active and move back and forth between the zoomed windows.
6. Unzoom both windows and restore the tree window.
7. Re-read the directory tree.

Using the Setup Configuration Pop-Up Menu

Figure 3.3 shows the **Setup Configuration** pop-up menu. Any changes you make using this menu can be saved so that they apply to all later PC Shell sessions by selecting **Save Configuration File** on the basic **Options** menu.

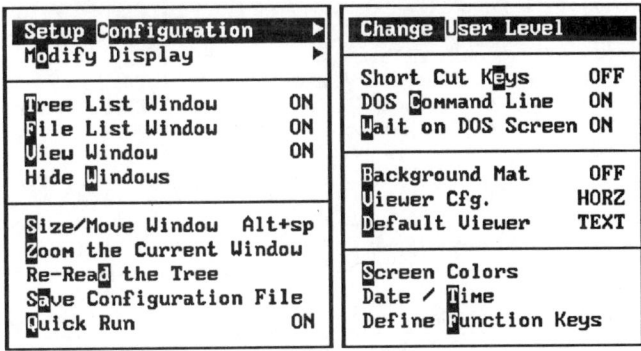

Figure 3.3   Setup Configuration Pop-Up Menu

Controlling Screen Layout

You can use this menu to switch between the **Short Cut Keys** and the **DOS Command Line**; only one can be displayed at a time but you can turn them both off if you prefer. When the short cut keys are displayed, you can activate a menu or a short cut key by pressing the highlighted letter; when the DOS command line is displayed, you need to press the Alt key with a menu letter to pull it down. When the DOS command line is active, PC Shell saves the commands you use; you can press the control key with the left arrow to see up to sixteen previously used commands. When the one you want is displayed, press Enter to process it. Control with the right arrow key moves the other way in the stored list. **Wait on DOS Screen** works with DOS commands; when it is ON, you'll be prompted to press a key or click a button to return to PC Shell after a DOS command is run. This gives you time to read the screen. If you turn it OFF, control returns to the shell automatically as soon as a command terminates.

Background Mat refers to the shaded background PC Shell puts behind the windows on the screen. If you turn it OFF, you will see underlying information on the screen. If you use DOS commands and want to see the results on screen while the shell is active, turn the mat off. When it is ON, you won't see DOS output on the screen behind the shell.

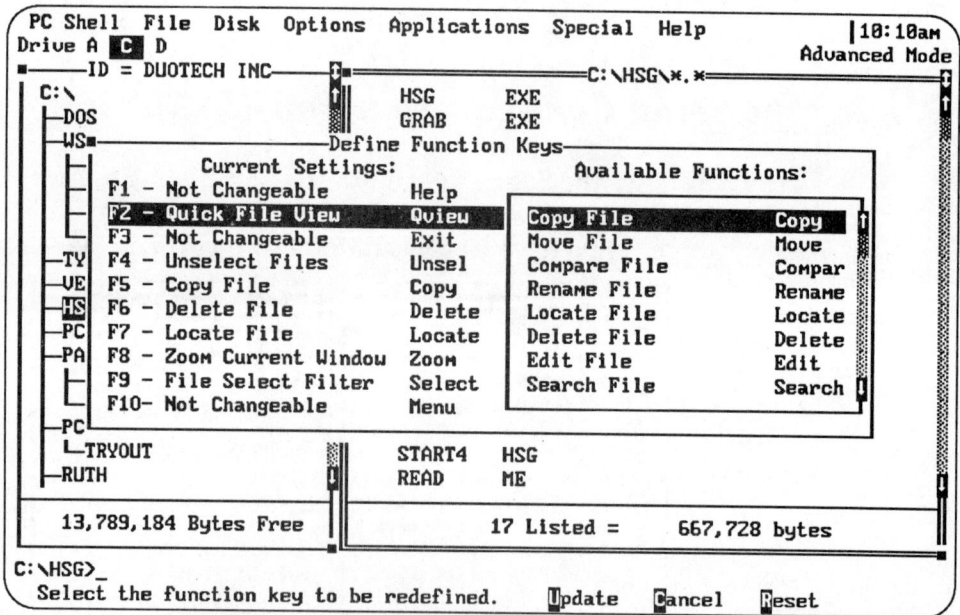

Figure 3.4   Define Function Keys Dialog Box

You cannot change the individual short cut keys, but you can redefine the function keys by selecting **Define Function Keys**. You may be asked to supply a password before you can use this function. If so, just type it in and the function continues as described. Figure 3.4 shows the resulting dialog box. The available function keys and the functions you can assign to them are shown. A message on the bottom screen line guides you through the process.

Notice that you can't change F1 (Help), F3 (Exit), or F10 (Menu). First you select a changeable key, then press Tab or click in the Available Functions box. Most of the menu commands are available; select the one you want associated with the selected function key. You can then select another function key to redefine or select Update, Cancel, or Reset from the screen. Update puts your changes into effect, Cancel restores the previous setting, and Reset restores the default function key settings.

Setting Viewer Defaults

When you select **Viewer Cfg.**, the displayed position of the view window toggles between VERT and HORIZ. Figure 3.5 shows how a vertical view window appears. You may not be able to see the entire text in the window. You won't be able to see much of the tree or file list. If you are working in a single directory, however, you could turn the tree window off; then the file list can be enlarged to occupy the entire left part of the screen.

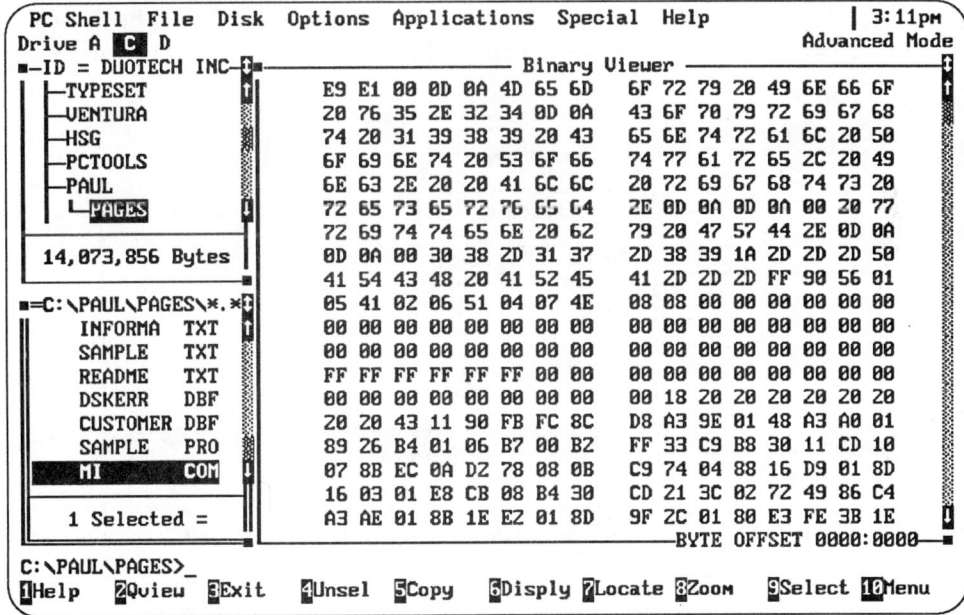

Figure 3.5   Vertical View Window

You can change the default view window format by selecting **Default Viewer**. The value toggles between TEXT and BINARY. Figure 3.1 shows the Text Viewer, while Figure 3.5 shows the Binary Viewer. If you view a file stored in a format PC Shell recognizes, it will appear in one of the specialized viewers. Any file with extension TXT or BAT is shown using the text viewer. Any file with extension COM, EXE, OBJ, BIN, or SYS is always shown with the binary viewer. Any other files are shown using the default viewer.

User Levels

Changing the user level affects what options are available on the menus. Advanced Mode includes all PC Shell commands. You can request a more restricted level by selecting **Change User Level**. The user level function may be password protected. If you wish to change your user level, you may have to obtain the password first. The resulting dialog box lets you choose a different level or allow for immediate running of an application.

Modifying the Screen Colors

PC Shell uses a set of colors it assumes are best for your equipment. If you don't agree, you can modify them. Bring up the **Setup Configuration** pop-up menu and select the **Screen Colors** option. You'll see a dialog box like the one in Figure 3.6. When you highlight one of the items in the list on the left, the color being used for that feature is marked with a dot between the parentheses.

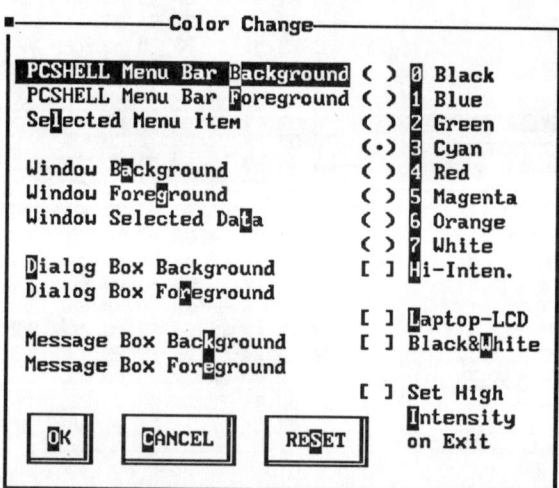

Figure 3.6   Color Change Dialog Box

You can change the color by clicking on a different one or by typing the highlighted number. The screen changes immediately so you can see the effect. When you select one of the dialog box or message box options, a small sample box appears showing the selected color.

The **Set High Intensity on Exit** option has no effect on colors within the shell but it handles a problem you may encounter if you hotkey into and out of PC Shell. If you find, on returning to an application, that colors that should be in high intensity are blinking, you can set this option to prevent it.

When you are satisfied with your selections, choose OK to put them into effect. CANCEL removes the dialog box without making any changes, and RESET restores the default colors.

Changing the System Date and Time

Most computers keep track of the date and time automatically. Such factors as daylight savings time and weak batteries may cause your system to have an incorrect date or time. You can correct either by choosing the **Date/Time** option on the **Setup Configuration** pop-up menu. The resulting dialog box shows the current system date and time and a sample format. You can type a new value for either or both; if you enter an invalid value, PC Shell gives you an error message. To cause the change to take effect, select the SET button. To cancel any change you've made, select EXIT.

The change will remain in effect when you leave PC Shell. If the problem was a weak battery, however, expect it to recur until you replace the battery.

✦ *Try It Out*

1. Change the status of the background mat, then remove the tree window and see the effect. Restore the tree window.
2. Reverse the display of the Short Cut Keys and the DOS command line. Leave it with the one you want to use.
3. Define a function key with a different command. Then restore it if you prefer the default definition.
4. Change the location of the view window and the default viewer. Display the view window if it isn't on, then examine a few files. Try a file with extension TXT as well as one with EXE.
5. Change the user level to **Beginner**, then examine the **File** menu. Set it back to **Advanced**.
6. Change the screen colors, date, and time if you wish.

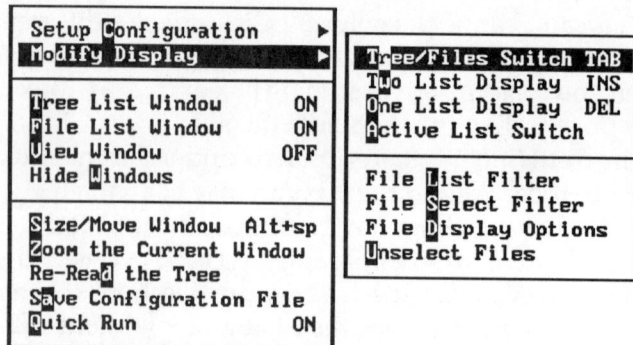

Figure 3.7   Modify Display Pop-Up Window

Using the Modify Display Pop-Up Menu

From the **Modify Display** pop-up menu, shown in Figure 3.7, you can control how the files are listed. We'll examine the lower half of the menu first.

Selecting and Unselecting Files

You can already select files using a global filename by selecting **9Select** or unselect them with **4Unsel**. You can achieve the same effects by choosing **File Select Filter** or **Unselect Files** from the **Modify Display** menu.

Displaying a Limited File List

By default, the file list includes all the filenames in the current directory in the order they appear in the DOS directory. Actually, there is more information available about all the files. If you ask, the shell can show it all to you. You can limit the number of files that are listed and modify the listed order as well.

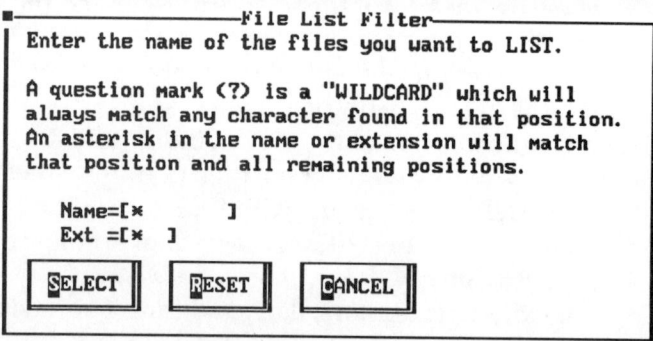

Figure 3.8   File List Filter Dialog Box

You can limit the number of filenames shown in the file list window by selecting the **File List Filter** option on the **Modify Display** pop-up menu. Figure 3.8 shows the resulting dialog box; it is very similar to the one you use when selecting files by a global filename. By default, PC Shell uses a filter of *.*, which lists all files.

Enter the **Name** and **Ext** specifications separately; you don't need a period. In fact, if you type a period, the cursor automatically moves to the **Ext** field, just as when you press Enter. As indicated in the dialog box, you can use the ? and * wildcard characters to specify which files you want to appear in the list. A specification of *.WS? causes all files with extension beginning with WS to appear in the list. A specification of A*.A* causes all files with name beginning with A and extension beginning with A to appear in the list.

A file list filter applies only to the current file list; if you make another directory active, the file list filter is reset to *.*.

Displaying More File Information

You can see more information about an individual file in the list by highlighting it and holding down the right mouse button. If you want the file list window to display more information about each file it lists, you can specify more fields. PC Shell can include the size in bytes, the date and time last modified, the attributes, and the number of clusters used by each file. The result takes up more space in the file list window, so you'll have to do more scrolling to examine the entire list.

Figure 3.9 shows the result of selecting the **File Display Options** on the **Modify Display** window. By default, the options for display are the filename

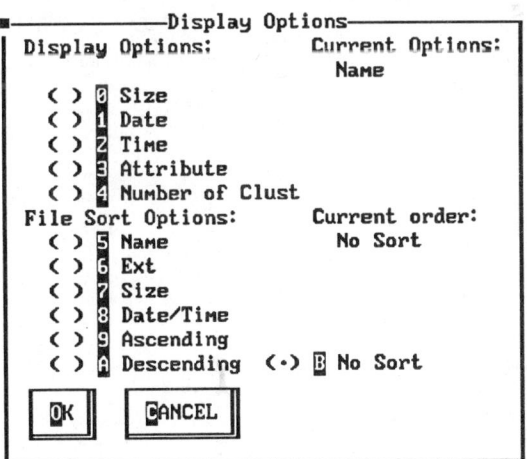

Figure 3.9 Display Options Dialog Box

and the extension. You can select any or all of the other display options by clicking or pressing the indicated number. A dot appears next to each selected option.

When copying or deleting a file, you sometimes need to know how much space it takes up. **Size** tells you how many bytes are in a file; **Number of Clust** tells how much space it occupies on disk. **Date** and **Time** can help you identify different versions of a file. The attributes are explained in Chapter 4. Figure 3.10 shows the effect when size and date are selected for display. While three columns of filenames are visible with only the name and extension displayed, just one shows in its entirety in this configuration.

As with the file list filter, the display options apply only to the displayed directory. If you switch to another, the default display reappears.

Rearranging the Directory List

By default, PC Shell shows you the files in the order in which they appear in the directory. This is the quickest way for the shell to work. You may want the files to be listed in some other sequence, such as alphabetically, by size, or by date. You can specify sort options through the **Display Options** dialog box (see Figure 3.9) as well.

You can select only one of the listed options for sorting. If you choose **Name**,

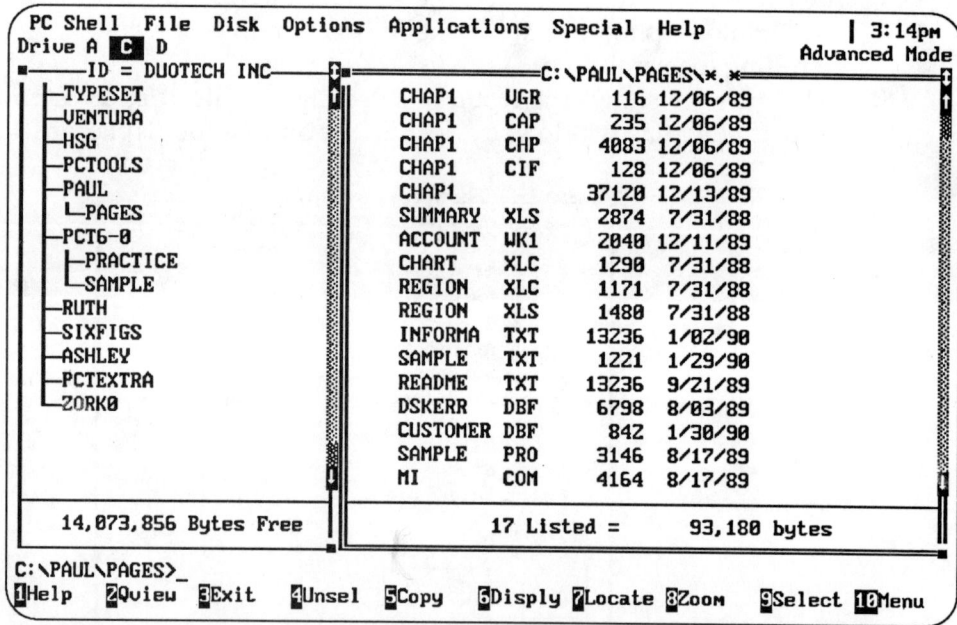

Figure 3.10   File List Window with Size and Date Displayed

the files are sorted in alphabetical order by filename. If you choose **Ext**, they are sorted in alphabetical order by extension. If you select **Size** or **Date/Time**, the files are sorted in that sequence. In addition, you can specify **Ascending** or **Descending** for the direction; if you don't specify, you'll get an ascending sort, with files beginning with A, the earliest date, or the smallest size first. You'll see a dot appear in the **Ascending** or **Descending** field when you select a sort option. You can change it to the other one if you prefer.

If two or more files have identical sort values, PC Shell determines their order. For example, if the sort field is extension and six files have EXE as the extension, they will be grouped together but the shell determines the order within the group. You cannot specify a secondary sort field.

Figure 3.11 shows the result of a name sort in ascending sequence. If two file lists are displayed, the sort affects them both. If you want a nondefault sort order to apply to all your PC Shell sessions, you can save the configuration.

The Directory Sort Option

You can also modify the directory sort order from the **Special** menu. Select **Directory Sort** to see the dialog box shown in Figure 3.12. Notice that this dialog box gives you an additional option; you can sort by select number as well. The real advantage of this method over the previous one, however, is that it can actually change the order of the files in the disk's directory. Then they will continue to be listed in the new order, even if you are working from the command prompt or some other software application.

```
════════════════════C:\PAUL\PAGES\*.*═══════════
 ACCOUNT    WK1
 CHAP1
 CHAP1      CAP
 CHAP1      CHP
 CHAP1      CIF
 CHAP1      UGR
 CHART      XLC
 CUSTOMER   DBF
 DSKERR     DBF
 INFORMA    TXT
 MI         COM
 README     TXT
 REGION     XLC
 REGION     XLS
 SAMPLE     PRO
 SAMPLE     TXT
 SUMMARY    XLS

           17 Listed =      93,180 bytes
```

Figure 3.11   Sort in Ascending Order by Name

58   Basic PC Shell Usage

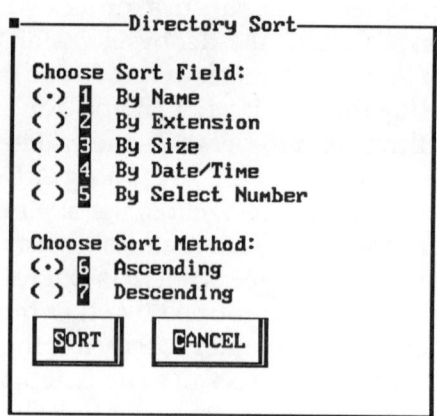

Figure 3.12   Directory Sort Dialog Box

When you sort by select number, the files are listed in the order they were selected. This is useful if you want to ensure that particular files appear in a specific place in the directory. For example, you might want to make sure a few files always appear first in a directory listing. Just select all the files so that each one has a select number on the screen. Start with the files you want to appear first. To force some files to appear last, select them last so they have the highest numbers. Then sort in select number order.

When you have chosen a sort field and either ascending or descending order, select SORT to put the sort into effect. You'll see the dialog box shown in Figure 3.13 next. Here you can choose VIEW to use the directory sequence

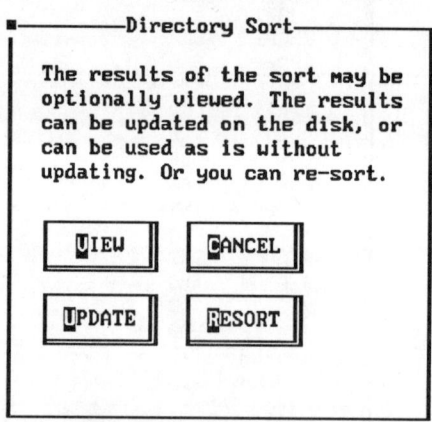

Figure 3.13   Completing the Directory Sort

on the screen without affecting the disk. Choose UPDATE to change the directory sequence on the disk as well as on the screen. If you sort the root directory, the UPDATE result won't be apparent until you re-read the tree. Sorting the root directory may rearrange the displayed sequence of its first level of subdirectories, but it has no effect on files stored in the various subdirectories.

If you choose RESORT, you'll return to the **Directory Sort** dialog box to choose an alternate sequence. This sort affects only the selected directory. Even if two file lists are displayed, the active one is the only directory affected. You don't have to save this configuration, because once you have selected UPDATE, the change is effective on the disk.

✧ *Try It Out*

1. Make the PC Tools directory current, then limit the display to files with extension OVL.
2. Display the date and time for each file.
3. Sort the directory by name.
4. Restore the standard listing (*.*) with no extra fields.
5. Copy two more files to TRYOUT, then make it current. Sort it by filename and update it on disk.

List Displays

You can also use the **Modify Display** pop-up menu to display two directory trees and two file lists at once; this can't be done when a view window is turned on. The default display status is the **One List Display**, seen in figures so far.

When you select **Two List Display** on the **Modify Display** pop-up menu, the screen changes to show two separate tree and file list windows as shown in Figure 3.14. The added set at the bottom reflects the same directory and drive, but you can change either set once the two lists are displayed. The drive selections apply to the currently active set of tree and file list windows.

By default, the two sets of windows take up the same amount of space on the screen. You can rearrange them by sizing and moving windows individually. The file display options affect both windows; you can't show the size in one window and not in the other. A sort through the **Options** menu affects both displays. A sort through the **Special** menu, however, affects only the active display.

While you can select files in both file lists, file operations affect only the active one. For example, if you select several files in both file list windows,

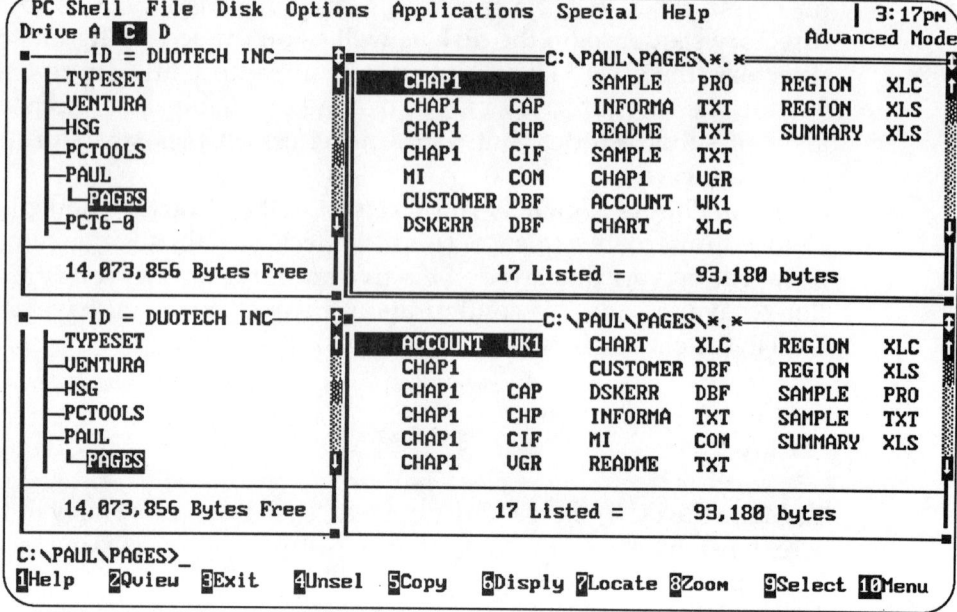

Figure 3.14   Two List Display

then start a copy operation, only the files in the active file list window will be copied.

Switching between Lists. As you know, a double border identifies the active tree or file list window. When you click in any displayed window, it becomes active. Pressing Tab switches between the active windows at one level. You can switch to the other set of windows by selecting **Active List Switch** on the **Modify Display** pop-up menu. If the upper set of windows was active, the lower set becomes active. If you work with two lists very often, you might want to define one of your function keys to perform the active list switch function. Once the correct set is active, you can Tab to make the other window at that level active as needed.

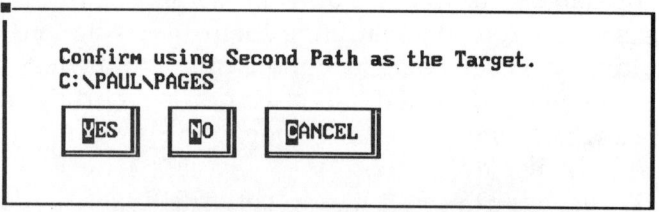

Figure 3.15   Copying to the Other Displayed Directory

Copying and Moving between Lists. When you have two lists displayed, you can copy or move files from one to the other more easily. When you select one or more files in one file list window and select **Copy** from the **File** menu, you see a dialog box like the one in Figure 3.15. If the selected files are to be copied to the directory in the other part of the screen, just select YES, and they are copied immediately.

To copy to some other location, just select NO. You can copy files between two displayed file lists by dragging as well. Select the files to be copied, press the mouse button, drag the pointer into the other file list, and release it.

You can move files between two displayed file lists by selecting them, then choosing the **Move** option. You can choose the YES button in the resulting dialog box to accomplish the move. To drag files from one displayed list to another, select the files, then press the Control key before dragging. You'll have to confirm the operation before the files are deleted from the original location.

✧ *Try It Out*

1. Make the TRYOUT directory active, then switch to a two-list display. Make the root directory active in the lower set of windows.
2. Practice making different windows active with both the mouse and the keyboard. Try the online help if you have any problems.
3. Display time and date in both file lists. Sort the root directory list by file name.
4. Copy two COM files from the root directory to TRYOUT using the **Copy** option.
5. Limit the root directory file list to files with extension COM.
6. If you have a mouse, use dragging to copy MYFILE.ZZZ from TRYOUT to the root directory.

You've learned to control what appears on your PC Shell screen and to manipulate how and where different items appear. You can use these features whenever you want their effects as you learn to use more file and directory utilities.

Section II
Using PC Tools Utilities

Chapter 4
File and Directory Utilities

PC Shell includes many utilities to manipulate files and directories. In this chapter, you'll see how to use PC Shell options to:

- Create and edit files
- Print a file
- Print a directory listing
- Locate a file by name
- Locate files containing a specified string
- Verify and compare files
- Interpret and manipulate attributes
- Display full file information
- Prune and graft directories

Editing a File

You can create or edit an ASCII or text file of any length using PC Shell. For example, you can modify your AUTOEXEC.BAT or CONFIG.SYS file using the PC Shell editing facility. Any file you create with this editor is an ASCII file by default.

The PC Tools Desktop includes another editor called Notepads, which has additional features and works somewhat differently. Chapter 7 deals with editing using Notepads.

Editing an Existing File

To edit an existing file with the PC Shell editor, select it, then pull down the **File** menu and choose the **Edit File** option or select **FileEdit** on the short cut keys line. If no file is selected, the shell assumes you want the highlighted file. You'll see a dialog box like the one shown in Figure 4.1. At this point you can choose to EDIT the named file, CREATE a new file, or CANCEL the file editor. If you happened to select a file with extension BAK, $$$, EXE, or COM, you will be told that these files can't be edited. In this case, you'll have only the CREATE and EXIT options available to you.

Once you confirm that you want to edit the named file, you'll see the text for that file on the screen.

Creating a New File

If you choose to create a new file, the next screen looks like the one in Figure 4.2. The commands and screen layout are the same whether you are creating a new file or editing an existing one. The only difference is that the filename of an existing file appears in the upper left corner and its text appears in the window. In the example in Figure 4.2, only the path appears since the new file does not yet have a name.

File Editor Screen

The menu bar is not active while the File Editor screen is displayed. The symbol shown on the line following the path is the end-of-file mark; it moves along with the cursor as you add text to a new file. The cursor itself appears onscreen as either an underscore when insert is off or as a shaded rectangle

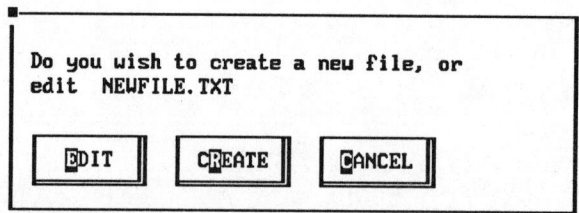

Figure 4.1   File Edit Dialog Box

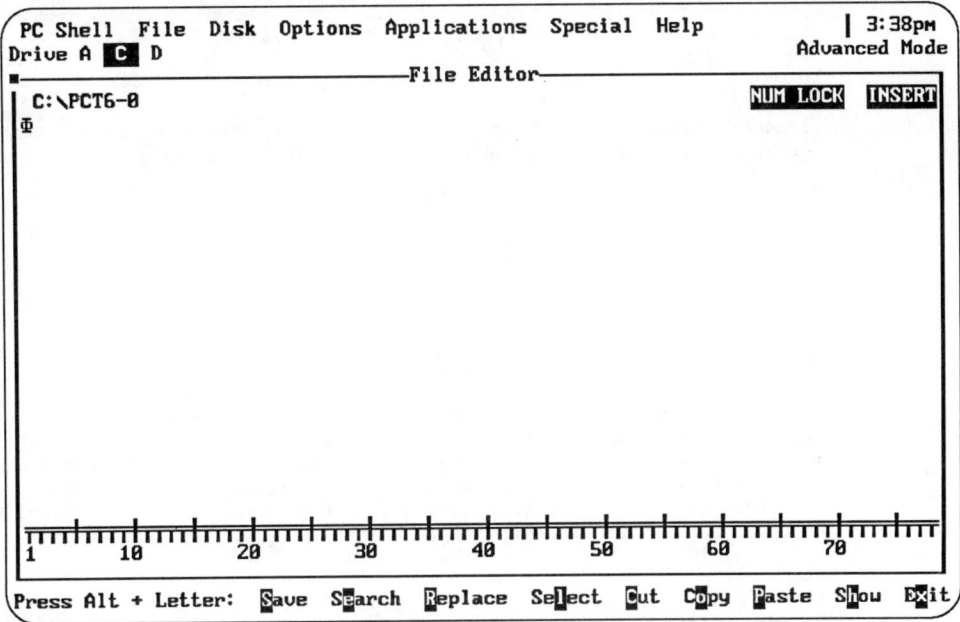

Figure 4.2   File Editor—Creating a New File

when it is on. The current status of NUM LOCK and INSERT are shown in the upper right. You can switch their status by pressing the NumLock or Insert key. The lower part of the window shows a ruler so you can format your text if you like. The ruler is especially useful if you are creating a table, a computer program, or any indented text. The bottom line provides special commands that you can use during editing. You can click on the words as on the main shell screen. From the keyboard, you must press the Alt key with the highlighted letter to activate the commands; characters typed without Alt or Ctrl appear in the text.

You create a file by just typing it. If you are creating a list or a computer program, press Enter at the end of each line. If you are typing paragraphs, you can let PC Shell handle line breaks; it wraps words to the next line, so you need to press Enter only to end the paragraph. To insert a blank line, press Enter twice in succession. One of the commands on the bottom line is **Show**; it displays every location where you pressed Enter, as you can see in Figure 4.3. Each highlighted left arrow shows where a carriage return occurs. Selecting **Show** again removes the displayed marks from the screen.

As you type, the characters automatically wrap to the next line, so the margins you see on the screen are not really part of the file. When you print the file, the margins will be as you request or as your printer defaults. You don't control the margins during text entry.

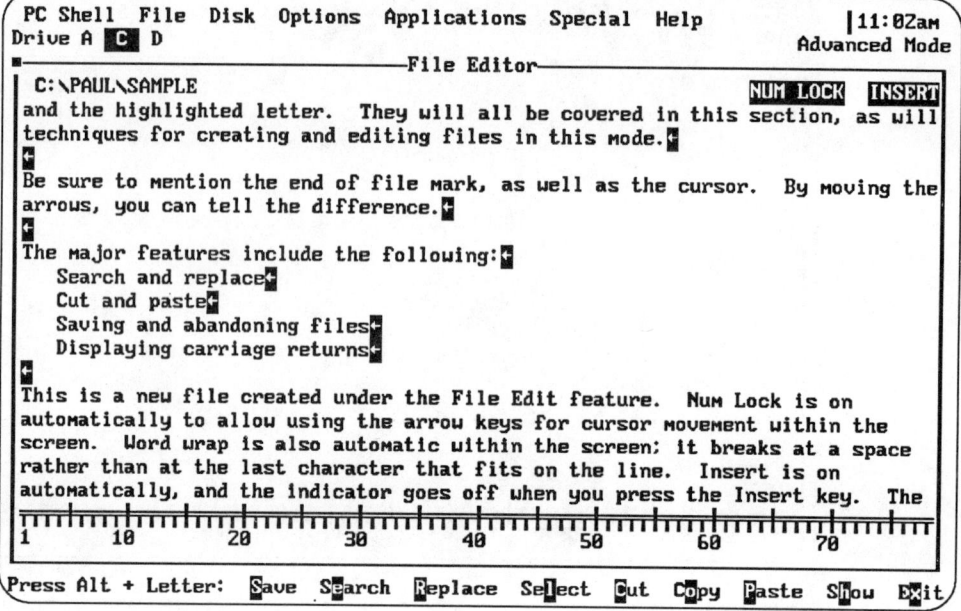

Figure 4.3   Displaying Carriage Returns

Moving the Cursor

While you are in the file editor, you must use keyboard keys for all operations except selecting commands. Most keys, listed in Table 4.1, function as you might expect. You can use these keys to move the cursor around in the file so you can examine it and make changes. Notice that Ctrl-Home and Ctrl-End move the cursor to the beginning and end of the file, while pressing the Home key twice in succession moves the cursor to the beginning of the window and pressing End,End moves the cursor to the end of the window.

Exiting the Editor

You can exit the editor by pressing Esc or by selecting **Exit** from the command line. If you have made changes to a file being edited, you'll be prompted to save the file. You can choose to save it or abandon any changes.

Saving an Edited File

When you have created or changed a file, you can save it to disk by selecting the **Save** or **Exit** command. If you select **Save**, you'll be prompted to enter a

Table 4.1   Keyboard Editing Keys

Delete	delete character at cursor
Backspace	delete character to left of cursor
Up arrow	move cursor up one line
Down arrow	move cursor down one line
Right arrow	move cursor right one character
Left arrow	move cursor left one character
Home	move cursor to beginning of line
End	move cursor to end of line
Ctrl-Home	move cursor to beginning of file
Ctrl-End	move cursor to end of file
Home,Home	move cursor to beginning of window
End,End	move cursor to end of window
PageUp	scroll text up one window
PageDown	scroll text down one window

filename if needed, then the changes you've made are saved and you remain in file edit mode. If you select **Exit** after changes have been made, you'll be asked if you want to save the file first. If you decline, any changes you have made are lost. If you were creating a new file, you'll be prompted to enter a name for it. If you were editing a previously existing file, you'll be asked if you want to provide a new name or use the current one.

When you edit an existing file, PC Shell doesn't modify the current disk file until you request that it be saved. Then PC Shell renames the old version with the BAK extension and applies the original name and extension to the saved version.

Cut and Paste Operations

You can perform minor editing using just the keyboard keys. Sometimes you'll need more extensive editing, however. You might want to remove a large block of text, for example, or repeat a group of sentences in several places. You can do these things using several commands from the command line: **Select**, **Cut**, **Copy**, and **Paste**.

Cut and copy operations work on already selected blocks of text. You select a block of text by highlighting it on the screen. Then you cut or copy it to an internal buffer. If you cut the block, it is also removed from the file onscreen; cutting a block effectively deletes it from the file. If you copy it, the text remains in its original location as well as being placed in the buffer. When you select

Paste, whatever is stored in the buffer is inserted into the file at the cursor. You can use **Paste** repeatedly to insert the buffer contents at several locations.

The buffer holds only one block of text at a time. If you have to work with several blocks, finish dealing with one block before selecting the next.

Selecting a Block. To select a block, first position the cursor at the first or last character of the block. Then select the **Select** command by clicking on it or pressing Alt-L. Now move the arrow keys until the entire block you want is highlighted. If you use Alt-L again at this point, the block is unselected. To put the selected block in the buffer, you need to use **Cut** or **Copy** while the block is highlighted; this cancels the selection and places the text in the buffer.

Deleting a Block. To remove a selected block from the file, select **Cut** by clicking on it or pressing Alt-C. The highlighted block disappears from the screen and is stored internally in the buffer. It will remain there until you use **Cut** or **Copy** again or leave the editor.

Moving a Block. To move a selected block to another location in a file, first select **Cut** to remove it from the original location. Then position the cursor at the desired location and select **Paste** by clicking on it or pressing Alt-P. The text in the buffer is inserted at the cursor. If you want to insert the same text in several locations, you can move the cursor again and repeat the **Paste** operation.

Copying a Block. To copy a selected block to another location in a file, first select **Copy** by clicking on it or by pressing Alt-O. Then position the cursor at the desired location and select **Paste**. The buffer contents is inserted at the cursor. You can repeat the **Paste** at different locations as needed.

✧ *Try It Out*

1. Use the editor to examine your AUTOEXEC.BAT file. Move the cursor around in the file and display the carriage returns, but don't make any changes. Exit the file without saving it.
2. Use the editor to create a file in your TRYOUT directory. Type your name and address as in a mailing label then save the file as MYSTUFF.ED without leaving the editor. Notice that the new name appears at the top of the screen.
3. Edit the file you just created. Type another name at the end of the file, then mark your address as a block and repeat it following the second name.

4. Type two or three short paragraphs of four or five sentences each at the end of the file. Type until the first set of lines is off the screen. Scroll back to the start of the file.
5. Move your original name and address to the end of the file.
6. Use a block command to eliminate the first copy of your name and address from the file. Exit the editor and save the file.

Search and Replace Operations

Even in basic editing, you may want to search for a string of characters. You might even want to do a search and replace operation. The PC Shell file editor lets you perform these operations using the **Search** and **Replace** commands. You'll be prompted to enter a string to search for. This string is limited to 32 characters and is not case sensitive; if you enter "john" it finds "John" and "JOHN" as well, either as separate words or as part of longer words. The search always begins at the first character in the file.

Searching for a String. When you select the **Search** command, a dialog box like the one in Figure 4.4 appears. You type the string you want to search for and press Enter.

If no matching strings are found, you'll see a message box containing "Search/Replace argument NOT found". When the editor finds a match, you'll see the message "Search Mode:" on the bottom line with the additional commands **Search** and **Exit**. Select **Search** to continue the search for the next matching string or **Exit** to terminate at this point and leave the cursor on the found string.

Replacing a String. If you want to replace a string, such as "Microcomputer" for "MC" or "Davidopolous" for "Davidopo", select the **Replace** command. You'll see a dialog box similar to the one in Figure 4.4, prompting you to enter the characters to be replaced. When you do, you'll see another dialog box asking you to enter the characters to replace them with. The strings need not be the same length, but both are limited to 32 characters. When you press Enter, the operation starts.

```
Enter characters to search for below:
[_                                    ]
```

Figure 4.4   Search Dialog Box

When PC Shell replaces a matching string, it stops and shows the result to you in context, as shown in Figure 4.5. In the first line of the last paragraph, the word "fitting" has replaced the word "right"; the cursor rests on the first character of the inserted string. You can choose to exit the replace operation or locate and replace the next occurrence of the string.

You can't skip a replacement; as soon as you choose to exit, the replacement operation is over. When no more matches are found, PC Shell displays an appropriate message.

✧ *Try It Out*

1. Bring up MYSTUFF.ED in the file editor. Search for a string such as "the" that appears several times in the file.
2. Search for a string that appears several times and change it to "$$$$".
3. Search for "$$$$" and replace it with the original string. Notice how the file is restored.
4. Practice replacing a string with one of a greatly different length.
5. Search for a string that doesn't exist in the file. Notice the message that appears when it can't be found.

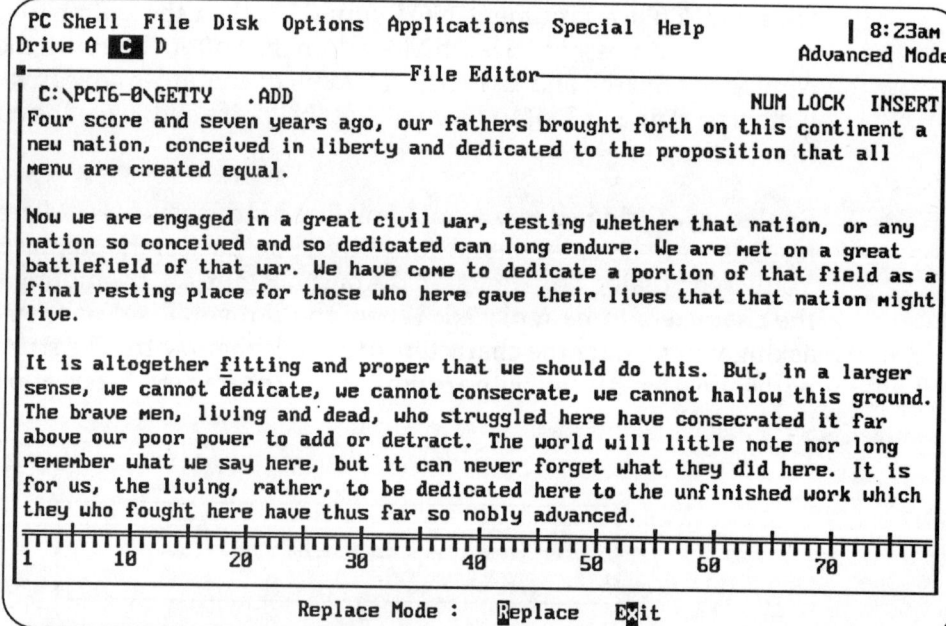

Figure 4.5   Replace Mode Choices

Printing

You can use PC Shell to print files you have edited as well as other files (if they are printable, of course) and directories. Printing takes place on the default printer, usually LPT1. If you have a printer connected to a different port, your AUTOEXEC.BAT file probably redirects LPT1 to it.

Printing a File

To print one or more selected files, select **Print File** on the **File** menu, after making sure the printer is ready. You'll see a dialog box like the one in Figure 4.6 in which you can select the type of printing you want done.

Printing Standard ASCII Text. The first choice prints the file as standard text; choose this if the ASCII file has carriage returns where you want every line to end. You might use standard text for lists, computer programs, or preformatted documentation. Standard text assumes a new line starts after each carriage return. If your file includes paragraphs in which word wrap occurred, the printed result with standard text depends on your printer. Many printers will show only the first part of a line and you won't see anything extending beyond the printer's default right margin. If a carriage return ends every line before the 80 character point, however, standard text prints just fine.

Printing Sectors in ASCII and Hex. The bottom print option in Figure 4.6 lets you print the hexadecimal form of the sectors in the file. Each disk sector (256 bytes) is printed in hexadecimal and the equivalent ASCII format. Figure 4.7 shows how a file appears printed in this mode. The sector dump is more useful for nonprintable files such as programs, if you can interpret the codes. Chapter 6 deals with hexadecimal format.

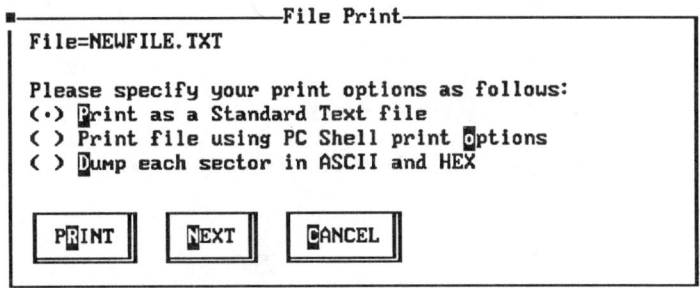

Figure 4.6   File Print Dialog Box

```
Sector 0000000
      0000 (0000)  0D0A0D0A54776169-6E2C204D61726B0D   ....Twain, Mark.
      0016 (0010)  0A48617774686F72-6E652C204E617468   .Hawthorne, Nath
      0032 (0020)  616E69656C0D0A42-656E63686C65792C   aniel..Benchley,
      0048 (0030)  2050657465720D0A-576F6465686F7573    Peter..Wodehous
      0064 (0040)  652C20502E20472E-0D0A4D6163446F63   e, P. G...MacDon
      0080 (0050)  616C642C204A6F68-6E20442E0D0A4D69   ald, John D...Mi
      0096 (0060)  6368656E65722C20-4A616D65730D0A43   chener, James..C
      0112 (0070)  6C61726B2C205374-657068656E0D0ARB   lark, Stephen..K
      0128 (0080)  696E672C20537465-7068656E0D0A4B61   ing, Stephen..Ka
      0144 (0090)  79652C204D2E204D-2E0D0A43726F7362   ye, M. M...Crosb
      0160 (00A0)  792C2042696E670D-0A4173686C65792C   y, Bing..Ashley,
      0176 (00B0)  205061756C0D0A52-61776C696E67732C    Paul..Rawlings,
      0192 (00C0)  204D61726A6F7269-65204B696E6E616E    Marjorie Kinnan
      0208 (00D0)  0D0A537465706865-6E736F6E2C204461   ..Stephenson, Da
      0224 (00E0)  6E69656C0D0A1A                      niel..
```

Figure 4.7   ASCII and Hex Dump Print

Printing with PC Shell Print Options. When you want to print files created with the editor that don't have a carriage return at the end of each line, you can use the second choice. This is ideal for files in which you let word wrap create your paragraphs. It uses a set of defaults to specify the page layout; it also lets you specify formatting options to override the defaults and control the layout to some extent. When you select this option, you see a dialog box like the one in Figure 4.8. The default values are shown in the box. You can modify any or all of the page layout values to get the page layout required by your file.

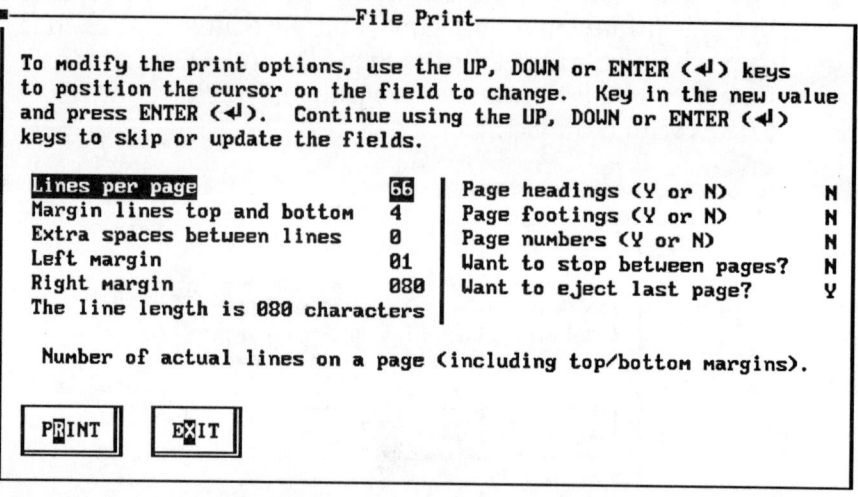

Figure 4.8   File Print Options Dialog Box

Exactly what the default values are and what values you can use depend on your printer. As you highlight each option in the box, a brief description of it appears above the PRINT and EXIT buttons.

If you want to use page headings or footings, you'll be given a prompt to type the text. You can use up to 50 characters in each. A heading is centered on the second line from the top of the page, within the top margin area. A footing is centered two lines up from the bottom of the page, within the bottom margin area. If you want page numbers, they'll start with 1. If you don't specify a footing, the first page number is centered as "Page 1". If you do, the footing is centered and the page number appears on the far right of the same line. More options for headings and footings are available through the Desktop Notepads if you find these too limiting.

When all your preferred options are set, select PRINT. The first selected file will be printed and this dialog box will return for the next. It will be set up just as you specified for the first file, but you can modify any options just as before. When you terminate PC Shell, the defaults are reestablished. Figure 4.9 shows the result of printing a file created under the file editor with nondefault margins, heading, and footing.

```
                        1991 Annual Conference Details


                           Registration Procedures


        Scheduling

        The registration booth will be open from 7 a.m. to 9 p.m.
        each day to accommodate both early and late arrivals.  At
        least five people will work the desk from 7 through 10 in
        the morning and from 2 to 4 in the afternoon.  Other times
        three people will be sufficient.
        One team leader will be on duty at all time. This will allow
        the registration directors to take care of specail problems
        and free them from supervision of the registration workers.


           ...
           ...


        Supplies

        The printouts and other records are available at the desk.
        They are for the use of the staff only; don't let the
        registrants get their hands on them.  Pens and pencils are
        supplied in abundance.



                              Confidential                      Page    2
```

Figure 4.9   Printing with Nondefault Print Options

Printing a Directory List

To print a list of the files in a directory, select the directory you want printed, then pull down the **File** menu and choose **Print File List**. The files currently listed in the file list window for that directory are printed; to get a limited list you can use a filter before printing the directory. To control the order of the list, you can perform a directory sort first. You'll get full file information in the listing, as shown in Figure 4.10, regardless of how much information is shown in the file list window.

The printed directory includes the filename and extension, the size of the file in bytes, and the number of clusters it occupies. The date and time it was created or last modified are shown as well. The rightmost column shows the current attributes for each file; you'll learn to interpret and change attributes later in this chapter.

✧ Try It Out

1. Print your AUTOEXEC.BAT file using the Standard Text option, then print a dump of it in ASCII and Hex mode.
2. Print MYSTUFF.ED using the Standard Text option.
3. Print MYSTUFF.ED using the PC Shell default print options.

```
PC Shell R5.5                      Directory Print              ID = DUOTECH INC
--------------------------------------------------------------------------------
Path=C:\WS5\TEST
      Name      Ext    Size #Clu   Date      Time  Attributes
      UNIX      PRO    7936    4  12/20/88   8:51a    A
      AWARD     LET    5760    3   1/19/89   1:30p    A
      LETTER    HD      256    1   1/13/89   3:01p    A
      ROGER     4-4    1792    1   4/04/89   2:50p    A
      NSPI      LET    1408    1   2/23/89   3:13p    A
      SCOXENIX  BF     1664    1   2/27/89   1:24p    A
      LHEAD2    PS     1536    1   4/04/89   2:16p    A
      ADDRESS   PS     1536    1   4/04/89   2:26p    A
      NEIGHBOR  WSF   33920   17   4/05/89  12:09p    A
      LHEAD2PS  SAV    1536    1   9/11/88   8:03a    A
      PSBOXES   PS      384    1   9/11/88   8:48a    A
      PSBOX2    PS      640    1   9/12/88   5:00p    A
      TELECOM   DEL    1152    1   5/15/89   9:47a    A
      DOWNES           3024    2   6/15/89   4:30p    A
      LET               896    1   6/16/89  12:54p    A
      INVOICE   MAR     896    1   7/15/89   4:15p    A

      16 files LISTed   =   64336 bytes.   16 files in sub-dir =   64336 bytes.
       0 files SELECTed =       0 bytes.   Available on volume = 14419968 bytes.
```

Figure 4.10   Printed Directory List

4. Print MYSTUFF.ED again. Modify the top, left, and right margin settings so that you notice the effect on the output.
5. Print MYSTUFF.ED with a page heading. Use any information you want for the heading.
6. Print the PC Tools directory list.

Locating Files

PC Shell offers several ways to locate files and text when you aren't sure where they are. You can locate files on the current drive by name, no matter which directory they are stored in, by specifying an individual or global filespec. You can limit the located files to ones containing a particular text string. If you aren't concerned with the filename, you can locate files in the current display that contain a particular string. This section covers both methods for finding files. Chapter 6 shows how you can search the disk itself for a string, even if it isn't currently part of a file.

Locating across Directories

You may not recall where a file is stored. You may not even remember the exact filename. Or you may want to perform file operations on files in several different directories at one time. PC Shell can locate a file by searching all the directories on the current drive. You can tell it the exact filename and extension, use a global filespec, or specify all files associated with an application. All files that match will be located, even if they are in different directories. The first step is to pull down the **File** menu and select the **Locate File** option. You'll see a menu like the one in Figure 4.11. The options listed depend on your

Figure 4.11   File Locate Pop-Up Menu

system. If you select the first option, you'll be prompted for specific or global information for both the **Name** and **Ext** fields, just as when you specify a filter for the file list or selection.

Next you'll see a search box in which you can enter a string. If you just want to locate files that match the name, press enter to bypass the search box. If you want to further limit the search to those files that contain a certain text string, type up to 32 characters before pressing Enter.

All the files PC Shell locates are listed in a special window. Figure 4.12 shows how the locate window might look if you use CH*.* as the global filespec. You can see the filename and extension on the left, while the appropriate path is shown on the far right. If you enter a string as well, the list will be further limited. You can select and process files in the locate window just as in a file list window. All the menu options and commands are valid while this screen is displayed. If you turn on the view window, you'll be able to examine each file; PC Shell uses the appropriate viewer. When the view window and locate window share the screen, you can resize and move them as needed to get the layout that is most useful to you.

If PC Shell is resident, you can hotkey out of it once the locate window is displayed. When you hotkey back into the shell, the same screen will appear. If you go to another screen within the shell, however, you'll have to run the **Locate Files** option again to restore the screen.

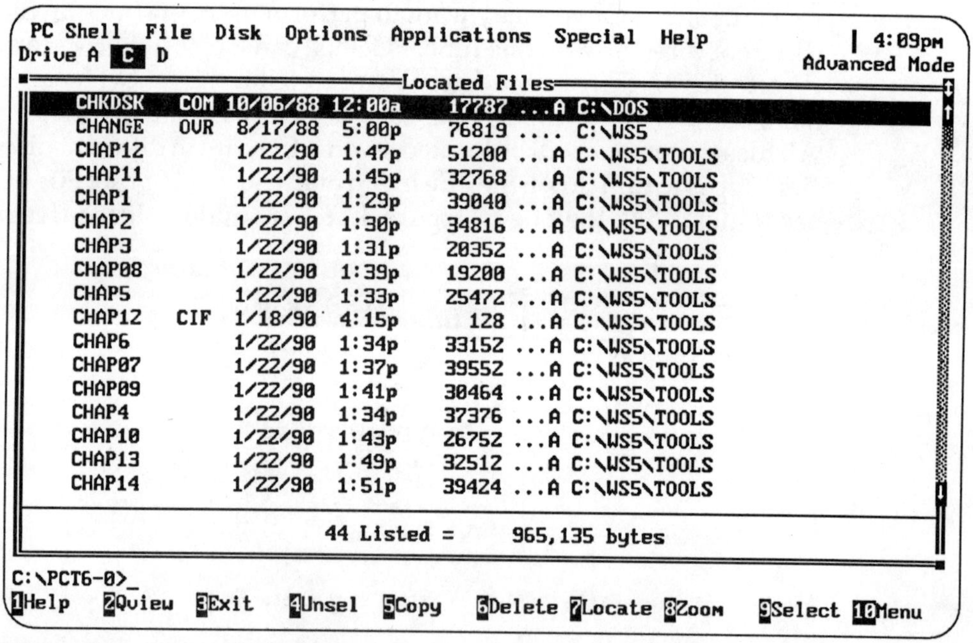

```
PC Shell  File  Disk  Options  Applications  Special  Help        | 4:09PM
Drive A  C  D                                                     Advanced Mode
===============================Located Files================================
   CHKDSK    COM  10/06/88  12:00a    17787 ...A  C:\DOS
   CHANGE    OUR   8/17/88   5:00p    76819 ....  C:\WS5
   CHAP12          1/22/90   1:47p    51200 ...A  C:\WS5\TOOLS
   CHAP11          1/22/90   1:45p    32768 ...A  C:\WS5\TOOLS
   CHAP1           1/22/90   1:29p    39040 ...A  C:\WS5\TOOLS
   CHAP2           1/22/90   1:30p    34816 ...A  C:\WS5\TOOLS
   CHAP3           1/22/90   1:31p    20352 ...A  C:\WS5\TOOLS
   CHAP08          1/22/90   1:39p    19200 ...A  C:\WS5\TOOLS
   CHAP5           1/22/90   1:33p    25472 ...A  C:\WS5\TOOLS
   CHAP12    CIF   1/18/90   4:15p      128 ...A  C:\WS5\TOOLS
   CHAP6           1/22/90   1:34p    33152 ...A  C:\WS5\TOOLS
   CHAP07          1/22/90   1:37p    39552 ...A  C:\WS5\TOOLS
   CHAP09          1/22/90   1:41p    30464 ...A  C:\WS5\TOOLS
   CHAP4           1/22/90   1:34p    37376 ...A  C:\WS5\TOOLS
   CHAP10          1/22/90   1:43p    26752 ...A  C:\WS5\TOOLS
   CHAP13          1/22/90   1:49p    32512 ...A  C:\WS5\TOOLS
   CHAP14          1/22/90   1:51p    39424 ...A  C:\WS5\TOOLS
                           44 Listed =    965,135 bytes
C:\PCT6-0>_
 1Help  2Qview  3Exit  4Unsel  5Copy  6Delete  7Locate  8Zoom  9Select  10Menu
```

Figure 4.12   Locate Window

Modifying the File Locate Pop-Up Menu

When PC Tools was installed, several general groups were added to your **Applications** menu, depending on what major software applications PC Setup identified on your disk. Files supporting these programs were also added to the **File Locate** pop-up menu, so that you can locate the files easily. Each one is associated with particular filespecs. You can remove entries from the **File Locate** menu, add new ones, edit existing ones, and rearrange the menu entries. While the **File Locate** menu is displayed, the function key line includes the options shown in Figure 4.11.

Each existing menu entry has two values associated with it. The groupname, which appears on the menu, can be up to 20 characters long. If one character is preceded by ^, that character is highlighted in the menu; the groupname ^Correspondence lets you press C to access the group. The filespecs consist of up to 100 characters of one or more filespecs that will be included or excluded from the locate operation. Suppose you want a group to locate all files with extension DOC except those in the root directory. You could use *.DOC –\ as the groupname. If you want to specify all files with extension SCR except those in the \HSG directory, you might use *.SCR –\HSG. You can use any combination you wish; each can include a dash to indicate exclusion. A path can be included with any filespec.

When you select **5Edit, 6Delete,** or **7Move,** you are first prompted to select the entry you want to affect. When you are deleting an entry, you'll have a chance to confirm it or change your mind first. When you are moving the position of an entry, you'll be prompted to use the arrow keys to place it in the desired position. When you press Enter, it is repositioned. When you are editing an entry, the complete entry appears in a box like the one in Figure 4.13. You can change the groupname or the filespecs as needed. Be sure and use at least one space to separate the filespecs.

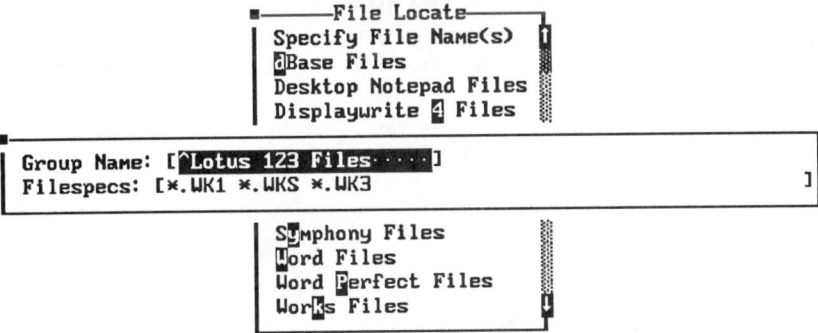

Figure 4.13   Modifying the File Locate Entry

To add an entry, select **4 Add**. A new line composed of <new entry location> appears at the end of the menu. You are prompted to move it to the position you want with the arrow keys. When you press Enter, an empty box like the one shown in Figure 4.13 appears; you fill in the groupname you want and the filespecs to be associated with it. For example, if you want to locate your correspondence files, which may be in any directory but always start with CO or LE, you might use this as a filespec: CO*.* LE*.* −*.COM −*.EXE. The last two filespecs eliminate any program files from the result. Or suppose you use a word processor called Amí® Professional that always uses SAM as the extension. You could use *.SAM as the filespec to locate the files.

If you make any changes to the **File Locate** pop-up menu, you can have them apply to later PC Shell sessions by saving the configuration through the **Options** menu; if you try to exit without saving them, PC Shell asks if you want your changes saved.

Finding Information in a File

You may want to locate a file from the displayed file list or locate window that contains a specific sequence of characters. You can use **Text Search** to search for a string in all files in a window, just the selected ones, or just the unselected ones. You can tell PC Shell to pause when the string is located or to select the file that contains the string and continue checking the other specified files and selecting the ones that contain the string.

After you pull down the **File** menu and select **Text Search**, you'll see the dialog box shown in Figure 4.14. You can enter a string of up to 32 characters. This function is not case sensitive; if you enter "macdonald", PC Shell finds "MacDonald", "Macdonald", "MACDONALD", and various other combinations as well.

If you prefer to search for a hexadecimal string, select **Hex** from the bottom screen line to see a dialog box specific for hex strings. The choices and string lengths are the same, but it is case sensitive; the hex code for "A" is different from that for "a", for example. If you enter an invalid hex value, PC Shell

```
■────────────Text Search────────────
    Enter case insensitive text to search for:
         [............................]
    in 1 file.

    Search:                 If found:
    ( ) All files           ( ) Select file and continue
    (•) Selected files      (•) Pause search
    ( ) Unselected files
```

Figure 4.14   Text Search Dialog Box

doesn't display it, so you'll have to correct it before going on. Corresponding ASCII values are displayed as you enter the hex string.

Once your string is typed, you can set the options. Specify which files to search and what to do when a match is found. Then press Enter or select **7Search** to start the search. If you chose **Select file and continue,** you'll be returned to the screen from which you started the search, with all files that contain the string at least once selected.

If you chose **Pause search,** you'll see these options on the bottom line each time a file containing the string is identified: **Select File, Continue Search, View File, Edit File,** and **Next File.** You can choose the appropriate option.

✧ Try It Out

1. Locate all the files on your disk with the EXE extension. Scroll through all the pages.
2. Locate all the files on your disk with the TXT extension that contain the string RE. View several of them from the locate window.
3. Use a text search to select all the files in the root directory that contain the string "REM". View a few of the resulting files.

Checking File Integrity

As you work with files on a disk, you expect that the media and the computer work perfectly. But actually, very little in life is perfect. Almost all the time, your media work correctly. You trust that a file copy is an exact match, that the files you stored on a diskette last month are still in the same condition as when you placed them there. You trust in the integrity of the system. Occasionally, you might want to check it, however. The commands in this section will help you do this.

Verifying Files

If the computer has trouble reading a file, or if you suspect it might, you can tell PC Shell to verify the file. It will then read all the sectors in the file to ensure that it is readable.

To verify files, first select one or more. Then pull down the **File** menu and choose the **Verify** option. PC Shell goes to work on the files immediately; you may see the sector numbers displayed on screen as it proceeds. If no errors are found, you'll see a message for each file that verified OK.

If PC Shell finds an error, you'll see a **File Verify** dialog box that displays the filename and the logical sector that contains the error. You can choose to continue VERIFYing files or to CANCEL the verify operation. A third choice is VIEW/EDIT, which lets you try to repair the error in that sector. Procedures for handling the sector edit are covered in Chapter 6.

Comparing Files

You can compare files to find out if they are identical. The two files can be in the same or different directories; they can have matching or different names. You can compare one set of two files or several pairs with one command.

The first step is to select the first of each set of files to be compared. If you want to compare just two files, select only the first one at this point. Then pull down the **File** menu and choose the **Compare** option. You'll see a dialog box in which you select the second drive for comparison. You can select the same drive if appropriate. Then you see a dialog box in which you choose whether the files on the second drive have names that match those already selected (MATCHING NAMES) or not (DIFFERENT NAMES).

Then you select the directory that contains the second file of each set to be compared; they must all be in the same one. If the screen shows a two-list display, you can just confirm that the second list is the one you want.

If you selected MATCHING NAMES, each set of files is compared, starting with the first one selected. If you selected DIFFERENT NAMES, you'll be prompted to enter the filename and extension for each selected file.

Before each comparison, you'll see the **File Compare** dialog box shown in Figure 4.15. It shows the names of the files being compared. In the example, different names were used.

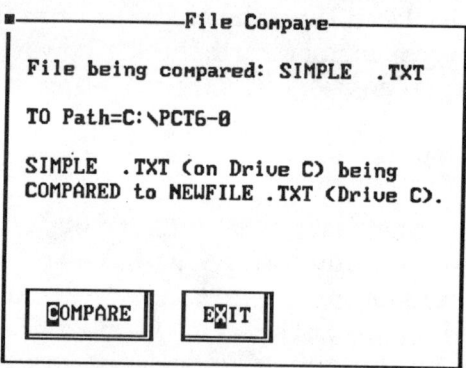

Figure 4.15   File Compare Dialog Box

If the files being compared are of different lengths, PC Shell assumes they don't match and reports an unsuccessful comparison for that reason. If they are the same size, the comparison proceeds. When a difference is found, it is displayed in the box, along with the sector and offset of the mismatch and the ASCII value at that location, as shown in Figure 4.16. You can select CONTINUE to continue the comparison or EXIT to end it. PC Shell continues to report errors until it reaches the end of the file or until you select EXIT. If you note the sector and offset for the beginning of a set of differences, you can examine the files under HexEdit to get further information. HexEdit is discussed in Chapter 6.

Attributes

Every file and directory can have up to four attributes. You can examine and change these attributes through the appropriate commands.

The *hidden* attribute determines whether or not the filename appears in a DOS directory; the file or directory name appears in the PC Shell directory even if it has this attribute. The *system* attribute has essentially the same effect. If you have a file that appears in lists under PC Shell but not at the DOS prompt, it may have either the hidden or system attribute or both. If you want to keep a file or directory from appearing in a DOS directory, give it the hidden attribute. Leave the system attribute to software distributors.

The *read-only* attribute makes the file or directory available only for reading. You won't be able to edit, change, or delete a file or directory that has the read-only attribute. If you can't delete a file, you will probably find that it has the read-only attribute.

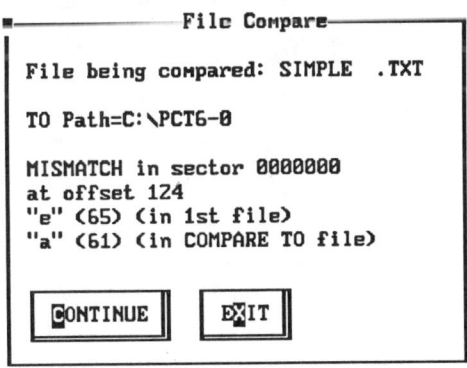

Figure 4.16   File Compare Error

The *archive* attribute indicates whether a file has been changed or copied since it was last backed up using this attribute. You'll learn more about the archive attribute and automatic manipulation of it in Chapter 14.

Examining File Attributes

You can display all the attributes for all your files by adding the attributes to the file list display through the **File Display Options** dialog box, reached through the **Options** menu and the **Modify Display** pop-up menu. Then all the file attributes will be displayed, as shown in Figure 4.17. The first position contains H if the file has the hidden attribute. The second position contains an S if the file has a system attribute, the third contains R if the file has the read-only attribute, and the fourth contains A if the file has the archive attribute. A period appears if the file doesn't have the attribute.

Changing File Attributes

You can check and/or change the attributes for selected files by pulling down the **File** menu and selecting **Attribute Change**. Figure 4.18 shows the result of selecting five files, then choosing **Attribute Change**. The **File Attribute** dialog box shows the four attributes following the extension.

The time and date the file was last modified are shown as well; you can change these if necessary. The file size is shown also, but you can't modify this

```
=C:\*.*=
  IO       SYS HSR.     TOOLS    BAT ...A
  MSDOS    SYS HSR.     EXTRA    FIL ..RA
  COMMAND  COM ...A  1  AUTO     SAV ...A
  AUTOEXEC SAV ...A     MIRROR   FIL ..RA
  MIRROR   BAK ..RA     AUTO     BAK ...A
  HOT      BAT ...A     AMI      BAT ...A
  LASER    BAT ...A     CONFIG   SYS ...A
  UP       BAT ...A
  MOUSE    COM ...A
  MOUSE    SYS ...A
  CON400   400 ...A
  AUTO400  400 ...A
  SCANEXCP RPT ...A
  AUTOEXEC OLD ...A
  MIRORSAV FIL HSRA
  AUTOEXEC BAT ...A
  PCTRACKR DEL ...A

           1 Selected =        336 bytes
```

Figure 4.17   File List with Attributes Displayed

value. You can change any of the attributes by clicking on it or by pressing the letter that indicates it; this toggles the letter and period in the appropriate position. When you press an arrow key, the cursor moves to the time field; alternatively, you can click in the field you want to change. Use the displayed format, with two digits for each part of the date and time if you change them. When you have made all the changes you want, select UPDATE to apply your changes or EXIT to restore the former status.

Don't change attributes on any copy-protected or system files unless you are specifically instructed to do so. It could cause programs to fail to run or your hard disk to fail to boot.

Changing Directory Attributes

Like files, directories can have the hidden, system, read-only, and archive attributes. If a directory has the hidden or system attribute, it still appears in the PC Shell directory tree, but it doesn't appear in the output from various DOS commands. The read-only attribute is applied to some directories in copy-protection schemes, as is the archive attribute. Don't change attributes of copy-protected or system directories; this could make your hard disk fail to boot or programs fail to run.

You can examine and change directory attributes by selecting **Modify Attributes** on the **Directory Maint** pop-up menu of the **Disk** menu. You'll first be prompted to select the subdirectory to modify in the tree window. Then you'll see the dialog box shown in Figure 4.19.

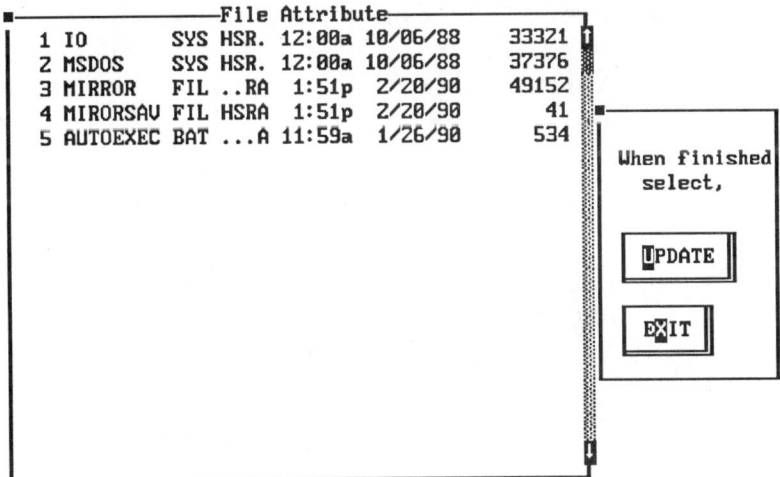

Figure 4.18   File Attribute Dialog Box

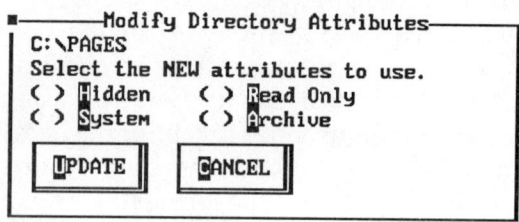

Figure 4.19 Modify Directory Attributes Dialog Box

Just select the attributes you wish to change, then select UPDATE to apply them to the selected directory. Remember what you changed, so you can change it back if your system works strangely after you change directory attributes.

Additional File Information

You can display full file information in the file list window if you wish. But sometimes you just want additional information about a few files. You can find it by selecting the files you are concerned with, then choosing the **More File Info** option of the **File** menu. You'll see a dialog box like the one in Figure 4.20. If several files are selected, a NEXT button appears as well.

The upper part of the dialog box gives the filename and extension, the complete path, and the attributes. The absence of the read-only attribute is called the normal attribute. You can also see the date and time the file was last modified and the file size. The starting cluster number and the number of clusters can help you locate the file on the disk, if that becomes necessary.

✧ Try It Out

1. Select two files in the TRYOUT directory and verify them.
2. Copy README.TXT from the PC Tools directory to the TRYOUT directory. Then compare the two files.
3. Edit TRYOUT\README.TXT by changing two characters in the first paragraph. Then compare it to PCTOOLS\README.TXT again. Notice the messages.
4. Examine the attributes of TRYOUT\README.TXT. Give it the read-only attribute.

5. Try to erase TRYOUT\README.TXT. Examine its full file information.
6. Remove the read-only attribute and give it the hidden attribute. Change the date to a different one.

Directory Maintenance

PC Shell also lets you maintain directories. You've already seen how you can create, delete, and rename directories, as well as change their attributes, using the **Directory Maint** pop-up menu. The shell also lets you move a subdirectory, with all its included files and subdirectories, to a new location in your directory tree.

Pruning and Grafting

Pruning and grafting are tree-surgery terms. When you prune a tree, you remove a branch; everything attached to that branch is removed as well. Grafting refers to attaching a free branch to a new location on a tree. With directories, the two are always used together; if you just want to remove subdirectories you can delete them. You can prune a subdirectory or remove it from its current location; all its files and subdirectories go with it. Then you can graft it to another location in the same directory tree, effectively moving the subtree.

You cannot prune the root directory or the current one; all other directories are fair game, however. Once pruned, the directory can be grafted to any existing directory, even the root or the current one. It becomes a child of that directory.

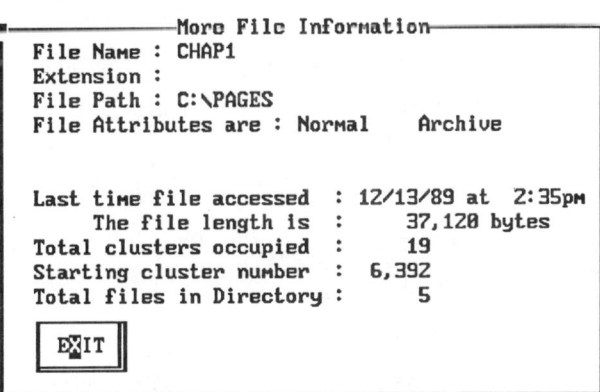

Figure 4.20   More File Information Dialog Box

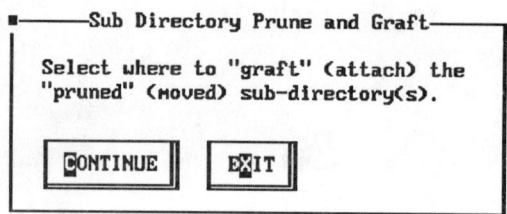

Figure 4.21   Grafting a Subdirectory

Moving a Directory

To move a subdirectory, first make its drive active. Then select **Prune and Graft** from the **Directory Maint** pop-up menu. You'll see a dialog box telling you to select the subdirectory to prune. The tree window is active for you to make the selection. Remember that all included subdirectories and files will be moved as well. You select only the top of the subtree to be moved.

After you select CONTINUE, confirm your selection. If you've selected the root or current directory, you'll see an error message. If the selection is valid, you'll see a dialog box like the one shown in Figure 4.21. The tree window is made active, with the symbol > indicating the top directory to be pruned. You select a different directory where the moved subtree is to be grafted.

Finally, you can select CONTINUE to confirm that the subdirectory marked with > is to be pruned from that location and grafted to the highlighted location. The function will be accomplished and you'll return to the main screen. The effect of the prune and graft operation will be apparent in the tree window.

✧ *Try It Out*

1. Examine your directory tree. Add a subdirectory below TRYOUT. Copy a few files from PCTOOLS to it.
2. Prune the TRYOUT subtree and graft it to another location in your directory tree.
3. Examine the directory tree again. Prune the TRYOUT subtree from its current location and place it under PCTOOLS.

Now that you can use most of the file and directory utilities, you are ready to start with some disk and system utilities. In the next chapter, you'll see how to manipulate your system at a different level.

Chapter 5 | Disk and System Utilities

PC Shell includes several features that you can use to manage your disks and directories, as well as some that give you additional information about how they are being used. These features are included:

- Rename volumes
- Find disk usage information
- Copy and compare diskettes
- Verify disks and diskettes
- Search a disk for a specific string
- Park a hard disk
- Map files on a disk

Rename Volumes

Every disk, including hard disk partitions and diskettes, can have a name. If you use volume labels appropriately, they can tell you the type of information that is stored on the disk and be a further prompt to disk usage. You can assign labels when disks are first used and never change them if you like. If you have more than one hard disk, you might use them for somewhat different purposes. Each diskette can have a label reflecting its purpose. You might label diskettes in accordance with the type of data or the person or project involved. The volume label can be assigned when the disk is originally formatted and changed at any time. The label is displayed during many disk operations.

To change a volume label, first make the drive current. You can click on the desired drive letter or hold down the control key while you press the desired drive letter. Alternatively, you can pull down the **Disk** menu and select the **Change Drive** option. Select the drive you want in the resulting dialog box.

The volume label of the current drive is shown in the top border of the tree window, where it is called the ID. Then pull down the **Disk** menu and select the **Rename volume** option. You'll see a dialog box like the one shown in Figure 5.1. The **Disk Rename** dialog box shows the current drive and its current label. If the disk has no label, you'll see "None" in the box.

You can type the new label at the cursor—up to 11 characters including letters, digits, and spaces. It cannot include such characters as comma and period. Then select RENAME and it is done.

Complete Disk Information

Much information is available about any disk in addition to the files and directories stored on it. You might want to know the disk size, the condition, even the basic structure in terms of clusters and sectors. You can get this information by making the relevant disk current, then pulling down the **Disk** menu and selecting the **Disk Info** option. You'll see a display like the one in Figure 5.2. This example reflects hard disk C. The drive name is not shown in the dialog box, but you can see it selected on the second screen line and displayed in the tree window.

The information includes details about the total and available space on the disk, as well as how much space is devoted to different categories of files and directories. You can also see a breakdown of the disk structure in terms of sectors, clusters, and tracks, as well as sides and cylinders.

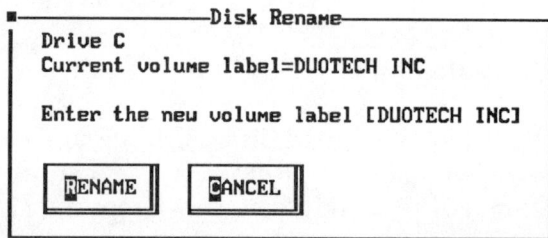

Figure 5.1   Disk Rename Dialog Box

Much of this information is not really useful unless you have a problem with a disk. Chapter 6 deals with clusters and tracks in more detail.

Copying a Diskette

You saw how to copy files in Chapter 2 and how to compare them in Chapter 4. The system also lets you copy all data on a diskette with a single command. You can already select all the files on a drive, then copy them with a single command. Copying a diskette as an entity is quicker than copying all the files on a disk, and it has a somewhat different effect. If you copy the files, DOS may rearrange them on the target diskette for more compact storage. And it can interfere with some security measures. If you copy the diskette as an entity, there is no rearranging; each sector on the source diskette is copied as is to the same location on the target diskette. The two are identical after the copy.

Disk Copy Principles

You can use the disk copy function only on diskettes, and the diskettes must be the same type. You can't use disk copy to transfer data from a 5.25" diskette to a 3.5" diskette. Similarly, you can't use disk copy to transfer files from a 360K diskette to a 1.2M one. It is possible to transfer files from a larger to smaller diskette of the same physical size, from 1.2M to 360K or from 1.4M to 720K, but the resulting diskette then can hold only the smaller amount of data.

When you do a disk copy, any previous data on the target diskette is

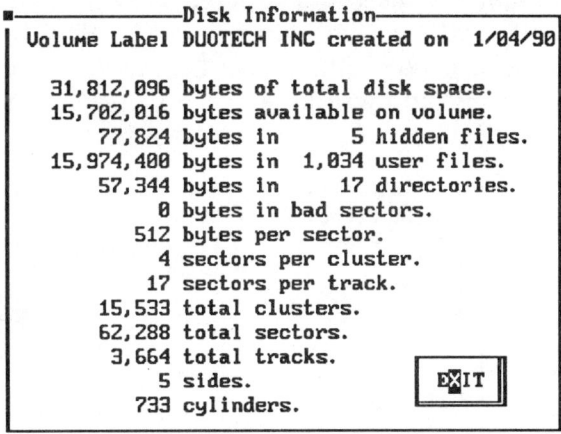

Figure 5.2   Disk Information Dialog Box

destroyed. If necessary, PC Shell formats the target diskette as it copies to give it the same format as the source diskette.

You can do a disk copy using one or two drives. If your computer has two drives that hold the same size diskette, you'll specify which drive will hold the source diskette and which will hold the target diskette, insert the diskettes, and PC Shell does all the work. If your system has only one of the needed diskette drive type, you specify the same drive for both the source and target diskettes, and PC Shell prompts you when to insert each. If the computer's available memory is smaller than the size of the diskette, you'll be prompted to remove one diskette and insert the other several times.

Copy Disk Process

When you are ready to copy a diskette, pull down the **Disk** menu and select the **Copy Disk** option. PC Shell displays a dialog box like the one shown in Figure 5.3. It first prompts you to select the source drive (notice the double border around the left box). After you select a drive by clicking or by highlighting the one you want and pressing Enter, the double border moves to the right box, which prompts you to select the target drive.

You can select the same drive for both the source and target if appropriate. PC Shell will keep track of them for you. Once you have selected both, you'll see the dialog box shown in Figure 5.4. It gives you some information and prompts you to insert the source diskette in the drive you selected for the source drive. You can select EXIT at this time if your diskette doesn't qualify according to the displayed message. After you insert the diskette, select COPY to begin the disk copy operation. If you selected two different drives, you'll next be prompted to insert the target diskette in the drive you specified.

Once the diskette(s) have been inserted, PC Shell begins to copy the source diskette to the target diskette. It does this by reading one track at a time from the source diskette and writing it to the same location on the target diskette. If necessary, it first formats the target track.

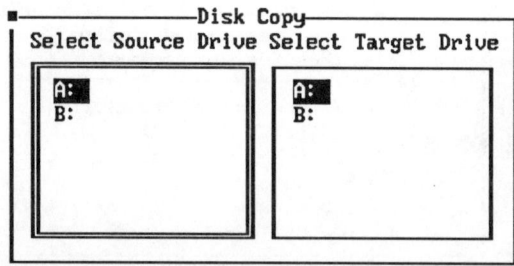

Figure 5.3   Disk Copy—Select Drives

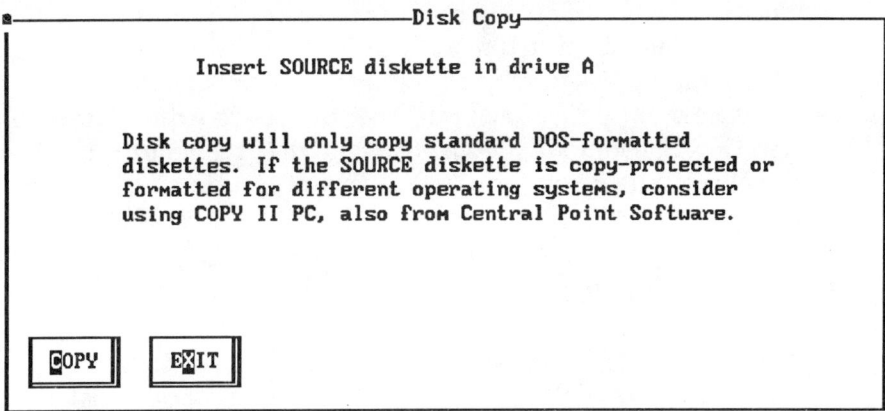

Figure 5.4   Disk Copy—Insert Source Diskette

If you specified the same drive for both source and target, PC Shell first reads enough tracks from the source drive to fill the available memory. Then you are prompted to insert the target diskette, and those tracks are written to it. You're prompted again to insert the source diskette, and the next group of tracks are read into memory. When memory is full, you are prompted to insert the target diskette and the data is written to it. The process is repeated as needed to complete the disk copy operation.

As the disk copy proceeds, PC Shell shows you a visual representation of what tracks are being copied. Figure 5.5 shows the dialog box that appears. When a source track is read, an R appears in its location. When a target track is formatted, an F appears. When a target track is written, the R in that location is replaced with a period. Figure 5.5 was produced near the middle of a

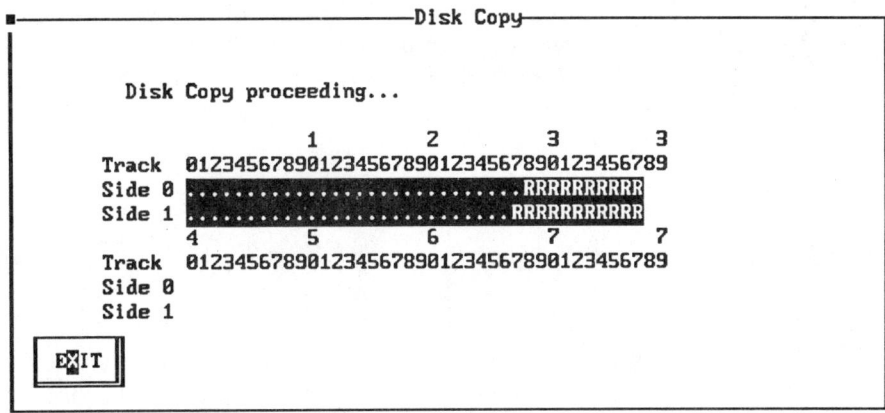

Figure 5.5   Disk Copy—Visual Display

one-drive copy of a 1.2M diskette. Notice that most of the tracks have been written. The shell is in the process of reading source tracks prior to prompting for the target diskette.

Once the target diskette is ready, you'll be returned to the main shell screen. The two diskettes will be identical, down to the volume label and the volume serial number, if any.

Comparing Two Diskettes

You might want to compare two diskettes immediately after making a disk copy to ensure that no errors crept in. If you made a disk copy to send to a client or colleague, you might want to be absolutely sure before sending it. Or you may have carelessly neglected to label several diskettes you have been working with. In any event, you can compare two diskettes using much the same procedure and restrictions as the disk copy operation itself.

Compare Disk Background

A disk compare is done on a track-by-track basis. If you copied all the files to a second diskette using the file copy method, the two diskettes will not be identical in a disk compare. The disk compare operation finds the two identical only if every bit on every track in one diskette matches the ones on the other diskette. The PC Shell diskette comparison checks every location on the diskettes; even differing volume serial numbers produce errors. A successful disk copy operation should produce two diskettes that compare successfully. If you have renamed the volume label on one of them, they will not compare identically. If a disk copy was done using the DOS command, the two diskettes compare as identical using the DISKCOMP command, but produce mismatches in the volume serial number field under PC Shell. This is no problem if you do all your disk copy operations using the shell.

Compare Disk Process

When you are ready to compare two diskettes, pull down the **Disk** menu and select the **Compare Disk** option. You'll see a screen much like the one you saw in Figure 5.3. This time, the dialog box prompts you to select the drives for the first and second diskettes; there is no source or target in a compare operation.

Once you have selected the drives, either one or two depending on your system and your situation, you are prompted to insert one or both diskettes. Then the comparison begins. Again, you'll see a visual representation of the tracks on the diskettes. The letter R indicates the track is being read; C indicates the track is being compared; a period indicates it compared successfully; E indicates a compare error. Figure 5.6 shows how the screen looks when an error was detected during the comparison of the first track of side one; notice the C in the location. The sector number and location of the byte, including the contents of that byte on each diskette, are shown near the top.

After you select CONTINUE, the compare operation continues with the next byte. You'll see a separate message for each pair of mismatched bytes in the track. When the end of the track is reached, PC Shell inserts an E in the location to indicate that an error was detected, but it doesn't indicate how many were found. If you want to track down the error, you can note the sector and offset numbers and check later under the hex editor after you are returned to the main shell screen for your next task.

Verifying the Disk

Suppose you have seen a message about a parity error, or you may have strange errors and activities you don't recognize in your computer. You can ask PC Shell to check that all sectors are readable. It will check all sectors, even the ones that aren't in use. You can verify any DOS formatted hard disk or diskette unless it is copy protected.

Verify Disk Process

When you want to verify a disk, first select the drive and make it current. Then pull down the **Disk** menu and select the **Verify Disk** option. PC Shell tells

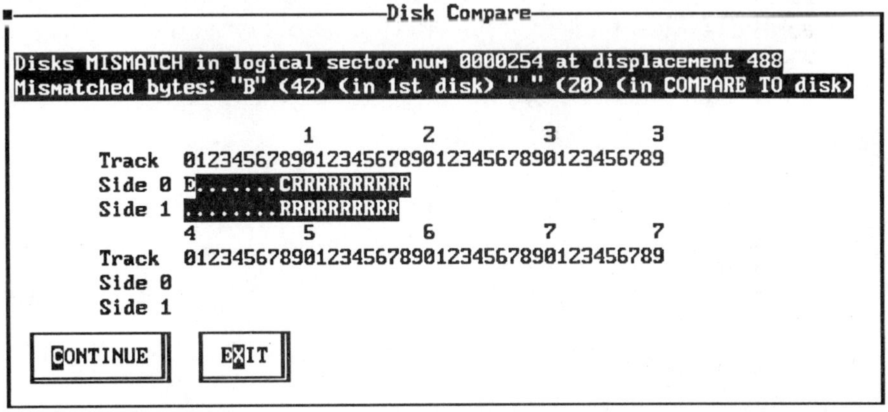

```
┌──────────────────────Disk Compare──────────────────────┐
│ Disks MISMATCH in logical sector num 0000254 at displacement 488 │
│ Mismatched bytes: "B" (42) (in 1st disk) " " (20) (in COMPARE TO disk) │
│                                                        │
│                    1         2         3         3     │
│         Track  0123456789012345678901234567890123456789 │
│         Side 0 E.......CRRRRRRRRRR                     │
│         Side 1 ........RRRRRRRRRR                      │
│                    4         5         6         7   7 │
│         Track  0123456789012345678901234567890123456789 │
│         Side 0                                         │
│         Side 1                                         │
│         ┌─────────┐   ┌─────┐                          │
│         │CONTINUE │   │EXIT │                          │
│         └─────────┘   └─────┘                          │
└────────────────────────────────────────────────────────┘
```

Figure 5.6   Disk Compare—Error Detected

you the current drive is about to be verified. You can select EXIT to cancel the operation or VERIFY to go ahead. When verification begins, you'll see a dialog box like the one shown in Figure 5.7. Notice that it keeps you posted on the sectors being verified. You can cancel the process at any time.

If no problems are detected in sectors that aren't marked by DOS, PC Shell simply returns to the main screen. If it detects a problem in a sector, you'll see a dialog box providing the sector number and information about whether the sector is part of the DOS system area, part of a file, or available. If it is available, PC Shell marks the sector so it won't be used again. If it is part of a file or a subdirectory, you'll be informed how to try a recovery to move the good parts away from the affected sector.

✧ Try It Out

1. Change the name of your hard disk or a diskette. Restore the original name if you like.
2. Check the disk information for your hard disk and a used diskette.
3. Verify the diskette to ensure that the data is all readable.
4. Copy the used diskette to a blank one, using a method that works on your computer. Then compare the source and target diskettes.

Searching a Disk

If you know or suspect that a file contains a character string you want, you can use the **Text Search** or **Locate File** command from the **File** menu to find it. Sometimes you may want to search for a character string when you really have no idea if it is in a file, but it probably was on the disk at some time. You can tell PC Shell to search the entire disk for a string of up to 32 characters. It will then search through each sector on the disk. If it finds a match, you can get further information.

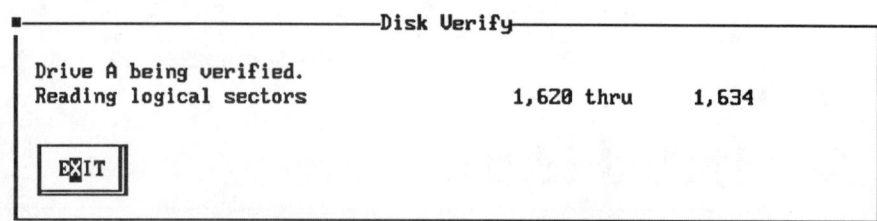

Figure 5.7   Verifying a Disk

Search Disk Process

When you pull down the **Disk** menu and select the **Search Disk** option, PC Shell gives you a dialog box much like the one when you ask it to find a string in a file with **Text Search**. You enter a string of up to 32 characters. The ASCII search is not case sensitive. If you would rather do a case sensitive hex search, select **9Hex** before entering the string. When you press Enter, the search begins. When a match is found, you'll see a display like the one in Figure 5.8. Notice that the string and a Found message are shown. Your options appear on the bottom screen line.

If you select **8Name**, you will next see the filename if the matching string occurred in an existing file. If not, you might see a message that the sector is a root directory sector or that it is not in an allocated area. No matter what the message is, you select EXIT to terminate it. Now you can make another choice. If you want to find another match for the same string, select **7Search**. If you want to examine the file containing the string, note the filename and press Escape or click on the close box to return to the main screen. If you want to see the context of the string that did not appear in a file, select **9Edit**. You'll see a standard Hex/ASCII Edit screen that you can process like any other HexEdit screen. The details of this are covered in Chapter 6.

Parking the Disk

When the computer reads data from a hard disk, it positions the disk head over the appropriate part of the disk. When you physically move a computer component containing a hard disk, it is possible that the motion may dislodge the disk head from a stable position and cause it to "crash" or bounce on the disk. Not surprisingly, this can cause loss of data and otherwise damage your hard disk.

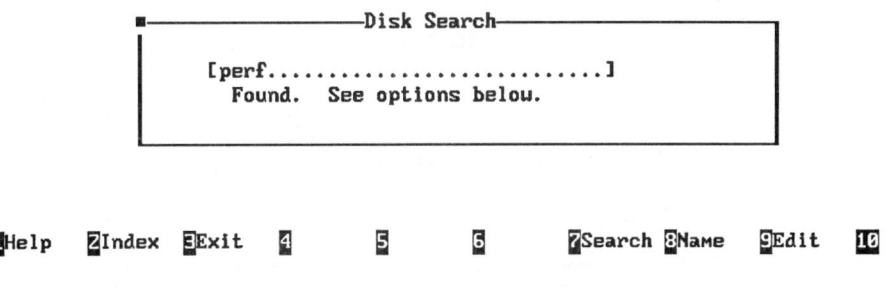

Figure 5.8   Disk Search—String Found

Some hardware setups automatically place the head in a safe position when you turn it off. Others don't. PC Tools provides an option that lets you specify that the disk head should be parked in a safe position. If yours already does, you won't need this option.

Before you move your computer, pull down the **Disk** menu and select **Park Disk**. You'll see a dialog box like the one shown in Figure 5.9. To complete the operation and leave the heads parked, turn off the computer while this dialog box is displayed. The heads remain parked and you can safely move the computer, whether to another desk or to another office or state.

If you want to continue using your computer rather than park the heads, select CANCEL and continue with your session.

Complete Computer System Information

You have seen how to get complete disk information using the **Disk Info** option. Much information is also available about your computer system itself. You might want to know how many ports you have available or when the BIOS programs on the mother board were dated. You might want to find out whether the system has a math coprocessor or how it compares in speed to the basic IBM PC. You can get this information by pulling down the **Special** menu and selecting the **System Info** option. You'll see a display like the one in Figure 5.10. The information shown does not reflect the current drive or any selected files; it deals with the computer system as a whole.

The information provided includes details about the computer as determined internally by PC Shell. Much of this information is not really useful to you, but it can be very interesting.

PC Shell gets the computer type and date of the BIOS programs internally; it recognizes most IBM models and close compatibles. The operating system displayed is the one with which you booted. If you boot with a different system, this line will change.

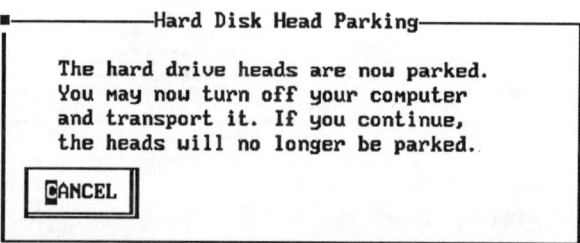

Figure 5.9   Hard Disk Head Parking Dialog Box

The number of logical disk drives has little to do with the number of actual disk drives. This number is 5 by default, with letters A through E. A special command in the AUTOEXEC.BAT file may increase it.

The next group of items has to do with the hardware. You can see the number of serial and parallel ports that are installed, as well as the CPU type. Notice that this one is an 80386 CPU, which PC Shell has interpreted above as an IBM/PC AT. The relative speed shown is compared to the original IBM PC 8088. This computer has no math coprocessor; PC Shell actually checks to see if the coprocessor socket is empty.

The rest of the items have to do with memory. You can see where user programs are loaded, how much memory is used by resident programs, and how much is available for other use. You can see whether PC Shell and DOS recognize the same amount of memory. The video adapter (EGA here) might have some memory of its own as well. The final item identifies any expansion boards that might contain BIOS extensions.

Mapping Disks and Files

If you are having trouble with your disks or finding many file read errors, you may want to know just where on a disk files are stored or where a particular file resides. PC Shell can give you a visual map of a disk so that you can see what parts of the disk are occupied. It can also show you just what parts of a disk are occupied by a particular file.

```
┌─────────────────────────System Information──────────────────────────┐
│                              Computer - IBM/PC AT                   │
│                   BIOS programs dated - 06/08/87                    │
│                       Operating system - DOS 4.00                   │
│               Number of logical disk drives - 7                     │
│                 Logical drive letter range - A thru G               │
│                               Serial Ports - 2                      │
│                             Parallel Ports - 1                      │
│                                   CPU Type - 80386                  │
│                 Relative speed (orig PC=100%) - 945%                │
│                     Math co-processor present - No                  │
│     User programs are loaded at HEX paragraph - 1C91                │
│     Memory used by DOS and resident programs - 117008 bytes         │
│          Memory available for user programs - 538352 bytes          │
│                   Total memory reported by DOS - 640K               │
│         PC Shell has found the total memory to be - 640K            │
│         Enhanced Graphics Adapter present (color) - 256K            │
│                        Extended memory installed - 384K             │
│    Additional ROM BIOS found at HEX paragraph - C000                │
└─────────────────────────────────────────────────────────────────────┘
```

Figure 5.10   System Information Dialog Box

Disk Map

To see the map of a disk, first make that drive current, then pull down the **Special** menu and select **Disk Map**. You'll see a display similar to the one in Figure 5.11 for a hard disk or large capacity diskette. Each position in the grid corresponds to one cluster; space is allocated in clusters. The number of sectors in a cluster depends on the type of disk; you can find out for sure by checking disk information for the disk. The display is for information only; you can't make any changes to the map.

You can see how much of the disk is available and what parts are allocated. The codes at the top of the window show you what the different symbols mean. Any sectors indicated with "x" are marked bad sectors, for example. This particular disk map shows that most of the allocated sectors are in the first part of the disk. This is a general pattern; clusters are allocated in order. When new clusters are needed, DOS starts looking at the beginning of the disk. Some of the later part of this disk is allocated as well. What probably happened is that additional files, since removed, once occupied the scattered disk areas that are currently available.

The special codes shown at the top of the screen are not always displayed in the map. They are used when you display a map of a smaller capacity diskette, however.

A disk map for a diskette with 80 tracks or fewer includes track numbers in the grid. This helps you to identify where clusters are located.

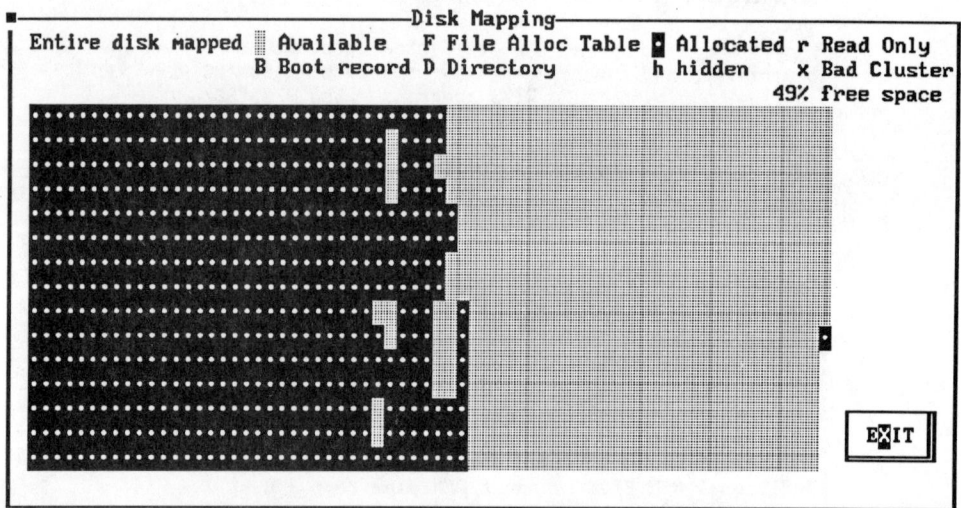

Figure 5.11   Disk Map

File Map

If you want to know exactly where and how a particular file is stored, you can check the map for a particular file. First select the file or files you want to check. Then pull down the **Special** menu and select the **File Map** option. The resulting grid resembles the one shown in Figure 5.12. The grid itself is much like the one for a full disk map, but only the clusters allocated to the particular file are indicated.

In the figure, file CHAP12 is allocated to five noncontiguous clusters. They are indicated in the map. Additional information gives the address of the first cluster allocated to the file (6598) and the relative sector on the disk. A file that is stored in noncontiguous clusters is said to be fragmented; access time may be increased for such a file. Later in this book, you'll see how to rearrange a disk to minimize fragmentation.

Only in maps of files on low capacity diskettes does the file map make use of the codes listed on the screen. A read-only or hidden file is marked with "r" or "h", for example, on a 360K diskette.

Memory Information

In addition to showing you how a disk is used and how a file uses the disk, PC Shell can also provide information on how memory is currently being used. For example, it can tell you which resident programs are currently loaded into

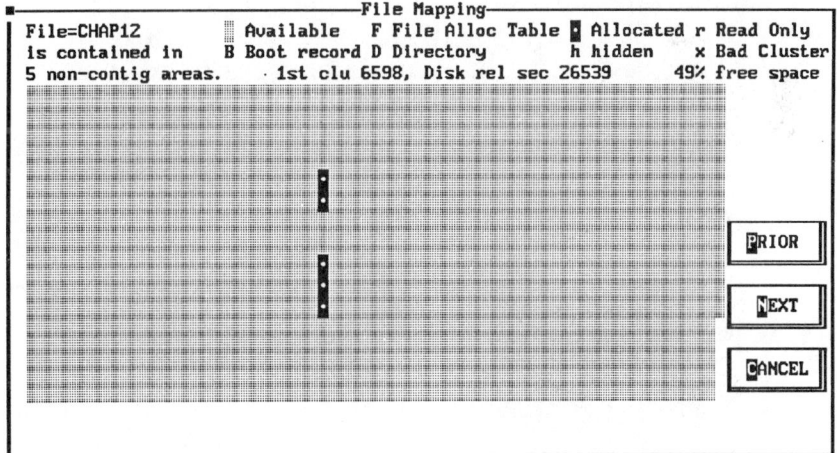

Figure 5.12 File Map

memory and how much memory each is using, as well as which memory it is and what interrupts affect it. This can be useful if your resident programs are interfering with each other or if you find you need to remove something from memory to allow other programs to run. In most cases, however, the information provided by a memory map is useful only to system programmers and troubleshooters. You might be asked to check this information if you call a software hotline, for example.

Memory Map

To check out through PC Shell what is occupying memory, pull down the **Special** menu and select the **Memory Map** option. You'll get a choice like the one shown in Figure 5.13. You can get information on only program memory blocks or on all blocks of allocated memory. In either case, you can get "hooked vectors" included as well. If you select an option that includes hooked vectors, you'll find out what system interrupts listed programs use as well.

Figure 5.14 shows information in the basic memory map; this one includes only program memory blocks. Notice that the "Type" of each is *Prog* for program. "Paragraphs" specifies the hexadecimal address of the program, "Bytes" gives the size, while "Owner" gives the program name. If the program does not reside in the root directory, the complete path is given as well.

If you select an option with hooked vectors, you'll get a listing of the interrupts it uses on the line following each program. If you ask for all memory blocks, you'll get types *Sys* for system blocks and *Env* for environment blocks as well, along with some free blocks interspersed among them. Figure 5.15 shows the result of selecting all memory blocks with hooked vectors. Notice that each line with *Prog* type is exactly the same as in Figure 5.14. Each is followed by a line with interrupt information representing the hooked vectors. The NEXT PAGE button lets you page through the output.

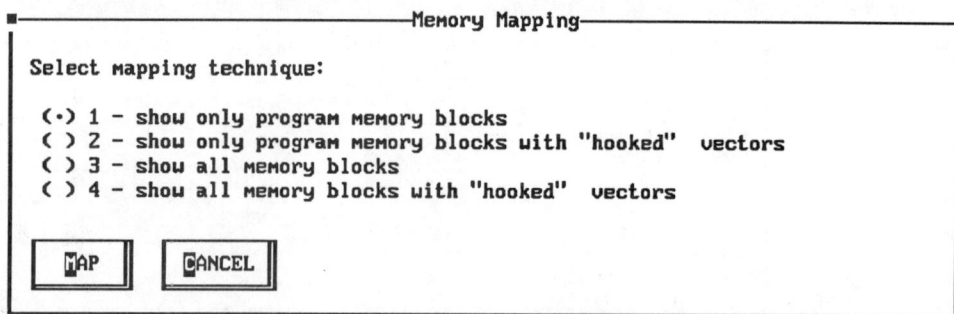

Figure 5.13   Memory Map Choices

Disk and System Utilities

```
┌─────────────────────────Memory Mapping──────────────────────────┐
│ Conventional memory.  Total:  640K                              │
│ Largest executable program:   526K                              │
│                                                                 │
│ Type  Paragraphs   Bytes    Owner                               │
│ Prog  128F-13F2H   5696     128FH COMMAND                       │
│ Prog  1410-15B1H   6688     1410H MIRROR   C:\PCT6-0\MIRROR.COM │
│ Prog  15BB-16C6H   4288     15BBH MOUSE    C:\MOUSE.COM         │
│ Prog  16D0-1C68H   22928    16D0H GRAB     C:\HSG\GRAB.EXE      │
│ Prog  1C72-1C8FH   480      1C72H MODE                          │
│ Prog  1C91-9FFFH   526K     1C91H PCSHELL  C:\PCT6-0\PCSHELL.EXE│
│                                                                 │
│   [MAP]      [EXIT]                                             │
└─────────────────────────────────────────────────────────────────┘
```

Figure 5.14   Program Memory Blocks

The additional lines describe other types of memory blocks. "Sys" identifies system blocks, "Env" identifies blocks devoted to establishing or maintaining the environment, and "Free" indicates available memory blocks that occur surrounded by otherwise established blocks.

The Memory Information Command

You can also check memory information with a stand-alone program called MI.COM, which is provided with PC Tools. When you type MI at the DOS

```
┌─────────────────────────Memory Mapping──────────────────────────┐
│ Conventional memory.  Total:  640K                              │
│ Largest executable program:   526K                              │
│                                                                 │
│ Type  Paragraphs   Bytes    Owner                               │
│ Sys   0BAC-128DH   28192    0008H < DOS >                       │
│   & using interrupt 02H,0AH,0CH-0EH,29H,2FH,70H,72H-74H,76H-77H,FFH.│
│ Prog  128F-13F2H   5696     128FH COMMAND                       │
│   & using interrupt 22H,2EH.                                    │
│ Free  13F4-13F6H   48       0000H < DOS >                       │
│ Env   13F8-1407H   256      128FH COMMAND                       │
│ Env   1409-140EH   96       1410H MIRROR                        │
│ Prog  1410-15B1H   6688     1410H MIRROR   C:\PCT6-0\MIRROR.COM │
│   & using interrupt 25H-26H.                                    │
│ Env   15B3-15B9H   112      15BBH MOUSE                         │
│ Prog  15BB-16C6H   4288     15BBH MOUSE    C:\MOUSE.COM         │
│   & using interrupt 0BH,10H,33H.                                │
│ Env   16C8-16CEH   112      16D0H GRAB                          │
│                                                                 │
│   [NEXT PAGE]   [EXIT]                                          │
└─────────────────────────────────────────────────────────────────┘
```

Figure 5.15   All Memory Blocks with Hooked Vectors

prompt, the result is screen output similar to the result of choosing the first choice on the screen shown in Figure 5.13. Several optional parameters are available; if you type MI ? at the DOS prompt, all the parameters will be listed on the screen.

You can use the /A option (MI /A) to get output similar to that produced by choice 3 in the same figure. If you want hooked vector information in addition, add /V to the command, as in MI /V or MI /A/V.

If the information results in more than a full screen, it will automatically pause at the end of each screenful; you can use the /N option to prevent the pause. If you want only a quick summary of the memory map information, use /Q instead of the other options.

One big advantage of using MI instead of the PC Shell memory mapping options is that MI allows you to have the information printed or sent to disk file. To send a complete listing of memory map information to a file, use a command like MI /A/V/N > MEMMAP.OUT. The output is sent to a file called MEMMAP.OUT in the current directory instead of to the screen.

◆ *Try It Out*

1. Check your system information.
2. Get a map of your hard disk then map the smallest capacity diskette you have available. Notice the format differences.
3. Make current a directory that you use frequently, then try a file map. Use NEXT to progress through the files until you find one with noncontiguous areas.
4. Examine a basic memory map using the menu, then try the same thing with the MI command.
5. If you would like to send a complete memory map to a disk file, try MI /A/V/N > MEMMAP.OUT at the DOS prompt. View the resulting file.

The disk and system utilities help you to understand and manipulate your equipment. The next chapter goes even deeper into the system; you'll learn to manipulate hexadecimal screens and help troubleshoot your system.

Chapter 6
Running Programs and Hexadecimal Processing

This chapter covers ways of running programs from within PC Shell as well as manipulating data on the hexadecimal level. Specifically, it includes the following:

- Running programs and PC Shell applications
- Adding and modifying applications
- Launching applications
- Interpreting hexadecimal screens
- Editing hexadecimal screens
- Using manual undelete techniques

PC Shell as a Program Launcher

PC Shell can be set up for use primarily to start other programs. When it is in this configuration, the shell comes up with the **Applications** menu pulled down and no other menus visible on the menu bar. To run a program, just select the appropriate option from the menu. The function key line includes **10Shell** to restore the standard PC Shell functions, if necessary.

You can establish the launch configuration through the **Change User Level** option of the **Setup Configuration** pop-up menu.

Running Programs under PC Shell

You can run programs under PC Shell whether or not it is resident. If you entered the shell from the DOS prompt, either through hotkeying or through the PCSHELL command, you can then run other programs without leaving the shell. When such a program terminates, you return to PC Shell.

If you are running PC Tools resident and hotkey from within a program, you can run other programs if your computer has enough memory left; in this situation, both the original program and PC Shell will be taking up memory. Active PC Shell uses about 170K of memory. Normally, it doesn't free up that memory when you run a program so that it can quickly load the program and quickly return when it terminates. PC Shell keeps track of the status of the original program. If you see a message reporting a problem with memory, you might need to hotkey back into the original program, terminate it, and return to the command prompt before reentering the shell.

From the Applications Menu

PC Setup puts several programs on the **Applications** menu. You can run one of these by selecting it from the menu, just as you select any other menu entry. The menu includes programs that are a part of the PC Tools package, such as PCBACKUP and PCFormat. You'll learn to use these later in the book.

The **Applications** menu may also include some widely used software that the installation process identifies in your directories. PC Tools recognizes and installs Lotus 1-2-3, dBASE, WordStar, and WordPerfect, as well as some other application programs. If any program is named in your **Applications** menu, it is already installed so that it can be launched from within PC Shell. In addition, you can add and modify menu options when you pull down the menu yourself. You'll see how later in this chapter.

From the DOS Command Line

You can run any program from the DOS command line that can be run from outside PC Shell, except for PC Shell itself or any resident program. Just type the command at the prompt. PC Shell generates a secondary command processor to run the program. You'll return to PC Shell automatically when the program has terminated. You can turn windows off to see the underlying screen output if necessary.

From the File List Window

If you highlight a file with extension COM, EXE, or BAT in the file list, then pull down the **File** menu and select the **Launch** option, the selected file will be run as a program; alternatively, you can double-click on the filename or select it and press Ctrl-Enter. If the extension of the selected file doesn't indicate that it's a program, you'll see a message box telling you so. If it is valid, however, PC Shell responds with a dialog box like the one shown in Figure 6.1. The name of the program you chose is displayed. You are prompted for parameters that will be passed to the program. When you select RUN, the program begins.

The parameters are determined by the program to be run. For example, if you run WordStar by selecting WS.EXE and choosing the **Launch** option, you can enter as a parameter the name of a file to be edited, as well as several other switches the program recognizes. If you run the DOS utility CHKDSK.COM, you could enter the drive name as a parameter. Whether or not parameters are required and which ones are valid depend entirely on the program you choose to run.

You can also launch an application from a data file instead of the program file. If several file specifications have been associated with your word processor, for example, you can launch the program by running an associated file directly from the file list as if it were a program. PC Shell examines the filespec, locates the program it is associated with, and launches that program, passing the selected file to it. If a file selected for launching is not associated with any program file, you'll be notified in a message box. You won't be prompted for parameters if you run a program through an associated file.

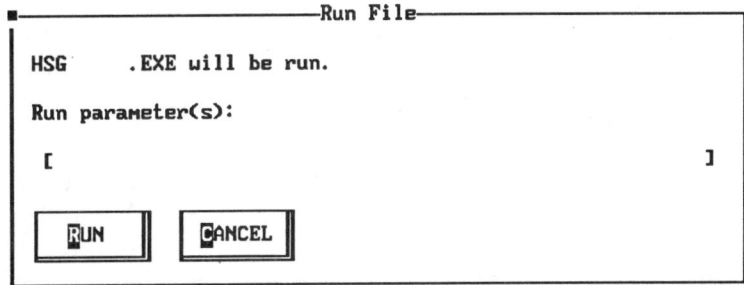

Figure 6.1   Run File Dialog Box

From the View Window

PC Shell also lets you launch programs from the view window. When data file contents are displayed in a view window, one of the options at the bottom of the screen is **Launch**. If you select this option, the associated application will be started to let you process the file currently being viewed. If the file being viewed isn't associated with any program, you'll see a message to that effect. When you end the application, you may be returned immediately to PC Shell, or you may be prompted to press a key, depending on how the application is installed. PC Shell will be in the same state as you left it, the same windows will be displayed and the same files selected.

Modifying the Applications Menu

When you pull down the **Applications** menu from within PC Shell, the function key line includes **4Add**, **5Edit**, **6Delete**, and **7Move**. You can use these commands to set up the menu for your own needs, adding other application programs, changing existing applications, removing ones you don't use, and rearranging the order on the menu. You can even add additional associated filespecs to installed applications. The process is similar to modifying the **Locate Files** pop-up menu.

When the menu appears as you want it, use **Save Configuration** to keep the changes as a permanent part of PC Shell. If you don't want the changes to be in effect next time you enter PC Shell, don't save the configuration.

Moving an Application

If you want to rearrange items in the menu, select **7Move**. You'll be prompted to select a menu item, then to reposition it to the desired location using the arrow keys. When you press Enter, the item remains in the new location. You'll be prompted repeatedly to allow you to rearrange as many options as needed. Press Escape to interrupt the cycle.

Deleting an Application

To remove an option from the menu, select **6Delete**. You'll be prompted to select the menu item you want to remove, then to confirm the deletion. If you delete an application in error, don't save the configuration; then the application will be restored next time you start up PC Shell.

Running Programs and Hexadecimal Processing

Adding or Editing an Application

To add a new application to the menu, select **4Add**; a new entry, labeled <location of new entry>, appears at the bottom of the menu. You are prompted to position it where you want the new entry to be placed. To edit an existing application, select **5Edit**; you'll be prompted to select the entry to be modified. In either case, you'll next see a dialog box in the form of the one shown in Figure 6.2. If you are adding a new application, all the fields in the upper part of the box will be blank; those in the lower part will show default values of N. You can add or modify information in each field.

Specifying the File and Path. Several fields are provided to let you fully specify the program file and its location. The first line provides the **Application** title; this value appears in the **Applications** menu. If you want one character to be highlighted in the menu for use in selecting that option, place a caret (^) before it. To use the XyWrite™ program by pressing "W", you would enter "Xy^Write" in the title field. Make sure you identify a unique letter in each title. If you highlight the same letter in two or more different titles, PC Shell uses the first one it finds when you press the letter. The brackets in the dialog box indicate how many characters you can use in the title.

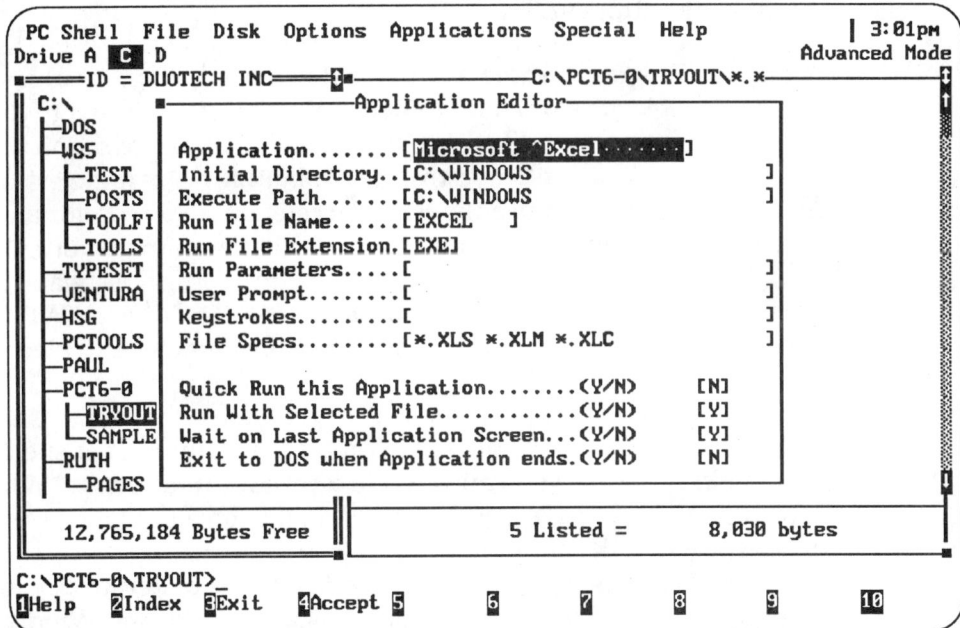

Figure 6.2   Application Editor Dialog Box

The **Initial Directory** field tells PC Shell to reset the current directory when the program is initiated. You would place a value in this field if the application requires that a certain directory be current in order to run properly, usually so that it can locate its support and data files. For example, the HotShot® Graphics program can be started from any directory, but it won't function properly unless the directory containing its support files is current. If you might start an application from a different drive, be sure to include the correct drive name in the directory path. You can omit the initial directory value if you don't want the default directory or drive to change. But if you have trouble running the application, check its documentation to see if it requires a certain directory to be current.

The **Execute Path** field tells PC Shell where to find the program to be executed. If you include a value in this field, it will be prefixed to the command that is issued when you select the application. For example, the command issued for the application shown in Figure 6.2 is C:\WINDOWS\EXCEL. You don't need an execute path if the program file resides in one of the directories in the DOS search path.

Run File Name and **Run File Extension** provide the actual name of the program file. The extension must be BAT, COM, or EXE. It must be in the directory named in the **Execute Path** field, if any, or in the DOS search path. PC Shell appends the filename provided in these fields to the execute path in creating the pathname.

Specifying Program Parameters. Several fields let you pass values to the program when it is started. The **Run Parameters** here are similar to those used to run a program from the file list. They depend on the application program you are installing. You can leave this field blank if no parameters are needed. Alternatively, you can use the **Run Parameters** field to tailor an entry for a specific application. For example, suppose you can start up your word processor in ASCII mode or in its standard mode. You might want to add two separate entries to the **Applications** menu: "WP-ASCII" and "WP-formatted". The "WP-ASCII" definition would include the parameter to place your word processor in ASCII mode.

The **User Prompt** field lets you provide a message to the user before the application starts. If the application has special requirements, such as a special diskette in drive A:, you can provide a prompt in this field. Whatever you enter, up to 128 characters, is displayed on the screen. When the user clicks or presses any key, the application begins.

The **Keystrokes** field lets you provide a series of keystrokes to be passed to the application. Some applications, including Microsoft Windows, can use keystrokes to perform various functions during startup. You can enter up to 128 characters worth of keystrokes in several different ways. When the cursor is in this field, **7Litkey** and **8Keywrd** appear on the function key line. You can just type the keystrokes; this works for character keys, such as letters, numbers, and symbols on your keyboard. You can use angle brackets to enclose key names as well, such as <Esc> or <Home>. If you select **7Litkey**, then perform the actual keypress, PC Shell converts it to the key name form. If you select **8Keywrd**, a dialog box of all the available command keywords appears for you to choose from. Figure 6.3 shows the words. Select the one you want, and it is inserted into the **Keystrokes** field. The descriptions in the box are fairly self-explanatory. If you use <Path>, for example, the full path of the selected file is inserted into the field. When the application is run, the selected file's path will be sent to the program. The <DelayN> keyword lets you specify a delay in seconds or tenths of seconds; <Delay1.2> requests a delay of 1.2 seconds. The <Typein> keyword requests the application to wait for user input.

Associating Files with the Application. The **File Specs** field in Figure 6.2 includes global file specifications to be associated with the application. Once associated here, it applies to launching from anywhere within PC Shell. The filespecs are often based on extensions that are generated by a particular application program. For example, Lotus 1-2-3 generates files with the WK1 extension, so *.WK1 associates those files with Lotus 1-2-3. Excel spreadsheets have extension XLS, so *.XLS refers to all the Excel spreadsheets. If you always use DOC, REP, or LET for your word processing files, you could associate global filenames that select all files with those three extensions with the word processor application. By associating filespecs with an application, you can run the application by running the data file. For example, if you use *.XLS with the Excel application, double-clicking on the file named BUDGET91.XLS causes the Excel program to be run and the filename passed to it.

You can enter up to 128 characters of filespecs for each application. Use complete filespecs, as shown in Figure 6.2; this one associates three extensions with the application. Use at least one space to separate filespecs. You can also

```
─────────────────KEYWORD LIST─────────────────
<Path>      Full path and filename of selected file
<Drive>     Drive letter of selected file
<Dir>       Path of selected file w/o drive
<Dir\>      Path of selected file w/o drive + \
<File>      Full filename with extension
<Filename>  Name of selected file without extension
<Ext>       Extension of selected file
<DelayN>    Delay passing characters
<Typein>    Variable-length field entry
```

Figure 6.3   Keyword List for Keystrokes Field

exclude a filespec by preceding it with a minus sign. The entry *.LET *.COR −B*.LET −B*.COR excludes files with the desired extension but with filename beginning with B. Don't associate the same filespec with more than one application; the results are unpredictable.

Controlling the Application. Several fields let you control how PC Shell starts and ends the application. In each of these cases, you can select **Y** (Yes) or **N** (No) to indicate your preference. **Quick Run this Application** specifies whether the program should be run in available memory or not. If you use **Y**, PC Shell doesn't free up its memory before running the program. This results in a quicker startup for the application and a quicker return to PC Shell when it is terminated. If you have memory problems, however, you may want to choose **N**. Then PC Shell frees up memory by writing much of its own data to a temporary disk file before running the application. This gives it more memory but takes more time, since PC Shell has to first create the temporary disk file, then reload memory from it after the application terminates. Generally, you'll want to use **Y** unless the application needs more memory.

Some software, such as word processors, spreadsheets, and databases, often use a data file. If you expect to always select a file for processing before selecting the application, specify **Yes** for the **Run with Selected File** field. PC Shell then passes the selected filename to the application program: if no file is selected, the highlighted filename is passed. If the program supports multiple files, you can select them all before choosing the application.

The **Wait on Last Application Screen** field lets you request a pause before PC Shell returns. Some utility programs that run at the command prompt end abruptly, and if you don't specify a pause here, you won't be able to read the last messages on screen. If you specify **Y** here, the user will be prompted to press a key or click to return to the shell.

Normally, control returns to PC Shell when a launched application terminates. If you prefer to return control to DOS, choose **Y** for **Exit to DOS when Application Ends**.

Saving the Changes. When the dialog box is completed the way you want it, select **4Accept**. Then try out the application. You can modify it from the **Applications** menu at any time. Be sure to select **Save Configuration File** before you terminate PC Shell.

✧ Try It Out

1. Make the DOS directory current. Then run the program named TREE.COM from the file list. Use the backslash (\) as a parameter.

2. Run CHKDSK.COM, using no parameters.
3. Examine your **Applications** menu. If a program you use outside of PC Shell is listed, select it and see the effect. Then exit the application to return to the shell.
4. Edit the application that you just ran. Add or modify the parameters if you didn't get the effect you wanted. If you didn't run one of the applications, edit any listed option to see how the fields are filled in.
5. Create a new application that will check the status of the diskette in drive A:. To do this, create a short descriptive title, use \DOS as the Execute Path, CHKDSK.COM as the filename and extension, and A: as the parameter. Have it wait on the last screen. Try out the new application.
6. Reposition the new application, then delete it.

Hexadecimal Manipulation

Several PC Shell functions can present a display in hexadecimal mode. Since all these screens are arranged in the same way, and many of the functions you can perform on them are similar, they are treated together in this chapter. If you are not a programmer and prefer to avoid these screens, you can do so; just select the EXIT option whenever one appears. But there are times you might want to know a bit more. A customer support person may direct you to get information from a hex display, for example.

This chapter doesn't cover all you ever wanted to know about hexadecimal; it is intended to help you get beyond the basics and to understand the choices available to you.

Background Concepts

Data is stored on a disk in a regular, structured form. Each disk has circular tracks in which data records are laid down. The circle is divided into wedge-shaped sectors, each generally containing 512 bytes of data. A cluster is a group of one or more sectors, specific to the type of disk. DOS allocates space for files in full clusters, so they are often referred to as file allocation units. All these components are numbered independently; a diskette has sides 0 and 1, tracks 0 through 79, sector 0 through the highest number, and clusters 0 through the highest number.

The first sector on a disk generally contains the codes the system needs to boot from; this is called the boot sector, and it is reserved even if the disk isn't bootable. The information about directories and files on the disk is stored next, in the file allocation table (FAT).

Just as our decimal system is based on the number 10, hexadecimal code is based on 16. Decimal digits are 0 through 9; hexadecimal digits are 0 through 9 and A through F. Each two-digit hexadecimal code represents one byte or a single ASCII character. A hexadecimal display includes the ASCII equivalent of each hexadecimal code.

Viewing The Hexadecimal Display

Most hexadecimal displays have the same layout and elements. Figure 6.4 shows the display that results when you select **Hex Edit File** on the **File** menu when a program file is selected; the data is formatted just as in the binary viewer. Sometimes when you select **Hex Edit File**, you get a full screen ASCII display; if so, select **Ascii/Hex** from the command line to see the screen in hexadecimal mode.

The top line in the window gives the display status. In the example, it shows the filename JOBAID.PLS. Then you see the *Relative sector*, indicating which sector is shown relative to the beginning of the current cluster. A sector generally contains 512 bytes; 256 bytes, or one-half sector, appear on one screen. Relative sector 0 refers to the first sector in a cluster. The *Clust* value gives the sequential cluster number on the disk. The example shows the beginning of the first sector in cluster 4357. The *Disk Abs Sec* value gives the absolute sector number on the disk; this example shows the first part of sector

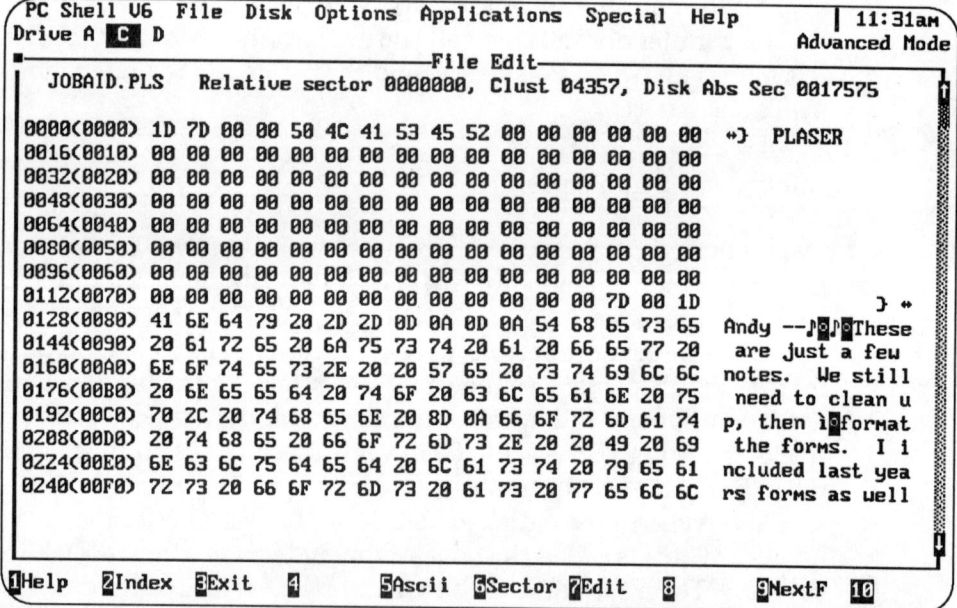

Figure 6.4   Hexadecimal Display

17575. Hexadecimal displays reached through other commands may show different values on the top line, but all serve to let you know where on the disk or in the file the displayed data appears.

The bulk of the hexadecimal display is taken up with three vertical sections: the address, the hexadecimal representation of the data, and the ASCII representation of the data. Each line includes 16 bytes of data; the first line shows bytes 0 through 15, the second bytes 16 through 31, and so forth.

The leftmost section gives the offset or displacement of the first byte in that line from the beginning of the sector. The first four characters give the decimal offset; the first line is 0 since it starts the sector. The offset of the last line is 240; that line includes bytes 240 through 255. The value in parentheses gives the hexadecimal equivalent of the offset. You can see that 0016 decimal is equivalent to 10 hexadecimal.

The large center section shows the hexadecimal value of each byte in the row. They are separated by spaces for easier reading. Only valid hexadecimal characters (0 through 9 and A through F) appear here.

The rightmost section shows the ASCII representation of the same 16 bytes. You may see graphic symbols if your monitor can display them. Unprintable characters appear as spaces. If the sector contains any readable characters, you may be able to interpret it. Many applications don't create files in ASCII format, but you can identify enough text to comprehend the contents. The example shows a file created under WordStar; it includes many unprintable characters, but also enough readable characters to recognize the contents of the sector.

The commands at the bottom of the hexadecimal screen vary somewhat according to how you reached the screen. In most cases, you'll be able to use **PgUp** and **PgDn** to page through the data, including the rest of the sector or cluster. **Home** returns you to the beginning of the file or cluster. **End** takes you to the end of the file or cluster. If the scroll bar is present, you can use it to move through the data. You can remove a hexadecimal screen by pressing Esc or clicking on the close box. If the choice **Ascii/Hex** is given, you can select it to see the entire screen in standard ASCII view format. If the choice **Next File** is available, it takes you to the next selected file or back to the PC Shell main screen. If the choice **Name** is available, it gives the name of the file that includes the data or the type of cluster being displayed.

Editing a Hexadecimal Screen

Most hexadecimal screens can be edited directly or after you select the **Edit** option. The window title changes to *Sector Edit*, the cursor moves to the first hexadecimal byte, and a new set of function key options appears on the command line. Figure 6.5 shows an example. Notice that you can choose **5Save** to save the modified sector or **8Asc/Hx** to switch the cursor from the hex values to the ASCII values and back again.

To edit, just position the cursor at the byte where you wish to begin making changes and type. Use the arrow keys or mouse to position the cursor in the hexadecimal section. Overtype anything you wish to change; your changes are immediately highlighted in both sections. If you prefer to edit in the ASCII section, select **8Asc/Hx** to move the cursor over; you must use the arrow keys rather than the mouse to move the cursor in the ASCII section. If you change your mind, exit the window without saving it. To make the changes a permanent part of the disk, select **5Save**. You'll automatically return to the hexadecimal view screen. To leave the screen without making any changes permanent, press Esc or click on the close box without selecting **5Save**.

Changing the Sector

While viewing a file or disk in hexadecimal mode, you will have the **Change Sector** option available. If you are viewing a file, this option lets you change to another sector relative to the beginning of the file. You'll see a dialog box like the one shown in Figure 6.6. Just type in the desired sector number, such as 4, and select CONTINUE. If you don't know what sector number you want,

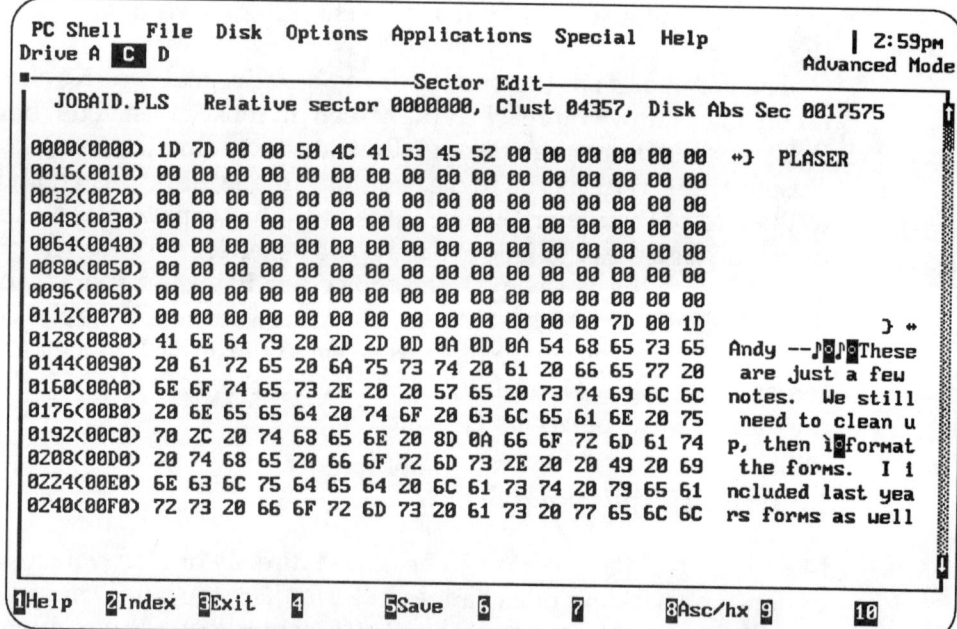

Figure 6.5   Hexadecimal Edit Screen

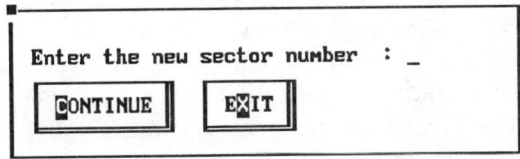

Figure 6.6 Changing Sector in a File

you can use PageDown to page through the file to find it instead of using **Change Sector**.

If you are viewing a disk rather than a file, changing to a different sector is a bit more complex. You can specify an absolute cluster or sector number relative to the beginning of the disk. When you select **Change Sector**, you'll see the dialog box shown in Figure 6.7. You can select any of several system sectors directly, including the BOOT sector, the first FAT (file allocation table) sector, the first ROOT DIR (root directory) sector, or the first DATA sector. If you prefer, you can request a specific cluster number (the range is given in the box) or an absolute sector number on the disk.

If you aren't sure what all these options are, you are probably better off avoiding them. If you choose to enter a specific cluster or sector number, you'll see a dialog box much like the one shown in Figure 6.6, but this time you'll have to provide an absolute number so that PC Shell can locate the sector or cluster you want.

Editing and Viewing Files

If you pull down the **File** menu and select **Hex Edit File**, you'll see either a standard hexadecimal screen for the selected or highlighted file, much like the one in Figure 6.4, or an ASCII screen on which you can select **8Asc/Hx** to see

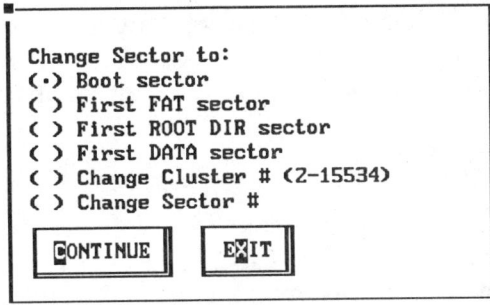

Figure 6.7 Changing Sector on a Disk

the hexadecimal screen. The binary viewer is formatted in the same way, so if you select **View** for a file with extension COM, EXE, or a few others, you'll automatically see the hexadecimal screen. If the binary viewer is your default, you'll see hexadecimal screens for many files that you view.

On any hexadecimal screen reached through the **File** menu, you can page or scroll to the end of the file. In fact, you can go beyond the end of the file to the end of the last cluster allocated to it. DOS allocates space for files in full clusters. Hexadecimal mode ignores end of file marks, so you can page further in hexadecimal mode than in ASCII mode. Before you can make changes, you may have to select **Edit**.

Disk View. To find a part of the disk that isn't currently in a file, or when you have no idea which file you want, you can select **View/Edit Disk** from the **Disk** menu. You'll see a standard hexadecimal display screen with the title *Disk View* in the upper border. You can use the standard paging commands or **Change Sector**, **Edit**, or **Name**. Selecting **Edit** puts you in hexadecimal edit mode, which works just as it does when you deal with a file. You get the SAVE option in edit mode, which lets you save changes to disk. It doesn't, however, put the sector in a file.

Selecting **Change Sector** on the Disk Edit screen results in the dialog box you saw in Figure 6.7. Selecting **Name** lets you see the name of the file the sector belongs to. You should check **Name** to make sure the sector is part of a file before you edit and save a sector. PC Shell lets you edit and save sectors to your heart's content, but it doesn't volunteer the information that a sector doesn't belong to a file. If you make changes in unallocated sectors, make a note of the cluster and sector numbers so you can assign them to a file in the **Undelete** function later.

Disk Search. When you do a disk search and the string is found, you may be informed that no file includes that sector when you ask for the filename. In that case, you can select **Edit Sector**, which results in a standard hexadecimal edit screen. You can page through only to the end of the current cluster. You can edit and save the cluster. To assign it to a file, you'll have to make a note of the cluster number, then use the manual undelete method.

✧ *Try It Out*

1. View your \AUTOEXEC.BAT file. Select **Hex Edit File**, then **8Asc/Hx** to see it in hexadecimal mode. Page to the end of the cluster to see what is stored after the end-of-file mark.

2. Select **Edit** to let you modify the file. Move the cursor within each section and between the Hex and ASCII sections. Change one letter in the ASCII section and see how the change is reflected in the Hex section. Restore the original letter.
3. Return to the main screen; don't save the changes.
4. Return to the main screen and try **View/Edit Disk**. Notice that a few words or character strings, such as DOS and FAT, are readable. Page 10 or 12 times to see more data.
5. Change to the first data sector. Check the file name, then page 10 or 12 times.
6. If you wish, try **Disk Search**. Search for a string you have used several times in files so it will be found in a reasonable length of time.

Undeletion Using Clusters

If PC Shell cannot undelete a file automatically using either the Delete Tracking or DOS Directory method, you still have two choices that may help you recover at least part of the file. A manual undeletion can be attempted when PC Shell can find some clusters that belonged to the file or when you have some idea which clusters should be included. Or you can create a new file using clusters from files that have been deleted in the past.

Manual Undelete. Manual undeletion is an option available under the DOS Directory method. You'll use it only if PC Shell can't undelete a file automatically. When the filename shown in a list of deleted files is followed by the * symbol, some of the clusters are available but not all of them; in this case, manual undeletion is often your only alternative. Some clusters that formerly made up the file may have been overwritten with data or assigned to other files. Manual undeletion is not likely to fully regenerate a file, but you may be able to get all except one cluster if you are lucky.

Manual undeletion requires that you recognize whether or not a cluster belongs in the file from its hexadecimal display. This generally works only with ASCII files or with files that are close to ASCII format. For example, word processors such as WordPerfect and WordStar don't create ASCII files, but you'll be able to recognize their contents on the hexadecimal view screen. Data files from most spreadsheet and database programs can also be recognized in hexadecimal format; you'll be able to recognize many labels, for example. You probably won't be able to recognize program files or most graphic data files well enough to reconstruct them.

After you select the DOS directory method and provide the first character of the filename, you may see a message that automatic recovery is impossible.

If you select UNDELETE at this time, you begin the manual process. Even if the file can be undeleted automatically, you can select MANUAL if you prefer.

The manual undelete screen, shown in Figure 6.8, is much like the standard hexadecimal display, with *Undelete* in the upper border. This screen displays only 128 bytes, half the number that appear in a standard hex screen; this is 1/4 sector in most disks. The line below the hexadecimal data shows how many clusters the file contained when it was deleted. The screen also provides additional information about the file at that time. You can use **PgUp** and **PgDn** to see other parts of the cluster. **Home** and **End** move to the beginning and end of the cluster.

If you select ADD, PC Shell adds the currently viewed cluster to the file being undeleted and shows you the beginning of the next cluster that might have been part of the file. If you select SKIP, the cluster is not added, and the next one appears. When you select SAVE, all clusters added so far, including the current one, are determined to make up the file being undeleted and you return to the main screen. You can keep track of how many clusters are added. The shell lets you add as many clusters as you want, no matter how many the file originally contained; it expects you to know what you are doing.

The remaining options let you locate or manipulate the clusters. When you select SRCH, you can enter an ASCII string to be located. Figure 6.9 shows the resulting dialog box. Characters appear in both ASCII and hexadecimal as you

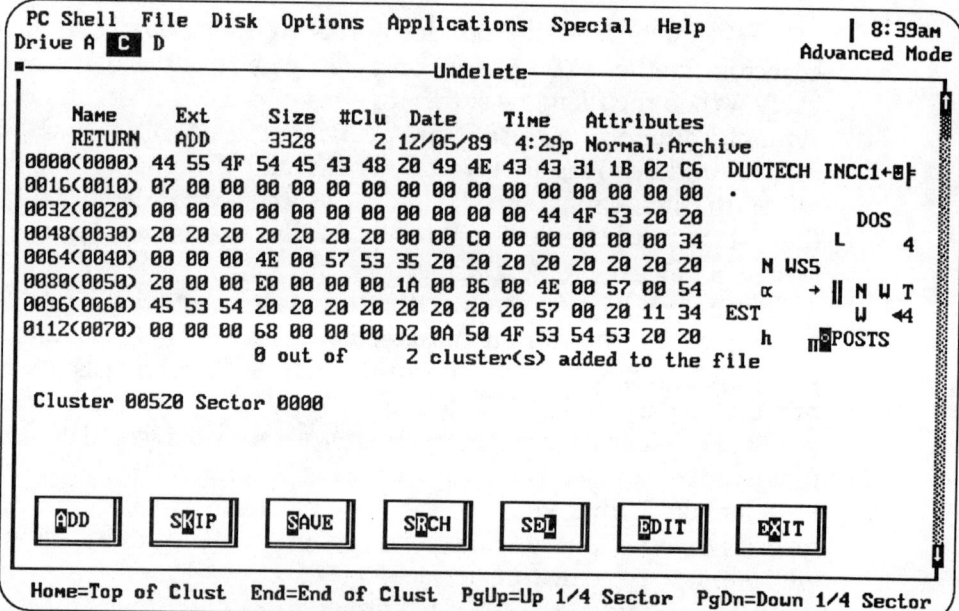

Figure 6.8   Manual Undelete Screen

type them; four ASCII characters have been entered in the figure. If you select HEX, you can type the string in hexadecimal instead. In either case, an exact match is located. The string is limited to 32 ASCII characters. When the string is located in an unallocated cluster, you can add the cluster to the file being undeleted if you want.

If you select SEL on the manual undelete screen, you can select a new cluster number by typing it in the resulting dialog box. You won't be allowed to add a cluster that is already part of a file. If you select EDIT, you can reorder the added clusters. You might want to do this if you have added too many clusters or if you know they are in the wrong order. Figure 6.10 shows the resulting screen.

You can select one cluster at a time and remove it from the file being undeleted or move it to another location in the file. Messages appear on the screen to prompt you through the process. When you finally select OK, you'll return to the standard undelete screen where you can save the result or continue to select clusters.

If you select EXIT on the undelete screen, all selected clusters are abandoned and no file is undeleted. You can start over or go on to another function.

Create through Undelete. If PC Shell has lost the directory entry for a file, you will not be able to undelete it automatically or manually. PC Shell can't tell

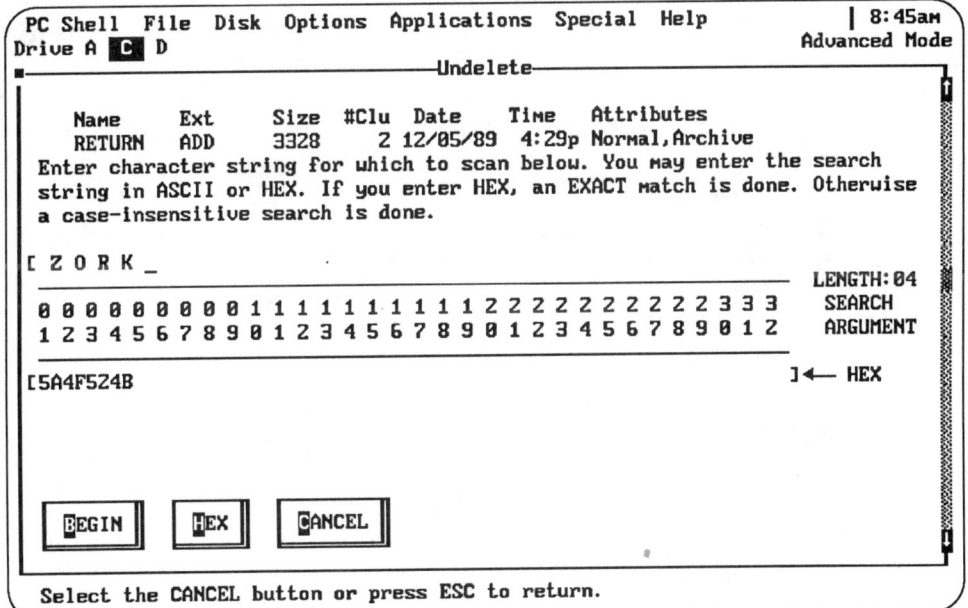

Figure 6.9   Search during Undelete

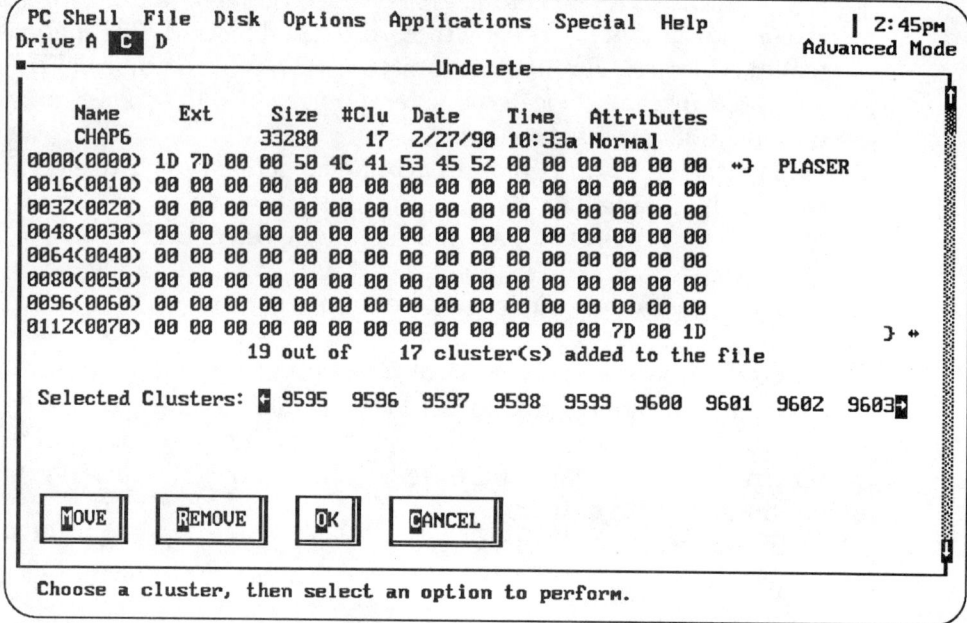

Figure 6.10   Edit during Undelete

what the filename was, where it started, or how many clusters it contained. If you expect some of its clusters to be intact or if you want to recover data in some free clusters, however, you may be able to create a new file through the Undelete function and add those clusters to it. To do this, return to the main screen and select **Undelete**. Confirm that the correct drive and directory to hold the new file are selected, then select **CREATE** instead of **FILE** or **SUBDIR** in the resulting dialog box. You will be prompted to enter a name for the file to be created from currently unassigned clusters.

The method is much like the one for manual undeletion. You'll be shown unassigned clusters in order. You can make any of the choices shown in Figure 6.8. When you have added the desired clusters to the file, you can use EDIT to rearrange them if you wish, then save the result. Finally, you can use **Hex Edit File** to check out the resulting file in detail.

✧ Try It Out

1. For preparation, make a copy of a file and name it COPYDEL.MAN. Then delete the copy.
2. Use the DOS DIR method and the MANUAL option to see how it is done.

After selecting the number of clusters in the original file, save the result. When it appears in your directory, delete it again.
3. Use the Undelete function to create a new file from four unused clusters on the disk. When it appears in your directory, examine the contents in hexadecimal mode, then delete the file.

You have learned to use the basic features of PC Shell. The next section of the book covers most of the functions you can accomplish using Desktop. If you prefer, you can skip to Section IV and learn to format disks before continuing with Desktop features.

Section III

PC Tools Desktop Manager

Chapter 7 | Notepads

PC Tools Desktop Manager is a separate facility on the same level with PC Shell. It comprises several common business applications that you will find handy. This chapter introduces the Desktop and shows you how to use Notepads to create and edit text documents. You will learn to:

- Start and terminate Desktop
- Manipulate Desktop windows
- Start and terminate Notepads
- Create, edit, print, and save a Notepad file
- Control Autosave
- Manipulate a Notepad file

Introduction to Desktop

PC Tools Desktop Manager is a collection of programs that provide the basic business computer services people use most often, along with some utilities that make both Desktop and PC Shell more useful. Desktop includes the following applications:

Notepads: Lets you create and edit text files.

Outlines: Lets you develop outlines and tables of contents.

Databases: Lets you develop and process databases.

Appointment Scheduler: Acts like a personal diary with a built-in alarm.

Telecommunications: Lets you send and receive messages and files through your modem and use your fax connection.

Autodialer: Dials telephone numbers through your modem.

Calculators: Simulates four different types of calculator—algebraic, financial, scientific, and programming.

Clipboard: Lets you transfer information from one application to another.

Macro Editor: Lets you create single-key commands for more complex procedures.

Utilities: Provides a variety of handy services, such as redefining hotkeys and displaying the ASCII character table.

The PC Tools Desktop interface (with such features as menus and screen layout) is similar to the PC Shell interface. The major difference from PC Shell is in the use of windows. Each Desktop application runs in a separate window, and up to 15 windows can be open at once. Figure 7.1 shows an example in which the user is using Outlines, Notepads, and Calculators on the same screen.

If PC Shell is in residence, you can also open it on the desktop. Thus, you could look up files, manipulate directories, and so on by using the shell while working with your desktop applications.

The chapters in this section deal with Desktop facilities. You'll learn how

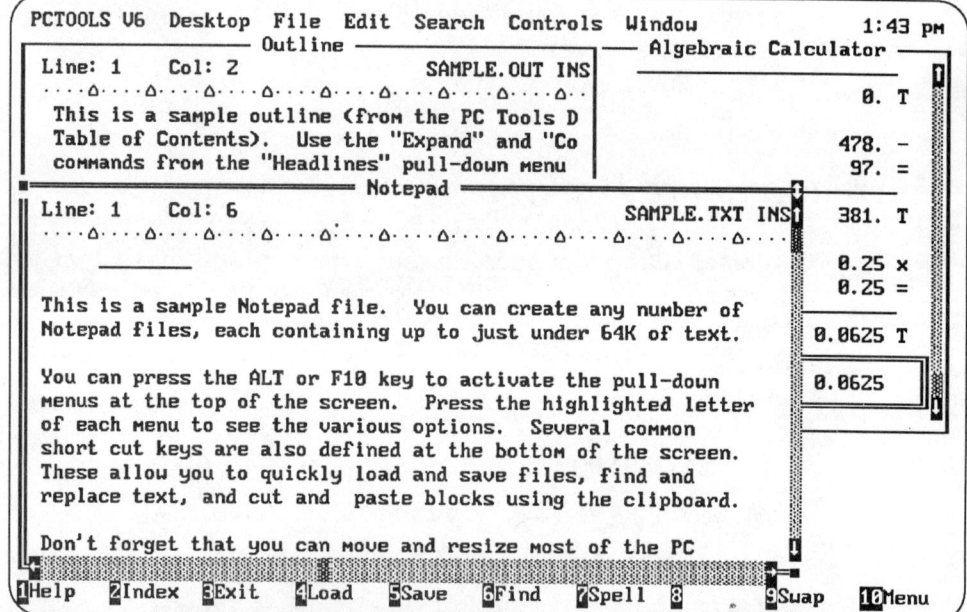

Figure 7.1   Sample Desktop Layout

to use Notepads in this chapter. The next chapter deals with Outlines and Clipboard. Chapter 9 covers Appointment Scheduler. Chapter 10 covers Databases. Chapter 11 covers Telecommunications and the Autodialer. And Chapter 12 deals with Calculators, Macro Editor, and Utilities.

Installing Desktop

You install PC Tools Desktop when you install PC Tools. If you used PC Setup to install PC Tools, then Desktop should be ready to go. If you have any problems, reinstall PC Tools, making sure to install Desktop also. Check Appendix A and your PC Tools reference manual for details.

Starting Desktop

Desktop can run in stand-alone or resident mode. Both modes operate just like PC Shell's modes. Resident mode offers some strong advantages because features such as macros and the clipboard are available even when you're working with non-Desktop applications such as WordPerfect and Excel. The disadvantage is that Desktop takes up memory space when it is resident (about 40K). Some applications might not be able to function properly because of the diminished memory space.

Starting Desktop in Stand-Alone Mode

To start Desktop in stand-alone mode, type DESKTOP at the DOS command prompt. You will see the **Desktop** menu shown in Figure 7.2. (It might be preceded by a copyright screen.) When you have finished working with stand-alone Desktop, you can terminate it by pressing Esc or F3 or by selecting **3Exit**. However, Esc and F3 close only the active window, if any are open, so you have to press the key repeatedly to close all the windows and get back to the **Desktop** menu. Pulling down the **Desktop** menu and selecting **Exit** closes all windows and terminates Desktop.

Starting Desktop in Residence Mode

You make Desktop resident by entering the command DESKTOP /R. A message appears that tells you how to hotkey into the program. To remove Desktop from resident memory, enter the KILL command, which removes both PC Shell and Desktop.

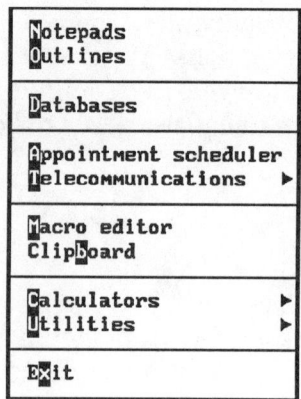

Figure 7.2   PC Tools Desktop Menu

After you make Desktop resident, the DOS command prompt returns. To activate resident Desktop from the command prompt or anywhere else, press Ctrl-Spacebar. The Desktop screen appears on the monitor, perhaps superimposed over the current application.

When you're finished with resident Desktop, you can exit by normal means (F3, for example) or by hotkey. A normal exit closes all windows. If you use the hotkey, the windows are left open for the next time you enter Desktop. You could hotkey into the Desktop once, open a calculator, then hotkey back to your previous application. The next time you hotkey into Desktop, the calculator will be waiting for you. (You could even keep a running total on it.)

Startup Options

The DESKTOP command includes several options, as shown in Table 7.1. Most of these options have the same effect as their PC Shell equivalents. This section discusses the unique options.

The /CS (clear screen) option affects the background in resident mode. Without /CS, the desktop windows are superimposed on the current screen. If you prefer a blank background, which makes the screen less cluttered, enter /CS with the DESKTOP command.

The /C3 and /C4 options are necessary only if you do not have a PS/2 and your modem is installed on COM3 or COM4. Since COM3 and COM4 are nonstandard except in the PS/2 environment, you must tell Desktop how to access the modem in such cases. See your Desktop reference manual for more details.

The /RA option, as opposed to plain /R, makes the Desktop resident and

Table 7.1   Desktop Startup Options

Monitor Control
- /BW   For monochrome monitors with color cards
- /CS   Clears the screen in resident mode
- /IN   Permits use of color with Hercules InColor card
- /350   Displays 350-line resolution on VGA monitor
- /LCD   Sets colors for an LCD display

Mouse Control
- /IM   Disables mouse in resident mode
- /LE   Exchanges mouse buttons

Other Hardware Control
- /C*n*   Identifies serial port 3 or 4 for modem
- /O*d*   Specifies drive for overlay files

Desktop Control
- /R   Installs Desktop in resident mode
- /RA   Installs Desktop in resident mode and starts it up immediately
- /DQ   Starts Desktop faster by not saving the DOS prompt screen

starts it immediately. If you have set up and saved an appointment file, the Appointment Scheduler is started. Otherwise, the main **Desktop** menu is displayed. If you use this option in the AUTOEXEC.BAT file, be sure the DESKTOP command is the last command in the file, because the /RA option activates the Desktop immediately, preventing the remaining commands in AUTOEXEC.BAT from being executed until Desktop is terminated.

Manipulating Windows

As you open more and more windows on your desktop, you'll want to arrange them so you can see the information you need. You can move them, resize them, and change their colors, much as you can in PC Shell.

The Active Window

Only one window can be active at a time, indicated by the double border. This is the window that receives input from the keyboard, mouse, menus, and dialog boxes. The easiest way to make a window active is to click on any part of it. If you don't have a mouse, press F9; a bottom line command **9Swap** reminds you. If more than two windows are showing, F9 calls up a dialog box in which you can select the desired window.

Moving and Resizing Windows

You can move, resize, and zoom a window just as you can in PC Shell. The mouse actions for resizing and moving a window are the same as those for PC Shell. The keyboard shortcut is the same (Alt-Spacebar) although the menu options are on the **Window** menu instead of the **Options** menu. Figure 7.3 shows an example of a **Window** menu; this one is from Notepads. To zoom, select **Zoom** on the **Window** menu or click on the Zoom icon. Some Desktop windows, such as the scientific calculator, cannot be resized. The **Video Size** option lets you change the number of lines displayed per screen.

Changing Window Colors

Sometimes changing the colors of a window helps to make it stand out. For example, if you are editing two different versions of a file in Notepads, you might want to place one version on a red background to help you differentiate between them. To change a window's colors, first make it active. Then pull down the **Window** menu and select the **Change colors** option. A dialog box similar to the one in PC Shell appears. The details of the box depend on the active window, but you can change the major features of each type.

Function Key Reminders

The bottom screen line shows the function keys available for the currently active application. That is, if a Notepad window is active, you will see function key commands for Notepads, but if a Calculator window is active, you will see a different set of commands. F1 gets help, F2 gets the help index, F3 exits,

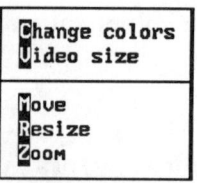

Figure 7.3   Window Menu

and F10 activates the menu bar, much as in PC Shell. F9 switches among the windows.

✧ *Try It Out*

1. Enter the KILL command to get rid of resident Desktop, if necessary. Then, start Desktop in stand-alone mode, using the same options you use to start PC Shell.
2. Exit back to the command prompt.
3. Make Desktop resident with a clear screen. Hotkey to it.
4. Open any calculator and hotkey back to DOS, leaving the calculator open.
5. Hotkey back to Desktop. The calculator should still be open. Then terminate and kill Desktop.
6. Make Desktop resident again using /RA. You should be able to see the difference.
7. Open the Clipboard window. Make it as small as possible. Then zoom it to full size. Zoom it back to its former size.
8. Make its background red and its border high-intensity white. Restore its original colors (cyan and blue).
9. Close the window.

Notepads

Notepads is a basic word processor that allows you to prepare and edit text files. It has more features than the PC Shell Edit function and is generally easier to use. You can create files in ASCII format or a special PC Tools Desktop format. You can also access and edit files in WordStar format, although you cannot create new files in WordStar format. The maximum file size is 60,000 characters.

Starting Notepads

You start Notepads by opening a Notepad window. Pull down the **Desktop** menu and select **Notepads**. You will see the dialog box shown in Figure 7.4. You must supply a filename in this dialog box; you can type one in the **Filename** field at the top of the box or select one in the list box. (If you don't supply a name, Notepads assumes WORK.TXT.)

To type a name, replace or edit the global name currently in the box (*.TXT in the figure). If you omit the period and the extension, Notepads supplies the extension TXT. If you don't want an extension, type the period but no extension. You can include a path in the filename if you don't want to use the current directory, shown on the line below the **Filename** field.

When the name is correct, select LOAD or NEW depending on whether you are trying to edit an existing file or create a new one. If you select LOAD and the filename doesn't exist in the designated directory, Notepads displays the message "File not found. Create a new file instead?" If you select NEW and the specified filename already exists in the designated directory, you will see the message "Warning! That file already exists. Continue anyway?" If you select OK, the new file overwrites the existing one. You can also delete the selected file with DELETE.

You can select the filename instead of typing it; the list box shows the files in the current directory that match the global filename, along with the available drives and directories. To change the drive or directory, click twice on the desired one or type its path in the **Filename** box. You can see the path change in the second line. To change the global filename, overtype or edit the current one. Whatever changes you make here pertain to future **Notepads** dialog boxes as well. When the list box contains the desired set of files, you can select the one you want by highlighting it and pressing Enter or by clicking twice on it. Both these actions load the existing file for editing. If you want to overwrite the existing file with a new version, highlight the filename and select NEW.

The Notepad Window

Once you open a new or existing file, it is displayed in a Notepad window much like the one shown in Figure 7.5. The menu bar shows names of menus specific to the Notepads application. The top line in the window is a status line showing the current position of the cursor, the filename, and the status of

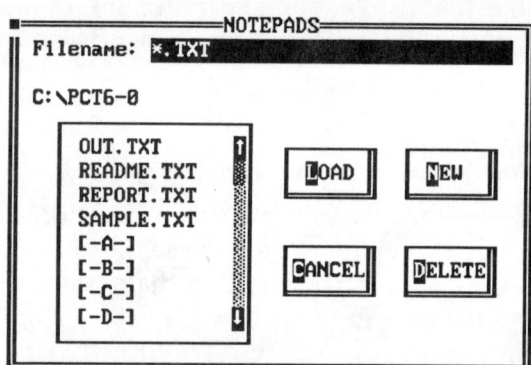

Figure 7.4   Notepads Dialog Box

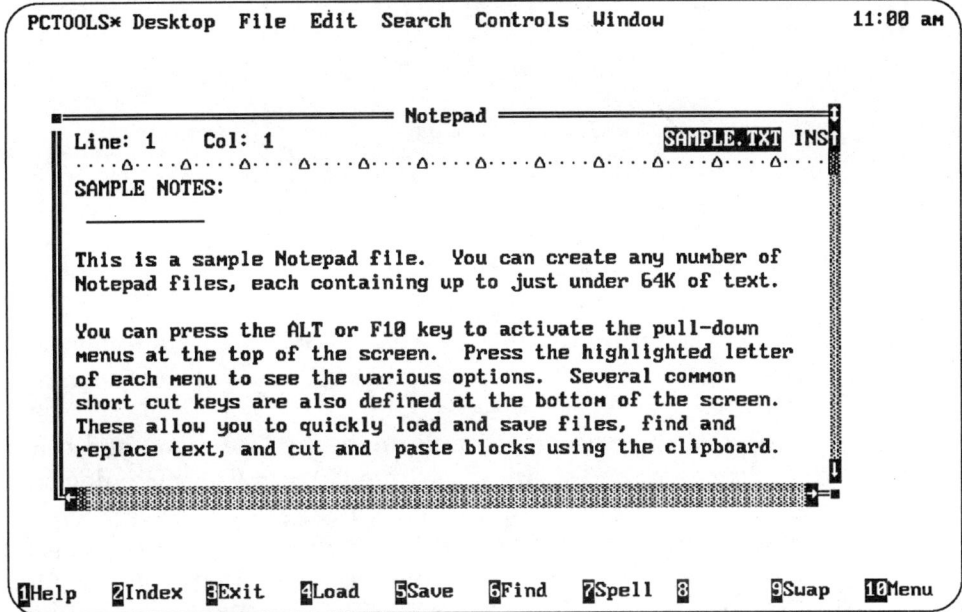

Figure 7.5 Notepad Window

insert mode. If you make the window very narrow, the filename disappears. The line below the status line shows the current tab settings, every fifth column by default.

The main portion of the window is the text area. What you see here is not what you get when the document is printed. Notepads formats the document when it is printed, but in the window, the text is displayed from border to border. If you make the window narrower or wider, the text adjusts to fit. So, don't worry about the margins you see in the window; they aren't the real margins.

The vertical scroll bar lets you scroll through documents longer than the window. The horizontal scroll bar at the bottom of the window displays the horizontal position of the cursor with respect to the ends of the current line. You can use it to move the cursor, but it's easier to just click on the desired position in the text area unless the line is wider than the window, which can happen when word wrap is turned off.

Printing

Printing is accomplished through the **File** menu, shown in Figure 7.6. The menu offers several functions to manipulate the file in the active Notepad

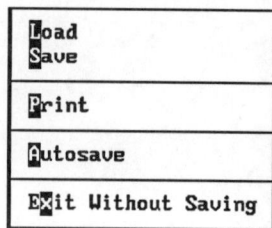

Figure 7.6   Notepads File Menu

window. You can print the file, save it, load a different file into the window, close the window without saving the file, and control when the file is automatically saved with Autosave.

To print the current file, pull down the **File** menu and select **Print**. The default device is automatically selected in the resulting dialog box. If you have more than one printer, you can select an alternate one by selecting its port. Set the number of copies if the default shown is wrong. Then select **Print**. While the file is printing, you will see a message in the status line of your window: NOW PRINTING. PRESS ESCAPE TO CANCEL.

Sometimes you need to format a file for printing but save the file on disk instead of actually printing it. The result is a file in ASCII format with margins, headers, footers, and so forth. To print to disk, select the **Disk file** option instead of a port in the dialog box. Notepads creates a file named *filename*.PRT containing the formatted version.

Saving the File

You can save the current file by simply closing its window or by pulling down the **File** menu and selecting the **Save** option. If you want to save the file under a different name or in a different format, then use the **Save** option, which results in the dialog box shown in Figure 7.7. You can replace or edit the filename, including the path if you want to put the file in a different directory.

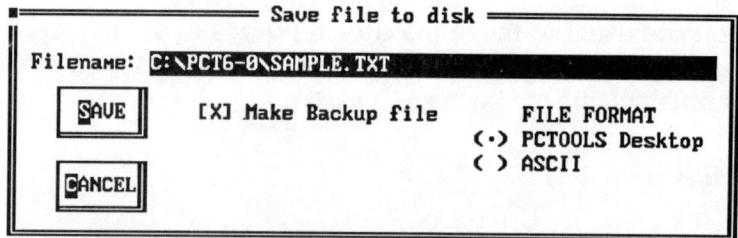

Figure 7.7   Save Dialog Box

If you change the name, you will have two versions of the file: the most recently saved version under the old name and the edited version under the new name.

You can select PCTOOLS Desktop or ASCII format. You can also elect to save a backup file. The backup feature saves the previous version of the file (the most recently saved version) under the name *filename*.BAK. You can turn the backup feature off by selecting the box.

Once the desired options are set, select SAVE or CANCEL. SAVE causes the file to be saved immediately. CANCEL closes the dialog box and records the options you have selected, but the file itself is not saved.

If the file is saved without going through the **Save** option, the text is saved according to the current condition of the **Save** dialog box. If you loaded an old file and did not change the dialog box, the previous filename and format are maintained. If you created a new file and did not change the dialog box, the PC Tools Desktop format is used. If you changed the dialog box, of course, the name and format you designated are used.

Four events cause a file to be saved without going through the **Save** option: closing the Notepad window via F3, Esc, or the close box; opening any other window on the screen; switching to a different window; and autosaving. If you want to save the original version of the file you are editing, you should make a backup copy under another name to protect its contents from all these various save situations. Keeping a backup version when you save a file is not good enough; the BAK file will contain the next most recently saved version, not necessarily the version you originally opened.

Autosave

Suppose after you work for three hours creating a new text file, the power goes out. Have you lost all your work? Not if you used the Autosave feature. With Autosave on, Desktop automatically saves all open windows to disk every so often to minimize the risk of loss due to power failure. You should always use Autosave unless there is no chance of a power failure.

To turn Autosave on from a Notepad window, pull down the **File** menu and select **Autosave**. Figure 7.8 shows the dialog box that results. If you select

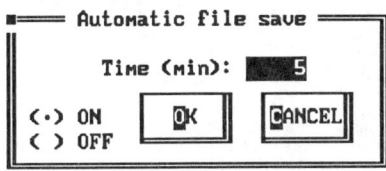

Figure 7.8   Autosave Dialog Box

OK without making any changes to the box, Autosave is turned on and all open windows will be saved every five minutes. You can change the time interval if you wish. If Autosave is already on, you use this same method to turn it off.

Even though you turn Autosave on and off in a particular file's window, the Autosave feature affects all Notepad, Outline, Appointment Scheduler, and Macro Editor windows; that is, all the Desktop applications that create and edit files. Turn it on once and it's on for all these applications until you turn it off again. Turn it off for one window, and you turn it off for all of them.

To rescue a file after a power loss, simply open it again. You should find the text as it was last saved. You might have lost a few minutes' work, but that's not as bad as losing several hours' work.

Exiting Notepads

You can exit a Notepad window by closing the window, which saves the file. Or you can pull down the **File** menu and select **Exit Without Saving**, which closes the window but doesn't save the file. (The most recently saved version of the file remains on the disk.)

✧ *Try It Out*

1. Start Desktop if necessary. Open a Notepad window for the existing file SAMPLE.TXT in your PC Tools directory. Read this file, scrolling as necessary.
2. Make the Notepad window narrower and wider. Watch how the text reformats itself to fit the window. Also watch the filename disappear and reappear. When you are finished, leave the window at about its original size.
3. Pull down the **Desktop** menu and open the Clipboard window. Arrange the windows on the screen so you can see them both at once.
4. Close both windows.
5. Open a Notepad window for a new file named PRACTICE. Turn on Autosave. Set it for one minute intervals. You should hear it saving as you work on the rest of this exercise.
6. Type a few paragraphs into the file. (Any text will do; don't worry about corrections yet.)
7. Print PRACTICE. Save it in Desktop format.
8. Turn Autosave off or set it for a longer time, as you prefer.
9. Exit by closing the window.

Cursor Movement and Scrolling

There are several ways to position the cursor in the text. You can use the cursor movement keys, the mouse, the Goto function, or the Search function.

The same cursor movement keys are available in Notepads as in the PC Shell editor. Most of the actions are fairly standard. Ctrl-← and Ctrl-→ move the cursor by words. Home and End take you to the beginning and end of the current line, while Ctrl-Home and Ctrl-End take you to the beginning and end of the file. Pressing Home twice jumps the cursor to the upper left corner of the window; pressing End twice jumps the cursor as close to the lower right corner as it can go (it can't go where no characters have been typed).

To move the cursor with the mouse, scroll as necessary, then click on the desired position. The cursor jumps to whatever position you click on.

Goto. The Goto feature moves the cursor to any specified line in the file. The current line number is shown in the status line at the top of the window. To skip forward or backward to another line, pull down the **Edit** menu and select **Goto**. A dialog box asks for the desired line number.

Search and Replace

You can select **6Find** or use the **Search** menu to locate text. The menu offers two options. **Find** moves the cursor to the next occurrence of a string. **Replace** finds a string and possibly replaces it with another. **6Find** lets you do either.

To move the cursor to the beginning of a particular string, pull down the **Search** menu and select the **Find** option. The dialog box shown in Figure 7.9 results. Fill out the **Search for** field with whatever string of characters you want to find. Also, select or deselect the **Case sensitive** option and the **Whole words only** option as appropriate.

When the dialog box contains the right information, select FIND NEXT. The search begins at the current position of the cursor and moves forward in the file. If a match is found, the cursor is positioned at the beginning of the matching string. The **Find** dialog box stays on the screen so that you can select

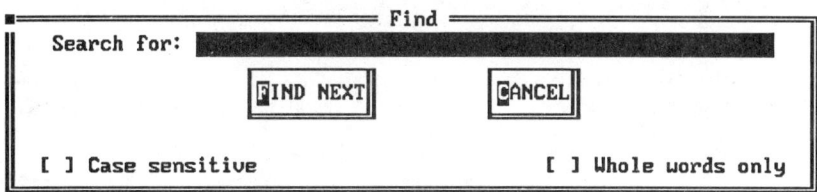

Figure 7.9   Find Dialog Box

FIND NEXT again to continue the search. (You can also change the search parameters if you don't like the matches you're getting.)

The dialog box clears automatically, accompanied by a beep, if no match is found. You can clear the dialog box when you find the desired string. The next time you select the find function, the last values you used will appear in the dialog box. You can start the same search again or overtype the parameters to start a new search.

To search for and replace a string, select **6Find** or pull down the **Search** menu and select **Replace**. You will see the dialog box shown in Figure 7.10. Fill out the **Search for** and **Replace with** fields and select the other options as appropriate. **Replace one time** means that only the next matching string will be replaced; the dialog box stays on the screen so you can continue the function. **Replace all** means that all the remaining matching strings will be replaced; the dialog box automatically clears after the replacements are completed. With **Verify before replace**, the cursor moves to the next matching string and a message tells you to press Enter to make the change, Spacebar to skip this match and go on to the next one, or Esc to abort the entire function. After you press Enter or Spacebar, the cursor jumps to the next match and the process repeats. If you press Esc, of course, the replace function is terminated.

Once you have chosen all your options, select FIND or REPLACE. FIND works just like the find function; the cursor moves to the next matching string, and no replacement takes place. REPLACE causes the selected replace function to take place.

Spell Checking

You can spell check an individual word, all the words showing on the screen, or the complete file. Figure 7.11 shows the **Edit** menu. The bottom section contains the three spell checking options. Selecting **7Spell** has the same effect as **Spellcheck File**. After you select an option, a message appears at the top of the window: SPELL CHECKING IN PROGRESS. PLEASE WAIT. If you are checking only one word, and it is spelled correctly, the message might flash by so fast that you don't see it.

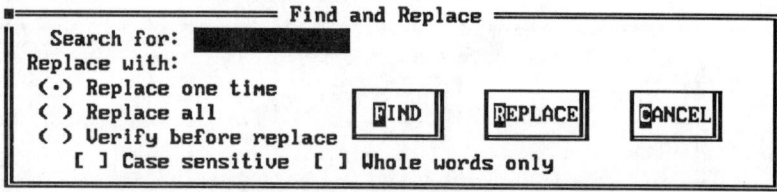

Figure 7.10   Find and Replace Dialog Box

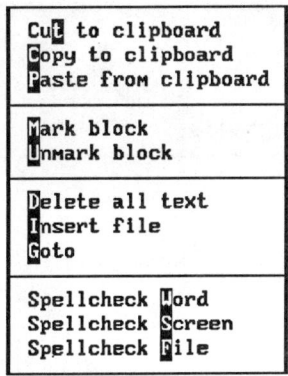

Figure 7.11   Notepads Edit Menu

If the spell checker finds a word that isn't in its dictionary, it highlights the word and displays a message similar to the one in Figure 7.12. This doesn't necessarily mean the word is misspelled, only that it isn't in Desktop's dictionary.

If you choose IGNORE, the spell checker leaves that word as it is for the remainder of the current spelling check. You can't tell it to ignore just one occurrence and alert you if the spelling appears again.

CORRECT brings up a dialog box in which you can enter or select the corrected spelling, much like the one in Figure 7.13. To type the corrected spelling, tab to where the incorrect spelling appears on the second line. Edit or overtype the word to correct the spelling. To select the correct spelling from the list box, highlight the correct spelling and press Enter or click twice on the correct spelling. (Clicking once won't do.) The incorrect spelling on the second line will be replaced with the correct spelling. Then select ACCEPT, and the corrected spelling will replace the incorrect one in the file. If at any time you select CANCEL, the **Word Correction** dialog box clears and the previous dialog box (shown in Figure 7.12) returns.

ADD adds the current word to the dictionary. Use this option to tailor your dictionary to your needs. But there is no way to remove a word from the

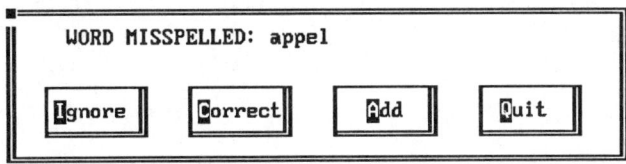

Figure 7.12   Word Misspelled Dialog Box

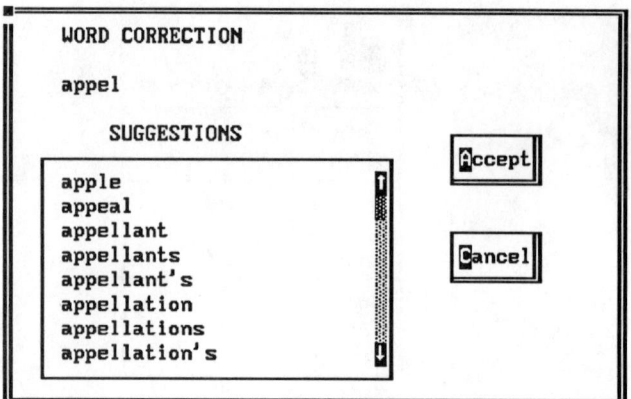

Figure 7.13   Word Correction Dialog Box

dictionary again, so don't add slang or intentional misspellings that are valid for this file only. If you do want to go back to the original dictionary as delivered by Central Point Software, you can copy the DICT.SPL file from the original PC Tools diskette to your PC Tools subdirectory. This will overlay the updated version of the dictionary with the original version, eliminating all the words you have added since installation.

The final option, QUIT, terminates the spell check.

✦ *Try It Out*

1. Open a Notepad window for PRACTICE, if necessary.
2. Try out various cursor movement keys.
3. Go to line 3.
4. Go to the beginning. Search for the letter "h". Repeat the search twice. Then quit the search function.
5. Replace the next "h" with "x".
6. Replace all remaining "h" with "x". Verify each replacement.
7. Spell check the PRACTICE file. If you get tired of making corrections, quit the spell checker and correct the rest of the errors by replacing all "x" with "h".

Formatting the Screen and Printed Documents

So far, we've been using the default format to create and print documents. To change the format, use the **Controls** menu, shown in Figure 7.14.

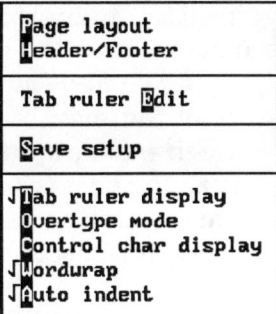

Figure 7.14   Notepads Controls Menu

Editing Toggles. The bottom section of the menu lists toggle switches that affect the editing environment. A check mark indicates the switch is on; no check mark means it's off. The default settings are shown in the figure. The following switches affect the screen display only, not the printed version of the file:

Tab ruler display: Determines whether or not the tab ruler is displayed on the second line of the window. Turn it off to remove the tab ruler and make one more line available for text.

Overtype mode: Determines whether typed characters overtype existing characters or are inserted between existing characters. This option functions just like the Insert key.

Control char display: When turned on, tabs, carriage returns, and spaces are shown on the screen. A tab appears as a right arrow (→); a carriage return appears as a bent arrow (↵); and a space appears as a small bullet (·).

Wordwrap: Determines whether or not paragraphs are word wrapped. Turn this off if you want everything between carriage returns to stay on one line on the screen. You can see a line wider than the window by scrolling sideways using the horizontal scroll bar, the arrow keys, or the other mouse button (drag to the left or right border).

None of the above options affects the way the file is printed. One switch affects both the screen display and the printed version: **Auto indent**. When this feature is on (the default), each new line is indented to the same level as the previous line. If you indent the beginning of a paragraph, subsequent lines are word wrapped to the same indentation, giving you an inset paragraph. When you press Enter to end the paragraph, the cursor moves to the same tab stop on the next line. Backspace removes the indentation. Automatic indentation is handy for typing lists, outlines, computer programs, and so on, in the middle of a text document. To type a list, outline, or computer program as a separate document, you might find Outlines easier than Notepads.

When **Auto indent** is off, no lines are automatically indented. Press the Tab key to indent; only the current line is affected. When you indent the first line of a paragraph, the remaining lines word wrap to the left margin.

Turning **Auto indent** on or off causes the entire file to be reformatted, so you can't have **Auto indent** on for some portions of the file and off for others.

Page Layout. Selecting the **Page layout** option brings up the dialog box shown in Figure 7.15, in which you can set margins, line spacing, and so forth. The default values are shown in the figure.

Left and right margins are measured in characters. If the print size is 10 characters per inch, the default left margin of 8 is 0.8 inch and the default right margin of 73 leaves 1.2 inches. If the paper is aligned in the printer to create a two-character offset on the left, which is very common, the default margins turn out to be one inch each. However, if your printer uses a different character size or paper alignment, or if you don't want one-inch margins, adjust the left and right margins to achieve the effect you want.

The top margin, bottom margin, and paper size are measured in lines. For devices that print at six lines per inch, the default margins are one inch each and the default paper length is 11 inches. If your printer prints at eight lines per inch or some other density, if your paper length is not 11 inches, or if you need different margins, then you will need to change the defaults.

Line spacing can be 1 or 2 for single or double spacing. The starting page number can be any number you like, but it must be Arabic, not Roman.

Header and Footer. If you want a header or footer printed on every page of the document, select **Header/Footer**. You can use either or both. The dialog box shown in Figure 7.16 results. By default, the header is blank and the footer is the page number (represented by #). Type whatever text you want for the header and footer, up to 50 characters each. They will be centered in the top and bottom margins. Use the pound sign (#) for the page number. If you want

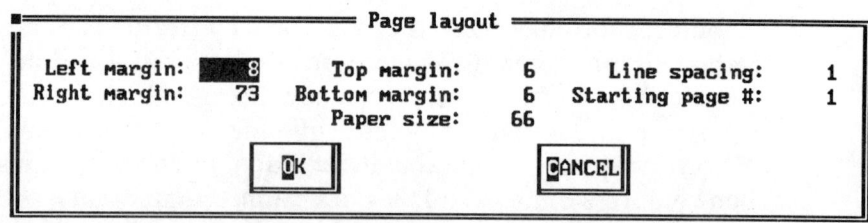

Figure 7.15   Page Layout Dialog Box

no header or footer, not even the page number, delete the pound sign in the **Footer** field.

Tabs. To change the tab stops, make sure the tab ruler display is on. Then select **Tab ruler Edit** on the **Controls** menu. The message EDITING TAB RULER appears on the top line and the cursor moves to the tab ruler line. Position the cursor as needed and press Ins to insert a tab stop, Del to delete one, and Esc to end the tab ruler edit. If you want to replace the current set of tab stops with evenly spaced ones, simply type a number between 3 and 29 representing the correct interval. The tab ruler changes immediately to show the new set of tabs. You can clear all the tab stops by typing 0.

Suppose you want tab stops in positions 8, 15, and 25. First type 0 to clear the tab ruler. Then move the cursor to column 8 and press Ins, to column 15 and press Ins, then to column 25 and press Ins; finally, press Esc. The file is automatically reformatted to the new tab stops. The tab edit message overlays the column number in the window, so you can't see column numbers while you are positioning the cursor. If you clear the existing tab stops, you'll have to count columns from the left margin to position the cursor accurately.

Generalizing the Setup. Every option on the **Controls** and **Window** menus is saved with the file in Desktop format. (With ASCII or WordStar format, formatting information is lost when you close the window.) Therefore, when you reopen the Desktop format file, its previous format and appearance on the screen are resumed. However, the decisions you make on the **Controls** and **Window** menu normally affect only the current file.

If you want to generalize the **Controls** and **Window** options to all future new files, select **Save setup** on the **Controls** menu. This sets the current tab stops, window size and colors, and so forth, as the defaults for files that don't have any format options stored with them; that is, all ASCII files, WordStar files, and any other new files. The options on the **Window** menu are generalized throughout Notepads. The options on the **controls** menu, however, are generalized for all printable files, including files in Notepads, Outlines, Macro Editor, and Databases.

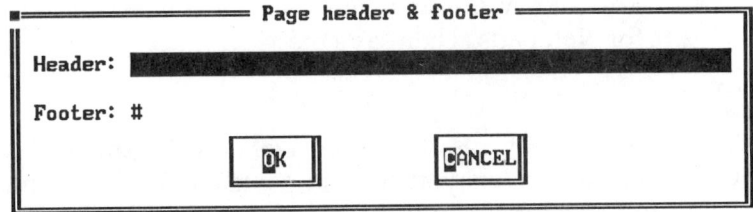

Figure 7.16   Page Header and Footer Dialog Box

When you're ready to start using Desktop, set up a Notepad window the way you like it—color, size, editing controls, page layout, and so forth. Then save the setup so you won't have to set up each file individually from then on.

File Manipulation

Three Notepads functions let you manipulate the entire file:

Load (**File** menu): Replaces the current file in the window with the designated file. The current file is abandoned without saving.

Insert file (**Edit** menu): Copies the designated file into the current file at the cursor position.

Delete all text (**Edit** menu): Erases all the text in the current file, but does not delete the file or remove it from the window.

✧ Try It Out

1. Open a Notepad window for the PRACTICE file, if necessary.
2. Turn off the tab ruler display. Turn on the control character display. Turn Wordwrap off; after you see the effect, turn it back on again.
3. Add an indented paragraph to the file. Press Tab to start the paragraph. Watch what happens when the paragraph wraps to the second line.
4. Type an indented list of items. (You can list the items on your desk.) Tab for the first item. The other items should indent automatically.
5. Turn Auto Indent off. The indented paragraph should reformat to the left margin, but the list should stay indented.
6. Set all margins to two inches. Turn on the tab ruler display and set the tabs at every 10th position. Add a header that says PRACTICE DOCUMENT PAGE followed by the page number. Eliminate the footer. Print the document.
7. Delete all the text in the file. Insert SAMPLE.TXT into the file.
8. If you would like to try saving the setup, set up all the features on the **Controls** and **Window** menus the way you would like them in the future for Notepads. Then save the setup.

Two Desktop features that often work in conjunction with Notepads are Clipboard, which lets you cut and paste blocks of text, and Outlines, which helps you develop an outline for a document you intend to write. In the next chapter, you will learn about both of these Desktop facilities.

Chapter 8 | *Outlines and Clipboard*

The Outlines facility helps you create outlines and other indented lists (such as computer programs). The Clipboard facility lets you transfer text among Notepads, Outlines, Macro Editor, Appointment Scheduler, and even non-Desktop applications. In this chapter, you will learn to:

- Create an outline
- Edit an outline
- Cut and copy text to the clipboard
- Paste text from the clipboard
- Use the clipboard with non-Desktop applications

Outlines

The Outlines facility is very similar to Notepads. You use both applications to create, manipulate, print, and save text files. The window appears the same, as you can see in the example in Figure 8.1. The menu bar is the same with the addition of the **Headlines** menu. The function keys are the same.

The difference lies in the handling of outline entry levels, as indicated by indentation. You can hide and reveal levels as needed to arrange the outline to suit your purposes. You can also change an entry to a higher or lower level, and all its subordinate entries will be raised (promoted) or lowered (demoted) as well. All the functions that manipulate entry levels are contained on the **Headlines** menu.

The other menus are much like their Notepads counterparts. The **Desktop** menu, which is standard throughout Desktop, lets you start other applications. The **File** menu lets you save, print, and so forth; you can also control Autosave from this menu, affecting all pertinent windows, not just the active one. The **Edit** menu lets you check spelling, insert a file, and so forth. The **Search** menu accesses the find and replace functions. The **Controls** menu lets you format the window and the printed document; you can select **Save setup** on this menu to set up the default format for future Outline windows and all printed documents. However, the word wrapping feature, available on the Notepads **Controls** menu, is not available in Outlines. The **Window** menu lets you control the appearance of the window.

Starting Outlines

When you select the **Outlines** option on the **Desktop** menu, you see an **Outlines** dialog box, which is much like the **Notepads** dialog box (Figure 7.4), where you enter or select the outline filename. The default extension is OUT, and the default filename is WORK.OUT. You can type a new filename and select NEW or an existing one and select LOAD. If a problem exists, you'll see a message box. Once you select LOAD or NEW, an Outline window appears. If you select DELETE, the file is gone.

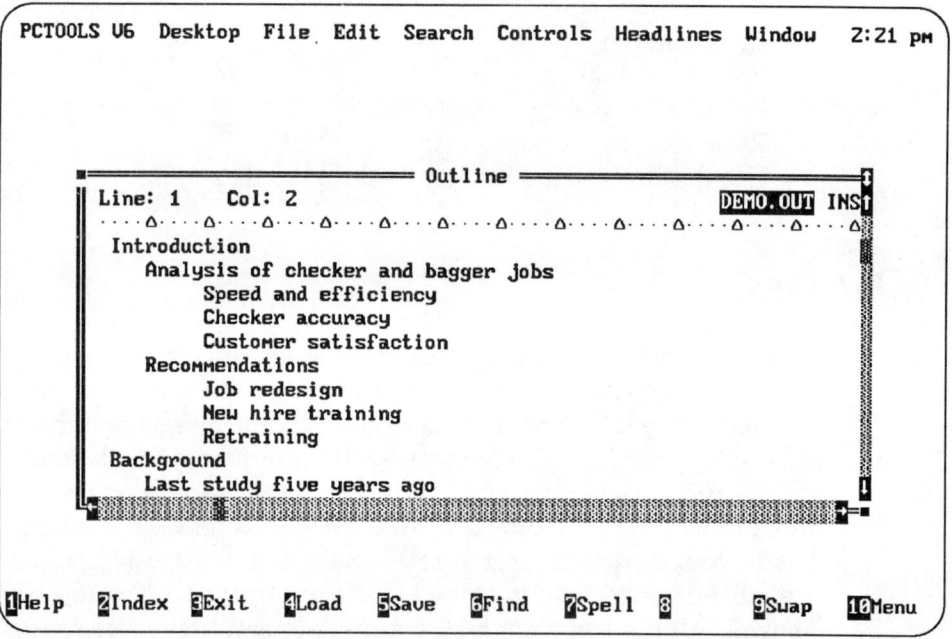

Figure 8.1   Outline Window

Creating a New Outline

To create a new outline, simply type the entries. If you want the entries numbered, you must number them yourself; Outlines does not generate numbers automatically. Each entry is considered a headline in the outline. Word wrapping is not available, so you have to press Enter at the end of each line. The text scrolls horizontally if you need a longer line; you can click on the horizontal scroll bar to see a different part of the line. When you press Enter, the cursor starts a new line at the same level of indentation as the previous line. You can keep the same level, press Tab to increase the level of indentation, or press Backspace to decrease the level of indentation. The following example shows when the Enter, Tab, and Backspace keys were pressed in Figure 8.1:

```
Introduction <Enter>
<Tab>Analysis of checker and bagger jobs<Enter>
<Tab>Speed and efficiency <Enter>
Checker accuracy <Enter>
Customer satisfaction <Enter> <Backspace>
Recommendations <Enter>
<Tab>Job redesign <Enter>
New hire training <Enter>
Retraining <Enter> <Backspace> <Backspace>
Background <Enter>
...
```

Once your outline has been created, you can save and print it just like a Notepad file. Lines that are wider than the margins are wrapped to the level of the beginning of the line in the printed version.

Editing an Outline

Edit the text of an outline entry just as you do a Notepad file; the cursor movement keys are the same. To alter the level of a single line, position the cursor at the beginning of the entry and press Tab or Backspace.

To insert an entry, position the cursor at the end of the preceding entry and press Enter. (Insert mode must be on.) A blank line will be inserted with the cursor indented to the same level as the previous line. Don't backspace to promote the level; backspacing in this particular situation deletes the inserted blank line. Type the entry first; then position the cursor at the beginning of the line and promote it.

◆ *Try It Out*

1. Create a new outline called TRYOUT.OUT. (Copy one from this chapter or make up one of your own, but use at least four entries and at least three levels.)
2. Delete the second entry. Add a new fourth entry that says "Inserted entry." Change the level of the last entry.
3. Print the outline. Close the window and save the outline.
4. Reopen it again.

Manipulating the Outline

The **Headlines** menu, shown in Figure 8.2, accesses the features that make Outlines unique. You can use this menu to hide and reveal entries as well as promote and demote entries and sections. These options affect the displayed version and the printed version. Thus, if you develop an outline with five levels of detail, you can print a full copy for yourself but an abbreviated version for your colleagues showing only the top two or three levels. You can compress and expand levels as needed while working with them.

Hiding Entries. The **Show level** option is used both for hiding lines and for revealing them again. Suppose you want to hide everything below the third level. Place the cursor on any line at the third level and select **Show level**. All the levels below the third level are hidden. Figure 8.3 shows the same outline as in Figure 8.1, but only the top two levels are showing. The triangular markers indicate entries with hidden subentries; the markers appear on the screen only, not in print.

The **Main headline only** option hides everything below the first level, which can be useful for checking the overall structure of your outline.

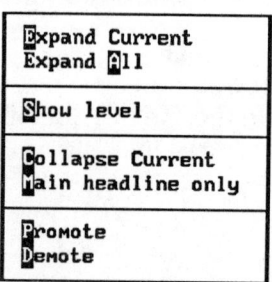

Figure 8.2   Headlines Menu

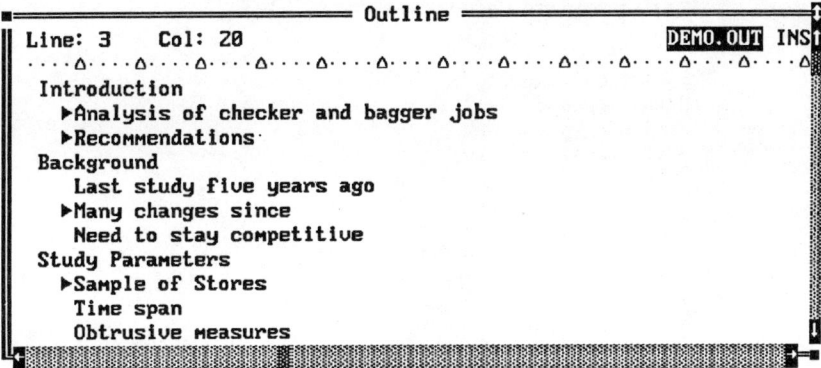

Figure 8.3   Outline with Hidden Levels

The **Collapse current** option hides all the subentries under the current entry (as identified by the cursor position). It has no effect on other entries at the same level. Figure 8.4 shows an example in which the first section has been hidden.

Revealing Entries.   Once you have hidden entries, you will eventually need to reveal them again. The **Expand current** option reveals all the subentries of the current entry. Suppose you want to see the detailed entries under "Sample of stores" in Figure 8.3. You would place the cursor on "Sample of stores" and select **Expand current**. The subentries of that particular entry would be revealed.

The **Show current** option reveals all entries at or above the level of the current entry, while hiding all entries below the level of the current entry.

```
========================= Outline =========================
Line: 2    Col: 14                            DEMO.OUT INS
····Δ····Δ····Δ····Δ····Δ····Δ····Δ····Δ····Δ····Δ····Δ····Δ
▶Introduction
 Background
    Last study five years ago
    Many changes since
          Checker stations
          Personnel
          Bags
    Need to stay competitive
 Study Parameters
    Sample of Stores
          Considerations
```

Figure 8.4   Outline with Hidden Section

```
═══════════════════════════ Outline ═══════════════════════════
Line: 6    Col: 12                                   DEMO.OUT INS
····∆····∆····∆····∆····∆····∆····∆····∆····∆····∆····∆····∆
►Introduction
►Background
 Study Parameters
     Sample of Stores
             Considerations
             Drawing of sample
     Time span
     Obtrusive measures
     Unobtrusive measures
►Results
►Conclusions
```

Figure 8.5   Outline with Headlines and One Expanded Section

Suppose you have used **Main headline only** to hide all but the top level. Then you used **Expand current** to show the detailed entries under "Study Parameters". The outline now looks like Figure 8.5. Now suppose you want to show all second level and above entries and hide any lower levels. You could place the cursor on "Sample of stores" and select **Show current**. All the second level entries throughout the outline would be revealed, while the third level entries under "Sample of stores" would be hidden.

The **Expand all** option reveals the entire outline, no matter what parts were previously hidden.

Promoting and Demoting Levels. You saw earlier that if you change the level of an entry by tabbing or backspacing at the beginning of the line, the subentries are not affected. To change the level of an entire section (an entry and all its subentries), use the **Promote** and **Demote** options from the **Headlines** menu. Figure 8.6 shows what happens if we place the cursor on the line in the first section that contains "Recommendations" and select **Demote**. Notice that its subordinate entries have also been demoted.

✧ Try It Out

1. Open an **Outline** window for TRYOUT.OUT, if necessary.
2. Reduce the display to main headlines only.
3. Expand one section.
4. Show only the top two levels. Print the result.
5. Expand the entire outline.
6. Demote the last section (one with subentries). Promote it again.

Clipboard

The Clipboard facility lets you copy blocks of text from one Desktop window to another. For example, you could copy a block from an Outline window to a Notepad window. When Desktop is memory resident, you can use the clipboard with non-Desktop applications as well. The clipboard is basically a memory area that can hold 4K or about 80 lines of text (not graphics). You can type data directly into the clipboard for pasting into other windows or applications, or you can copy data to and from it. You can also view, edit, and print the clipboard contents. There is no file associated with the clipboard; you cannot save it. When you terminate Desktop, the text in the clipboard is forgotten.

Using the Clipboard with Desktop Applications

The clipboard functions appear on every Desktop **Edit** menu; you saw them in the Notepads **Edit** menu in Figure 7.11. These commands let you mark a block and cut or copy it to the clipboard, as well as paste clipboard contents into the active window. The clipboard **Edit** menu lets you mark and erase blocks, as well as perform standard edit functions.

To place text from another Desktop application onto the clipboard, the first thing you must do is mark it as a block. First, place the cursor at either end of the block. Then you can select **Mark block** from the **Edit** menu, but it's easier to just hold down the Shift key and move the cursor to the other end of the block using the arrow keys. As the cursor moves, the block highlights, so you can see what it contains at all times. If you have a mouse, the process is even easier. Simply drag the mouse pointer over the block. If you change your mind,

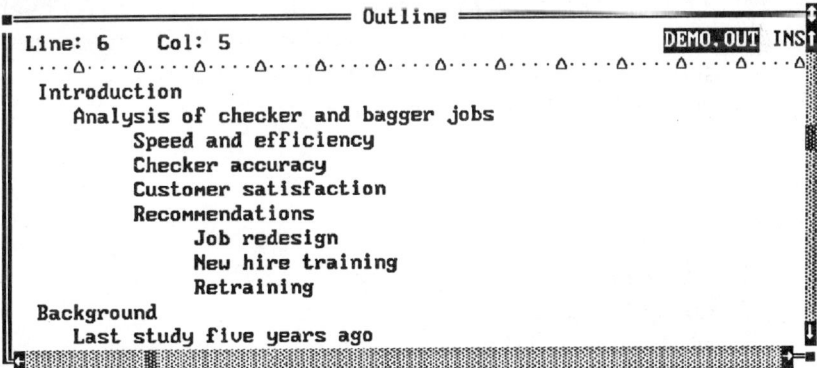

Figure 8.6   Demoted Section

you can unmark the block by selecting **Unmark block** or by pressing Esc or clicking anywhere.

Once the block is marked as desired, you pull down the **Edit** menu and select **Cut to clipboard** or **Copy to clipboard**. If you select **Cut to clipboard**, the block is removed from the current file and placed on the clipboard. You would do this if you want to move the block from its current location. Shift-Del has the same effect as **Cut to clipboard**. If you select **Copy to clipboard**, the text is copied to the clipboard but not removed from its current location. (There is no shortcut.)

The clipboard can hold only one block at a time. Whenever you use cut or copy to place something on the clipboard, the new contents always replace the previous contents.

To copy a block from the clipboard to your file, position the cursor, pull down the **Edit** menu, and select **Paste from clipboard**. You can use Shift-Ins as a shortcut. The block is copied to the cursor position, but it is not removed from the clipboard. Thus, you can copy it as many times and in as many places as needed.

Suppose you want to move a paragraph from the beginning of a document to the end. Block it, cut it to the clipboard (Shift-Del), move the cursor to the end of the file, then paste it from the clipboard (Shift-Ins). Suppose you want to copy a paragraph from one file to another. Block it in the source file, copy it to the clipboard, make the target file window active, position the cursor, and paste it from the clipboard (Shift-Ins).

Suppose you need to type the same line five times in a row. Type it once, block it, copy it to the clipboard, move the cursor down a line, and press Shift-Ins. Continue to move the cursor down and paste until all five lines have been created. (If you include a carriage return at the end of the line in the block, then you don't need to move the cursor down. Just press Shift-Ins four times.)

The text remains in the clipboard, and can be used over and over again, until you cut or copy another block to the clipboard or terminate Desktop. If Desktop is resident, the clipboard remains intact until you kill Desktop, reboot, or shut down the system.

✧ *Try It Out*

1. Open an Outline window for TRYOUT.OUT, if necessary.
2. Using the clipboard, copy the first section to the end of the outline.
3. Move the second section to the end of the outline.
4. Copy the third section to the end of the PRACTICE.TXT file that you created under Notepads.

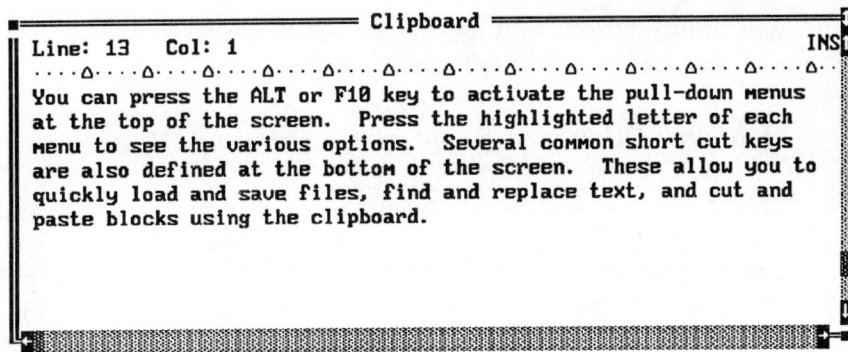

Figure 8.7   Clipboard Window

Viewing the Clipboard

You can view the contents of the clipboard in a Desktop window. You might simply want to peek at the current contents to find out what you're about to paste, or you might want to keep the Clipboard window open so you always know what it contains. To view the clipboard, select the **Clipboard** option on the **Desktop** menu. A window such as the one in Figure 8.7 appears. You can resize, move, scroll, and change the colors of this window just like a Notepad or Outline window.

Editing the Clipboard Text

You can edit the text in the Clipboard window as you can with other Desktop applications. Insert and delete text in the normal manner. The **Edit** menu, shown in Figure 8.8, gives you access to some other editing functions, including a block erase function that you have not seen before. To delete a block of text from the clipboard, block it and select **Erase block**; this has no effect on

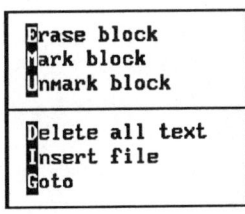

Figure 8.8   Clipboard Edit Menu

text in any other windows. The options in the bottom section of the menu function just like their Notepads counterparts.

Using the Clipboard with Non-Desktop Applications

When Desktop is resident, the clipboard is available to all your applications, even the non-Desktop ones. To paste the current contents of the clipboard into a non-Desktop application, first position the cursor in the application where you want the pasted text to go. Then hotkey to Desktop and close any windows other than Clipboard. If any other windows are open, the clipboard will be pasted into one of them instead of the application, so you must close all Desktop windows in order to reach the application. Then open the Clipboard window, if necessary, and pull down the **Copy/Paste** menu. Select **Paste from Clipboard** and the contents of the clipboard are pasted into the application at the cursor location. Desktop then automatically hotkeys out.

To copy a block to the clipboard from a non-Desktop application, make sure you can see the block you want to copy on the screen (remember the 80 line limit), then go to the Clipboard window. Select **Copy to Clipboard**, which causes the application screen to reappear. However, you have not actually returned to the application; you are still in Clipboard, as you can see by the appearance of the Clipboard menu bar at the top of the screen. Figure 8.9 shows an example using a WordStar screen. Notice that the top line provides the Desktop Clipboard menu bar. The application's normal functions are not available. All you can do is mark a block using special methods. Even if the application has its own methods for marking a block, they won't work now.

To mark the block, you must build a rectangle surrounding it. In the example in Figure 8.9, the sentence starting with "It's not a scrolling list" and ending with "cable channel" is the desired text, but we had to block extra text in order to enclose the desired block in a rectangle. To block the text with the keyboard, position the cursor in the one corner of the rectangle and press Enter. Then move the cursor to the diagonal corner and press Enter again. When you press Enter the second time, the text is copied to the clipboard. With the mouse, position the pointer at one corner and drag it to the diagonal corner. When you release the mouse button, the text is copied to the clipboard. In either case, you'll see the Clipboard window on the screen. You can edit it to eliminate any unwanted text you were forced to include in the rectangle.

You might find differences in the text as it appears in the clipboard and in a non-Desktop application. Formatting codes might be lost; the clipboard might add carriage returns. Other problems might appear, depending on the application. Usually, a little editing is all it takes to get the effect you want. Some applications do not receive text from Clipboard well. For example, if

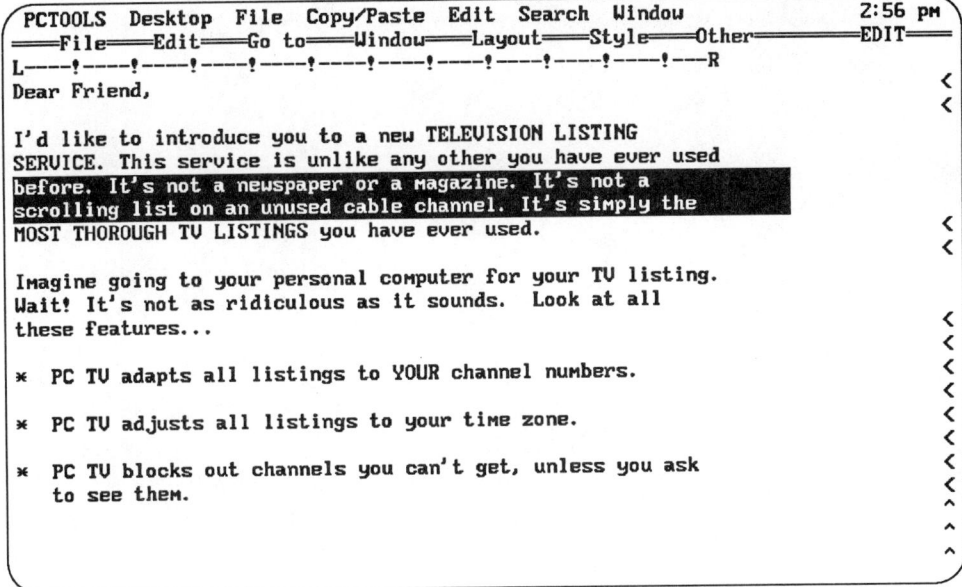

Figure 8.9   Blocked Text in Non-Desktop Application

you try to paste a block of text into a WordStar file, it will probably trigger several WordStar functions and copy only a few words of text.

◆ Try It Out

1. View the current contents of the clipboard.
2. Try editing the clipboard. Add some text to the end. Delete a block.
3. If you have a non-Desktop word processor, try transferring some text between it and a Notepads file. Don't forget that Desktop must be resident for this to work. (If you don't have another word processor, try using the editor under PC Shell.)

Desktop will pop up alarms on whatever Desktop window you are working with, such as Notepads, Outlines, or Clipboard, to remind you of important appointments. You'll learn how to control this feature in the next chapter, which covers Appointment Scheduler.

Chapter 9 | Appointment Scheduler

Appointment Scheduler can help you make and keep appointments, maintain a list of things to do, and analyze how you use your time. In this chapter, you will learn to:

- Open an appointment file
- Manipulate the Appointment Schedule window
- Create, edit, and delete to-do entries
- Create, edit, and delete appointments
- Attach notes to to-do and appointment entries
- View and edit attached notes
- Set up automatic activities
- Search for appointments and free time
- Examine your time usage
- Manipulate schedule files
- Print your schedule

Introduction to Appointment Scheduler

Appointment Scheduler functions like a daily appointment book combined with an alarm clock and a memo pad. The basic window, shown in Figure 9.1, displays the three main functions in subwindows. At the upper left is a calendar for the current month, which you can scroll to any month in any year; as you do, the other two subwindows change. Below the calendar is a to-do list, which you can edit throughout the day to keep current. The subwindow on the right is a list of appointments and memos for whatever day is highlighted on the calendar.

Any item on the list of appointments can have an alarm attached to it. If Desktop is resident, the alarm will sound on your computer at the appointed time, and a message box will appear on your screen, no matter what application you are working in. If several people have appointment schedules, only the last one used will take effect. You can also attach a Notepad file to the appointment so that you can have a longer memo than appears on the basic screen. And, as you will learn in Chapter 12, you can attach a macro to the appointment; the macro could be used to place an automatic telephone call through Autodialer, for example.

Each person who uses the computer can have a separate Appointment Scheduler file, just as each would have a separate appointment book.

Starting Appointment Scheduler

To start Appointment Scheduler, select it from the **Desktop** menu. You will see an **Appointment Scheduler** dialog box, virtually identical to the **Notepads** and **Outlines** dialog box, in which you select or name the appointment file you want to open. The default extension is TM, and the default filename is

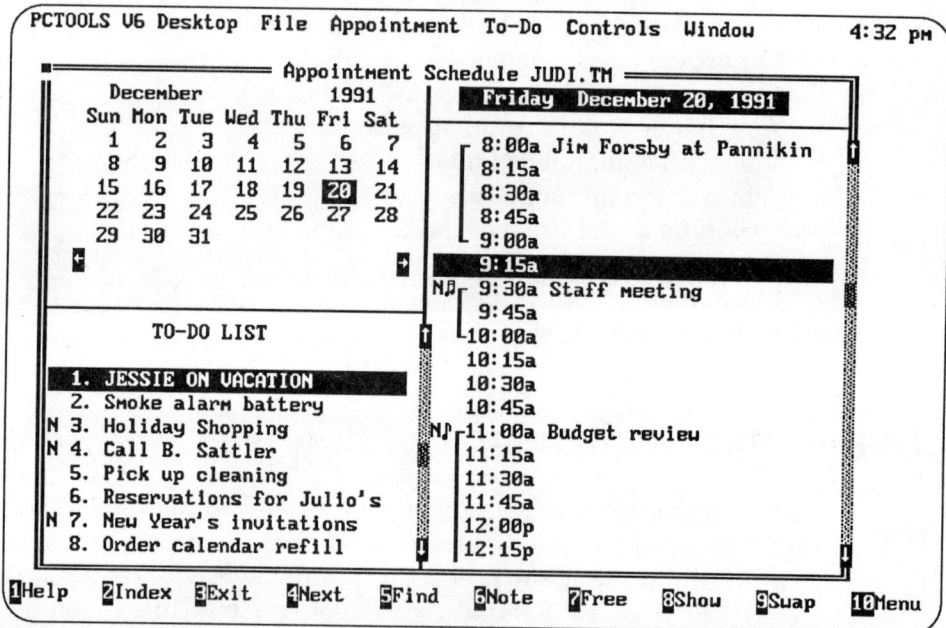

Figure 9.1 Appointment Schedule Window

WORK.TM. If you are the only person using your computer, then you might as well use the default name. If more than one person will use Appointment Scheduler, then name your file something like JUDI.TM or RUTH.TM.

Once you have identified the appointment file, you will see an Appointment Schedule window much like the one in Figure 9.1. The name of the file is shown with the window title to remind you whose file is showing.

You can also open Appointment Scheduler by making Desktop resident with the /RA option. When you use this option, if any appointment file exists, Desktop will be started immediately with the Appointment Schedule window open for the appointment file. If more than one appointment file exists, Desktop chooses the most recently opened one to open again.

If you use Appointment Scheduler as your main daily appointment calendar, you might want to make sure your AUTOEXEC.BAT file contains the command DESKTOP /RA as the last command in the file. (Remove any other DESKTOP command from the file.) Then, each time you boot, your appointment schedule and to-do list will appear on the screen.

Manipulating the Window

The Appointment Schedule window contains three sections that act like subwindows: the calendar, the to-do list, and the appointment schedule. Only one can be active at a time. The active section is indicated by the highlighted title; in Figure 9.1, the schedule subwindow is active.

You select an item in a section much as you do in other windows. If you have a mouse, click on the desired item. If you use the keyboard, tab to the desired section, move the highlight with the cursor movement keys, and press Enter.

Table 9.1 shows the effect of cursor movement keys in the various sections. Most of them are exactly what you would expect. Notice, however, that the left and right arrow keys always affect the calendar no matter which subwindow is active. As the calendar day changes, the appointment and to-do sections change accordingly.

If you use a mouse instead of the cursor movement keys, you can click on the scroll bars to scroll the various sections. In the calendar, click on the left and right arrows in the bottom row to change the month. To change the year, you'll need either to change 12 individual months or to use the Ctrl-PageUp and Ctrl-PageDown keys.

The window itself can be moved but not resized; notice there is no zoom icon. However, you can eliminate the calendar and to-do lists and use only the appointment list, reducing the size of the window. To do this, pull down the **Controls** menu and select **Wide display** to turn it off. To restore the window to its default display, turn **Wide display** on again.

System Date/Time vs. Current Date/Time

As you move about in the appointment calendar and schedule, the date and time slot you are working with change. This does not affect the system date and time that are determined by your computer's internal clock/calendar. Some Appointment Scheduler functions are based on the system date and time. For example, if you ask Appointment Scheduler to find your next appointment, it starts at the system date/time and searches forward until it finds an appointment. Some functions are based on the date/time currently selected, regardless of the system date/time. For example, if you display your time usage, Appointment Scheduler shows a graph for five days starting at the currently selected date, not the system date. In this chapter, the "current date and time" means the date and time currently selected on the calendar and appointment schedule; "system date and time" means today's date and time as the system understands them.

The To-Do List

The to-do list can hold up to 80 entries. They carry over from day to day until you delete them or they expire. They can be repeated yearly, so that you can remind yourself to send a birthday card or change the battery in the smoke alarm. They can be prioritized so that new items can be positioned above

Table 9.1   Cursor Movement Keys in Appointment Scheduler

Key	Calendar	To-Do	Appointment
Left arrow	back one day	(see calendar)	(see calendar)
Right arrow	forward one day	(see calendar)	(see calendar)
Up arrow	back one week	up one row	up one row
Down arrow	forward one week	down one row	down one row
PageUp	back one month	up one page	up one page
PageDown	forward one month	down one page	down one page
Ctrl-PageUp	back one year	first item	first time slot
Ctrl-PageDown	forward one year	last item	last time slot
Home	today's date	first item	first time slot
End	—	last item	last time slot

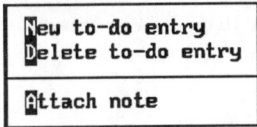

Figure 9.2   To-Do Menu

existing items. And you can attach a notepad file to an entry to provide room for more text.

The **To-Do** menu, as shown in Figure 9.2, offers access to the basic to-do functions of adding a new entry, deleting an entry, and attaching a note to an entry. But you never need to use the menu. In the following sections, you'll see how to accomplish each function without using the menu.

Adding a New To-Do Entry

To add a new entry to the to-do list, pull down the **To-Do** menu and select **New to-do entry**. A **New to-do entry** dialog box, as shown in Figure 9.3, appears. Alternatively, you can position the cursor on a blank line in the list and type the new entry (up to 24 characters). When you press Enter, the same dialog box appears with the entry you typed in the **Note** field.

Start date defaults to the current date and **End date** defaults to **none.** These fields control when the item will appear on your to-do list. Suppose you want the entry "Holiday shopping" to appear from November 25 to December 24. Enter 11-25-91 as the start date and 12-24-91 as the end date. If you want the item to appear for one day only, enter the same start and end date. If you want to item to continue to appear until you delete it, leave **none** as the end date.

You must enter a year with each date, and the date itself must be valid, but

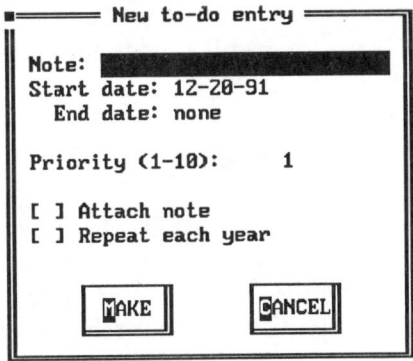

Figure 9.3   New To-Do Entry Dialog Box

you can ignore leading zeros. For example, 2-31-90 is not considered valid; there is no February 31. When you select MAKE, if the dialog box doesn't clear and the highlight returns to one of the date fields, that date is not valid for some reason.

The **Priority** field lets you assign a value from 1 (high priority) to 10 (low priority). Items in the to-do list are displayed in order of priority. Items with identical priorities are listed in the order that they were created.

Attaching Notes to To-Do Entries

If you want to record more than 24 characters for an entry, attach a note to it. You can then choose to view the note whenever you wish. Select **Attach note** in the dialog box. An X will appear in the check box. When you select MAKE, a Notepad window appears with the to-do note, start date, end date, and priority on the top line. You can add any text you want. For example, you might want to include your holiday shopping list, an address for the birthday card, or the type of battery to buy for the smoke alarm.

When you close the Notepad window, the note is saved in a file named *filename.nnn*, where *filename* is the name of the current appointment file (such as WORK, JUDI, or RUTH), and *nnn* is a serial number. If you see such filenames in your directory, don't erase them; they are notes attached to to-do and appointment entries.

To-do entries with attached notes have an "N" in the left margin on the to-do list. To see the attached note, highlight the item and press F6. Once the appropriate Notepad window appears, you can view and edit the note. Close the box normally to return to the Appointment Scheduler window.

Repeating Entries Yearly

To repeat a to-do entry yearly, select the **Repeat each year** box. An X in the check box means it is on. (You still have to fill in the first year in the **Start date** field and none for the **End date** field.

Editing or Deleting a To-Do Entry

To edit or delete a to-do entry, select it by clicking or highlighting the entry and pressing Enter. The dialog box shown in Figure 9.4 appears. Select DELETE to delete the item. Select EDIT to call up the **New to-do entry** dialog box containing the current information for the entry, which you can edit. Select ALTER NOTE to call up the Notepad window for the attached note, which you can edit. This is another way to view the note attached to a to-do entry,

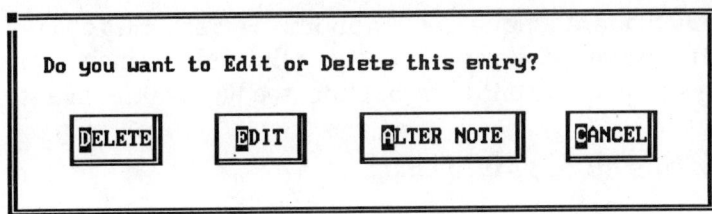

Figure 9.4   Affect Existing Note Dialog Box

but pressing F6 is faster because you don't have to respond to the dialog box shown in Figure 9.4.

✧ Try It Out

1. Start an Appointment Scheduler file named PRACTICE.TM.
2. Get to the page for January 1, 1992.
3. Enter a to-do entry to do your income tax. Give it an end date of April 15 and a priority of 3.
4. Scan through the calendar to April 15 to see the repeated entry. Go to April 16; the entry should disappear.
5. Edit the to-do entry to make it yearly. Scan forward a couple years to see the entry.
6. Attach a note to the to-do entry that lists all the documents you must collect: W-2 forms, interest statements, etc.
7. Enter another to-do entry to make New Year's resolutions. Give it a priority of 2. In the resulting list, notice that it precedes the income tax entry because it has a higher priority.
8. Close the Appointment Scheduler. Open it again. Add another to-do entry. Close it again.

Daily Appointment Schedule

The major portion of the Appointment Schedule window is the daily appointment schedule. You can enter appointments here, attach notepads to them, and set off alarms when they come due. You can repeat them daily, weekly, or monthly. You can ask Desktop to search for a particular appointment and to find you some free time. You can even display a graphic analysis of your time usage over a five-week period.

The **Appointment** menu, shown in Figure 9.5, contains most of the functions that are unique to the appointment schedule. Many of these functions can be accomplished without going through the menu, however. The function keys displayed on the bottom line (see Figure 9.1) save steps.

Making an Appointment

To make an appointment, you can select **Make new appointment** on the menu. The dialog box shown in Figure 9.6 appears. Default values may appear in some fields, but you can change them. Alternatively, you can make the appointment section active and type the memo in the appropriate time slot. When you press Enter, the same dialog box appears. The memo, date, and time are filled in for you, but can be changed if you wish. You might want to change the time from 10:00 to 10:10, for example.

In its default state, Appointment Scheduler assumes A.M. for all times unless you specifically add a "p" for P.M. or change to 24-hour time.

Fill out the rest of the dialog box as needed to describe the appointment. The **Note** field contains the memo you entered; it appears on the schedule and in the alarm box if you request an alarm. **Type** can be a single character, to mean whatever you choose. The Find Appointment function, which you will learn shortly, can search for appointments by type, which could be very handy if you have a packed schedule and need to know the next time you have a doctor's appointment or a sales presentation.

The **Duration** fields can be used to indicate the length of the appointment in days, hours, and minutes. The value need not correspond to the time periods; you could use 5 minutes, for example. The duration will be shown by a bracket on the appointment schedule, extending to the next higher time period; this can help to prevent conflicting appointments. Another good reason to always fill out the duration is that the Find Appointment function cannot find appointments that have 0 duration.

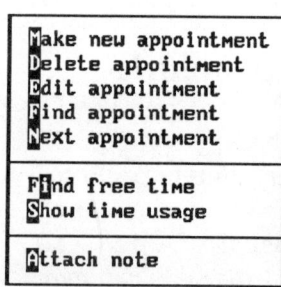

Figure 9.5   Appointment Menu

If it is a recurring appointment, select the desired recurrence under **When**. Appointment Scheduler will automatically fill out the necessary time slots for all appropriate future dates. You might want to fill out the end date. For example, if you are scheduling a class on Tuesdays from November 9, 1991 through December 18, 1991 from 3:00 to 5:00, you would enter 11-9-90 as the **Start date**, 12-18-91 as the **End date**, and 3:00 as the **Time**. Then you would select **Weekly** under **When** and fill out **Hours** under **Duration** as "2". Be sure to use "p" to indicate the correct time.

When you have finished describing the appointment and selecting options, select MAKE. You might see some warning messages at this point if the date precedes today's date or if a scheduling conflict occurs. Scheduling conflicts are also marked by a highlight in the bracket that marks the durations of the two appointments.

If you indicated that you want to attach a note, a Notepad window appears in which you can type the text of the note. As with the to-do list, the name of the file is automatically assigned by Appointment Scheduler.

A bracket is added to the appointment schedule showing how long the appointment lasts. If you request an alarm, a musical note appears on the schedule. A single note indicates a nonrecurring appointment; a double note indicates a recurring appointment, such as weekly or monthly. If you attach a note, an "N" appears on the appointment schedule. In Figure 9.1, you can see that the 9:30 staff meeting is a recurring appointment and has an alarm and note attached; the 11:00 budget review meeting is not recurring and has an alarm and note attached.

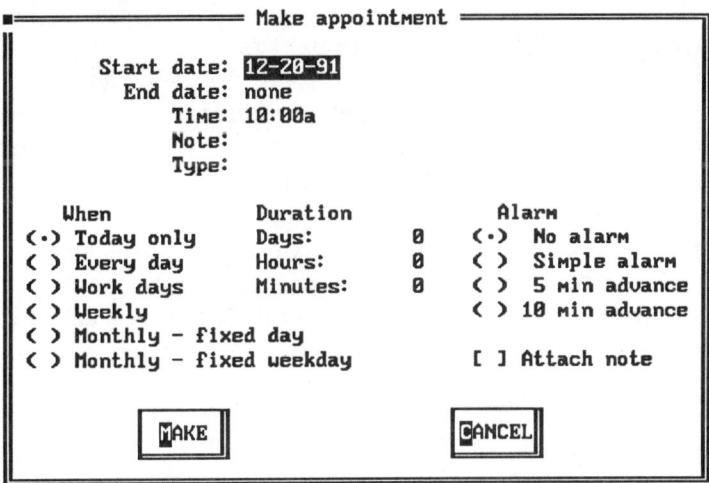

Figure 9.6   Make Appointment Dialog Box

Figure 9.7   Alarm Message Box

Using the Alarm

Figure 9.7 shows how the screen looks when an alarm pops up. The message comes from the **Note** field in the **Make appointment** dialog box; any attached note is not displayed. Select OK to turn the message off. Select SNOOZE to pop up the message again in five minutes.

If Desktop is not resident, the alarm works only when Desktop is active. If Desktop is resident, then the alarm will pop up no matter what program you are working with. If more than one appointment file exists, only the alarms in the most recently opened file are executed. The file does not need to be currently open.

Viewing an Attached Note

The letter "N" in the margin shows which entries have attached notes. To view the attached note, highlight the entry and select **6Note**. The appropriate Notepad window appears; you can both view and edit the note.

Editing and Deleting Appointments

To edit or delete an appointment, highlight it in the appointment schedule and press Enter or click on it or select the appropriate menu option. A dialog box just like the one you saw in Figure 9.4 appears. If you select DELETE, the appointment is deleted. If it is a recurring appointment, a dialog box asks if you want to delete all occurrences or only the present one. If you select EDIT, the **Make appointment** dialog box appears with the current description of the appointment filled in for you to edit. If you select ALTER NOTE, the appropriate Notepad window appears with the note text for you to edit.

Setting Automatic Actions

You can use the Appointment Scheduler to set up operations to run at at a preset time. For example, you may want to back up your hard disk in the evening or do a long sort operation on your database while the staff is out to lunch. You might want to load a file into Notepads at a specific time, just before a meeting or expected call. You might want to start a macro at a particular time. The format for establishing automatic actions is the same for all three.

An appointment for an automatic action includes an alarm setting as well as a vertical bar (|) in the note text. A filename with extension BAT, COM, or EXE following the vertical bar is executed. Any other file is loaded into a Notepad. If no text precedes the vertical bar, the program is run or the file loaded without prompting you. Any text preceding the vertical bar is displayed in the Alarm message box; at that point you select OK to run the program or load the file. If you select SNOOZE you can put it off, just as with a standard alarm.

To make sure that Desktop can find the file, you must include the complete path unless it is in the standard search path or in the current directory.

Running a Program

When you run a program automatically, you include the complete filename as well as any parameters it needs. When the program is started from the filename, the parameters you supply are passed to it. If your program, and the prompt and path used, takes more than 24 characters, you can create a batch file to run it, then name the BAT file in your appointment note. For example, suppose you want to perform an extensive sort that requires the command SORTB F/2A/5D I/MEMBERS.OLD O/MAILOUT.10. You can create a file named SORTBB.BAT under Notepads, then make the appointment with the text "Do sort | sortbb.bat" to run the command. Be sure to set an alarm and leave Desktop resident or the program won't run.

Loading a Notepad

Any filename that doesn't have extension COM, EXE, or BAT can be automatically loaded into a Notepad if you define it as an appointment with an alarm and the vertical bar. You'll be prompted first if the file isn't in Notepad or ASCII format. Once the file is loaded, you can process it normally.

✧ Try It Out

1. Create an appointment for right now to "Phone home". Assign type P to the appointment.
2. Create an appointment for the next time slot (15 minutes from now) to

"Phone ET". Assign type P to it. Request an alarm to ring ten minutes in advance. When the alarm pops up, which it should do during this exercise, put it on snooze. Turn it off the second time.
3. Set up SAMPLE.TXT to be automatically loaded into a Notepad file in the next timeslot. Use a brief prompt before the vertical bar. Be sure to set the alarm.
4. Create a recurring appointment for 10:00 every morning, starting tomorrow morning, to "Take a break". Request a simple alarm. Give it type B.
5. Attach a note to the first appointment you set. Enter the appropriate phone number in the notepad.
6. Add two appointments for tomorrow morning. Give the first one type R.
7. Delete the "Phone ET" appointment after you have handled its alarms.
8. Use Notepads to create TESTING.BAT. Include the two lines VER and VOL in it. Then have TESTING.BAT executed in the next time slot.

Finding Appointments

Sometimes you need to search for an appointment. The **Next Appointment** menu option returns from anywhere in the appointment schedule to show you what your next appointment is based on the system time. The **Find Appointment** option searches through all your scheduled appointments to find a specific one.

You can find the next appointment by selecting **Next Appointment** or by selecting **4Next**. Appointment Scheduler uses the system date and time to determine when your next appointment is. Thus, even if you were currently displaying a date sometime in the future, Appointment Scheduler reverts to the actual date and time and finds your next appointment.

You can locate a specific appointment by selecting the **Find Appointment** option on the **Appointment** menu or by selecting **5Find**. The dialog box shown in Figure 9.8 appears. If you want to look for an appointment containing a specific string of characters as part of the **Note** field, fill out the **Text** field.

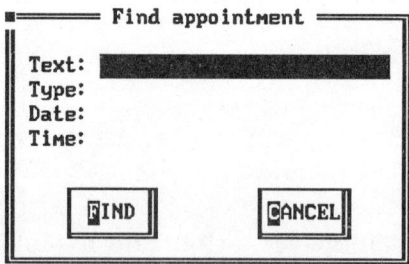

Figure 9.8   Find Appointment Dialog Box

Desktop will not search associated Notepad files, just the **Note** field that appears in the appointment schedule. As you can see in the figure, you can also search for a specific type of appointment according to the types you assign when you create the appointment, a particular date, and a particular time.

If you enter a specific date, Appointment Scheduler searches only that date. To search for your first appointment on *or after* a particular date, don't use the **Date** field in the dialog box. Instead, set the calendar to the first date you want to search, then use the Find Appointment function to search forward.

If you enter a specific time, Appointment Scheduler searches only that time slot for a matching appointment. To locate your next appointment scheduled at 3:00, no matter what the day, fill out **Time** with "3:00p" and leave **Date** blank. Appointment Scheduler will find appointments in the designated time slot only if you have indicated some time duration in scheduling them. If you left all the **Duration** fields (**Days**, **Hours**, and **Minutes**) at 0, then those appointments aren't found by a designated timeslot search.

You can combine two or more search fields. For example, suppose you want to search for a quarterly review meeting (type Q) with John Wilcox on 12-7-91. You would fill out "John Wilcox" in the **Text** field (you could probably get away with just "Wilcox"); "Q" in the **Type** field; and "12-7-91" in the **Date** field. The next meeting that matches *all three* characteristics would be selected.

When you select FIND, Desktop searches forward from the current appointment to find the first appointment that matches the search fields and highlights it. The dialog box remains onscreen so that you can search for the next appointment; you can also change the search fields, if necessary. If no appointment matches the search fields, an alarm sounds, the dialog box disappears, and the highlight remains on the current appointment.

If you provide no search fields, the next appointment (after the current one) is found. So, if you want to find the next scheduled appointment after the system date and time, use the Find Next function; to highlight the next scheduled appointment after the currently displayed one, use the Find Appointment function with no search fields.

Finding Free Time

If your appointment schedule is very full and you need to find some free time in a hurry, perhaps while a client is waiting, you can use the menu or select **7Free** to bring up the **Find free time** dialog box, as shown in Figure 9.9. The fields in this box let you describe the characteristics of the appointment you would like to schedule. The default settings are shown in the figure.

Suppose a client wants a two-hour appointment on any weekday morning before noon. Fill out **Stop time** as "12:00p" and change the **Duration Hours**

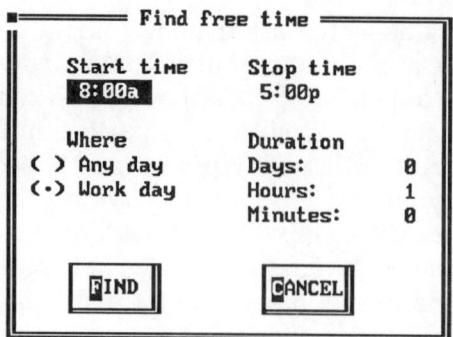

Figure 9.9   Find Free Time Dialog Box

field to "2". When you select FIND, Desktop searches forward from the system date and time until it finds an unscheduled appointment slot that meets your needs. It highlights the qualifying time and removes the dialog box.

The Find Free Time function ignores the currently selected date and time and uses the system date and time to begin the search. Thus it will never find a time slot before today's date and time (as long as your system date and time are correct). However, it also means you can't repeat the search to find another eligible time slot. Desktop will always find the same time slot until the system date/time change or you schedule an appointment in the qualifying time slot. Suppose Desktop finds a qualifying time slot next Tuesday at 8:00 A.M., but the client says "Oh, I can't do it on Tuesday. Any other day will be fine." Either search forward manually to find another time slot, or make a fake appointment in the Tuesday, 8:00 A.M. time slot, then use **Find free time** again. (Don't forget to delete the fake appointment.)

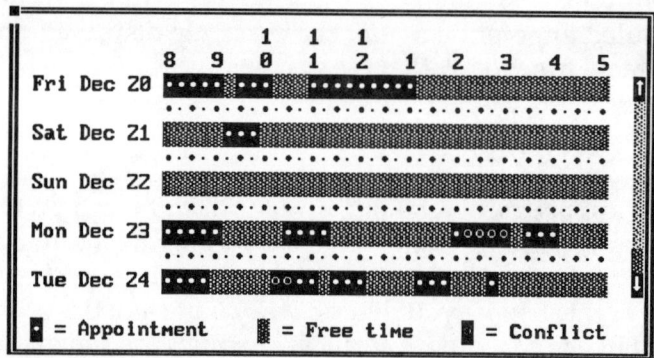

Figure 9.10   Time Usage Dialog Box

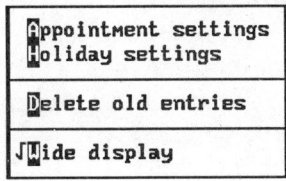

Figure 9.11   Controls Menu

Examining Your Time Usage

For a quick scan at what your schedule looks like over a five-week period, select **8Show**. A dialog box like the one in Figure 9.10 appears. You can't see the details, but you can get a general feel for how full or empty your schedule is and where the conflicts are. You can scroll to see other five-week periods.

Personalizing Appointment Scheduler

The options in the **Controls** menu, shown in Figure 9.11, can be used to personalize the Appointment Scheduler display.

As you have seen, the daily schedule by default starts at 8:00 in the morning and stops at 5:00. The time slots are 15 minutes apart. You can adjust the default settings with the **Appointment settings** option, which results in the dialog box shown in Figure 9.12. You can change the **Start time**, the **Stop time**, the time **Increment**, the **Date format**, and the **Time format**. You can also indicate which days should be included when you search for an appointment or free time on work days only. **Start time**, **Stop time**, and **Increment** affect

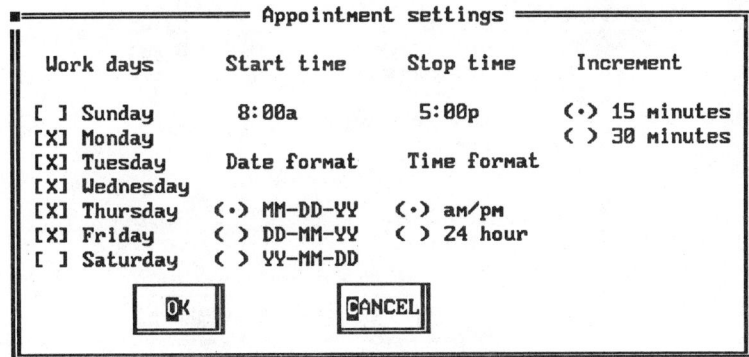

Figure 9.12   Appointment Settings Dialog Box

the displayed schedule, the time usage display, and the search for free time. **Date format** and **Time format** affect not only how times are displayed, but also how you must enter them in other Appointment Scheduler dialog boxes. If you prefer to use 24-hour time, you can make the appropriate selection for **Time format**.

The Appointment Scheduler skips your designated holidays when searching for free time or scheduling recurring appointments. To check and modify holidays, select **Holiday settings**, which results in the dialog box shown in Figure 9.13.

The left column lists most standard holidays. The Appointment Scheduler knows the dates for these holidays, no matter what the year. By default, they are all selected; deselect the ones you don't want to block out. The column on the right can be used to block out up to 10 additional holidays. They will recur on the same calendar date each year, so you will need to redefine movable ones each year. Even though they recur yearly, you must include the first year affected when you define them.

When you leave old entries in your appointment file, the Appointment Scheduler can act like a diary. You can look back to see when you sent a proposal, when you met with a particular person, or when you had your annual checkup. However, after a while, the appointment file gets very long and the Appointment Scheduler performance begins to slow down. To avoid this, you might want to start a new appointment file every year, every quarter, or every month. Or you might want to delete your old entries. To delete old entries, select **Delete old entries** on the **Controls** menu. You will be asked for a cutoff date. All entries before that date will be deleted.

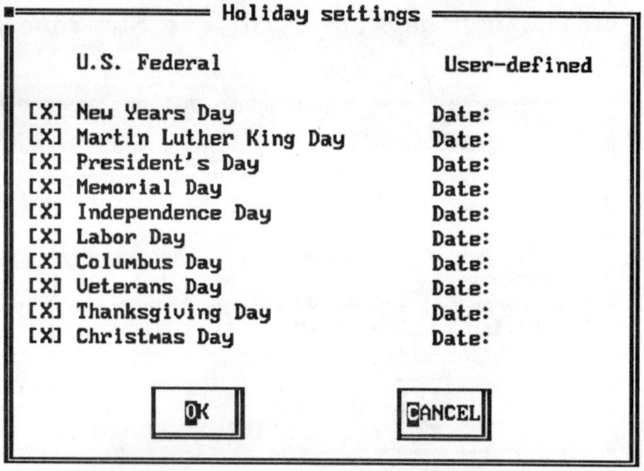

```
================ Holiday settings ================

         U.S. Federal              User-defined

    [X] New Years Day              Date:
    [X] Martin Luther King Day     Date:
    [X] President's Day            Date:
    [X] Memorial Day               Date:
    [X] Independence Day           Date:
    [X] Labor Day                  Date:
    [X] Columbus Day               Date:
    [X] Veterans Day               Date:
    [X] Thanksgiving Day           Date:
    [X] Christmas Day              Date:

               [ OK ]              [ CANCEL ]
```

Figure 9.13   Holiday Settings Dialog Box

Manipulating Schedule Files

The **File** menu lets you load, save, and print schedule files, as well as control Autosave. Suppose you are working with your 1991 schedule file and want to look back to 1990. Select **Load**, then select the name of the file you want to load. The current file will be automatically saved before the next file is loaded.

When you are working on a schedule file, making additions, changes, and deletions, you need to save the file to record the changes. If you have Autosave on, the file will automatically be saved every so often. If you switch to another window or load another file, the current file will automatically be saved. If you close the Appointment Schedule window, the current file will automatically be saved. You can also force the file to be saved without any of the other options by selecting **Save**. Select **Exit without saving** to abandon changes to the file, but you might find that at least some of the changes have been saved automatically.

Printing Your Schedule

You don't have to carry your computer with you to meetings to know what your current schedule is. You can print out your schedule. The **Print** option on the **File** menu pops up the dialog box shown in Figure 9.14. As you can see in the figure, you can print your schedule and to-do list for the day, the week, and the month. You'll print some examples for yourself in the next exercise.

Desktop can't print the musical symbols indicating alarms as they appear on the screen. Instead a single note is printed as a pound sign (#) and a double note, indicating a recurring appointment, is printed as a percent sign (%). You will probably also want to select **Translate graphic characters**. The lists and

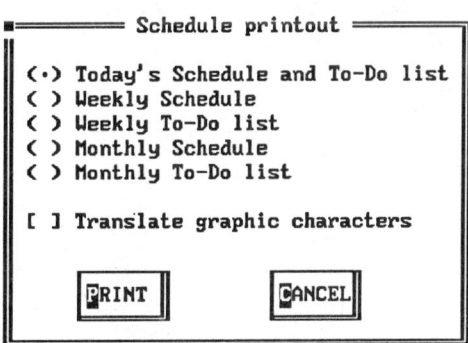

Figure 9.14   Schedule Printout Dialog Box

schedules are organized into sections separated by lines, much like the Appointment Scheduler screen, and the lines don't print well on all systems. This option prevents characters that appear as vertical lines on the screen from being printed as "3"s, and so forth.

✧ *Try It Out*

1. Find an appointment on tomorrow's date, then find your next appointment.
2. Find an appointment of type R.
3. Find two hours of free time between 11:00 A.M. and 2:00 P.M. Schedule it to study Chapter 10.
4. Examine your time usage. Scroll backward and forward if you have appointments on several different days.
5. Set your workday to 10:00 A.M. to 4:00 P.M. and show half-hour increments. Examine the result on your appointment schedule.
6. Set your birthday and Groundhog's Day (February 2nd) as holidays.
7. Print several versions of your schedule, using different print options. Try it with and without translating the graphic characters. Decide whether you need to translate graphic characters for your printer or not.
8. Delete a few entries in your appointment schedule file, then delete the file itself under DOS or PC Shell. Set up a real appointment file if you plan to use Appointment Scheduler.

So far, you have learned how to use Notepads, Outlines, Clipboard, and Appointment Scheduler. The next chapter covers another major Desktop application, Databases.

Chapter 10 | *Databases*

The Databases facility lets you create a database and use it to manage data and print form letters, mailing lists, and other documents. Databases is compatible with dBASE® in many aspects. In this chapter, you will learn to:

- Create a new database
- Use browse mode to see several records at a time
- Add, edit, and delete records in a database
- Format and print database records
- Select and hide database records
- Sort the database
- Transfer records to another database

Database Structure

Figure 10.1 shows the structure of a database. Each row represents one record. The record is divided into fields. All the records in the database must have the same structure—that is, the same fields in the same sequence. When you create

Name	Year	Credits	GPA	Resident	Enrolled
McCrumb, John D.	C	91	3.250	Y	09/05/89
Myerson, Milo X.	A	0	0.000	N	09/03/91
Voigt, Cecile A.	C	92	2.750	Y	09/05/89
Young, Donna E.	B	63	1.792	N	01/03/90

Figure 10.1   Sample Database

a new database, you define its fields; each record will contain all the fields. Then you fill data into the records. You can change the structure later.

Creating a Database

To create a new database, select the **Databases** option on the **Desktop** menu. The **Databases** dialog box, which is virtually identical to the **Notepads** dialog box, appears. Fill in the name of the database you want to create, such as STUDENT, CUSTOMER, or INVENTRY. Databases will supply the required DBF extension.

When you select NEW, the **Field Editor** dialog box, as shown in Figure 10.2, appears. You use this dialog box to define each field in the database; you'll use it again later if you edit the field definitions.

Defining Fields

Each field must have a name of up to ten characters, starting with a letter. You can use letters, digits, the underscore character, and any ASCII graphics characters. All letters are converted to uppercase. Invalid characters either result in a message that the name is invalid or are automatically converted to underscores. Thus, G_P_A is a valid name but G.P.A. is not.

Field Number. The **Field number** field is assigned by Databases and cannot be changed. You can't rearrange the field numbers, but you'll see later how you can rearrange the order in which fields are displayed.

Field Type. The **Field type** field lets you select from among four types of data. It specifies the format of the field and the type of data it can hold.

Character fields can contain any text data and can be up to 70 characters long. Since dBASE fields can hold up to 254 characters, you may lose some data if you transfer it from a dBASE file.

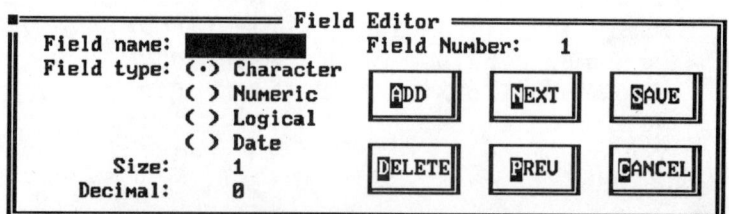

Figure 10.2   Field Editor Dialog Box

Numeric data contains digits, a sign, and a decimal point and can be up to 19 characters long; the default value is 0. The sign and the decimal point each count as a character. Numeric fields can be used in dBASE formulas, but they have no special features in Databases except for decimal point alignment and restricting data entry.

Logical fields are exactly one character long and can contain T, t, Y, or y to represent true and F, f, N, or n to represent false; the default value is F.

Date fields contain exactly eight characters in the format *mm/dd/yy*; the default value is 00/00/00. Databases assumes the twentieth century; the date 01/13/29 refers to 1929.

Field Size. The **Size** field can be filled in if the field type is either character (up to 70) or numeric (up to 19). Both character and numeric fields default to 1 position if you don't change it. For logical fields the size is fixed at 1, and for date fields the size is fixed at 8.

Decimal Places. For numeric fields, you can also fill in the number of decimal places in the **Decimal** field. A value you enter into a numeric field will be aligned at the decimal point you type.

Recording the Definition. Once you have filled out the **Field editor** dialog box to describe field number 1, select ADD to record the description. You will then see the same dialog box for field number 2. Continue filling out **Field editor** dialog boxes until all the fields are described.

When all the fields are described, select SAVE. You can use PREV to go back to earlier fields and NEXT to go forward again before you choose SAVE, which saves the DBF file. If you wish to change the structure later, select **Edit fields** on the **Edit** menu any time the database is loaded.

Effect of SAVE. When you define a new database, Desktop creates three files that it uses to store data and process it. The *filename*.DBF file contains the field definitions and the record data. *Filename*.REC contains information such as the sort order. *Filename*.FOR contains the default display format, which you see in the **Database** edit window.

Edit vs. Browse Mode

After you select SAVE, the **Field editor** dialog box disappears and you can begin entering data. What you see depends on whether Edit mode or Browse mode is the current default. You can switch modes by selecting **Browse** on the **File** menu; when it is checked, Browse is on. The same menu bar and function key commands are available in both modes.

The Edit mode screen contains the structure of a record in the database, as shown in Figure 10.3. This example shows the STUDENT database from Figure 10.1; each field name and any initial values are taken from a default format stored in *filename*.FOR. You can type data for each field, using Tab or Enter to move between fields; Shift-Tab moves up a field.

Browse mode is different; it shows the first several fields for each record, displaying several records at a time, one per line. Figure 10.4 shows an example; several records have already been added to the database. Both edit and browse mode work much the same. An action on an edit mode record affects the displayed record. An action on the browse screen affects the selected record.

Entering Data into the Database

To enter data into a field, position the cursor in the field, type the value, and press Enter. If the value is unacceptable, Databases beeps and displays an error message. When you have completed the fields for a record, select **8New** to record it and start adding data for a new record. Alternatively, you can select the **Add new record** option from the **Edit** menu, shown in Figure 10.5. When you exit databases, all records you have entered are saved, unless you have not finished adding the last one.

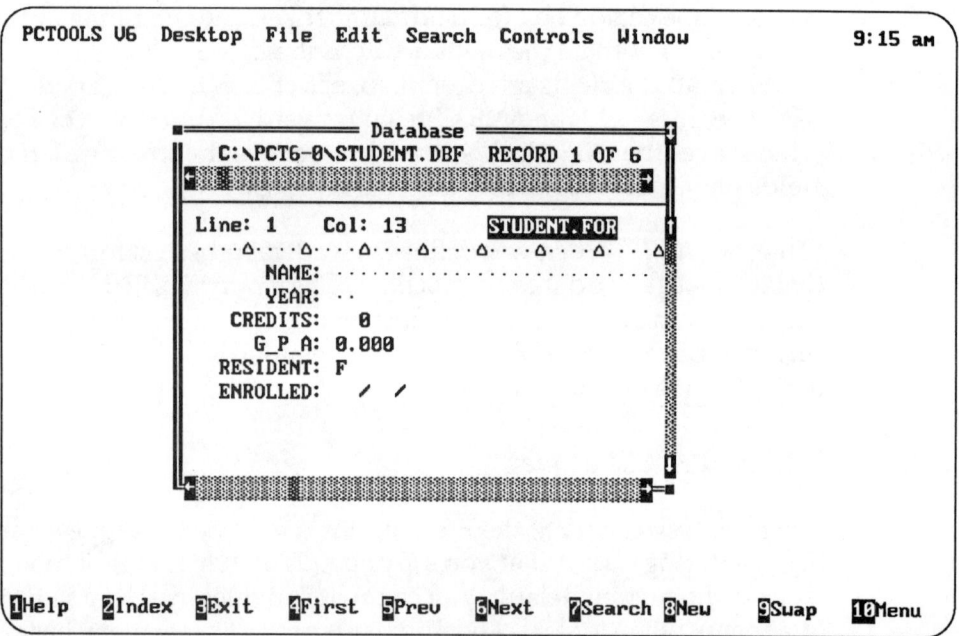

Figure 10.3   Database Window—Edit Mode

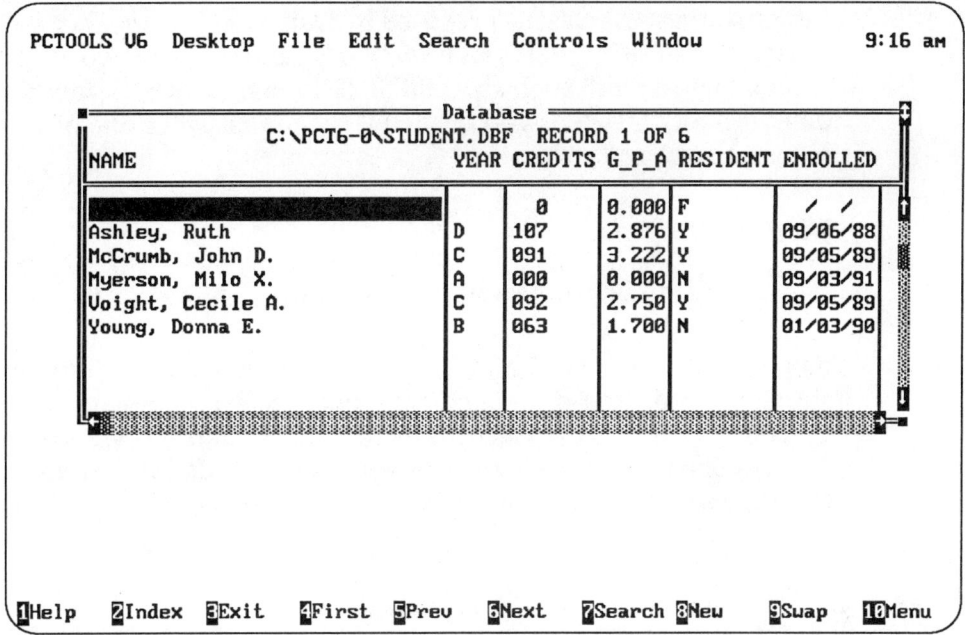

Figure 10.4 Database Window—Browse Mode

No values are unacceptable in a character field. Dots show the maximum size of the field in Edit mode. In Figure 10.3, you can see from the dots that NAME is a 30-character field and YEAR is a one-character field.

In numeric fields such as CREDITS and G_P_A, a default value of 0 is supplied, showing the number of decimal places defined for the field. You don't need to align your numeric data with the default value; just type the desired value in the first positions in the field. Desktop will move it to the correct position after you press Enter.

To type a date, such as ENROLLED in Figure 10.3 or 10.4, you must type all eight characters, including the slashes. Either use the arrow keys to move

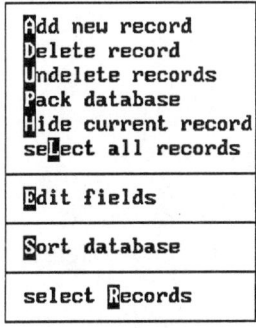

Figure 10.5 Edit Menu

the cursor past the slashes provided by Databases or type them yourself. You must include leading zeros, as in 05/03/90, and use only two digits in the year.

In a logical field, such as RESIDENT in Figure 10.3, Databases supplies a default F for "false". If you change it, you must enter one of the acceptable values: F, f, N, n, T, t, Y, or y.

Viewing Records

The function keys listed on the bottom line (see Figure 10.3 or Figure 10.4) let you save and view records at any time. Once you have finished filling out a database record, select 8New or the **Add new record** option. The record is stored in the database, and another empty record is displayed.

You can view existing records by selecting 4First, 5Prev, and 6Next. Record 1 of 1 is usually blank so you can add new records. (If you delete the blank record, you can restore it by selecting **Add new record**.)

Handling an Existing Database

You can view records in an existing database at any time, using the same function keys as when first entering records. You can make changes to the data in a record any time it is on the screen. Just move the cursor to the field and make your changes. The cursor keys move much as they do in other Desktop applications. Use the scroll bars for faster movement through the database. Table 10.1 lists the effects of various keys on the cursor; they are similar in both Browse and Edit mode.

Adding Records

To add a record to an existing database, position the cursor in the blank record, enter data, then select **Add new record** or 8New. If the blank record doesn't exist, select the command and it will appear.

Deleting Records

To delete a record, display it, then select **Delete record** from the **Edit** menu. This option marks the record for deletion but does not actually erase it from the database. However, you can no longer view it or select it. To undelete a record, you must undelete all records currently marked for deletion by selecting **Undelete records**.

To erase the deleted records from the database, select **Pack database**. You'll

Table 10.1   Cursor Movement in Databases

Tab	Move to next field
Shift-Tab	Move to previous field
Home	Move to beginning of field
End	Move to end of field
Up arrow	Move up one line
Down arrow	Move down one line
Left arrow	Move left one character
Right arrow	Move right one character
Ctrl-Left arrow	Move left one word
Ctrl-Right arrow	Move right one word
Home, Home	Move to beginning of record (Edit mode)
Ctrl-Home	Move to start of file
Ctrl-End	Move to end of file
Home, Home	Move to beginning of window (Browse mode)
End, End	Move to end of window
PageUp	Scroll up one window
PageDown	Scroll down one window
Ctrl-PageUp	Scroll up one line
Ctrl-PageDown	Scroll down one line
Esc	Cancel edit

need to do this every so often in a large, active database because you are limited to 3500 records. Even in smaller databases, you might want to pack the database periodically; otherwise, every time you undelete records to rescue a particular deleted record, you'll undelete all past deleted records, and you'll have to find and delete many records again. Once you have packed a database, of course, you can't undelete any records that were deleted before the packing.

Modifying the Database Structure

You may find that you need to change a field size, add a field, remove one, or even make more drastic changes to a database structure. You can do this by selecting **Edit fields** on the **Edit** menu. You'll see the **Field Editor** dialog box (see Figure 10.2) for the current database. Use NEXT and PREV to locate the field you want to change. You can change any or all aspects of it, just as when you originally defined the field; select ADD when you are satisfied with your changes to each field. Select SAVE to record them all. Most changes to existing fields are reflected immediately in the displayed database. An added field or a change in field name won't be included in the default form. You'll have to modify the form file that was created when the database was first set up to reflect changes in field names.

✧ Try It Out

1. Define and save the STUDENT database (refer to Figures 10.1 and 10.3 for details).
2. Add in the records shown in Figure 10.1.
3. Examine the records thoroughly in both Edit and Browse mode.
4. Change the year field to hold two characters, then add two more records. Delete one of them, then undelete it.
5. Open the DSKERR database and examine it in both modes. Try the cursor movement keys.
6. Open STUDENT again and change data in two fields. Add a new record, then close the database.

Formatting the Database

When you create a new database, Databases creates a default format named *filename*.FOR that it uses to display records in Edit mode. Once the records have been entered, you can format them any number of ways to suit your needs. You can apply several different formats to the same database. You could have one format where the fields are stacked in a column, much like the default format but with your own headings instead of the field names. Such a format is good for entering data into the database. You might have another format that displays selected information for clerks who access the database and who don't need to see everything. You can put your own text in a format, so you can create and print personalized form letters using a special format and information from records in your database. There is no way to modify the default browse mode format.

Creating a Column Format

Figure 10.6 shows an example of a column format. You can see that it is a little more attractive than the default format shown in Figure 10.3. The columns have been neatly stacked. The labels are in mixed case. The order of the items has been changed. And spacing has been used to set off the credits and GPA.

Figure 10.7 shows how you define the format demonstrated in Figure 10.6.

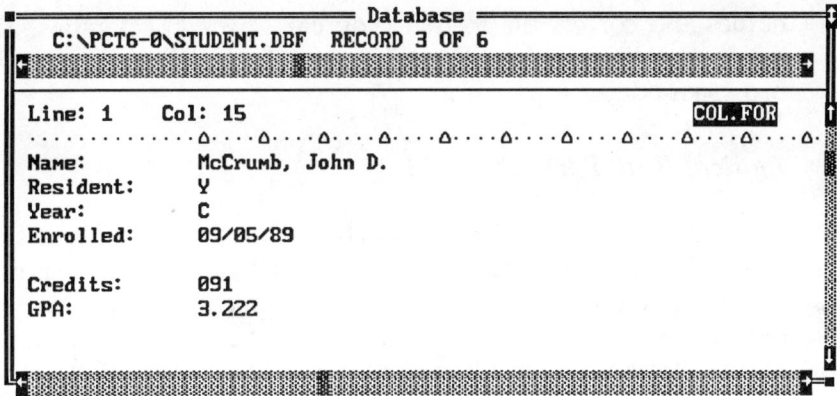

Figure 10.6   Sample Column Format

You use Notepads to create a file named *name*.FOR, where *name* is different from any existing database name. (The default format created automatically by Databases is named *database-name*.FOR.) For example, you might name the format shown in Figure 10.7 COL.FOR.

You can place any text you want in the format file. It shows on the screen and in print just as you type it in the file. In the example, the labels for each line come from the format file. They are not the same as the field names, since upper- and lowercase letters are used; they are aligned differently as well.

Wherever you want a field filled in from the database, type "[*field name*]". The field name must exactly match the name you supplied when you defined the field in the **Field editor** dialog box. You do not have to use all the fields in the record, you can use the fields in any order, and you can use the same field more than once. However, you cannot use more than one record in the format.

When you look at the database using the format, if you can't see data in a field or you can't type in the field, the field name you used in the format doesn't match the field name you defined for the database. Check the database field

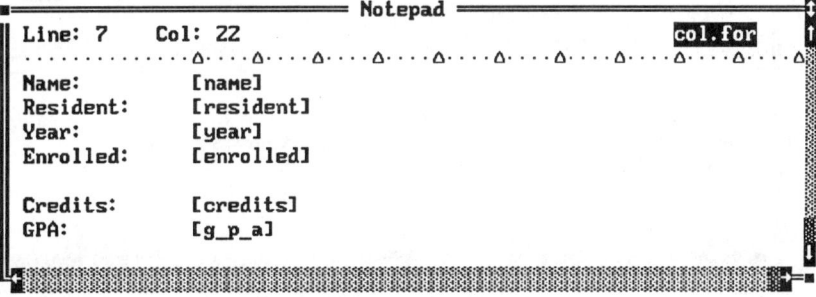

Figure 10.7   Sample Column Format Definition

names and correct the format. You can check the database field names by selecting **Edit fields** on the **Edit** menu or by checking the default Edit or Browse mode screen.

Typical Row Format

Another common format displays the fields across a row, as shown in Figure 10.8. This format is handier for displaying data than for entering it, especially when you don't want to show all the data in the record. Also, you might want to print records this way, printing several per page. For printing, you would define a format without fixed text so that it isn't repeated with every printed record.

Defining a format for data across the screen is more complex, primarily because the field names are not the same length as the data. You can set tabs in Notepads to match your needs, but the definition will probably look out of alignment. You'll have to practice a bit until you come up with a layout you like. The Desktop Manager documentation includes hints on handling row-oriented formats. In most cases, you'll find that Browse mode is adequate.

When designing formats, you can have both the **Database** window and the **Notepad** window for the FOR file open simultaneously. (You can arrange them side by side, but every time you swap windows, Desktop superimposes them again.) Switch to the **Notepad** window and make some changes. When you switch back to the **Database** window, you will immediately see the effect of the changes.

Sample Form Letter

Figure 10.9 shows an example of a short form letter. You can use similar techniques to create advertising mailers, appointment reminders, or whatever

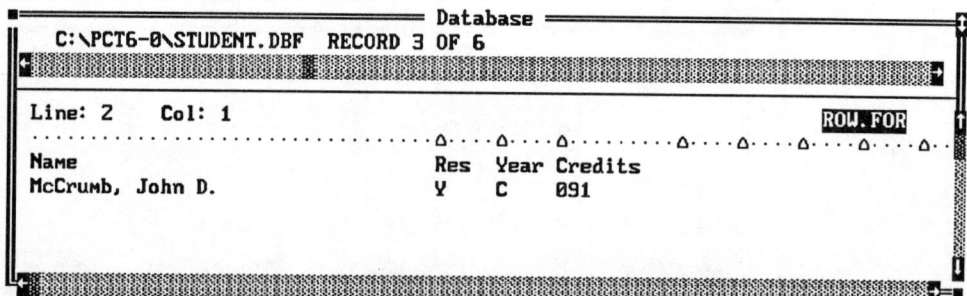

Figure 10.8   Sample Row Format

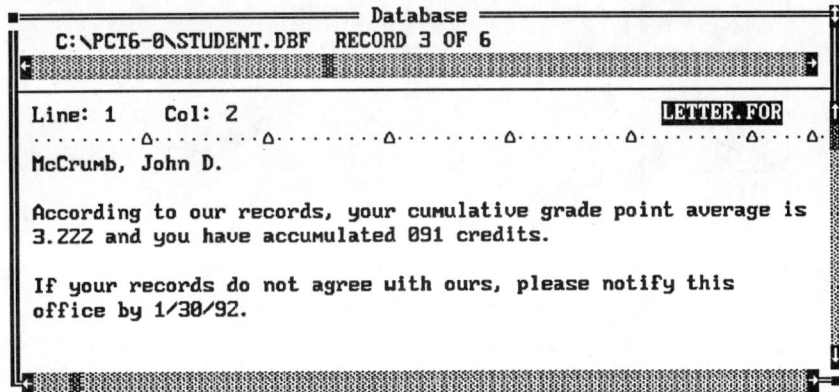

Figure 10.9   Sample Letter Format

you need from your database. Figure 10.10 shows how the form letter is defined by intermixing fixed text with database fields. Spacing can be tricky. For example, if the NAME field, which is defined as 30 characters long, were used within a sentence, the actual paragraph could turn out to be longer than the defined paragraph, perhaps affecting the page layout.

Applying the Format

To apply a particular format to a database, use the **File** menu, shown in Figure 10.11. When you select the **Load Form** option, a dialog box shows you the list of available formats so that you can select the one you want. You can switch to other drives and directories as needed to find the desired format file. The current format name appears on the third line of the **Database** window unless the window is too narrow.

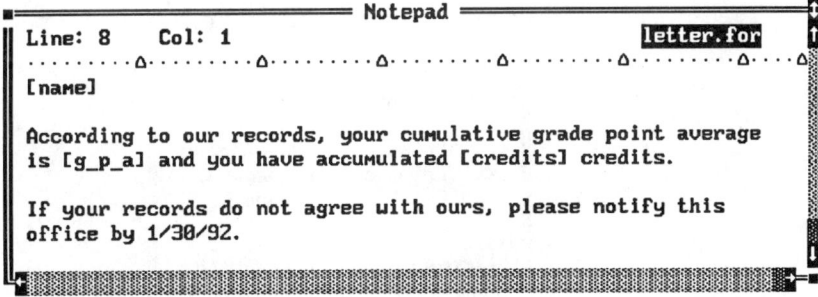

Figure 10.10   Sample Letter Format Definition

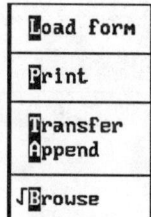

Figure 10.11   File Menu

Printing the Database

You can print the database in the current Edit format. If Browse mode is active, only the fields that appear in the window will be printed, for all selected records. Use the **Page Layout** option on the **Controls** menu to define margins, tabs, and so forth before printing. The resulting dialog box is the same as for Notepads, Outlines, and the other Desktop applications that print. When the page layout and the database format are correct, select **Print** from the **File** menu. In Edit mode, you will see the dialog box shown in Figure 10.12. In Browse mode, the windowed portion of all selected records will print with the field names in the first line.

In Edit mode, **Print selected records** prints all the records in the database, one record per page. (You will learn shortly how to select a subset of records.) **Print current record** prints only the record that is currently showing on the screen. **Print field names** prints a list of all the field names in the database. After you select the PRINT button, you will see the same **Print** dialog box that appears in Notepads, Outlines, and all the other Desktop applications that print. You'll have a chance to select the port or specify a disk file when you print from either mode.

You can print multiple formatted records per page by redefining the page length to two lines, three lines, or whatever. Use at least one line more than the format to cause space between records. The top and bottom margins will also appear with every record, so don't forget to redefine them; you can set them to zero if desired. To avoid spanning records over page breaks, be sure

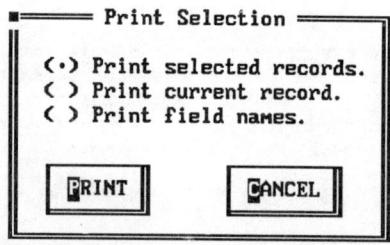

Figure 10.12   Print Selection Dialog Box

the actual page length is an even multiple of the redefined page length. For example, if the real page length is 66 lines, you could print logical pages of two, three, or six, or 11 lines, but four or five lines would cause problems.

Working with a Subset

You will often want to work with some subset of the entire database. For example, you might want to print a letter only to seniors or to list those students with grade point averages below 2.000. Several ways exist to select records for viewing and printing. You can view the entire database one record at a time and hide the ones you don't want to work with. Or you can enter selection criteria and let Databases hide records that don't match the criteria.

Hiding Records

To hide a record, display it and select **Hide current record** from the **Edit** menu. That record disappears, and the next is highlighted or displayed. The record number and total in the first line of the window are revised. You cannot view, edit, or delete the hidden record until it is revealed again. The only way to reveal an individual record is to reveal all hidden records with the **seLect all records** option from the **Edit** menu.

You cannot hide all the records in the database. If you try, you will see the dialog box shown in Figure 10.13. You must select an option to continue.

Selecting Records

To select records for processing instead of individually hiding the ones you don't want to process, choose the **select Records** option on the **Edit** menu. The

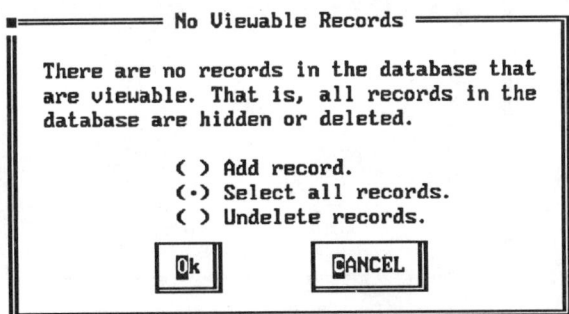

Figure 10.13   No Viewable Records Dialog Box

dialog box shown in Figure 10.14 appears. Type a field name in the left column and the value or values it should contain in the right column. For example, to select all students in year B, you would type "YEAR" in the left column, because that is the defined name of the field, then Tab and type "B" in the right column. When you choose SELECT, all records containing a "B" in the YEAR field will be selected.

Databases selects all fields that begin with the value you enter. If you enter "Name" for the field and "Smith" for the value, Databases would select records not only for Smith, but also for Smithson, Smithy, and Smithers. However, it will not select Highsmith or Grant, Smithley. To select just the Smiths, you could use "Smith," as the field criteria in the STUDENT database. In other databases, a terminal space can be used to limit the records that are selected.

You can use a question mark as a wildcard character in your field criteria. For example, suppose you want to select all students with a whole number in the G_P_A field. You would enter "?.0" as the field criteria. This would select values of 0.000, 1.000, 2.000, and so on.

You can use two dots to specify a range of values. To select all students in years A or B, enter "A..B". You could also enter "..B" since that will select all values up through B. To select B and above, enter "B..". To select all students with a G_P_A of 2.5 or less, you would enter "..2.5". To select all students with at least 60 credits, you would enter "60..".

If you fill out more than one set of selection criteria, a record must match all the criteria to be selected. For example, you could select all students in year B with a G_P_A above 3.500. However, there are some limitations. You can't select all students in year A or C, but not B. And you can't select all students who are in year D or who have a G_P_A of at least 4.0.

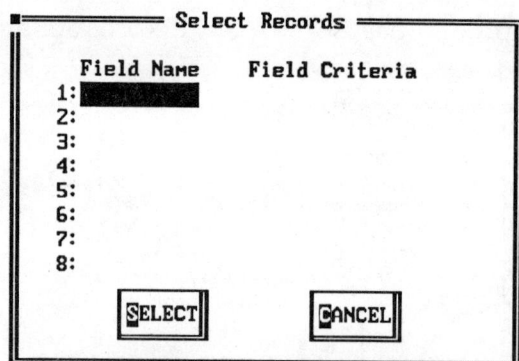

Figure 10.14   Select Records Dialog Box

When you choose SELECT, all the records that match the selection criteria are selected and all those that do not match the selection criteria are hidden. If some records are already hidden, only unhidden records are considered. Therefore, if you want to consider the entire database, you should select **seLect all records** first.

You can view, edit, and print the selected records. To go back to the full database, select **seLect all records** on the **Edit** menu.

✧ Try It Out

1. Format the STUDENT database like this:
   ```
   Name:                              Year:
   Resident:
   Credits:                           GPA:
   ```
2. Examine the results. View several records.
3. Select only students in year C. Print the results using the above format. Select all records again.
4. Select all students with a GPA below 3.0. Design a format and page layout so that you can print just the student name and GPA for all records on one page. Then print the database.
5. Select all records again. Delete the records for John McCrumb and Cecile Voigt. Undelete them.
6. Delete the record for Milo Myerson and pack the database to completely remove the record.

Searching for Records

You don't have to use the function keys to view each record in sequence in order to find a particular record to view, print, edit, hide, or delete. There are several ways to search for the record you want, all accessed from the **Search** menu shown in Figure 10.15.

The **Find text in all fields** option searches all the fields in each record for

```
Find text in all fields
find Text in sort field

Goto record
```

Figure 10.15   Search Menu

text you enter. It stops and displays the first record it finds that contains the text. You can ask it to continue until you locate the record you are searching for. When you select this function you see the dialog box shown in Figure 10.16. It reappears every time a match is found so that you can continue searching for more records that meet the criteria.

You fill in the **Search Data** field at the top of the box with the text string you want to search for. If you enter "Smith" in the box, for example, Databases will search for a record containing "Smith" in any position in any field. Notice that this search function is different from the record selection function, where the specified text must match the beginning of a specified field.

The search function is not case sensitive. If you use "Smith" as a search parameter, Databases will find "SMITH" and "smith" as well. Unlike the **select Records** option, you cannot use wildcard characters with the search function.

If you select **Search all records**, Databases searches viewable records, hidden records, and deleted records, starting at the beginning of the file. If any records are deleted or hidden, the message on the top line of the window changes from RECORD n OF x, where x is the number of viewable records, to RECORD n OF y (ALL), where y is the total number of records in the database, including hidden and deleted records. When a matching record is found, Databases displays it but retains the dialog box, making **Search from current record** the default option. To search for the next record that matches the search criterion, just select SEARCH again. When the record you want is displayed, select CANCEL to get rid of the dialog box and access the found record.

When the found record is hidden or deleted, it is displayed as long as the dialog box is on the screen. Selecting CANCEL will bring up an error message box explaining that the found record is not viewable. After you clear the message, the found record disappears from the window. The only way to access the record is to select or undelete all records. Unfortunately, Databases does not tell you whether the record is hidden or deleted, so you might have to do both to access it.

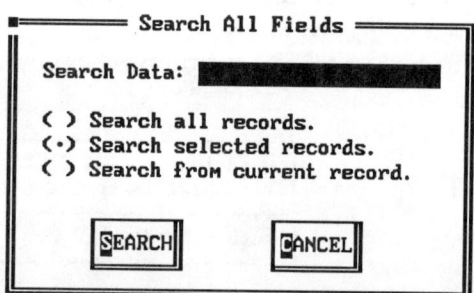

Figure 10.16   Search All Fields Dialog Box

Another way to search for records is the **Find text in sort field** option. If you want to find the students in year A without also selecting records with "A" in the name field, you could first sort by the year field, then use **Find text in sort field** to find the records you want. The **Search Sort Field** dialog box is much like the **Search All Fields** dialog box; only the result is different.

If you know the record number of the record you want, you can use the **Goto record** function to display the record. A dialog box asks you for the number of the record you want to display.

Sorting Records

By default, Databases sorts records based on the first field. As you add new records, they are placed in their correct order. You might need to change the order for certain applications. For example, you would probably print a membership list in alphabetical order but print mailing labels in zip code order.

To sort the database, select the **Sort database** option from the **Edit** menu. You will see the dialog box shown in Figure 10.17. Use this box to select the field on which to sort the records. Select the NEXT and PREV buttons until the desired field name appears in the box. Then select SORT. You will see a message box telling you to wait while the records are sorted.

Records are always sorted in ascending order. There is no way to select more than one sort field. For fields longer than 12 characters, only the first 12 characters are used.

Copying Records to Another Database

Databases lets you copy records from one database into another without having to retype them. The Transfer function lets you copy selected records

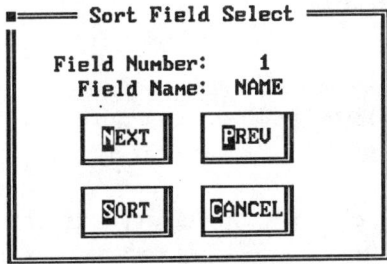

Figure 10.17   Sort Field Select Dialog Box

from the active database into another one. The Append function lets you copy all records from a different database into the active one. Both functions are selected from the **File** menu, and the process is much the same. In neither case is any change made to the source database.

The database records need not have the same structure. The fields are matched by name. If field names match but the definitions don't, the result is unpredictable. If fields don't match, only part of each record may be copied. If the source database record contains fields that aren't in the destination database, those fields aren't copied. If the destination database contains fields that aren't in the source database, you'll be prompted for a default value to be inserted in every record. Records are automatically sorted in the destination database according to the current sort order.

Transferring Records

This process lets you transfer some of the records in a database to another one. To copy selected records, first select them in the active database. Then select **Transfer** and select a destination database in the resulting file selection box. Respond to prompts for default values if necessary, then close the dialog box. When the process is finished, you can activate the destination database to see the result.

Appending Records

When you want to copy all the records in a database into another database, you want to append one file to another. In this case, you first open the destination database, the one that will receive the records. When you choose **Append**, you are prompted to select the source database. After you respond to any prompts for default values, close the dialog box. When the process is finished, you can check the result in the database.

Interface with dBASE

Databases and dBASE files are interchangeable except for some restrictions. You can interchange database files with a colleague who uses dBASE, for example. However, the following restrictions apply:

- Databases is limited to 10,000 records. If you load a larger dBASE file, Desktop cuts it off at 10,000 records. You can perform all Databases functions except adding records and packing the database.

- Databases does not recognize memo fields.
- Databases limits character fields to 70 characters whereas dBASE allows 254. Values longer than 70 characters will be truncated by Databases.
- Numeric fields can be used in formulas in dBASE, but formulas aren't supported in Databases. Date fields can also be used in dBASE formulas.

✧ *Try It Out*

1. Start at the beginning of the STUDENT database. Search for Cecile Voigt's record.
2. Return to the beginning. Search for the next person who enrolled in 91. See if you can figure out a way to avoid finding records containing 91 in the CREDITS field.
3. Sort the database by CREDITS and view the results. Then sort it by YEAR and view the results.
4. Create a new database containing just a 30-character name and the GPA. Add one record to it. Then copy all the records in STUDENT into the new database. Examine the contents of the new database.

If your database record includes a phone number, you can use Autodialer to dial the number for you, as you will learn in the next chapter.

Chapter 11

Telecommunications and Autodialer

Desktop includes features that let you connect with remote computers via modem as well as send and receive fax communications via an internal fax board. If you don't have a modem or a fax board, you should skip this chapter. In this chapter you will learn to:

- Configure Telecommunications for modem and fax board
- Dial a number using your modem
- Connect with an electronic bulletin board
- Send and receive files using a modem
- Send fax communications
- Manage a fax log
- Configure Autodialer
- Call any number displayed on the screen

Telecommunications

The Telecommunications component of PC Tools Desktop Manager lets you use a modem and control an internal fax board. Selecting **Telecommunications** on the **Desktop** menu results in the pop-up menu shown in Figure 11.1.

Modem Telecommunications assumes that you have a fully connected Hayes-compatible modem, but you can change defaults to handle other modem types. The other menu options let you send a fax or check the fax log.

Modems come in many different styles and forms. Yours may be internal or external; it may be very fast or very slow. Desktop assumes your modem is Hayes-compatible and can handle a transmission rate of 1200 or 2400 baud. If you have a different type of modem, you can change the Desktop defaults; check your modem documentation to see what you have.

Your modem may have been configured during installation. PC Setup allows you to do much of the modem configuration, including entering the speed and dialing information for selected services. You can also add the information through the Telecommunications component.

Modem Telecommunications

In order for two computers to communicate, they must match in several ways. The software and the modem together help to balance their different features. Most of the decision-making work is done by the software, while the modem handles data transmission. Through Desktop's Modem Telecommunications component, you specify the settings that match the requirements of the system you will be connected to.

You have to indicate whether the connection will use full or half duplex. The *duplex* refers to how the telephone lines are shared, and both must be the same. Most transmissions at a speed of 1200 baud or less use half duplex; faster ones generally use full duplex.

You have to specify how the data is transmitted so that both systems can

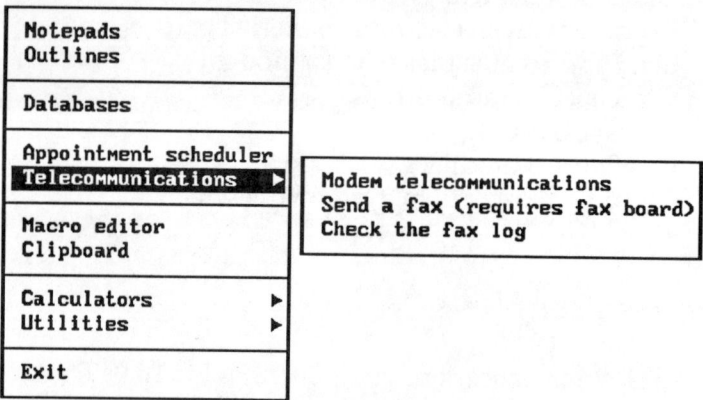

Figure 11.1   Telecommunications Pop-Up Menu

interpret it correctly; this involves the parity, the data bits, and the stop bits. *Parity* is a built-in form of error checking; it can be even, odd, none, mark, or space. Many systems these days use none; if you don't know which to use, try no parity as your first choice. *Data bits* refers to whether the system sends seven or eight bits from each byte. If you don't know which to use, try eight first. *Stop bits* indicate where a byte ends. Most systems use one stop bit.

The *baud rate* is the speed at which data is transmitted; while it is often referred to as bits per second or bps, the values aren't quite the same. In any case, however, a higher number indicates a faster rate. Desktop can support from 300 through 19200 baud; use the highest speed that both systems support.

Telecommunications Phone Directory

After you select **Modem telecommunications**, you see the Telecommunications screen shown in Figure 11.2. The bulk of the screen contains entries from the phone directory file named in the upper right corner of the window. You can use the keys on the bottom window line or scroll to see additional entries in the directory. The **File** menu lets you load a different directory file or save the current one. The **Edit** menu lets you manipulate entries in the current directory. The **Actions** menu lets you place and interrupt calls. The **Window** menu lets you move the dialog box and change its colors.

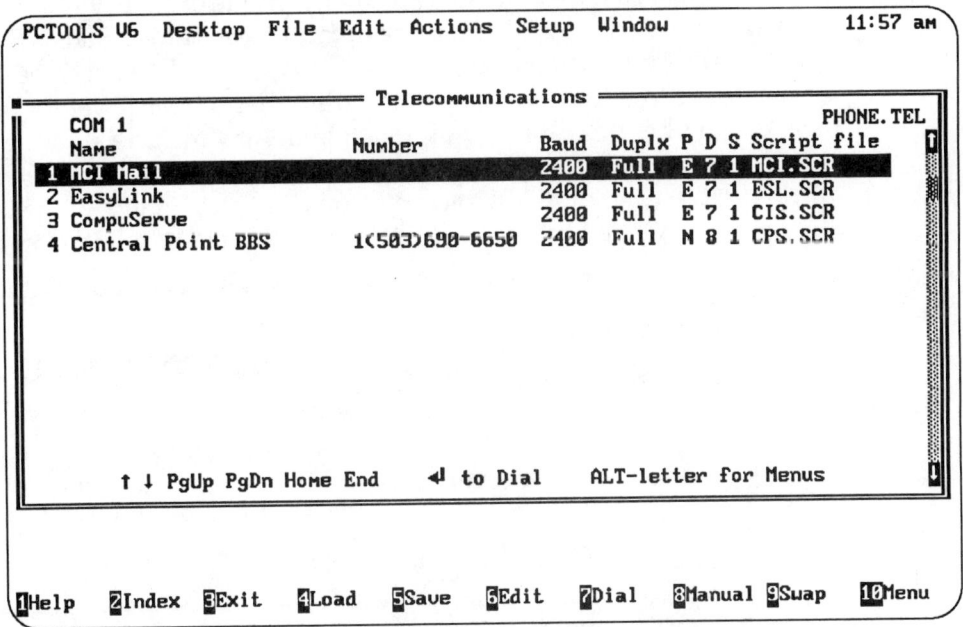

Figure 11.2   Telecommunications Phone Directory Window

Pressing Enter dials the selected entry, prompting you for a telephone number if necessary. Before you can call, however, you have to make sure the modem is prepared. You do that through the **Setup** menu.

Modem Setup

Every modem needs to receive an initialization string that tells it how to process the telephone number that follows. The standard Hayes string is set by default. When you pull down the **Setup** menu and choose the **Modem setup** option, you see the dialog box shown in Figure 11.3. It shows the standard Hayes modem initialization string for three different transmission rates. It will use the string that corresponds to each call you place. You can edit the strings if necessary; be sure to refer to your modem documentation for the correct information. If your modem is Hayes-compatible, try using the default string first. The dialog box also shows the connect string; this is the message that is sent to the computer when a connection is established. You can change this string also, if necessary.

The Telephone Directory File

The telephone directory you see in the Telecommunications window includes items you can call. You can have as many phone directory files as you want, each containing up to 200 items. The default file is named PHONE.TEL. When you install Desktop, it contains four already-entered items; three commercial services and the Central Point Software bulletin board system (BBS) where you can get help using PC Tools. Each item may include a phone number or it may not; if there is no phone number when you try to call an item, you'll be prompted to enter one. After you do, you can press Enter and the call is dialed using the displayed baud rate, duplex, parity, data bits, and stop bits.

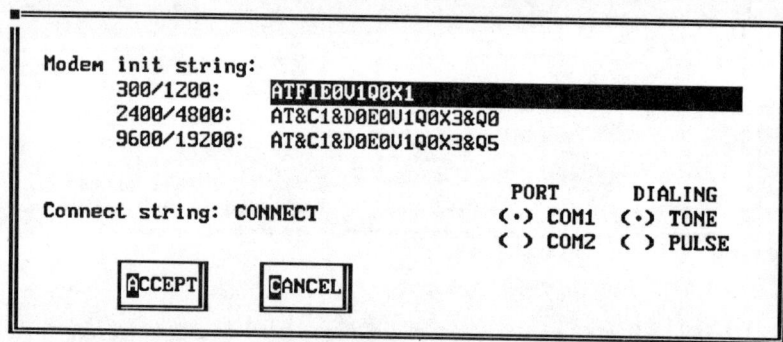

Figure 11.3   Modem Setup Dialog Box

Once you know the correct phone number, you can add it to an existing item or you can create a new entry. The values displayed for each item in the Telecommunications window represent just a few of the values associated with it. You can see the rest if you edit the item. If a script file is listed, it will be used in making the connection; script files are covered later in this chapter.

Editing the Phone Directory. As you can see in Figure 11.2, you have to fill in telephone numbers for most of the supplied directory items. You may have done this during PC Setup. If you want to change any parameters, you'll have to edit the item. When you pull down the **Edit** menu, you have three choices; to edit the highlighted entry (select **6Edit**), to create a new entry, or to remove the highlighted entry. If you select **Remove entry**, it is gone immediately. If you select **Edit entry**, you'll see a dialog box like the one in Figure 11.4; this one shows values associated with the Central Point BBS.

The dialog box shows the current setting for each value. You can change any of them, but you won't want to unless you know your modem requires different values. Check the baud rate especially; the Central Point BBS can handle up to 2400 baud, but your modem may have a lower limit.

Each directory entry can include a **NAME** and a **PHONE** number to be dialed. If a script file is included, it will be processed after a connection is estabished. You can also include a **USER ID** and **PASSWORD** for the system if you wish, but they will be transmitted only if included in a named script file. If you supplied a phone number, user ID, and password during PC Setup, they will appear here. If you wish, you can name a Desktop **DATABASE** and

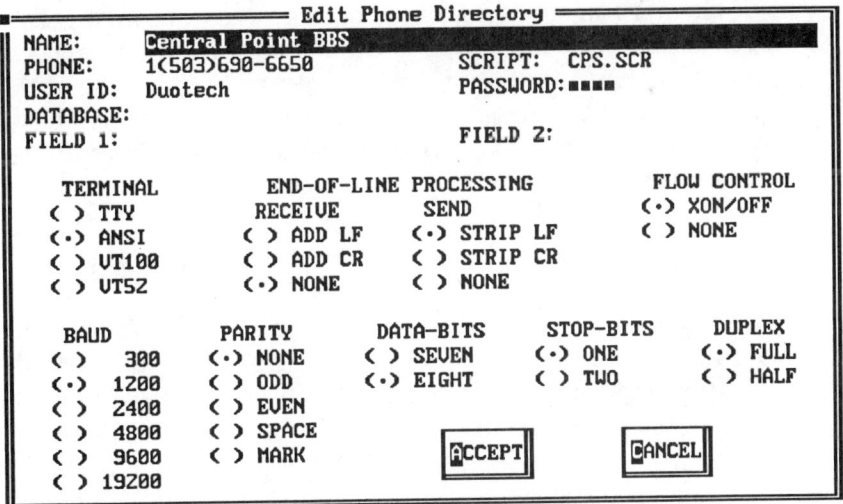

Figure 11.4   Edit Phone Directory Dialog Box

one or two fields to contain information to be used in sending electronic mail or faxes after the connection is ready. The script file and database elements are optional; both are covered later in this chapter.

The **TERMINAL, END-OF-LINE PROCESSING,** and **FLOW CONTROL** values depend on your system and on what the remote system does. You won't want to change these unless you have trouble exchanging data with the remote system. The Desktop documentation includes details about these features. When you are satisfied with the entries, select ACCEPT.

Adding Items to the Phone Directory. When you add an item, you see a dialog box much like the one for editing; but no values are provided in the upper part of the box. You type the name and phone number, add script and database information if any, change any parameter defaults that aren't right, and select ACCEPT. The item is added to the current phone directory.

Using Multiple Phone Directories. When Desktop is installed, there is a single phone directory, PHONE.TEL, that can hold up to 200 entries. You can create and load others as needed using the **File** menu, which allows you to load and save phone directory files. To start a new phone directory, pull down the **File** menu and select the **Load** option. You'll see a standard file selection box in which you can enter a new filename or select an existing one.

Highlight a filename and select LOAD to bring up an existing file or type a new name (with TEL as the extension) and select NEW to create one. When you complete the selection, the requested file is displayed on screen. If it is a new phone directory, all the items will be empty.

Changes to a phone directory are saved automatically when you leave Telecommunications. You can make sure they are saved at other times by using the **Save** option on the **File** menu; you have the option of providing a new filename at this time to create a copy of your file. The only time changes aren't saved is when you load a different phone directory; be sure to use **Save** first if you have made any unsaved changes.

Placing a Straightforward Call

Once your modem is connected and configured, you can try out your telecommunications features by dialing a remote computer. While script files can automate the process, you should know how to place a call when all you know are the telephone number and the communications parameters.

You can create a generic phone directory item and use it to place a call to any BBS or computer system. Once the connection is made, the rules of the remote system are in control.

Create a new item in your phone directory using a name like "Generic Call".

Use the same parameters Central Point uses for its own BBS, making sure to use your modem's top rated speed (up to 2400 baud) and the correct port. Don't enter a script file or a database name. Select ACCEPT to place the item in your directory.

To dial the item, highlight it on the screen, then press Enter, select **7Dial**, or pull down the **Actions** menu and select the **Dial** option. Since there is no telephone number in the item, a small dialog box prompts you for a number.

Once you type the number and press Enter or select ACCEPT, you'll see a message on the bottom line; the process of dialing may take a few minutes, so be patient. If you have a speaker phone, you may hear the sounds of dialing; if not, just wait a few minutes and you'll see some messages on screen. When you see something recognizable, you most likely have made a connection.

Manual Dialing

To dial a number manually, first highlight a directory item that has the baud rate and other values you want to use, then select **8Manual** or pull down the **Actions** menu and select **Manual**. You'll see a full screen window, in which you can type the desired phone number preceded by the standard string for your modem; use ATDT for tone phones or ATDP for pulse (rotary) phones connected to a Hayes-compatible modem. To call the Central Point BBS from a touch-tone phone, you would enter ATDT1-503-690-6650. Once the connection is made, the way you dialed makes no difference.

Using a Connected Service

Once you are connected to an online service or another computer, it generally prompts you for activities. If you want to have a full screen devoted to the online activity, you can select **Full online screen** on the **Setup** menu; otherwise you'll see command reminders and messages on the bottom two lines.

Terminating Connections

You can terminate a connection in several ways. If the system is still dialing, just press Esc to break the connection. Once the online screen is displayed, you can select **Hangup phone** from its **Actions** menu; this works at any point. Physically hanging up a connected phone can also break a connection. Once you have connected to a BBS or other remote system, use its commands to disconnect before you hang up your phone. This keeps the records of the remote system in order. If it is a system with connect charges, you may pay extra if you don't disconnect before hanging up.

Using the Central Point Software BBS

The Central Point Software bulletin board included in PHONE.TEL is available 24 hours a day. There is no charge for using the bulletin board except for normal long distance charges (generally lowest on nights and weekends).

Once you reach the Central Point Software BBS, most of the process is self-explanatory. You'll have menus to choose from on the screen, and the BBS has a built-in help system. The first message you'll see is this:

```
Can you display ANSI graphics?
If you are not sure select "N".
Would you like ANSI? (Y/N) _
```

The ANSI graphics affect how data is displayed on your screen. You'll be able to use the BBS quite effectively even without ANSI graphics, so type "N" if you aren't sure. And especially type "N" if you see strange characters on the screen before you reach this point. After you respond, you'll see general information, including the address and phone number for technical support.

Next you'll be asked if you already have a user ID on this system. If not type "new" and press Enter. When you do, the BBS starts preparing a record for you so you won't be asked the same questions every time you call. It asks several general questions about your computer, then you are asked to create your own user ID; this can be from three to nine characters long with no spaces or punctuation. The BBS automatically capitalizes the first letter and uses lowercase for all other letters so it looks like a name. If the value you enter is not unique, you'll be asked to type a different one. Use any value that will identify you; your user ID appears in messages you receive from the BBS.

Next you create a password that keeps other people from using your name without your permission. It should be short and easy to remember, but not easy to guess. The security of your account depends on nobody else knowing what your password is. The BBS displays both your user ID and password and suggests you write them down. You won't be able to get them from the BBS if you forget them.

Finally, you see the main menu of the BBS, as shown in Figure 11.5. Once you reach this point, you can use the full BBS. If you have never used one before, try several options and follow instructions on the screen. Try **BBS Information** even if you have used bulletin boards in the past. Try **Technical Information** to see what is included there.

Once you have a user ID and password, you can return to the BBS whenever you want. You can leave messages and questions about any aspect of PC Tools or other CPS products. Later, you can check **Read your messages** for answers.

✧ Try It Out

1. Your modem must be connected and turned on. Make sure you know what communications port it is attached to and its maximum speed. If it is not Hayes-compatible, you'll need to check its documentation and update the initialization strings.
2. Bring up Desktop and get into the Modem Telecommunications component. Examine the screen and check out a few of the menus.
3. Create a generic item that corresponds to your modem without a telephone number. If you know that any of the default parameters need changing, change them.
4. Leave the **Edit Phone Directory** dialog box, highlight your new item, then select **Dial**. When prompted, type the phone number of the Central Point Software BBS. If you prefer, you can use a local bulletin board if you know the number and the parameters it uses.
5. If you reach a BBS, log on and get a user ID and a password. Take some time to explore the BBS if you like, then sign off as instructed by the system. Use the **Hangup phone** command in Desktop.
6. If you don't reach a BBS, read any messages that appear. Check the modem switches. Check the parameters for the system. If you can't make it work, consult a colleague or call the Central Point Software technical support voice number provided in the PC Tools documentation.

Script Files

Using script files with phone directory entries simplifies the logon process. A script file generally includes commands to respond to routine prompts from a connected system, including a user ID and password. As soon as a connec-

```
1 ... Central Point Software Inc.
2 ... Technical Information
3 ... Sales Information
4 ... Download files
5 ... BBS Information
6 ... Leave a message
7 ... Read your messages
X ... EXIT the system

Select an option, X to EXIT or ? for help: _
```

Figure 11.5   Central Point BBS Main Menu

tion is made, the script file named in the phone directory item is processed. Telecommunications can't find the script files, however, unless they are located in the same directory as the PC Tools Desktop programs. Script files are included for all four entries that come with PC Tools. Except for the CPS script, they assume you added telephone number, user ID, and password information during PC Setup or while editing the phone directory item. The script for Central Point Software can work and provide prompts even if you haven't entered a user ID and password. You can edit script files under any ASCII editor, including the PC Shell Editor or Notepads.

Basic Script File Commands. Some script file commands appear in virtually all script files. Figure 11.6 shows part of the script file provided for calling the Central Point Software BBS. It uses very basic commands. Script files can also include some DOS commands, such as ECHO. The ECHO command in a script file causes all the information to appear on the screen.

Script files include special commands and symbols. Each line that begins with an asterisk (*) is a comment; it explains something to the reader but has

```
* Central Point Software BBS script.
*
ECHO ON
PRINT "Logging on to CPS's BBS.  Please wait..."
WAITFOR "(Y/N)"
SEND "Y"     * Change to N if you cannot display ANSI Graphics
WAITFOR "new"
WAITFOR ":"
IF USERID <> "" GOTO USEROK
PRINT ""
PRINT "User ID not specified in phone directory:"
GOTO NEEDLOG
:USEROK
IF PASSWORD <> "" GOTO PASSOK
PRINT ""
PRINT "Password not specified in phone directory:"
:NEEDLOG
   ...
GOTO BYE
:PASSOK
SEND USERID
WAITFOR "Password"
SEND PASSWORD
:BYE
```

Figure 11.6   Partial Contents of CPS.SCR

no effect on the script file itself. The three most common commands in script files are these:

PRINT specifies something to be displayed on the screen. You will see a message displayed while the script file is being processed.

WAITFOR specifies a string of characters that will be sent by the other computer; the next command won't be processed until the specified string is received.

SEND provides a string of characters to be sent to the remote computer; SEND frequently follows WAITFOR.

The script file for the CPS bulletin board is called CPS.SCR. You can examine and edit it under Notepads. Notice that it has several sets of WAITFOR and SEND commands. The first sends a response to the ANSI question. If your system doesn't support ANSI, you should change the "Y" to "N". The second WAITFOR deals with the user ID; if there is one stored in the phone directory item, control branches to another location where the SEND command occurs. Another WAITFOR handles the password request.

If the user ID and password aren't entered, the bulletin board will help you get them. Once your user ID and password are entered in the phone directory dialog box, the script will log you in automatically when you call the bulletin board. The other script files provided by CPS assume that you have provided the user ID and password in the phone directory entry. You'll have to call these services manually or remove the script file reference until you have signed on the first time and established these values.

Additional Script File Commands. If you are at all familiar with computer programming, you may want to expand your script files to further automate your use of modem telecommunications. Many additional commands are available that you can use. The RECEIVE command captures a message from a connected system and saves it in a variable for later use in the script. The INPUT command lets the user enter a variable at the keyboard. The SEND command sends a string or a variable to the connected system. The IF and GOTO commands, in combination with labels and variables named V1, V2, and V3, let you include decision making in your script. In Figure 11.6, the IF commands check to see if the phone directory item includes values for USERID and PASSWORD. If not, it transfers control to a label. UPLOAD and DOWNLOAD let you send or receive files by name or from a variable from within the script file. The HANGUP and PAUSE commands let you terminate the connection or cause it to pause for the specified length of time to give you more control over the script file.

You can also use predefined variables from a database in your script files. If you entered a database and two fields, you can refer to them in scripts as DATABASE V1, DATABASE V2, and DATABASE V1 V2; you can use these fields in scripts you write to automate sending electronic mail or faxes. When the script file encounters a reference to the database variable, it opens that database for you to select the appropriate record. Then it uses the value in the fields you named. This is most useful for sending electronic mail or faxes over your modem. Several of the provided script files include examples of how to use this feature.

Sending and Receiving Files

Once you are connected to an online service or another computer system, you can send (upload) and receive (download) files over the telephone lines. You must first set up the remote computer for the transfer. Use the instructions on the screen to start the process. If you want to send a file, you will have to know where it is stored and what its name is. If you want to receive one, you must be able to indicate which one to the remote computer.

In either case, both computers must use the same protocol. The protocol is a set of rules that specify how the data is exchanged. Two major protocols, ASCII and XMODEM, are supported by nearly every telecommunications software package.

ASCII Protocol

ASCII protocol is generally used to transfer ASCII or text files. It works for electronic mail as well. This protocol does not do error checking; if you want to be absolutely sure the data is transferred perfectly, use the XMODEM protocol instead. ASCII transfers work with either seven or eight data bits.

Receiving an ASCII File. Once you have identified a file to be received or downloaded, press F6 or pull down the **Receive** menu and select **ASCII**. When the **Save** dialog box appears, type the name of the file to be received; include a pathname if necessary. Select SAVE and the file transfer begins. The screen shows the text as it is transferred. In many systems, you'll have to press a key at the end of each displayed page to bring up the next one; other systems send the file as a continuous stream. ASCII transfer is fairly slow, since all the data must be written to the screen. When the download is complete, you'll be notified and you can select **End Transfer** from the **Actions** menu. If you want to interrupt the transfer early, just press Esc, click on the close box, or select **End Transfer** early.

Recording a Complete Session. You can use ASCII protocol to create a file containing a record of anything that prints on the screen during a session. Just select ASCII protocol and provide a file name early in your session, without having selected a specific file to download. Everything that appears on the screen, whether sent by you or by the connected system, will be sent to that file. Be sure to choose **End Transfer** before you disconnect from the system.

Sending an ASCII File. You can save connect time to a BBS by preparing your messages using Notepads or another ASCII editor, then uploading them to the remote computer. To send or upload a file, press F4 or pull down the **Send** menu and select **ASCII**. When the **File Load** dialog box appears, select or type the name of the file to be sent. Select LOAD and the file transfer begins. You'll see the text on the screen as it is transferred. When the upload is complete, the remote computer may not respond or may ask for more data. Just press Shift-Esc to indicate the end or to interrupt the transfer earlier.

XMODEM Protocol

XMODEM protocol is widely used because it allows very different computers to exchange files of any type. The files can be text, programs, data, or graphics. XMODEM includes error checking routines to ensure that data is transferred accurately. It is somewhat slower than ASCII, but more reliable, so use it when accuracy is important to you. You must use eight data bits in the connection for XMODEM to work properly.

Receiving Files with XMODEM. After a file to be received or downloaded has been identified to the remote computer, press F7 or pull down the **Receive** menu and select **XMODEM**. When the **Save** dialog box appears, type the name of the file to be received; include a pathname if you wish. Select SAVE and the file transfer begins. You'll see information on the screen telling you how much time has elapsed, how much of the file has been transferred, and how many errors have occurred. Use the **End Transfer** option (from the **Actions** menu), press Esc, or click on the close box to terminate the transfer.

Sending Files with XMODEM. To send or upload a file, press F5 or pull down the **Send** menu and select **XMODEM**. When the **File Load** dialog box appears, select or type the name of the file to be sent. Select LOAD and the file transfer begins. A box on screen lets you know how the transfer is progressing. If you see many errors, you might want to disconnect and try again later when the lines are quieter or using a lower baud rate. When the upload is complete, you'll return to the standard communications screen to continue your session.

Telecommunications in the Background

When Desktop is resident, Telecommunications can send and receive files in the background while you do other work at your computer. For example, you could download a file that takes more than an hour to transfer while you work at Lotus 1-2-3 or WordPerfect. To do this, you must install the background telecommunications option. If you didn't specify this during installation, type BACKTALK at the DOS prompt before making DESKTOP resident. Use BACKTALK /2 if your modem is connected to COM2; use /3 or /4 if appropriate. Don't use that port for anything else while BACKTALK is resident. If you expect to use background communications regularly, add the command to your AUTOEXEC.BAT file before the DESKTOP command. BACKTALK is a TSR program that requires about 64K of memory.

You can do file transfers in the background as long as no script file is in progress. If your script files are used just for the login process, however, they'll be completed by the time you use background communications and won't cause any problems.

To use the background communications, first establish the connection and start the transfer as usual. Then press Alt-B to put it in the background. You'll be returned to the main Desktop screen or the application that was in progress. You can continue to work, hotkeying in and out of Desktop as needed. You'll see a blinking "B" in the upper right corner of the screen while the file transfer is in progress. When the transfer is complete, a beep advises you.

When communications is used in the background, Telecommunications sets up a TRANSFER.LOG file to document file transfers and keep track of errors. If a transfer does not complete successfully, error messages are placed in the file as well. You can check the log to see the status of transfers or to find out what happened. Each file transfer in the background creates another file with the same name, so be sure to move or rename the file between transfers if you want to save the log files.

✧ Try It Out

1. Add your CPS BBS user ID and password to the phone directory. Then try accessing the BBS with the script file.
2. Download (receive) a file from a bulletin board such as CPS using ASCII protocol. Try an information file with a name such as README.
3. Download the same or a different file using XMODEM protocol.
4. If you expect to use Telecommunications in the background, try downloading the same file in the background.

Fax Telecommunications

If your computer contains an internal fax board compatible with the Connection™ CoProcessor from Intel Corporation or the SpectraFax® from SpectraFax Corporation, you can send faxes from your computer and receive them in the background. You can send faxes to a standard fax machine or to another internal fax board. Once a request has been made, you can return to other work at your system. Your fax board should be installed and connected according to its instructions. The Desktop Manager reference manual includes additional information.

To use the fax component of Telecommunications, select **Send a fax** from the **Telecommunications** pop-up menu. You'll see a screen like the one in Figure 11.7. Notice only four menus appear; the **Actions** and **Configure** menus are unique to Fax Telecommunications.

As you can see on the bottom screen line, function keys F4 through F8 let you perform various functions. You can add a new item (**4Add**), edit (**5Edit**), or delete (**6Delete**) an item, send a file to the selected item (**7Send**), or check the fax log (**8Chklog**).

Most screen entries are self-explanatory. The **Type** field contains "FAX" to send to a stand-alone fax machine or "FILE" to send to an internal fax board.

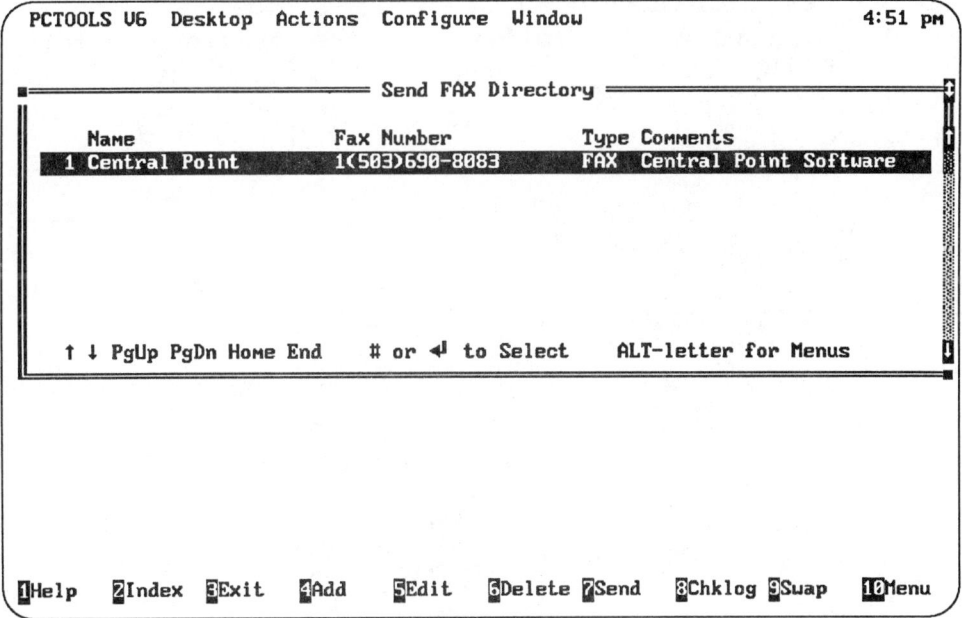

Figure 11.7   Fax Telecommunications Screen

Configuring Fax Telecommunications

Before you send your first fax, you must make sure your system is configured properly. Once you set the values, they apply to all future faxes you send; you can change individual settings for special occasions. You establish your default values through the **Configure** menu, shown in Figure 11.8. The **FAX Drive** may have been set during PC Setup; it must contain the path of the directory that contains Fax Telecommunications. That is probably the PC Tools directory.

The **Page Length** should be 11 inches if you normally send letter-size pages. When you send very short faxes, however, you can reset the value two inches or whatever is appropriate to avoid wasting paper at the receiving end.

If you turn the **Cover Page** option on, you'll be offered a chance to create one in a Notepad window every time you send a fax. A logo will automatically be included on every fax cover page. You can replace the default one (stored in PCTOOLS.PCX) with a personalized logo if you have one that you can convert to a PCX file. Be sure to use the same filename.

Whenever a fax is sent, the top line includes various information about the fax, including the recipient's name, the sender's name, the date and time the fax was sent, and the page number.

You can change the format from 24-hour time to AM/PM format if you wish. Be sure to include "p" for P.M. if you change the format.

To specify a standard **Sent From** value, just type your name. That name will be used unless it is changed when a specific fax is sent.

Sending a Fax

To send a fax, select the appropriate item and press Enter, select **7Send**, or choose **Send files to the selected entry** on the **Actions** menu. You'll see the dialog box shown in Figure 11.9. It shows the current date and time; if you want the fax sent later, you can change these values.

If you provided a **Sent From** value earlier, it will appear in the dialog box; you can change it if you wish. The **To**, **FAX Number**, and **Comments** fields

```
FAX Drive...
Page Length:    11
Cover Page:     YES
Time Format:    24 hr
Sent From...
```

Figure 11.8   Configure Menu

are filled in from the selected entry. If you want to send the fax somewhere else, you can change all these values. If you do, a new item is automatically created for your FAX directory.

You can select the resolution or destination type here. **Normal Resolution** is reasonably clear and is adequate for most purposes; it is transmitted more quickly than **Fine Resolution**. If you are sending to another fax board, choose **FAX Board to FAX Board**; resolution has no impact on fax boards.

If the files are ready to send, select **Select Files and Send**. You'll see a file selection box and can select as many files as you wish. If you selected **Cover Page** in your configuration, you'll be prompted to create one; you can decline if you wish. If you want a cover page, you'll be given the COVER.TXT Notepad file to prepare it. The same file is always used and erased after using. If you have a standard format, you can tailor it and load it into COVER.TXT before sending each fax.

If the files aren't ready yet, select **Create a File and Send**. You'll be prompted for a filename, then given a Notepad window to create it in. When you are finished, you'll be prompted for a cover page if necessary.

Finally, the fax is sent. You are returned to the standard Fax Telecommunications screen.

The FAX Log

Desktop keeps a record of all faxes sent and received. You can check it directly from the **Telecommunications** pop-up menu, by selecting **8Chklog**, or by pulling down the **Actions** menu and selecting **Check FAX Log**. When you do, you'll see a screen like the one in Figure 11.10. The log contains information on the last 99 faxes sent or received.

Most of the information is self-explanatory. The status value can be any of these: Dialing, Sending, Sent, Receiving, Received, Aborted, Error messages,

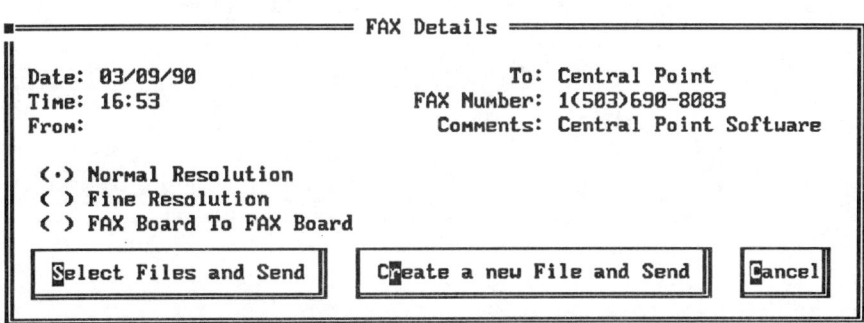

Figure 11.9   Fax Details Dialog Box

or Bad Phone Drop. Try to send it again if you get either of the last two. You can delete fax entries by highlighting them and selecting **5Delete**. This helps keep the log to a manageable size. You can search for a particular entry by selecting **6Search** and entering search text.

❖ *Try It Out*

1. Configure your fax board.
2. If you have information about future FAX recipients, add some entries to the FAX directory.
3. If you have a reason to, prepare a file and send a test fax.
4. Check the fax log.

Autodialer

The Autodialer feature of Desktop lets you dial a telephone number through your Hayes-compatible modem from the screen automatically. You can use it to place voice calls to numbers in database records, notepad files, or any Desktop application. The number could also be in a non-Desktop application or at the DOS prompt, as long as Desktop is resident.

Number Criteria

When you use Autodialer, it scans the characters on the current screen, until it finds a number it recognizes. The first string of three or more digits, ignoring such characters as spaces, dashes, parentheses, and "x" for extension, is considered a valid telephone number. A value such as a zip code or a social

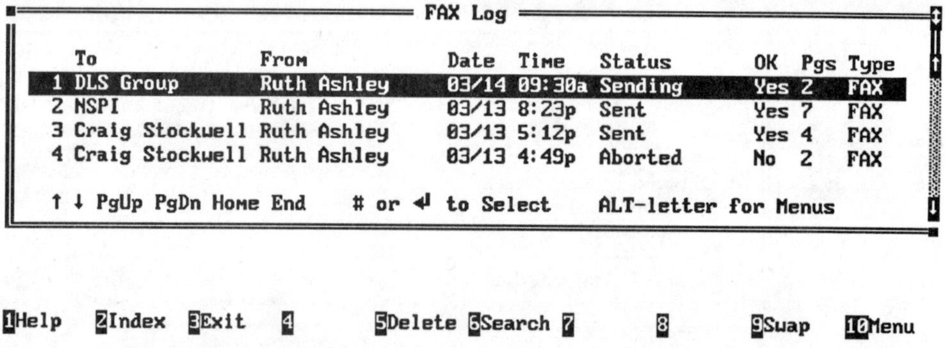

```
============================ FAX Log ============================
     To             From           Date   Time   Status     OK  Pgs Type
  1 DLS Group      Ruth Ashley    03/14 09:30a  Sending    Yes  2   FAX
  2 NSPI           Ruth Ashley    03/13 8:23p   Sent       Yes  7   FAX
  3 Craig Stockwell Ruth Ashley   03/13 5:12p   Sent       Yes  4   FAX
  4 Craig Stockwell Ruth Ashley   03/13 4:49p   Aborted    No   2   FAX

  ↑ ↓ PgUp PgDn Home End      # or ↵ to Select    ALT-letter for Menus
```

1Help   **2**Index   **3**Exit   **4**   **5**Delete **6**Search **7**   **8**   **9**Swap   **10**Menu

Figure 11.10   FAX Log

security number might get dialed! The following are all considered valid telephone numbers:

```
1-800-555-1212
10288-1-800-555-1212
555-8888x1410
1(800)5551212
376-40-9988
92111-1278
```

You can also include the following standard Hayes characters in a phone number field in a database:

P	For a pulse or rotary dial phone
T	For a touch-tone phone
,	For a two-second pause (use several commas for a longer pause)
* or #	If needed in the number
W	To wait for dial tone before dial
K	To delay until you press another key
@	Wait for dial tone (no answer)

Since many character strings, including address lines, social security numbers, and dollar values, may be recognized as phone numbers, put the phone number first in a database record if you expect to use Autodialer with it. It also makes sense to place a phone number early in a note so you don't have to select NEXT too often.

Configuring Autodialer

Before you can use Autodialer, it must be configured for your system and modem. The modem itself must be set so that Data Carrier Detect (DCD) and Data Set Ready (DSR) reflect the actual state of the electronic signals the modem receives. Many telecommunications software packages, including the one in Desktop, work with other settings of these switches. If you can use modem telecommunications just fine but Autodialer doesn't work, set these switches as required; check the modem documentaion. Desktop Telecommunications will continue to function, although some other communications software may not.

Autodialer itself must be configured from within Databases, but once configured, you can use it in other locations. Once you enter Databases and load any file, pull down the **Controls** menu and select **Configure Autodialer**. You'll see the dialog box shown in Figure 11.11.

Autodialer must know whether your telephone uses tones or pulses. It

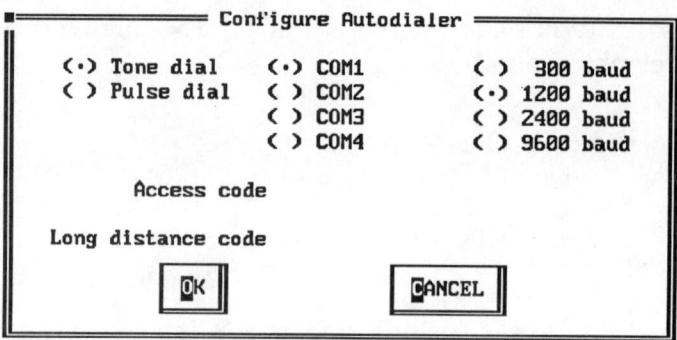

Figure 11.11   Configure Autodialer Dialog Box

must know which communications port the modem is connected to. And it must know the rated speed of the modem. If you use a special access code, such as 9, or a long distance code such as 10288, enter it as well. When these are set correctly, choose OK. You shouldn't have to worry about the modem configuration again.

Using Autodialer

When Desktop is not resident, you can use Autodialer only within Desktop applications. To dial a number in the currently displayed database record, you can select **Autodial** from the **Controls** menu. The first recognized telephone number will be dialed immediately. If your telephone has a speaker, turn it on so you will know when the connection is made and the ringing starts. Picking up the receiver terminates the Autodialer involvement.

You can also use Autodialer in other Desktop applications. To cause the first telephone number on the screen in a Notepads file or an Appointment Scheduler note to be dialed, press the hotkey established for Autodialer. The default hotkey is Ctrl-O. You'll see how to change this in the next chapter.

When Desktop is resident, you can also use Autodialer with the hotkey in other applications or at the DOS prompt. In some applications, such as WordStar, Ctrl-O has another meaning. In that case, you'll want to change the hotkey so it doesn't override the application function.

When you invoke Autodialer with the hotkey, and everything is properly set up, you'll see a message box like the one in Figure 11.12. If the number displayed is the one you want dialed, select DIAL. If you select NEXT, Autodialer looks for the next valid phone number on the screen. Choose CANCEL to stop the operation. If your database records include several phone number values, you'll want to use the hotkey instead of the menu selection to run Autodialer so that you can select the desired number.

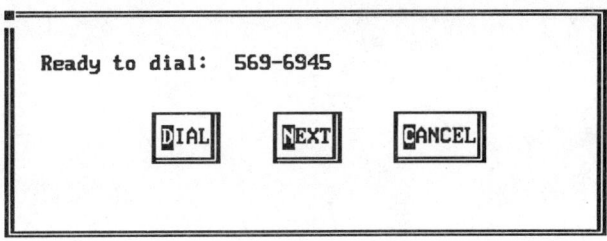

Figure 11.12   Hotkey Autodialer Dialog Box

If Autodialer can't locate your modem, you'll see a message such as MODEM IS NOT CONNECTED. This may mean the modem is not available or it is not turned on. Sometimes it means the modem switches (DCD and DSR) are set wrong. Once you get Autodialer to work, the worst problem should be that the modem is not turned on or that it is already in use.

◆ Try It Out

1. Configure Autodialer from within Databases. Check the current hotkey from the **Desktop** menu.
2. Add a database record that includes a valid telephone number, perhaps to a friend. Display the record.
3. Use the **Controls** menu to dial the number in the record.
4. Create a Notepads file that includes at least one valid telephone number. Use the hotkey to dial the number.

The next chapter shows you how to change the hotkeys used in PC Tools applications, including Autodialer. You'll also learn to create macros that use Autodialer as well as other PC Tools features.

Chapter 12 | *Utilities, Calculators, and Macros*

The remaining three areas in Desktop comprise a variety of applications that make your work easier. Utilities include an ASCII chart and hotkey selection, among others. Four kinds of calculators meet most people's math needs. And Macro Editor lets you create macros that work with any application. In this chapter, you will learn to:

- Change Desktop hotkeys
- View the ASCII table and insert ASCII characters into your file
- Change Desktop system colors
- Unload Desktop without unloading PC Shell
- Use the Desktop calculators appropriate to your work
- Create and use macros

Utilities

Desktop utilites are programs that make using other Desktop applications more convenient. The **Utilities** menu, shown in Figure 12.1, includes four items. **Hotkey Selection** lets you set your own Desktop hotkeys if the standard ones aren't appropriate to your system. **Ascii Table** displays a table of all 256

ASCII characters, so that you can find out how to type such characters as í and ¿. **System menu/window colors** lets you change colors of widows, backgrounds, and so forth. And **Unload PCTOOLS Desktop** lets you remove Desktop from residence without also unloading PC Shell. Each function is explained in the following sections.

Hotkey Selection

When you select the **Hotkey selection** option, you see the current hotkey combinations that activate resident Desktop, Clipboard paste, Clipboard cut, and Autodialer. Once the dialog box appears, you select the item you want to change, type the key combination you would like to use as a hotkey, then close the box. The new hotkey takes effect immediately. If you change the Desktop hotkey, the new one will be displayed the next time you install Desktop as a resident program.

The most compelling reason to change a hotkey is because the application you want to use it with has another definition for the hotkey. For example, if you want to use Autodialer with a WordStar file, you would have to change the hotkey definition because WordStar uses Ctrl-O to trigger its Onscreen Format Menu.

ASCII Table

Your computer keyboard includes all the standard English letters and digits and many symbols. But many more characters are available to you—up to 256 characters in all. You can include characters such as £ and ≈ in Notepads, Outlines, Appointment Scheduler, Clipboard, Databases, Macro Editor, File Edit, and non-PC Tools applications such as WordPerfect and WordStar. Desktop will pop up a dialog box showing the complete set and how to type each character.

Figure 12.2 shows two pages of the information that results when you select the **Ascii table** option. The first and last page are shown. You can page through with the up and down arrows or click on the scroll bar. The first 32 ASCII codes can represent either a graphic character or a control code depending on the application and the device, so the first two pages are formatted differently

```
Hotkey selection
Ascii table
System menu/window colors
Unload PCTOOLS Desktop
```

Figure 12.1   Utilities Menu

from the remaining pages. The left column contains the hexadecimal representation of the code, followed by its graphic character and the decimal representation of the code. Following the vertical line is the Ctrl-key combination that may represent the code and the control function that can result. For example, the code represented by decimal 7 might display a bullet or it might ring the hardware's alarm bell. It might also do nothing or display some other character. The control functions have been standardized, so it is unlikely to trigger any other control function.

The codes from decimal 32 to decimal 127 represent the letters, numbers, and symbols that appear on your keyboard; you can type these directly. These codes have been standardized and should have the same result everywhere. The codes from decimal 128 to decimal 255 have not been standardized; they generally result in graphic characters such as the ones shown in the last page in the figure. But they might have one result on your monitor and another on your printer; different software might also yield different results. You might also be able to change the codepages in your monitor and printer to produce different characters for these codes. The characters shown in the table are the best guess as to what you will get by inserting these codes in your file.

To insert codes, hold down the Alt key while typing the decimal number on your numeric keypad (the numbers from the top row of your regular keyboard won't do it). When you release the Alt key, the graphic symbol appears on your screen (if your screen can create it). For example, to insert the character Σ into your file, type Alt-228.

```
 ═══ Ascii Table ═══           ═══ Ascii Table ═══
| HEX  DEC | CTL CODE |       | HEX   DEC | HEX   DEC |

  00          ^@  NUL           E0 α  224   F0 ≡  240
  01 ☺     1  ^A  SOH           E1 ρ  225   F1 ±  241
  02 ☻     2  ^B  STX           E2 Γ  226   F2 ≥  242
  03 ♥     3  ^C  ETX           E3 π  227   F3 ≤  243
  04 ♦     4  ^D  EOT           E4 Σ  228   F4 ⌠  244
  05 ♣     5  ^E  ENQ           E5 σ  229   F5 ⌡  245
  06 ♠     6  ^F  ACK           E6 μ  230   F6 ÷  246
  07 •     7  ^G  BEL           E7 τ  231   F7 ≈  247
  08 ◘     8  ^H  BS            E8 Φ  232   F8 °  248
  09 ○     9  ^I  HT            E9 θ  233   F9 ·  249
  0A ◙    10  ^J  LF            EA Ω  234   FA ·  250
  0B ♂    11  ^K  VT            EB δ  235   FB √  251
  0C ♀    12  ^L  FF            EC ∞  236   FC ⁿ  252
  0D ♪    13  ^M  CR            ED ø  237   FD ²  253
  0E ♫    14  ^N  SO            EE ε  238   FE ■  254
  0F ☼    15  ^O  SI            EF ∩  239   FF     255
```

Figure 12.2   First and Last Pages of ASCII Table

System Menu/Window Colors

The **System menu/window colors** option lets you alter the colors of menus, dialog boxes, and message boxes on a global level that can't be controlled from the individual **Window** menus. Figure 12.3 shows the dialog box that results when you select this option. It works just like the dialog boxes you have seen before. You can select RESET to restore the default colors.

The **Set High Intensity on Exit** option should be used only if you are having trouble when exiting resident Desktop to an application that uses high intensity colors. Under certain conditions, the return to the application causes the high intensity colors to be blinking instead. You can cure that problem by selecting this option. If you never notice a problem, then leave this option alone.

Unload PCTOOLS Desktop

The final option on the **Utilities** menu unloads Desktop from residence. It is equivalent to the KILL command except that it doesn't also unload PC Shell. You should use the **Unload PCTOOLS Desktop** option only under certain conditions:

Desktop was the last resident program loaded. Resident programs must be unloaded in the reverse order from the way they were loaded. That is, the last one in must be the first one out.

Desktop must have been initiated from the DOS command prompt. If you

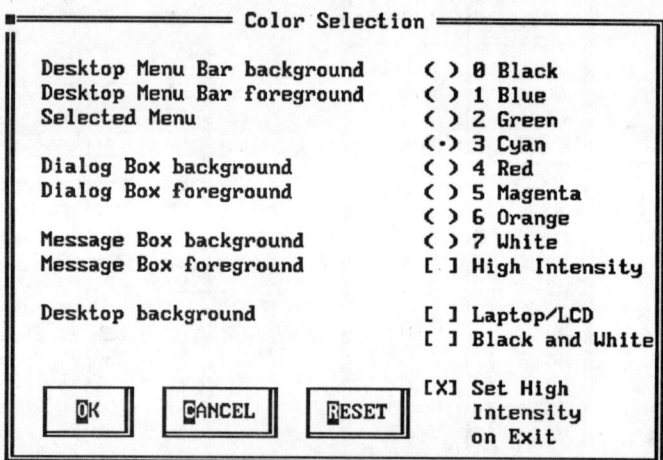

Figure 12.3   Color Selection Dialog Box

hotkeyed to Desktop from any other program, do not use this option. Return to the command prompt and type KILL.

✧ Try It Out

1. Change the **Clipboard Paste** hotkey to Alt-X. Change it back to Ctrl-Ins again.
2. Open any Notepad file. Type the character â. Erase it and close the file.
3. Change Desktop menu colors (**Menu Bar background**) to green. Check out a couple menus to see the effect. Change them back to cyan again.
4. Unload Desktop if possible. Load it again if you'd like.

Calculators

Desktop emulates four calculators. Algebraic Calculator is like the hand-held calculator that most people use for everyday purposes. Financial Calculator emulates the Hewlett-Packard HP-12C to help you calculate loan payments, calculate compound interest, perform discounted cash flow analysis, and so forth. Programmer's Calculator helps programmers convert among several number systems and also emulates the Hewlett-Packard HP-16C, except for its programming capabilites. Scientific Calculator emulates the Hewlett-Packard HP-11C (except for its programming functions) to help you compute logarithms, reciprocals, trigonometric functions, and so on. The following sections explain how to get started using the calculators. Read only those sections for the calculators you will actually use.

Algebraic Calculator

Algebraic Calculator, shown in Figure 12.4, works much like any algebraic calculator with a paper tape, except that you can edit the tape and recalculate the totals. The three parts of the window are the keypad on the right, the display at the bottom left (the single number inside a double border), and the tape above the display.

You can enter numbers into the calculator from the numeric keypad or the number keys along the top row. You can also click on the keys represented on the screen. Table 12.1 shows how to use the keyboard for keys such as MC and CLR. Getting help (**1Help**) produces a complete list onscreen.

To enter a number, type or click out the number, including decimal point, followed by one of the operation keys: +, -, *, /, =, or Enter. Use exactly the

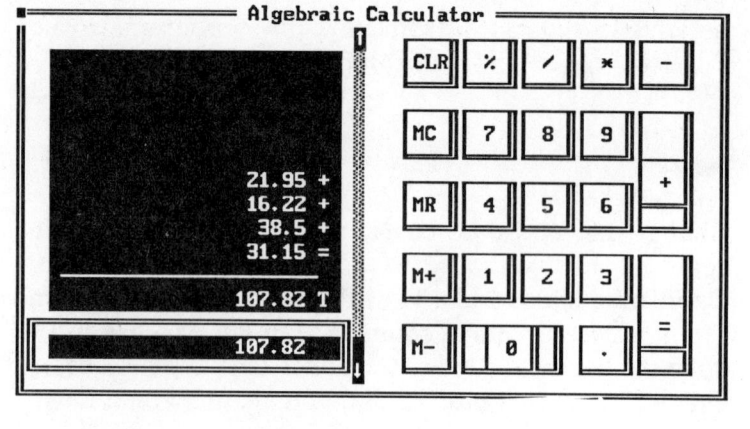

Figure 12.4   Algebraic Calculator

same sequence that you would use to write out an equation. That is, if you want to subtract 7 from 12, type 12 followed by a minus key. Then type 7 followed by = or Enter. When you press = or Enter, the total is calculated, "printed" on the tape, and displayed in the display. If you want to use that total as the first number in the next problem, imagine that you have typed the number in the display and start by pressing the appropriate operation key to place that number on the tape.

Table 12.1   Algebraic Calculator Keyboard Equivalents

```
Addition                +
Subtraction             -
Multiplication          * or x
Division                /
Percentage              %
Total                   = or Enter
Clear                   C

Add to memory           M followed by +
Subtract from memory    M followed by -
Recall from memory      M followed by R
Erase memory            M followed by C

Set decimal places      D followed by number of places
Comma display           ,
```

Figure 12.5 shows how to multiply the value in the display (from Figure 12.4) by 7.4%. Press * or x for multiply, which places the displayed value on the tape. Then type 7.4 and press or select %. If you wanted to add 7.4% of the value to the value, as you might in adding sales tax to a total, press + while the value is displayed. Then type 7.4 followed by %.

The algebraic calculator automatically edits numbers with commas and a decimal point. You can set the number of decimal places by pressing D followed by the number of decimal places. If you press D2 while the tape in Figure 12.5 is displayed, the result changes to 7.98. You can toggle the comma display off and on by typing a comma. When entering data, you can type commas if you wish.

Clearing. You can clear the display and the tape using function keys. Clearing the display (**4Clear**) erases only the number currently in the display. It does not affect the rest of the problem you are working on, as recorded on the tape. Clearing the tape (**5Erase**) sets the display to zero and erases the tape, setting it up for a new problem. However, memory is not cleared.

Using Calculator Memory. The algebraic calculator has a memory that you can use during calculations. To enter the currently displayed value into memory, press either M+ or M- depending on whether you want to add it to or subtract it from any current value in memory. An M appears to the left of the tape whenever a value is in memory.

To recall a value from memory into the display, press MR. You can then use the number just as you would a number that you had typed yourself. To clear memory, press MC.

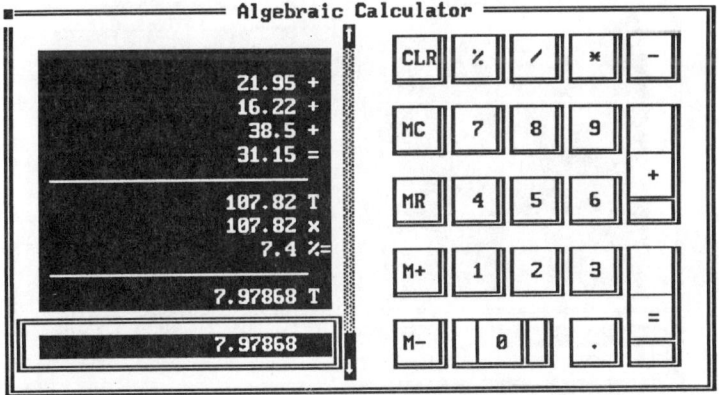

Figure 12.5   Calculating a Percentage

Editing the Tape. If you make a mistake or if you just want to play "what if", you can edit any value on the tape that was entered from the display; it holds about 1,000 lines. You can't edit values that resulted from calculations. When you edit a value, all values that were calculated from it automatically change.

To edit a value, use the up and down arrow keys or the scroll bar to reposition the tape so that the desired value appears in the display. Then change the value as needed. When you scroll to the end of the tape again, totals affected by the edited value are recalculated, but M+ and M- aren't redone. You can scroll quickly by pressing End.

Suppose you clear memory, the display, and the tape. Then you multiply 123 by 725, resulting in 89,175, which you add to memory. Then you multiply 42 by 899, resulting in 37,758, which you subtract from memory. Recalling memory shows a result of 51,417. Now you go back and edit the original number, 123, to read 125. When you scroll back down the tape, the total 89,175 is changed to 90,625. But the value that was added into memory is not affected by the recalculation; it is still 89,175. Figure 12.6 shows what the tape looks like at this point. If you need to correct the value in memory also, the easiest way is to clear memory and add 90,625 to it.

Options Menu. The **Options** menu, shown in Figure 12.7, contains several useful options. You already know how to clear the display and erase the tape without using the menu. The Print tape option sends the tape to the printer. This could be useful to attach documentation to a worksheet, for example.

The **Wide Display** option toggles the calculator window back and forth between the wide version, which is the default, and a narrower version. The narrower version contains only the left half; the keyboard half is eliminated so you enter all values from your keyboard.

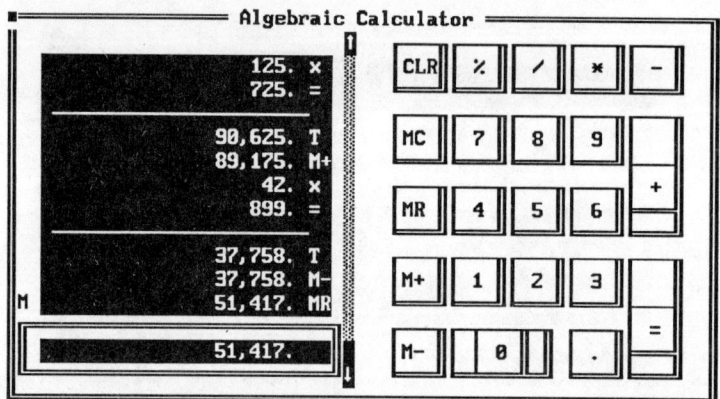

Figure 12.6   Changing Values on the Tape

Utilities, Calculators, and Macros

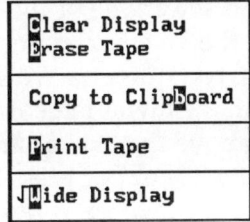

Figure 12.7   Options Menu

The **Copy to Clipboard** option copies the entire tape to the clipboard, where you can edit it and then copy it into another application. For example, suppose you want to copy a total into your word processing document. Select **Copy to Clipboard**. Then close the calculator window and open up the **Clipboard** window and edit out all the lines except the total. Then copy the result to your word processing application.

✧ *Try It Out*

1. Open the Algebraic Calculator. Clear the tape and memory. Calculate 39 times 722.
2. Press comma several times to toggle the comma display off and on. Notice the result on the screen.
3. Type D2 to set two decimal places. Set five places. Set no places.
4. Edit the tape to change 39 to 47. Scroll to the bottom of the tape to see the total change. Add the result to memory.
5. Subtract 65 from memory.
6. Recall memory. Calculate 4.35% of the result.
7. Try out some of the options on the **Options** menu.
8. Print the tape.
9. Practice using the calculator until you feel comfortable with it.

Financial Calculator

Financial Calculator emulates the Hewlett-Packard HP-12C calculator, which is a highly complex device. Showing you how to use it in detail is beyond the scope of this book. If you need to learn how to use it, check your bookstore for books on the HP-12C. Figure 12.8 shows the **Financial Calculator** window.

The display emulates the appearance of the calculator. Each "key" has multiple functions. Function names on the top half of the "keys" are the standard functions. To select one of these functions, you click on the key or type the letter beside the key. For example, to select the RCL function in the bottom row, you could type the letter M. Other functions are accessed by using the F and G prefixes in the lower left corner of the calculator.

Functions shown above the "keys" are accessed by the F prefix. To select the F prefix, click on the F "key" or press F7. Do not press the letter F; that key will give you the Δ% function. Suppose you want to access the AMORT function in the top row. Select the F prefix, then select the AMORT "key", which can be accessed by typing Q.

Functions shown on the bottom half of the "keys" are accessed with the G prefix. To access the 12X function that shares a key with AMORT, select the G prefix (F8), then select the 12X "key" (type Q).

We will walk through one simple problem to show you how the display, the mouse, and the keyboard relate to the actual calculator. If you expect to use this calculator, try it out following these instructions.

Suppose you want to calculate the monthly payment on a 125,000 dollar loan at 10.2 annual percentage rate for 48 months. Payments are made at the end of the month. Your basic strategy is to enter values into the n (number of payments), i (monthly interest), PV (present value), and FV (future value) registers and solve for the remaining financial register, PMT (payment). Then follow the steps listed below.

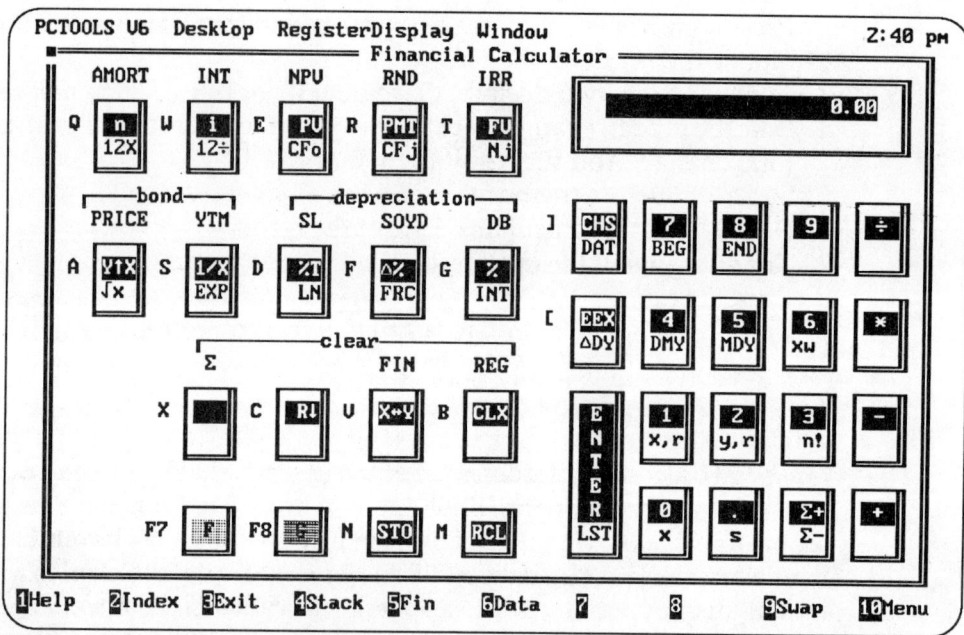

Figure 12.8   Financial Calculator

1. Clear all five financial registers.
    Select the F prefix. An "f" will appear in the display window to show that the next key will use the F function. In the **clear** section, select the REG key.
2. Check the registers to make sure they are clear.
    Pull down the **RegisterDisplay** menu and select **Financial registers**. A dialog box showing the five financial registers will appear. All five should be 0.0. If not, repeat steps 1 and 2.
3. Tell the calculator that month-end payments are intended.
    Select the G prefix; a "g" appears in the display window. Select the END function that appears on the 8 key; it is not the same as the End cursor movement key.
4. Enter values into the n, i, PV, and FV register.
    Type 48 (the number of payments) and select n (in the upper left corner). The interest rate needs to be converted from annual to monthly. Type 10.2, select the G prefix, and select the 12÷ function. This divides the number by 12 and places 0.85 in the i register.
    Type 125000 (Financial Calculator will insert a comma automatically) and select the PV function.
    Type 0 and select the FV function.
5. Check the registers to make sure they are correct. If not, try the whole process again.
6. Select the PMT function. The payment will appear in the calculator display. It should be -3,182.34.

Programmer's Calculator

Programmer's Calculator emulates many functions of the Hewlitt-Packard HP-16C. It converts numbers and performs simple arithmetic in any of the four number systems that are used by many programmers. In addition, it performs arithmethic in 1's or 2's complement notation or unsigned mode. You can also use it to isolate bits using logical operators, shift and rotate bits, and perform double precision functons. To learn all the functions in detail, you'll want to acquire the detailed HP-16C instruction manual. Figure 12.9 shows the programmer's calculator onscreen. The **RegisterDisplay** menu shows the contents of the stack and data registers; selecting **4Stack** and **5Data** accesses these functions as well.

The upper part of the screen is the display area. You can convert numbers using only this area. Just select the base to enter the number, type it, and it immediately appears in all five modes. This part of the screen also displays the current word size, the complement mode, and indicators of flags. The letter

"Z" indicates that the zero flag is set, "C" indicates that the carry flag is set, and "G" indicates an overflow flag. The letter "f" appears when the F function has been selected, and "P" appears when more input is required.

The rest of the window includes calculator buttons. Each button has two functions, one plain and one preceded by the F function. The plain function is highlighted on each button. You can select buttons with the mouse or by pressing the keyboard key shown to the left of the displayed button; in plain mode this activates the highlighted function named in the lower half of the button. If you first select the F button or press F7, the function in the upper half of the button is activated. Notice that the simple arithmetic buttons are all F functions along the right edge of the calculator.

Simple arithmetic is done in Reverse Polish Notation. To do a simple calculation, type the first number and press Enter, then type the second number followed by +, -, *, or /. (You can also type "x" for multiplication.) To operate on a third number, type it followed by its operator. As you continue, a running total appears in the display area, in all bases. This value is always the current value in the X register.

You perform logical operations (F value of the arithmetic operators) in the same way: press Enter after the first value, then type the second and select the operator. To select AND, for example, you would select F, then the button that has AND and x. With the keyboard, you would press F7, followed by the x or asterisk key.

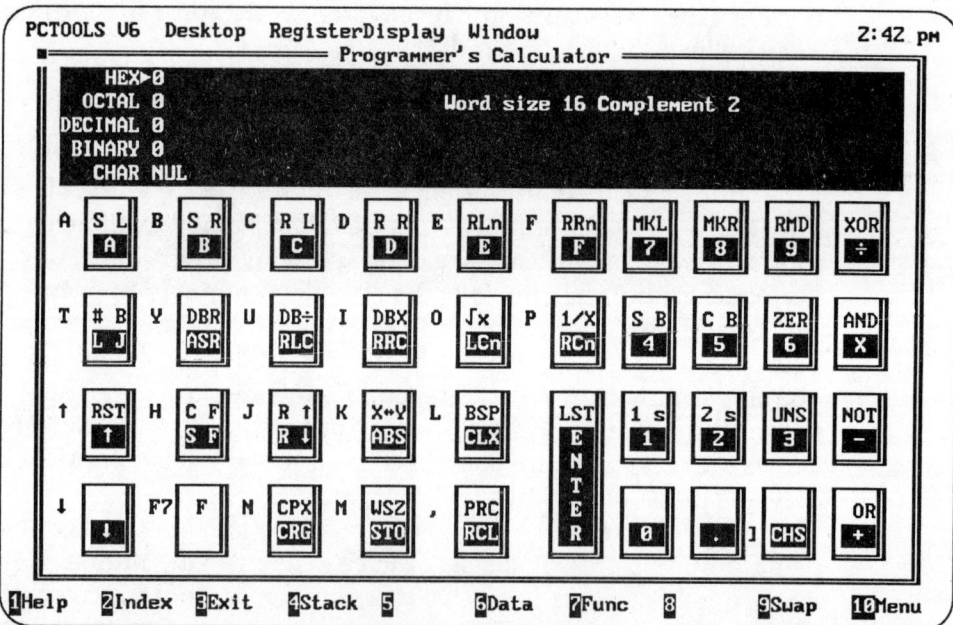

Figure 12.9   Programmer's Calculator

You can store and recall numbers with the STO and RCL buttons at the bottom center. You can view the contents of the data and stack registers by selecting menu options of bottom line commands. You can scroll through the stack registers with the R↑ and R↓ buttons (third row down, third button from the left). The X↔Y button (next to R↑) exchanges data in the X and Y data registers.

Scientific Calculator

Scientific Calculator, shown in Figure 12.10, can be used for calculations beyond the capabilities of Algebraic Calculator. Here you can calculate exponents, roots, logarithms, trigonometric functions, hyperbolic functions, and more. It emulates the Hewlett Packard HP-11C calculator except that it is not programmable. Explaining that calculator takes an entire book; check your bookstore if you need more help in using the calculator.

We'll show you a couple of examples to demonstrate how the monitor display, mouse, and keyboard relate to the actual calculator. If you plan to use this calculator, try out the examples on your computer.

The display emulates the appearance of the calculator. Each "key" has multiple functions. Function names on the top half of the "key" are the standard functions. To select these functions, you click on the key or type the

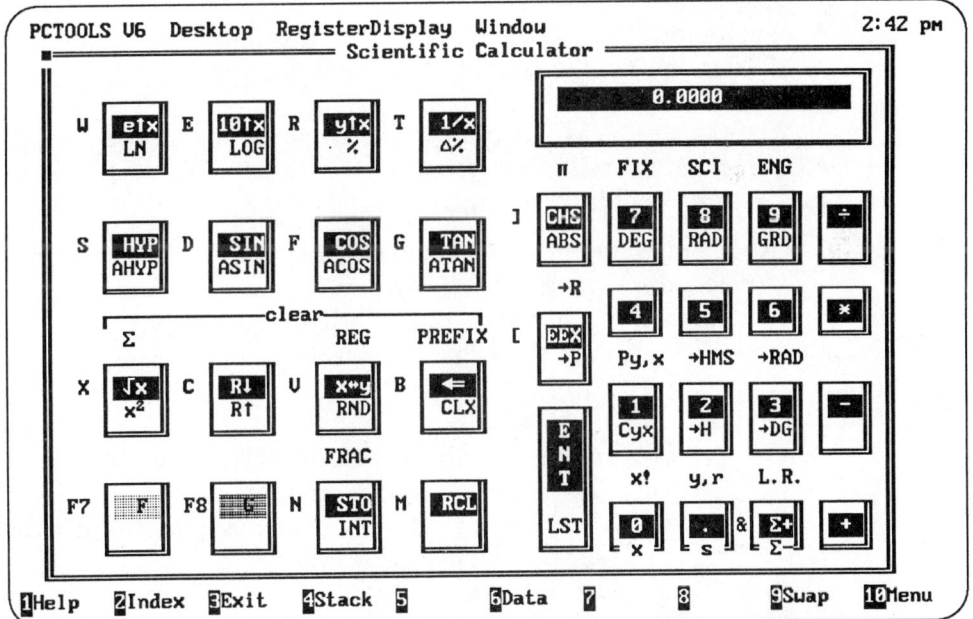

Figure 12.10   Scientific Calculator

letter to the left of the key. For example, to select the HYP function (left end of second row), you would type the letter S. Other functions are accessed by using the F and G prefixes in the lower left corner of the calculator.

Functions shown above the "keys" are accessed by the F prefix. To select the F prefix, click on the F "key" or press F7. Pressing F gives you the COS function. Suppose you want to access the π (pi) function directly below the display window. Select the F prefix, then select the CHS "key" or press].

Functions shown on the bottom half of the "keys" are accessed with the G prefix. To access the ABS function that shares a key with the CHS function, select the G prefix (F8), then select the ABS "key" or press].

Here's how to raise 2 to the 7th power (2^7). It is not necessary to clear the registers first.

1. Store 2 in the Y register.
   Type 2 and press Enter. When you press Enter, the value in the display is automatically stored in the Y register.
2. Place 7 in the X register.
   Type 7 but don't press Enter. The number you are currently typing is always stored in the X register until you select a function or press Enter.
3. Select the y↑x function (in the center of the top row).
   This function raises the number in the Y register to the power in the X register. The answer (128) replaces 7 in the X register and appears in the window.
4. If you would like to view the stack at this point, press F4. You will see 128.0 in the X register and 7.0 in the LSTX (last X) register.

It is not necessary to clear the stack register before starting the next problem. New numbers push old numbers out of the stack. The next problem calculates the percentage of increase from 2.56E+7 to 6.16E+8.

1. Use scientific notation with two decimal places in the mantissa.
   Select the F prefix. An "f" appears in the calculator display. Select the SCI function (centered underneath the display window). The calculator waits for the next key. Press 2. The display changes to scientific notation with two decimal places. The exponent is shown on the right.
2. Enter 2.56E+7 into the Y register.
   Type 2.56. Select the EEX function (above the enter key) to tell the calculator that you want to type the exponent (00 appears in the exponent position). Type 7. Press Enter to place the value in the Y register. (Press F4 to see the stack registers for confirmation.)
3. Type 6.16E+8 but don't press Enter.
   Type 6.16. Select EEX (above the enter key). Type 8. This value is now in the X register.

4. Select the Δ% function.
     Select the G prefix. Then select the Δ% key (to the left of the display). The value in the display shows the percent change (2.31E+03).

✧ Try It Out

1. Open the specialized calculator you expect to use.
2. Check out the menus, then do a simple calculation.
3. For practice, try out one of the procedures outlined in the preceding section. Then develop a new one.

Macro Editor

By now, you probably realize that you repeat certain procedures over and over again. If they involve several keystrokes and/or mouse actions, you could save time by creating a macro to execute them. With a macro, one keystroke takes the place of many. You can use macros anywhere in Desktop. For example, printing a Notepads file normally takes three steps; using a macro can reduce it to one. Opening a database named PARTS.DBF normally takes 12 keystrokes; you could create a macro to do it in one keystroke.

If Desktop is resident, you can also create macros that work in non-Desktop applications. For example, you could create a macro to open WordPerfect, switch to a particular directory, and display the list of files in that directory.

Working with the Macro Editor

Macro Editor is the facility that lets you create macros or individually defined short cut keys. To start it, select the **Macro Editor** option from the **Desktop** menu. A dialog box virtually identical to **Notepads** appears. You can select an existing macro file or name a new one.

A macro file contains a set of related macros. You could place all the macros that you create into one file, but it makes more sense to divide them into related groups. For example, you might have a set of macros to use with WordStar, another set to use at the DOS command prompt, a set to use with Databases, and so forth. You can use several macro files at once. You activate the macro files that you currently want to work with and deactivate the others.

Once you have selected or named a macro file, a **Macro Editor** window appears. Figure 12.11 shows an example of this window with an existing macro file. It works just like a **Notepads** window, but some of the menu options and bottom line commands are different, as you will see as you progress through this chapter.

Loading the macro file lets you view and edit it, but does not activate it. You'll learn shortly how to activate a macro file.

You can type any text you want in the macro file; everything not enclosed between <begdef> and <enddef> is considered a comment. The comments help to document the macros you create both for yourself and for others.

Macro Format

You can see several macro definitions in the figure. Every macro definition must have this format:

<begdef><trigger>script<enddef>

The <begdef> and <enddef> markers identify the beginning and end of the macro definition. They must appear exactly as shown including the angle brackets. You can either type them out yourself or press the key combination Alt-+ for <begdef> and Alt-– (that's Alt and the minus key) for <enddef>.

The <trigger> is the key or key combination that invokes the macro. It must appear inside angle brackets. (In macros, all key names must appear

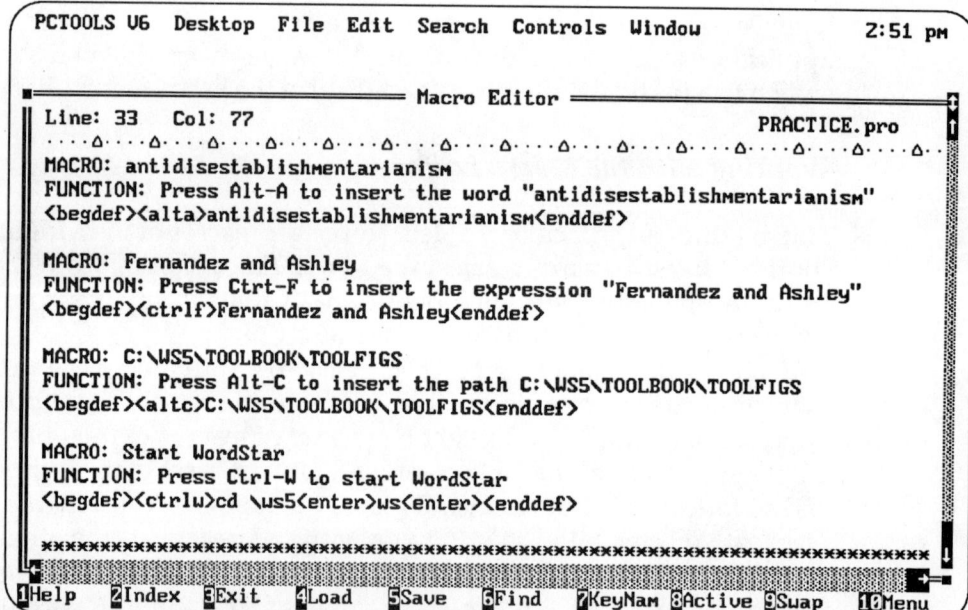

Figure 12.11   Macro Editor Window

inside angle brackets to distinguish them from text strings.) You'll see shortly how to type a key name.

The *script* is the sequence of keystrokes that is executed when you invoke the macro. It might be a text string, such as "antidisestablishmentarianism", a sequence of key names, such as "`<f10><f5><enter><enter><enter>`", or, more commonly, a combination of both text and keystrokes, as in the macro "`<shiftf8>135.2<enter><enter>N<enter>`". You can either type out the script yourself or let Macro Editor record your keystrokes as you perform the function you want made into a macro.

Typing Key Names

If you want Macro Editor to generate the key names for you, select **7KeyNam** followed by the key or key combination. For example, if you press F7 followed by Ctrl-E, Macro Editor places `<ctrle>` at the cursor position. **7KeyNam** tells Macro Editor that the next key or key-combination should be turned into a key name. Without it, Macro Editor processes the keystroke just as Notepads or any other application would.

You can also type the key name yourself. Just enclose it in angle brackets, typing "shift", "alt", and "ctrl" as appropriate. The function keys are named f1 through f10. (Case doesn't matter.)

Not all key combinations are supported by Macro Editor. For example, you cannot assign a macro to `<ctrlq>`. The Desktop reference manual contains a complete chart of keys you can use. The advantage of letting Macro Editor generate the key name is that it will not generate invalid ones. Thus, by pressing F7 followed by the key combination, you can find out right away whether the key combination is valid.

Choose your trigger carefully. If you are creating a macro to work with WordStar, for example, you would not want to use one of the key combinations that pull down a menu, such as `<ctrlo>` or `<ctrlp>`. For macros to be used within any PC Tools application, don't use an Alt key combination. Even if you think you are not duplicating or overriding an existing function, you could create problems with the software. Use Ctrl key combinations for all PC Tools macros.

Creating a Text-Only Macro

Text-only macros are fairly easy to create. Type whatever documentation is appropriate. You can see some good examples of documentation in Figure 12.10; try to at least describe the function, name the trigger, and tell where it should be used. You don't have to start a new line after the documentation, but the macro will be easier to find when editing the file if you do. Then press Alt-+ to enter <begdef> into the file. Press F7 followed by the key or key combination to enter the name of the trigger into the file. Then type the text that should be displayed whenever you press the trigger. Finally, press Alt-– to enter <enddef> into the file.

Suppose you want to define macros to type â when you press Ctrl-A and ä when you press Alt-A. You would define these two macros:

```
<begdef><ctrla>â<enddef>
<begdef><alta>ä<enddef>
```

A macro to type "Intercity University Relocation and Rehabilitation Service" when you press Ctrl-I would be defined this way:

```
<begdef><ctrli>Intercity University Relocation and
Rehabilitation Service<enddef>
```

Once you have typed a macro, it is immediately available as long as the macro file is active. But be sure that the file eventually gets saved by one of the usual Desktop methods for saving files.

Activating Macro Files

To activate the current macro file, select **8Active**, which brings up the dialog box shown in Figure 12.12. Select the appropriate option to make the macros in the file available only when Desktop is active, only when Desktop is not active (but it must be resident), or both inside and outside Desktop.

Be careful to define only one macro per trigger in a macro file. If you activate multiple files, check to make sure the same trigger is not defined twice. You can deactivate all macros by selecting **Erase all macros** from the **Controls** menu. (This doesn't erase them; it just deactivates them.) Then activate only the files you want to use now.

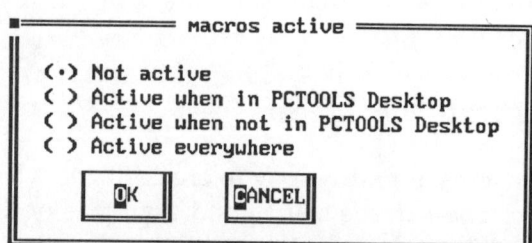

Figure 12.12   Macros Active Dialog Box

Using Macros

To use a macro, press the trigger. The macro should begin to work. You can interrupt it, if necessary, by pressing Esc.

If the macro doesn't begin to work, the macro file is probably not properly activated for the screen you are currently using. If it begins to work but something goes wrong, check the macro definition. Check first to make sure you included <enddef>. Then check that the script is defined correctly. If the macro seems to be defined correctly, try rebooting. Sometimes that clears up problems that were created by an earlier incorrect version of the macro.

If all else fails, try deactivating all macros. You can do this by returning to Macro Editor, pulling down the **Controls** menu, and selecting **Erase all macros**. Once all macros have been deactivated, activate only the macro file you are trying to use. Then try again. If it still fails, the problem must be in the script.

Once the macro works correctly, you can activate the other macro files that you deactivated. Then try the macro again to make sure it is still working. If it stops working, the problem might be in conflicting definitions for the same trigger.

You can override the trigger so that it does not start the macro by preceding it with a backward apostrophe (`). Thus you can use the trigger for other functions in an application.

✧ Try It Out

1. Start a new file called PRACTICE.PRO. Create a macro to type your name when you press a trigger.
2. Activate the macro file to work within Desktop.
3. Open any Notepad file. Try out your macro. It should insert your name in the file. Correct the macro until it works.

Action Macros

An action macro performs some kind of operation. For example, you could write a macro to open the algebraic calculator with one keystroke. The definition would look like this:

```
<begdef><ctrla><altd>ca<enddef>
```

As always, <begdef> and <enddef> are the macro definition delimiters.

The trigger is defined by <ctrla>. The rest of the keystrokes comprise the script. First, <altd> pulls down the **Desktop** menu from any location in Desktop. (Remember that you can pull down any Desktop menu by pressing Alt plus the highlighted letter in the menu name.) Once the menu is down, c selects the **Calculators** option, which pops up the **Calculators** dialog box. You press a to select the **Algebraic Calculator** option.

You can't use mouse actions in defining a macro. Every action must be done through the keyboard. You can define an action macro in either of two ways: by writing out the script yourself, and by capturing your keystrokes with Learn Mode.

Writing the Action Script. To write out the action script yourself, first figure out what keystrokes you must press to accomplish the operation from the keyboard. You might need to walk through the operation once or twice and write down the keystrokes you need (especially if you normally use a mouse).

Letter, number, and symbol keys can be typed as is, as with c and a in the above example. (Case doesn't matter unless you are inserting text strings.) Keys with multiple-character names, such as <altd> in the above example, need to be placed in angle brackets just like the trigger. You can write out the key name yourself, if you know it, or get Macro Editor to generate the key name by pressing F7 followed by the desired keystroke. This is true not only for Alt and Ctrl key combinations, but also for <enter>, <esc>, <home>, <up>, and so forth.

Learn Mode. Learn Mode captures your keystrokes for you. All you have to do is turn it on, go through the operation that you want to capture, then turn it off. Afterwards, you can open the macro file and edit the captured script if necessary.

To turn Learn Mode on, pull down the **Controls** menu, which is shown in Figure 12.13. Select **Learn Mode**. A check mark appears next to its name when it is on. Then you can remove the menu. Learn mode stays on, but it doesn't capture keystrokes until you tell it to start with Alt-+ for <begdef>.

Next, get to the place where you want to start capturing keystrokes. For

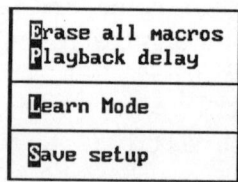

Figure 12.13   Controls Menu

example, you might want to get to a **Notepads** window. If Desktop is resident, you can exit Desktop and go to the DOS prompt or some other application.

When you are ready to begin capturing keystrokes, press Alt-+, which triggers Learn Mode and places `<begdef>` in the macro file. While capture is on, the cursor changes from an underscore into a complete rectangle. Next, press the trigger key, just as you do when defining a macro yourself. Don't press F7 in Learn Mode or it will capture F7 as the trigger. If you get no visible response to the trigger, you have done it right. If an alarm sounds, you have pressed a key that is invalid for the trigger, so press a different one. You can change it later by editing the macro file.

After the trigger is quietly accepted, begin the operation you want to capture, using the keyboard, not the mouse. Try to do it cleanly, but don't worry if you make some mistakes. You can edit the macro file later to clean out the mistakes, backspaces, escapes, and so on. When the operation is complete, press Alt-– to terminate capturing. The cursor will return to its normal shape. Learn Mode stays available so that you can capture another macro if desired. You must return to Macro Editor and specifically turn off Learn Mode to terminate it.

Most people have trouble using Learn Mode at first. After you turn it on, be sure to press a trigger first. Then work through the desired procedure slowly and deliberately. A beep tells you something is wrong; terminate the macro (Alt-–), start it again (Alt-+), and try again. After a while, Learn Mode becomes easy to use.

Macros you create through Learn Mode are always placed at the end of a file called LEARN.PRO, no matter which macro files are currently open or active. To view and edit a learned macro, open LEARN.PRO through Macro Editor. Look at the very end of the file for the most recently learned macro. You might have difficulty finding it because Macro Editor doesn't automatically start a new line when it records a macro. Once you have found it, place it on a new line, if necessary, for easier reading. Also, add some documentation. Finally, clean out any mistakes and make any other changes you wish. Be sure to activate LEARN.PRO so that you can test the macro. You can copy the macro to a different macro file using Clipboard if you wish.

Sample Macros

Suppose you want a macro to delete all BAK files in the current directory through PC Shell. At the keyboard, you would go through the following steps to delete BAK files:

1. Press F9 for the **Select** function.
2. Press Enter to get to the **Ext** field.

3. Type BAK.
4. Press Enter to select the files.
5. Press T to select the delete function.
6. Press A to select DELETE ALL.

The macro to automate this function with a trigger of Ctrl-B would be defined like this:

```
<begdef><ctrlb><f9><enter>BAK<enter>ta<enddef>
```

Suppose you want a macro to open Algebraic Calculator from another Desktop application and add 25 to the current total. At the keyboard, you would add 25 to Algebraic Calculator this way:

1. Press Alt-D to pull down the **Desktop** menu.
2. Type C for **Calculators**.
3. Type A for **Algebraic Calculator**.
4. Type + to place the current total on the tape.
5. Type 25 to add 25 to it.
6. Type = to total it.

The macro would be defined this way:

```
<begdef><ctrla><altd>ca+25=<enddef>
```

This macro works only from within Desktop and only if the **Desktop** menu is not already down. (If the menu is already down, the `<altd>` key selects the **Databases** option.) Later you will learn how to write this macro so that it works under any circumstances.

◆ Try It Out

1. Enter the two sample macros above. Try them out and correct them until they work well.
2. Create a macro to print a Notepads file, letting you type in the filename. Test it until it works.

Special Macro Functions

Macro Editor offers several special functions that you can use in your macros, as shown in Table 12.2. They are explained in the following sections.

Activating Desktop. Macros can get to the **Desktop** menu using the `<desk>` function, rather than Ctrl-Backspace and `<altd>`. `<Desk>` causes Desktop to be activated, if necessary, and the **Desktop** menu to be pulled down, if necessary. If Desktop is already activated, that portion of the function is ignored. If the **Desktop** menu is already pulled down, that portion of the function is ignored. Thus, by using `<desk>` at the beginning of the macro, you know where you are no matter where the macro was triggered from.

The calculator macro shown before could be revised so that it would work from anywhere. The definition would look like this:

```
<begdef><alta><desk>ca+25<enddef>
```

Date and Time. To cause the current date and time to be inserted when the macro runs, place `<date>` and `<time>` in your macro. For example, suppose you define a macro like this:

```
<begdef><ctrll>DuoTech, Inc.<enter>2122 S. Main Street
<enter>Fort Washington, Arizona 55555<enter>(205)
555-1212<enter><enter><tab><tab><tab><date><enddef>
```

When you execute the macro, the display will look something like this:

```
DuoTech, Inc.
2122 S. Main Street
Fort Washington, Arizona 55555
(205) 555-1212
5-10-92
```

Suppose you want to define a trigger that will insert the date and time at the cursor location. You might define this macro:

```
<begdef><ctrld><date>, <time><enddef>
```

Table 12.2 Macro Functions

`<desk>`	Activates Desktop and pulls down **Desktop** menu
`<date>`	Inserts today's date
`<time>`	Inserts current time
`<ffld>`	Accepts fixed-length field from keyboard
`<vfld>`	Accepts variable-length field from keyboard
`<cmd>d`	Pauses for specified amount of time

When you press Ctrl-D, you will see something like this at the cursor:

```
5-10-92, 4:15pm
```

Suppose you want to define a macro to build a file of telephone memos throughout the day. The macro would open the file in a Notepad window, position the cursor at the end of the file, enter the current date and time, start a new line, and terminate. You could then type the text for the telephone memo and close the file again. The macro would look like this:

```
<begdef><ctrlm><desk>nc:\daily\phonmemo.txt<enter>
<ctrlend><enter><date>, <time><enter><enddef>
```

Following the trigger, `<desk>` gets to the **Desktop** menu. The letter n selects the **Notepads** option. The filename `c:\daily\phonmemo.txt` will get typed in the **Filename** field, overlaying the default name. It's important to include the absolute path because you don't know what directory will be the default when the macro is triggered. The `<enter>` key causes the file to be selected and opened. The `<ctrlend>` key jumps the cursor to the end of the file. The `<enter>` key starts a new line since the cursor may be positioned at the end of a line of text. Then `<date>, <time>` causes the current date and time to be placed in the file. The final `<enter>` starts another new line. Then the macro quits and you can type the text of the telephone memo.

Entering Data. Two functions cause a macro to pause to receive data from the keyboard before continuing. The `<ffld>` function (fixed field) waits until a fixed number of characters have been typed. The `<vfld>` function (variable field) lets you enter a variable number of characters when the macro runs. To use `<ffld>`, code two `<ffld>` symbols; type any characters between them to create the size field you want to enter. For example, to define a three-character input field, you could use `<ffld>###<ffld>`, `<ffld>abc<ffld>`, or `<ffld>123<ffld>`. You must also code two `<vfld>` symbols to create a variable length field. Place exactly two characters between the symbols; any characters can be used, but there must be two of them.

When Desktop encounters `<ffld>` in a macro, it pauses and waits for keyboard input. It continues to wait until the required number of characters have been typed. (No prompt is displayed unless you write one into the macro.) As soon as the last character is typed, the macro continues to the function following the second `<ffld>`. It works much the same way with `<vfld>`, but input continues until you press Enter.

Suppose you are creating a macro to issue a FORMAT command at the DOS prompt. A drive name must be included in the command, and you want to enter the drive name when you invoke the macro. You could define the macro this way:

```
<begdef><ctrlf>FORMAT <ffld>1<ffld>:<enter><enddef>
```

When you press Ctrl-F, the word "FORMAT" followed by a space is displayed at the cursor. Then the system pauses. As soon as you type any character, a colon is displayed and an Enter key signal is generated. The overall effect at the DOS prompt is to enter a command of FORMAT *d:*, where *d* is the drive name entered from the keyboard.

You could adapt the telephone memo macro to enter a local phone number as a fixed-length field. The macro might look like this (new functions are shown in bold):

```
<begdef><ctrlm><desk>nc:\daily\phonmemo.txt<enter>
<ctrlend><enter><date>, <time><enter>Phone:
<ffld>999-9999<ffld><enter><enddef>
```

Now, after entering the date and time and starting a new line, the macro types "Phone:" followed by a space; then it waits for you to enter exactly eight characters. Then it starts another new line and quits.

Of course, if you need to enter some long distance phone numbers, some local phone numbers, some phone numbers with extensions, and so forth, then the phone number field should be variable length. You could define the macro this way:

```
<begdef><ctrlm><desk>nc:\daily\phonmemo.txt<enter>
<ctrlend><enter><date>, <time><enter>Phone: <vfld>
##<vfld> <enter><enddef>
```

Now the macro starts a new line, types "Phone:" followed by a space, and waits for you to enter data. It continues to accept and display whatever you type until you press Enter. The Enter key terminates the variable length field. Then the macro starts a new line and terminates.

You could go on to accept the text of the phone memo as another variable length field, then close the file automatically. The macro would look like this:

```
<begdef><ctrlm><desk>nc:\daily\phonmemo.txt<enter>
<ctrlend><enter><date>, <time><enter>Phone: <vfld>
##<vfld><enter><vfld>##<vfld><esc><enddef>
```

Notice that you could not start a new paragraph in this telephone memo.

As soon as you press Enter, the variable length field would be terminated and the file closed.

Macros that accept input data have a common problem. You cannot backspace and correct errors when entering data in them. If you mistype the phone number or any text in the phone memo, you cannot correct it until the macro ends. This feature limits the application of <ffld> and <vfld> in macros.

Time Delays. A macro executes very quickly unless you build some time delays into it. Some applications can't receive codes and data as fast as the macro transmits it. Or you might want the macro to pause long enough for you to read a message before continuing. Or you might want the macro to slow down while you are testing it so you can see the various menus and dialog boxes it goes through. After the macro works correctly, you can remove the time delays to let it run at normal speed.

There are two ways to build time delays into a macro. The first is to insert time delays at specific points in the macro using the <cmd> function. The other is to slow down the rate of macro execution using the **Playback Delay** option on the **Controls** menu.

The <cmd> function has this format:

<cmd>d*time*

The time is expressed as *hh:mm:ss.t*. You can omit zero leading sections and their colons, so that 5:10 is assumed to be 5 minutes and 10 seconds, while 7 is assumed to be 7 seconds. To build in a delay of 4 hours, you should use 4:0:0. The following macro opens a Notepad file called DEMO.TXT and displays it one page at a time for a total of three pages, pausing 10 seconds between pages:

```
<begdef><ctrld><desk>nc:\tooldemo\demo.txt<enter>
<cmd>d10<pgdn><cmd>d10<pgdn><cmd>d10<enddef>
```

To cut short a time delay, press Esc, which causes the macro to continue. To slow down the rate of macro execution, pull down the **Controls** menu and select **Playback Delay**. Figure 12.14 shows the dialog box that results. Set the

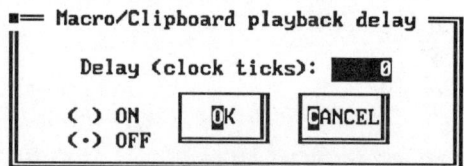

Figure 12.14   Macro Playback Delay Dialog Box

amount of delay between each character, key, or function in the **Delay (clock ticks)** field in 18ths of a second. In other words, for a full second delay between each item the macro executes, enter 18 into the field. If you find that too slow, try a half second delay by entering 9 in the field. Be sure to select ON to turn the function on.

As long as you leave the Playback Delay function on, all macros are affected. Turn it off or set it to zero when you don't need it any more.

Invoking Macros from Appointment Scheduler

You can automatically trigger a macro from your appointment schedule. This facility lets you do such things as automatically print the notes you need for a meeting, automatically dial a scheduled phone call, and do an automatic backup. In fact, if you set it up properly (and if nothing goes wrong), you could have your computer work all night for you. It could do an automatic backup at midnight, print a long job starting at 2:00 A.M., print your daily schedule at 4:00 A.M., send data to the East Coast at 6:00 A.M., and give you a wakeup call at 7:00 A.M.

You trigger a macro from your appointment schedule much the same as you do a note file or program. Following a vertical bar (|) in the **Note** field, type the name of the key that triggers the macro. For example, if the macro is triggered with `<ctrld>`, you would enter this in the **Note** field: `|<ctrld>`. If you put text before the note and select one of the alarm options, the text is displayed in an alarm box along with the message: PRESS "OK" TO EXECUTE ATTACHED MACRO. In this case, the macro doesn't start automatically; it waits until you select OK.

To use Autodialer to automatically place a call at 7:00 A.M., you would place the desired number in a Notepad file, then define a macro to open the file and start Autodialer. The macro would look like this:

```
<begdef><ctrlc><desk>nmyphone.txt<enter><ctrlo>
<enddef>
```

Printer Macros

You can enhance your output printed by any of the Desktop applications with boldface type, underlines, italics, and whatever other features your printer is capable of. Printers are controlled by special code sequences, usually beginning with Esc. Desktop includes printer macro files to support the Epson® FX-80, the IBM Proprinter®, the HP Laserjet™, and Panasonic printers. These macros will place the appropriate code sequences in your file. Activate the file that is appropriate for your printer. Then examine it to find out what triggers to use to turn bold face on and off, underlines on and off, and so on.

When you use a printer macro, Desktop inserts a phrase such as |BOLD ON| or |BOLD OFF| in your file. At print time, that phrase is replaced by the appropriate codes to control the printer. Don't try to use printer macros outside of Desktop applications; other printer programs will not replace the phrases with the correct set of codes.

The first macro in each file is a |SETUP| macro. Desktop automatically issues this macro whenever it prints a file. By default, it contains nothing, so it does nothing. You can insert codes into the macro to set up the printer the way you like it: select a font, turn on near letter quality printing, and so forth. Insert the codes after |SETUP| and before <enddef>. Examine the other macros in the file and your printer manual to find out what codes to use.

If your printer isn't included in the files provided by Desktop, you may be able to define your own macros, using one of the provided files as a guide to the format of the macro definitions. Check your printer manual and/or contact the manufacturer to find out what codes you can use.

Nested Macros

You can call another macro from within a macro; simply include the trigger in the macro script. In fact, a macro can call itself. For example, because the following macro calls itself, it repeats until you press Esc:

    <begdef><altd><pgdn><altd><enddef>

The macro pages through a file until Esc is pressed.

✧ Try It Out

1. Try out some of the macros in this section.
2. Try writing a macro to open a Notepad file named PRACTICE.TXT and inserting the date and time. Make the macro work from anywhere inside or outside Desktop.
3. Try out any printer macros that pertain to your printer.

Now that you know how to use Desktop to create and edit numerous files, you'll find the programs in the next section of this book useful for keeping your disks in good shape.

Section IV

Disk Management and Recovery

Chapter 13 | *Formatting and Rebuilding Disks*

New disks must be formatted before they can be used. You can also format disks containing data for reuse. PC Tools supplies a format program that differs from the standard DOS format program. You can still use the DOS program when necessary. A corresponding program can be used to recover data from formatted disks. In this chapter, you'll learn to:

- Format data and bootable diskettes
- Format hard disks
- Format from the **Applications** menu
- Use Mirror to save system information
- Use Mirror for delete tracking
- Use Rebuild to recover a formatted disk
- Use Diskfix to repair a damaged disk

Background Information

PC Tools provides several programs that help you prepare, maintain, and rebuild your disks. The most common of these programs formats disks in various ways. Each disk must be initialized by a format program before it can be used. The installation procedure renames files so that the FORMAT command runs PC Format, which uses different techniques to initialize disks.

The MIRROR program keeps track of how a root directory is structured; it keeps a record of the files and subdirectories defined in the root directory. The information Mirror saves can be used to rebuild the disk if necessary. Another feature of Mirror keeps track of deleted files so they can be undeleted easily using the delete tracking (DEL TRACK) method.

The REBUILD program is used only in a real crisis. It lets you reconstruct the contents of a disk after it has been accidentally reformatted or erased. Rebuild works best if the disk has been initialized with PC Format and if Mirror recently saved the first level of disk entries.

You'll learn to use all three programs in this chapter.

Formatting Disks

Every disk you use must be formatted to prepare it to store data and to be accessed by programs. If you have installed PC Tools on your hard disk, it has evidently been formatted at some point. If you have been using diskettes, they have been formatted. New hard disks and diskettes must be formatted before they can be used.

You would reformat a hard disk only under special circumstances. For example, you might have a disk crash, you might start getting lots of read errors for bad sectors, or you might want to use a different version of DOS. You can reformat diskettes for many reasons. You might want to clean off old data to reuse the diskettes. If they are fairly old, you want to make sure they don't have any bad sectors. Perhaps they have been formatted to a lesser density than they are capable of, and you want them to hold more.

During PC Shell Installation

The PC Shell formatting program works somewhat differently from the DOS formatting program. The differences allow more types of formatting and make it possible to recover data from an inadvertently formatted disk. If you use one of the PC Shell formatting options, you can even format a disk without destroying any of the data on it. You can also do a quick format that leaves the disk formatted but usable in a very short time.

When PC Shell is installed, PC Setup replaces the DOS FORMAT program with one named PCFORMAT.COM. The DOS FORMAT.COM program in the root directory or in the /DOS subdirectory is renamed as FORMAT!.COM; you can still use it by that name. A batch file named FORMAT.BAT is placed in the PC Tools subdirectory. This file calls the PCFORMAT program, passing any parameters to it. You can start the program from the shell or by using the PCFORMAT or FORMAT command. If you really want to use the DOS program, use FORMAT! as the command.

Methods of Formatting Disks through PCFORMAT

PC Shell offers several ways to format diskettes and hard disks through PC Tools. You can process diskettes through commands on the **Disk** menu. Or you can select the **PCFormat** option on the **Applications** menu. If you select the PCFORMAT.COM file in the PC Tools directory, you can format any disk or diskette if you enter the appropriate parameters in the resulting dialog box. Alternatively, you can enter the PCFORMAT command at the DOS command prompt with appropriate parameters. You'll learn to use all these methods in the following sections.

Making a Data Diskette from the Disk Menu

You can format diskettes from within the shell. You might want to do this when you are using some other program and need a newly formatted disk. If PC Shell is resident, you can hotkey into it, format the diskette, hotkey back into the other program, and use the diskette. (If the shell isn't resident, you might just as well format the disk with the FORMAT command at the prompt.) Once a data disk is formatted, you can also ask PC Shell to make it bootable; that is, you can have the diskette made into a system diskette once you have formatted it to hold data.

Just pull down the **Disk** menu and select the **Format Data Disk** option. You'll see a dialog box that lets you select the drive to format; all your diskette drives will be listed. If you have only one drive, you'll see A: and B:, both of which refer to the same drive. After you make your selection, you'll see a **Disk Initialization** dialog box in which you can select the format for the diskette. PC Shell lists the options available for the type of diskette drive you selected. Figure 13.1 shows the result for a 5.25" drive.

You have to know the type of drive you have. If you have a drive that can handle a 1.2M diskette, it can handle all the others as well. If your drive is a standard double-sided 360K drive, it can handle all the options listed above it in the dialog box too. You probably won't want to use the first three choices, unless you are preparing a diskette for use on a lesser system. If you have a 3.5" drive, you'll be given choices that correspond to that type of diskette.

After you select the type of diskette you want to format and choose

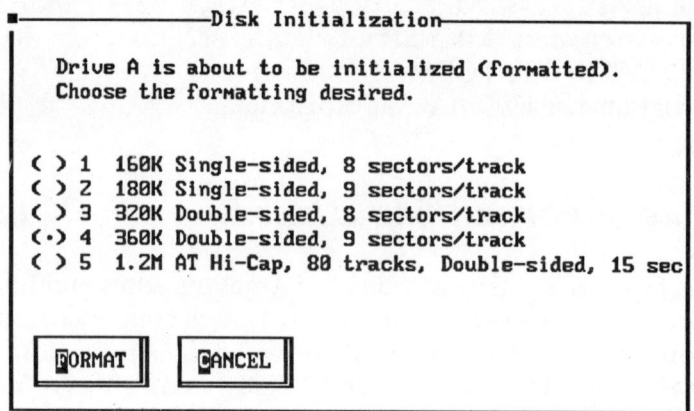

Figure 13.1   Disk Initialization Dialog Box

FORMAT, PC Shell begins formatting the diskette immediately if it is available. You'll be prompted to insert a diskette if there isn't one present. You'll see a dialog box in which you can track the progress. Figure 13.2 shows the display for a 1.2M diskette. The letters "F" for format and "V" for verify appear briefly at each location. When the track is ready, a period appears in the location. You can interrupt the formatting at any time, but the disk will be pretty much unusable if you do.

When the formatting is complete, you'll be prompted to enter the volume name. You can type up to 11 characters, just as when you use the **Rename volume** option of the **Disk** menu. Then you'll be asked if you want to make

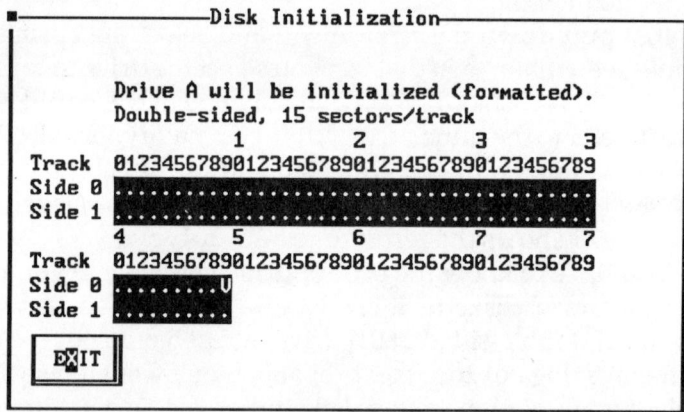

Figure 13.2   Disk Initialization in Progress

the disk bootable. Selecting BOOTABLE here doesn't really complete the process; you'll still have to copy COMMAND.COM to the disk. After you deal with that, you'll be shown details about the diskette—how much disk space is available, how much of the diskette, if any, is in bad sectors, and what files are placed on the diskette.

Making a System Diskette

If you want to be able to boot your system from a diskette, you want to make a system diskette. If you respond appropriately during the format process, PC Shell allocates space for system files at the beginning of the diskette. Then it copies two required hidden files to it. The disk is not yet bootable, however, since it doesn't have the COMMAND.COM file on it. You can put it there in two different ways. One is to copy it from the root directory using the standard file copy procedure. The other is to select **Make System Disk** on the **Disk** menu after making sure the target drive isn't current. When asked, select the drive containing the diskette. Then PC Shell proceeds to copy all three files that are required to make a diskette bootable. This option has the same effect no matter what you responded when asked if PC Shell should make the disk bootable.

If the diskette already has other files placed on it, you can still select **Make System Disk**, but it might not work. PC Shell has to rearrange the directory and file allocation table to make sure the two required hidden SYS files are in the first two slots in the directory. It does this just fine if you use the SYS command at the DOS command prompt, but the **Make System Disk** option occasionally has problems with in-use diskettes within the shell.

Recovering from Format

Normal diskette formatting with PCFORMAT doesn't totally destroy the diskette. Most of the data is still there. You can use the REBUILD utility to recover most or all of the files that were previously on the diskette. REBUILD is covered later in this chapter.

Formatting from the Applications Menu

If you want to format a diskette for drive A:, you can use the **PCFormat** option of the **Applications** menu. You'll see a display much like the one in Figure 13.3. PC Format tells you that it is about to format the diskette in drive A: as a data disk; it gives you the parameters of the drive so you know what form of diskette will result. You don't get to enter or select any options here, but you can cancel the operation with Ctrl-C. For example, if you want to format a 360K diskette in a 1.2M drive, the application tries to format it to match the drive and hold 1.2M. You might press Ctrl-C and format the diskette from the **Disk** menu instead, since you can select the format from the dialog box shown earlier in Figure 13.1. If you press Enter and the diskette contains any data, you'll be reminded that the process will destroy it. You'll have to type "YES" (all three letters) to reassure PC Format that you want to continue before it will format the diskette.

If you examine the **Modify Applications List** dialog box for the **PCFormat** application by selecting **5Edit** while the menu is pulled down, you can see a single run parameter, A:. You can modify the format to apply to a different drive or to use nondefault formatting, using any of the options covered in the next section. PC Format, as mentioned earlier, is used instead of the DOS FORMAT command. If you used a nondefault directory for your PC Tools files, you'll have to change the **Initial Directory** and **Execute Path** fields to reflect the actual PCFORMAT.COM location.

When you use **PCFormat** from the **Applications** menu, the process keeps you updated in a different way from the **Disk** menu process. The track, cylinder, and percentage of disk completed are continually updated onscreen. After the diskette is completely formatted, you'll be prompted for a volume name, then shown diskette information and asked if you want to format another diskette. If you respond with anything except "Y", you'll be returned to the shell.

If you regularly format different types of diskette drives, you might want to install an option on the **Applications** menu for each one. Suppose your A: drive supports a 1.2M 5.25" diskette and the B: drive supports a 1.44M 3.5" diskette. You might edit the **PCFormat** application so its title is **PC^Format A:**. Then create a new application called **PCFormat ^B:**, so that you can press "B" to select it. Use all the same values as in the other application, but type "B:" in the **Run Parameter(s)** field. Now you have two PC Format applications, one for each diskette drive. If you want to format bootable diskettes with a single selection, you could create an additional application for that.

```
PC Tools Disk Formatter v6
Copyright 1987-90 by Central Point Software, Inc.  All rights reserved.

Will format drive A:   (physical # 00h, type= 1.2M 5.25-inch)

Formatting 15 sectors, 80 cylinders, 2 sides.
Press Enter when ready...
```

Figure 13.3   Using the PC Format Application

✧ Try It Out

1. Format a data diskette in your A: drive using the **Disk** menu.
2. Convert the diskette into a system disk using the **Disk** menu.
3. If you ever use a different format or diskette drive, reformat the diskette using those parameters.
4. Examine the **Modify Application List** dialog box for the **PCFormat** application. Change it if your requirements warrant.

Formatting from the File List

You can run PCFORMAT from the file list for the PC Tools directory by double clicking on the filename PCFORMAT.COM or by selecting it and choosing **Run** from the **File** menu or pressing Ctrl-Enter. You'll see the standard dialog box that prompts you for run time parameters. If you type "A:", the effect will be exactly the same as selecting **PCFormat** from the **Applications** menu. You could type B: or E:, depending on what other drives you have. If you don't enter at least the drive name, you are in danger of reformatting your hard disk, which is generally the default. You'll be prompted heavily before this occurs, however.

You can also enter parameters to control how the format is performed. All the parameters explained in the next section are valid in the **Run Parameter(s)** field as well.

Formatting from the Command Prompt

You can use the FORMAT or PCFORMAT command at the command prompt to format a disk through the PC Format program. If you are working from the DOS command prompt within PC Shell, don't format the disk that contains the PC Tools directory.

In its pure form, the PC Format program reads each track to see if it has been formatted and if it contains any errors. If no read errors occur and the track has been formatted in the past, it is okay, so PC Format goes on to the next track. If the track has never been used, PC Format formats it. If it encounters a read error, PC Format reads what data it can from the track, reformats the track, then rewrites the data it read.

PC Format clears the root directory and writes an empty file allocation table (FAT) so the diskette can be reused as a clear disk. The root directory is cleared in such a way that it can be recovered with the REBUILD command. All that is lost is the FAT. Once the root directory is restored with Rebuild, you can recreate the FAT from remaining data on the disk if there wasn't any fragmentation. If the disk was compressed recently before formatting, recovery is more likely to be successful.

There are many parameters you can use in the PCFORMAT command to specify formatting details; the most useful ones are shown in Table 13.1. All are applicable to diskettes, but only a few to hard disks. You probably won't format hard disks very often, if you're lucky.

Diskette Parameters. When you enter a FORMAT or PCFORMAT command at the command prompt, you can include parameters. The parameters can also be included in the **Modify Applications List** dialog box to specify how the application should be performed. You should include at least the drive to be formatted. If you omit the drive, PC Format uses the current drive. If you want to format your primary hard disk (the one you boot from), you should have the PCFORMAT.COM program on a system diskette ready for use.

Each parameter except for the drive name must be preceded by a slash. You don't have to separate them with spaces, but you may if you wish.

Several parameters let you specify the type of diskette to be formatted. You can use the /F:*nnn* parameter to request a diskette formatted to hold a specific number of kilobytes. In a 5.25" drive, you can use 160, 180, 320, 360, or 1200. PCFORMAT A:/F:360 requests a diskette formatted to hold 360K prepared in the A: drive; this prepares a double-sided double-density diskette. In a 3.25" drive, you can use 720 or 1440. You shouldn't have to use 1200 or 1440, since the type of format defaults to the density of the drive itself, and you can't format to a greater density than the drive allows for. Additional parameters are available for you to get more specific with the format type, but the /F: parameter should meet your density needs.

If you want the diskette to be bootable, include the /S parameter. When you use a command such as PCFORMAT A: /S, the disk is formatted, then made bootable. In the process of making it bootable, PC Format copies the

Table 13.1   PC Format Parameters

/F:*nnn*	Specify number of kilobytes
/F	Full format (for disks with read errors)
/S	Make disk bootable
/V	Ask for volume label
/Q	Quick reformat
/R	Reformat each track (very slow)
/P	Print format messages
/DESTROY	Format and destroy all data
/TEST	Show effect without actual formatting

system files to it, including two hidden files and COMMAND.COM, so that you can place the diskette in drive A: and boot or reboot. You will have to add any CONFIG.SYS and AUTOEXEC.BAT files you want to use. (See your DOS manual for details.)

Early versions of DOS FORMAT (before 3.3) did not automatically allow for a volume label on a disk being formatted. If the process does not automatically ask you for a volume name, you can use the /V parameter to tell it to ask you for one. If you format through the **Disk** menu **Format Data Disk** option, you'll be prompted to enter a volume label. You can always add a volume label later with the **Rename Volume** option.

You can request special effects with several additional parameters; these effects are not available through standard DOS formatting. If you've been having problems with a diskette, you may want to make sure each track is fully formatted. In that case, use the /F parameter; don't include a number with this one. You'll get a full format. PC Format will read, format, then rewrite each track. This results in a slower formatting process, but it has the effect of cleaning up some rare disk read problems, such as marginal sector IDs. In the formatting process, the FAT is cleared. You can still recover the data on the diskette later using the REBUILD command before you have placed other data on the diskette. PCFORMAT B: /F requests a full format of the diskette in drive B:. PCFORMAT A: /F:360 /F requests a full format of a double-sided 360K diskette in drive A:.

If you want to reformat the disk quickly, you can use the /Q parameter. A diskette that has been in use and hasn't been giving any trouble probably doesn't need a full format. When you use the /Q parameter, PC Format completely erases the root directory and FAT but doesn't do a scan of the tracks. PCFORMAT A: /Q requests a quick reformat of the diskette in drive A:, using the maximum density supported by the drive.

On the other hand, if you want to force a thorough format of every track on the disk while leaving all the data, the FAT, and the directory structure intact, you can use the /R parameter; you must use the /F: parameter as well. This leaves all the data and values available, while clearing up any marginal sector ID's. The result is a very slow formatting, since all the data must be rewritten. The type of errors cured by this method are very rare, but may occur occasionally. Since it leaves the disk fully readable and usable with the existing data, it may come in handy if your system can't read a diskette that contains valuable data.

If you want progress information and messages sent to the screen during formatting to be printed as well, include the /P parameter. All data is automatically directed to your computer's default printer.

As you've seen, most uses of PC Format do not actually get rid of data on the disk. If you want to make sure no trace of the former data is left for security reasons, use the /DESTROY parameter. The diskette will be formatted and there is no possibility of recovery of any of the data.

If you want to see the effect of formatting a diskette without actually performing the operation, use the /TEST parameter. This simulates the format without actually writing to disk. You might use this option to find out if formatting will locate any bad sectors.

Hard Disk Parameters. When you use PC Format to format a hard disk, you can use only a few parameters. The PC Format program must be on a different drive from the one you are formatting, so you must specify the drive to be formatted in the command. You can include the /S parameter to make it bootable if you are formatting your primary hard drive. You can include the /V parameter if the DOS version you use is prior to 3.3. You can use /P to print messages on the default printer. And you can use /Q to do a quick reformat that erases the FAT and root directory only. Normally, if you are reformatting your hard disk, you will want a standard format, so you won't include /Q. As long as all your data is backed up and about to be made difficult to recover, you might as well take the time to do a thorough format. If you want to check out your command first, you can use the /TEST parameter to simulate the operation before trying it for real.

✧ Try It Out

1. Try a quick format of a diskette.
2. Create a system diskette with full format.
3. Take a diskette that contains data, and do a format with /F. See if you can access data after formatting it with /F.

The MIRROR Program

The MIRROR program keeps a copy of the FAT and root directory in a read-only file. If you have used Mirror, rebuilding the disk can be easier and more effective. In general, you can't use Mirror with diskettes. Mirror has other effects as well. It maintains a record of files deleted, including which clusters are allocated to them; this is used in the Delete Tracking method of undeleting files. Mirror can also be used to set up a permanent record of the partition structure of the hard disk in case you have to reconstruct it from scratch.

If you do much DOS work outside of PC Tools, you'll want to run Mirror regularly to keep the records up to date. During installation of PC Tools, the MIRROR command was probably placed in your AUTOEXEC.BAT file so that it runs automatically when you start up your system.

The MIRROR command can have several different effects. In its basic form, it makes a copy of the system area on the default or specified drive. You can tell it to maintain delete tracking for any disks. Or you can tell it to save the partition information.

Copying the System Area

When you use the MIRROR command with no parameters or with just a drive name, as in MIRROR C:, it makes a copy of the system area, including the root directory, the FAT, and the boot record, in a file called MIRROR.FIL in the root directory of the affected drive. By default, it saves two versions, renaming the previous one to MIRROR.BAK and using MIRROR.FIL for the most recent. If you want to keep only the latest, you can use the /1 parameter as well; you would do this only if you have a real space crunch on your disk. Any changes to the root directory made after the last running of Mirror may be lost if the disk crashes.

The security of having two versions is useful if you have problems with your system, then reboot. During the reboot procedure, Mirror runs again and replaces the former values. If you want to fall back to the status before the problem occurred, you can use the older version of the Mirror file.

You can't use Mirror with diskettes, since they are removable. The system would get confused by changed diskettes. You can use it for all your hard disks, however. If the command in your AUTOEXEC.BAT file has MIRROR C:, you can change it to MIRROR C: D: if you have two hard disk partitions.

Establishing Delete Tracking

You can request delete tracking for any of your hard disks through Mirror. When you do, a small resident program is started that intercepts all delete commands in the shell and in DOS and records the information in a root directory file named PCTRACKR.DEL. From this information, the undelete function can reestablish files with all their clusters intact if no clusters have been assigned to other files. If you use MIRROR C: /TC, the system information on drive C: is saved and the delete tracking program is established to track files deleted from drive C:. The command MIRROR C: D: /TC /TD saves system information and tracks deletions from two hard drives. You can't use delete tracking for diskettes.

Delete tracking simplifies undeletion and has no real negative aspects, since the resident program takes very little memory. If you compress a disk, however, all the delete tracking is invalidated, since clusters have changed. Compressing a disk includes erasing any delete-tracking files. A Mirror file is invalid after compression as well. However, rebooting after compression sets up a valid Mirror file unless you have removed the MIRROR command from your AUTOEXEC.BAT file.

Saving Partition Information

If your hard disk contains more than one logical partition, you can use Mirror to save the partition information on a diskette; you'll need it if you ever try to rebuild the disk. Use the command MIRROR /PARTN, insert a diskette that you will save in drive A:, and let it run. The partitioning information will be stored on the diskette in PARTNSAV.FIL. Save the diskette with your original PC Tools diskettes in the unlikely event you will need it.

Running MIRROR Other Times

If you use your system heavily, you might want to run Mirror more often than just at boot time. You can do this from the command prompt or from the **Applications** menu. You can also cause it to run automatically by creating batch files to run any applications that involve heavy file use. For example, suppose you use WordPerfect as your word processor and do most of your document file processing through it. You generally start the program with WP. You can create an ASCII file called WPERF.BAT that contains these commands:

```
WP
MIRROR C: D:
```

Then add "WordPerfect" to your **Applications** menu. For the program, use WPERF.BAT instead of WP.EXE. When you select the application, you'll enter WordPerfect as usual. But when you leave it, Mirror will run automatically (you don't have to start delete tracking again) and you'll be prompted to press a key or click to return to the shell.

✧ Try It Out

1. Examine the MIRROR command in your AUTOEXEC.BAT file.
2. If the MIRROR command doesn't specify all your hard disks for saving

system information and delete tracking, add the parameters needed. Reboot after making the change.
3. Run MIRROR from the **Applications** menu to see the effect.

The REBUILD Program

The REBUILD program is one of those programs you hope and expect never to use. It helps you recover from an accidental erasure or reformat of a disk. Rebuild restores the root directory and the FAT using the latest Mirror file, or the earlier one if you request it. If there is no Mirror file, Rebuild uses other methods depending on how the disk was formatted. If you used PC Format (with any parameters except /DESTROY) on the disk, Rebuild can reconstruct the FAT and root directory files. You can even rebuild a diskette that didn't have Mirror files as long as you used the PC Shell format program.

Be sure not to try any other programs between the formatting and the attempt to rebuild a disk. If you use the DOS FDISK program on your hard disk, for example, you won't be able to rebuild it even if FDISK fails. Don't try searching sectors on the disk. Just grit your teeth and try Rebuild.

If you formatted the disk with the DOS FORMAT command, Rebuild can probably identify the first level subdirectories, but the files in the root directory are gone. The subdirectories won't have their original names, but you can use undelete on them to restore files. Once you've done this, you'll be sure to put Mirror in your AUTOEXEC.BAT file.

You need a separate system diskette containing the REBUILD.COM program in order to restore a hard disk after accidental formatting.

Rebuilding a Disk after MIRROR

If you have been using Mirror regularly, rebuilding a hard disk after inadvertent formatting is straightforward. Boot with the system diskette that contains the REBUILD program. At the command prompt type REBUILD C:. You can add the J parameter to see the possibilities without actually rebuilding or destroying anything. You'll see a message with the date of the last Mirror file. If you want to continue, accept it. If not, you'll be offered an earlier Mirror file if there is one. If you reject that as well, you'll have a chance to request that the disk be rebuilt anyway.

Once you have accepted one of the Mirror files, Rebuild proceeds to search the disk directly to restore the subdirectories, files, and data. When it is finished, you'll be prompted to reboot.

Rebuilding a Disk with No Mirror Files

If Rebuild doesn't find any mirror files, you can try again from disk data when offered that choice. Rebuild tries to recreate what it can. It can recover most of the files and data if you formatted the disk using PC Format. If it doesn't work, try running PC Format and trying Rebuild again.

You can use Rebuild on any disk that has been formatted. REBUILD A: can be used if you have formatted a diskette by mistake. REBUILD B: performs the process on the diskette in drive B:. If the diskette was formatted with PC Format without the /DESTROY parameter, it should all be recoverable.

If you used a DOS format you won't get any of your root directory files back, no matter what drive you are trying to rebuild. You should get first level subdirectories, but they won't have their original names since they were destroyed in the format process. You can then use undelete to restore files in those subdirectories.

REBUILD Parameters

The REBUILD command has options similar to some of those available for the PCFORMAT command. You must name the drive to be rebuilt. You can use /P to cause messages and reports to be sent to the printer. You can use /L to cause all files and directories to be listed to the screen as they are located. You can use /? to see a help screen; if you do this, DOS won't try to rebuild the disk until you enter the command again. You can use /TEST to see what would be the effect without actually rebuilding the disk. You might do this if you want to see whether it would work better with one Mirror file than the other or if you suspect the Mirror files have been corrupted.

While Rebuild is rebuilding files, you may be prompted for input. If the file was fragmented, Rebuild may not know which cluster to use next. You'll be asked to decide whether the file should be truncated or deleted. If you choose truncated, you'll have at least the first part of the file. If you choose deleted, you'll be able to try to undelete it manually and restore more of the file. Any file you aren't asked about is probably fine. The only way to tell for sure is to run programs and examine data files to see if they do work.

✧ Try It Out

1. Take or create a diskette that has a few root directory files and a few subdirectories. Place it in drive A: and use PC Format with any parameters except /DESTROY.

2. Check its file list on the screen, then exit the shell.
3. Rebuild the diskette in drive A:
4. Check its file list on the screen.

Repairing a Disk

The PC Tools package includes a stand-alone program called DISKFIX.EXE that you can use to repair many disk problems on both hard and floppy disks. In fact, if you use it regularly, you can even prevent many disk problems. Diskfix can often read sectors that DOS has trouble with and thus it can recover more data. And it can lock out bad sectors it does find so that no more data is stored there.

Starting Diskfix

To start Diskfix, type DISKFIX at the DOS prompt. (You can't run this through the **Applications** menu). When the program starts, it checks the hardware for the drive configuration. Before allowing any specific disk fixing, Diskfix checks the BIOS, the CMOS, the partition table, and logical boot sector data.

Handling Errors

If Diskfix detects any problems during the initial phase, you'll see an error dialog box like the one shown in Figure 13.4, with information about the detected error. Every error dialog box you'll see in Diskfix has much the same

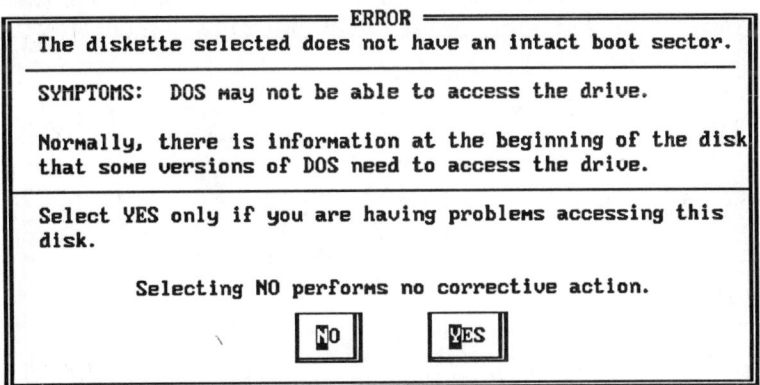

Figure 13.4   Diskfix Error Dialog Box

structure. The upper part of the dialog box describes the problem. The central part gives symptoms and possible effects of the problem, and the lower part gives you an opportunity to have Diskfix attempt to fix the problem (YES) or to bypass it (NO).

The Diskfix Main Menu

At the end of the equipment checking phase, Diskfix asks you if you want to repair a disk now. If you respond YES, you'll go immediately to that part of the program. If you respond NO, you'll see the Diskfix Main Menu, shown in Figure 13.5.

Your choices are to fix a disk, do a surface scan of a disk looking for potential errors (this is a subset of fixing a disk), revitalize a floppy that has been experiencing read errors, and exit to DOS.

Fixing a Disk

The Diskfix program goes through a series of steps in checking and fixing a disk. The first step is to select the disk. Diskfix displays a dialog box containing a list of the drives it identified. If you want to fix a floppy, insert the diskette before selecting the drive. Once the selection is made, Diskfix displays a status box like the one shown in Figure 13.6 and starts analyzing the first item on the list. If it doesn't encounter any problems, Diskfix doesn't pause until it reaches the **Media Surface** item.

If any problems are detected, you are notified in an error dialog box; you can have Diskfix try to fix any problems.

Cross-linked files occur when a particular cluster is identified as belonging to more than one file. A problem like this must be fixed before Diskfix can continue. Lost clusters occur when clusters are marked as allocated but the

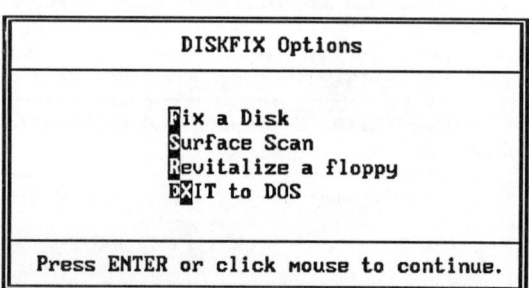

Figure 13.5   Diskfix Main Menu

```
            Status of Drive A: Analysis

         Areas tested:              Result:

       √  DOS Boot Sector             Ok
       √  Media Descriptors           Ok
       √  File Allocation Tables      Ok
       √  Directory Structure         Ok
       √  Cross Linked Files          Ok
       √  Lost Clusters               Ok
          Media Surface

          Select CONTINUE or press ENTER.
                    [CONTINUE]
```

Figure 13.6   Diskfix Status Dialog Box

FAT doesn't show them as assigned to a particular file. If you ask Diskfix to recover these, lost cluster groups will be given names such as PCT00000.FIX, PCT00001.FIX, and so forth. You can examine them later under the viewer to see if the data must be saved or deleted.

If Diskfix reaches the bottom item in the status box, it displays the dialog box shown in Figure 13.7. It provides information about how you can look for any missing data, if that is your problem. If you don't have a special reason, don't do this, since it may find directories that have been erased for perfectly legitimate reasons.

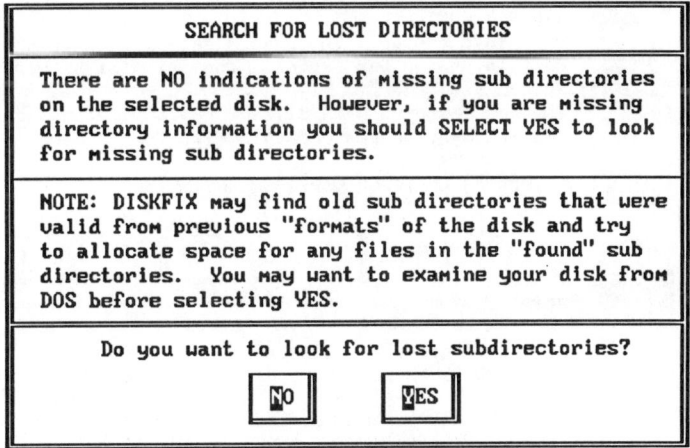

Figure 13.7   Search for Lost Directories Dialog Box

Media Surface Scan

The media surface analysis is the same procedure as the **Surface Scan** you can select from the Diskfix main menu. Each cluster is checked for errors. You'll see a visual display of the disk on the screen, with indicators of what is stored in each cluster. As the analysis continues, the display keeps you updated on the progress. If a read error is detected, a dialog box like the one in Figure 13.8 appears, overlaying the visual display. You'll know what file, if any, contains the sector and you'll see advice about what to do. If you choose to LOCK the sector, Diskfix copies all the data in the involved cluster to another location on the disk, using dashes for data that it couldn't read from the affected sector. The cluster is blocked out in the FAT, and an X then appears in the locked position in the visual display.

If you select CONTINUE, the surface scan continues without solving the encountered problem. CANCEL stops the process and returns you to the Diskfix Main Menu.

Revitalizing a Floppy Disk

Sometimes a floppy diskette may have occasional read errors and other erratic problems that aren't easily detected. You can ask Diskfix to revitalize such a

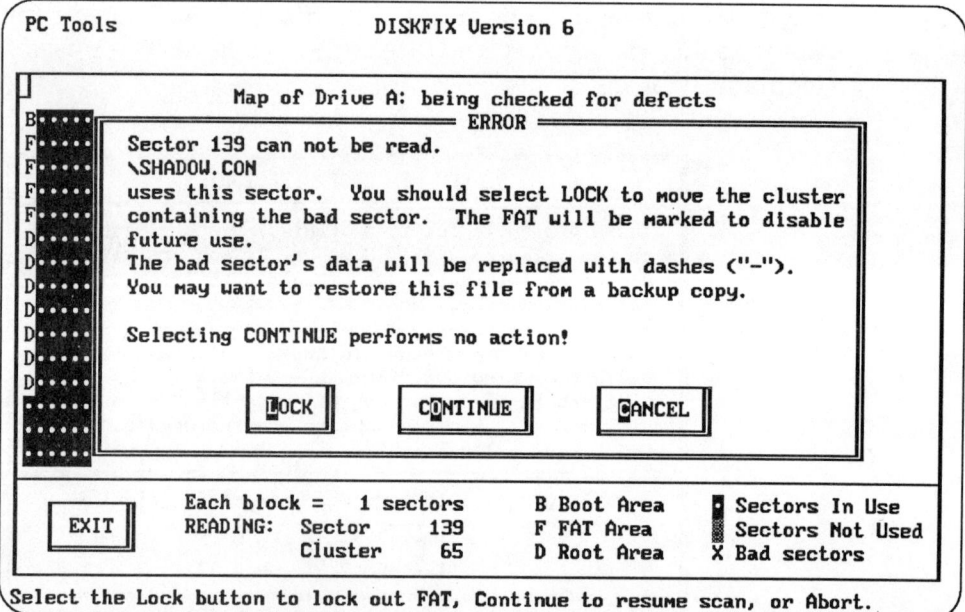

Figure 13.8   Media Error Dialog Box

diskette. It then reads data from tracks into memory, reformats those tracks, and rewrites the data. Any major errors are detected during the formatting process and the clusters are blocked out. After they have been revitalized, most diskettes will not encounter any more problems.

✧ *Try it Out*

1. Exit PC Shell and get to the DOS prompt. Start Diskfix.
2. When asked, choose not to repair a disk immediately.
3. From the Diskfix Main Menu, choose to repair a disk. Insert an old, well-used diskette into drive A: and select it.
4. Let Diskfix repair any errors it finds. When the process is complete, try revitalizing the diskette.

Once you have tried to rebuild a disk, especially without Mirror, you'll be more convinced of the virtues of a good backup system. That is covered in the next chapter.

Chapter 14 | Backing Up Files

Working with computers requires that you regularly back up data on your hard disk in case of disaster. With luck, you'll never have to use the backup diskettes. But just in case, this chapter shows you how to handle the following operations:

- Configure PC Backup
- Set options for a complete backup
- Select directories and files for a partial backup
- Select files by attributes, date and time, or extension
- Create a complete or partial backup
- Compare backed up files to verify accuracy
- Restore data completely or in part from backup diskettes
- Identify type of information on a backup diskette

Backup Concepts

No computer disk is 100 percent reliable. You'll want to back up files from the hard disk regularly so that you have a copy if anything goes wrong with your hard disk or the controlling hardware or software. Most people who have used hard disks for a few years have experienced some sort of problem. It might be a head crash or disk controller problem. It might be a virus or other software problem. It might even be a fire, hurricane, or earthquake. But it makes data on the hard disk inaccessible, at least temporarily. The best solution is to have a safely stored backup of your files. Then you can restore the files from your backups to the same or another hard disk.

Backup Decisions

There are several methods of backing up hard disks. Your DOS software includes programs called BACKUP and RESTORE that you can use to make backup copies and restore them if necessary. But these DOS programs have some built-in limitations. Other commercial software can also be purchased.

PC Tools includes a stand-alone program named PCBACKUP.EXE that lets you create backups very easily and restore files if necessary. It includes more options and has more reliability than does the equivalent DOS software. For example, PC Backup has several built-in features to speed up the process. It can read files from the hard disk at the same time it writes to diskette. It can use a special option board if it is installed. It can compress files during backup to save space and time. It even gives you a time and space estimate in advance. PC Backup lets you specify exactly which files you want backed up as well as which ones you want to ignore.

One major decision you have to make, and stick to, is which software you will use. The PC Backup system is more flexible and reliable than the DOS method, but its output is not compatible. If you back up files using PC Backup, you must restore them with the same version of PC Backup. You can't use the DOS RESTORE command or an earlier version of PC Backup to interpret the backed up output. If you try to restore files using an earlier version of PC Backup, it creates a new directory named OLDPCT and stores the files there.

Result of Backup

Backing up to diskette results in a set of diskettes containing data. The directory of each shows a single file, PCBACKUP.*nnn*, with 001 as the first diskette of the set. The final diskette of a set of seven would contain a directory entry for PCBACKUP.007; there is no special indication that it is the last diskette. The last diskette of a set contains summary information about the entire backup set, including the complete path, size, and date of each file backed up. It also has information about which diskette in the set contains each file. PC Backup uses this information to compare or restore files later.

You can also back up files to other media; most of the procedure is the same. Special considerations for using tape backups are included later in this chapter. If you use another hard drive, you can specify that when you configure PC Backup.

You can have PC Backup store the history of the backup set in a file on the hard disk as well. If the history is saved, PC Backup generates a file containing all the same information as in the history component of the last diskette and stores it in the directory where the PCBACKUP program is stored. The filename takes the form *hyymmdda*.DIR, where *h* indicates the hard disk being backed up, *yymmdd* gives the date with the year first, and *a* indicates the backup sequence number on that day. The file named C921201B.DIR is a history file of the second backup of drive C prepared on December 1, 1992.

You can also request a report of the backup, containing much of the same information as the history file. If the report is printed, it appears on your default printer after the backup is complete. If it is sent to disk, the file is named in the form *hyymmdda*.RPT and stored in the same directory as the PCBACKUP program.

Starting PC Backup

When you select **PC Backup** from the **Applications** menu or type PCBACKUP at the command prompt for the first time, you have to configure it and set your chosen defaults.

Configuring PC Backup

The first time PC Backup is started, you see a **Welcome** dialog box that tells you the program is not yet configured. This box explains that the information you provide is used to configure PC Backup, then stored in a file called PCBACKUP.CFG in the same directory as PC Backup. You can change the configuration file through PC Backup later if appropriate. Once you select CONTINUE to remove the **Welcome** dialog box, you see a dialog box like the one shown in Figure 14.1. In this dialog box, you specify the type of diskette drives you have available.

Next, you'll have to select the drive and media for the output. The resulting dialog box is shown in Figure 14.2. You can select one media type for output. The diskette density can be less than in the drive type selected earlier, but it cannot be greater. If you have two identical drives, you'll have the opportunity to select a one- or two-drive backup. If you select a two-drive backup, PC Backup will use the diskette drives alternately, which can be much faster than a one-drive backup.

Instead of a diskette, you can specify a second fixed disk or a removable drive and path if necessary. This works with tapes that aren't diskette-compatible or a Bernoulli box that can be configured as a DOS device. You'll see an additional dialog box that lets you enter information about the device.

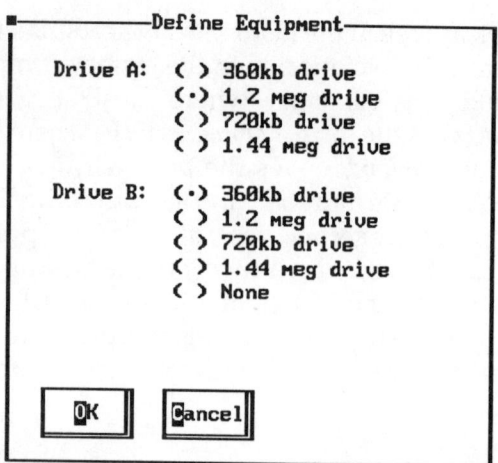

Figure 14.1 Define Equipment Dialog Box

PC Backup then offers to perform a confidence test and recommend the speed setting; you can bypass the test if you wish. You can modify the configuration later from within PC Backup if your needs or system change.

The PC Backup Screen

Once the configuration is done, you see the PC Backup screen, as shown in Figure 14.3. The PC Backup screen and menu interface are much like the one in PC Shell. You can use the mouse or the keyboard, just as in the shell. F1 accesses context-sensitive online help.

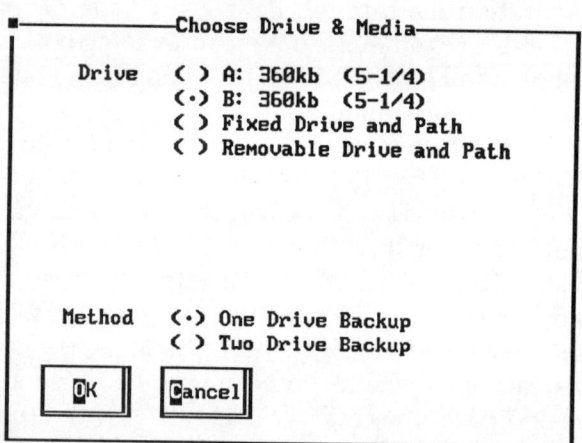

Figure 14.2 Choose Drive and Media Dialog Box

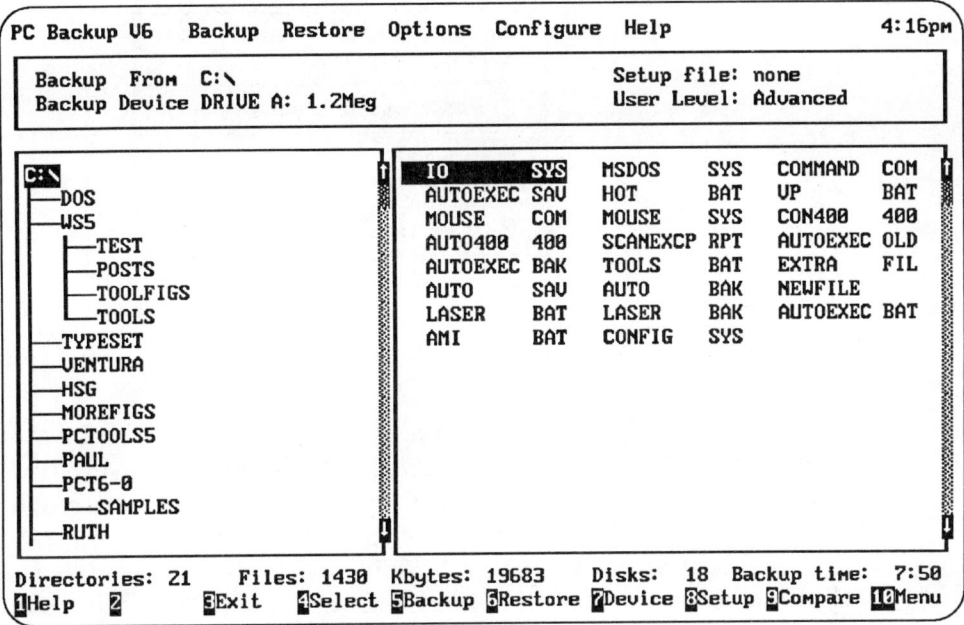

Figure 14.3   PC Backup Screen

Notice that the menu bar at the top of the screen and the status and command bars at the bottom of the screen are similar to those in the shell. The directory tree and file list are also similar to those in the shell.

Below the menu bar is the backup specification information, including the default hard disk and the media you specified to hold the backups. You set these the first time you use PC Backup or through options on the **Configure** menu. On the **Options** menu, you can set various selection and processing features. The **Backup** and **Restore** menus control the backup and restore processes.

Changing the Configuration

After PC Backup is configured for the first time, you can change any part of the configuration from the **Configure** menu, as shown in Figure 14.4. You can get the dialog box from Figure 14.1 by selecting **Define Equipment**. You can get the dialog box from Figure 14.2 by selecting **Choose Drive and Media**. Changes made through the menu apply only to the current PC Backup session unless you select **Save as default** before leaving PC Backup.

PC Backup defaults to the highest possible speed, which uses high speed direct memory access (DMA). Most PC and AT compatible computers include

274 Disk Management and Recovery

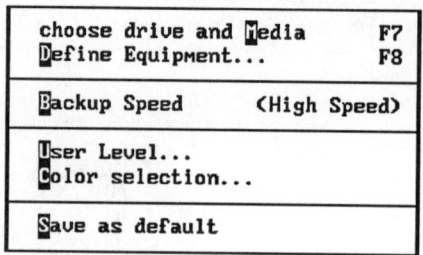

Figure 14.4   Configure Menu

a DMA controller, which this method uses; the computer can then read from the hard disk and write to a diskette at the same time, overlapping the input and output operations. This lets the system work much faster when you back up to a diskette or diskette-compatible tape, but it has no effect if you back up to another hard disk or a nondiskette device.

If your system has problems using high speed DMA, select medium speed, which allows no overlap in input and output operations. If necessary, you can request a low speed or DOS compatible backup, which lets you back up files to any DOS device. You must use this type to back up files to any device not handled by DMA. Even though it is called "DOS compatible", you'll still have to use PC Backup to restore files from it.

Like PC Shell, PC Backup supports three user levels: Advanced, Intermediate, and Beginner. The only difference is the number of commands available on the **Options** menu. The user level function may be password protected.

You can also change the colors used in the PC Backup displays through this menu. If you choose **Save as default**, all changes you make on this menu will affect later sessions as well.

✧ *Try It Out*

1. Start PC Backup from within the shell. If you get a memory error message, exit the shell and type PCBACKUP at the DOS prompt.
2. If you see a Welcome dialog box, read it and then select CONTINUE. In the next dialog box specify the types of diskette drives in your computer. In the next dialog box, specify the type of diskette you will use to store backup files. In most cases, this will be the same as the drive type to store as much on a diskette as possible.

3. When you see the PC Backup screen, examine it in detail. Pull down each menu and see what options are available. Change to Advanced user level if possible.
4. Examine the drive and media option dialog boxes from the **Configure** menu and make any changes you need. Modify the colors if you want. Save the changes if you want them to be permanent. Then terminate PC Backup.

Startup Parameters

If you find that the display or function of PC Backup isn't quite right, you may want to specify one or more of the optional parameters, listed in Table 14.1. If you enter the command at the prompt, just type any parameters following PCBACKUP. If you use the **Applications** menu to start PC Backup, you can edit the menu option to add the parameters.

/BW starts PC Backup in black and white mode. Use it when you have a color card but a monochrome monitor. If you use /BW to start PC Shell, you'll want it here as well. It doesn't carry through from PC Shell even if you use the **Applications** menu. If you use /LCD to start PC Shell, you'll need to use it here as well.

/DOB forces PC Backup to use the Copy II PC Deluxe Option Board, if it is present. It lets you back up using unformatted disks, speeding the process.

/NO turns off simultaneous hard disk and floppy disk direct memory access (DMA). If you use /NO to turn it off, the backup is slower. Some machines can't handle the simultaneous DMA. If you find that your system

Table 14.1   PC Backup Parameters

/BW	Use black and white mode
/LCD	Use LCD display
/DOB	Suppress Deluxe Option Board usage
/NO	Suppress DMA (simultanoues read and write)
/LE	Exchange mouse button functions
/PS2	Control mouse appearance
/R	Start in Restore mode
d:	Start on nondefault drive
<setname>	Start with loaded setname
/?	Display command parameters

hangs up or acts strangely during backups, try the /NO option to see if it works better. It has the same effect as selecting a medium backup speed.

/LE and /PS2 affect how the mouse works, just as in PC Shell. You'll want to use them with PC Backup if you use them with PC Shell.

The *d:* parameter lets you specify a nondefault hard drive for backing up. It will be reflected in the tree window that appears.

/R brings PC Backup up in restore mode; this saves time since the program doesn't have to read the hard disk directories in the process.

The *<setname>* parameter causes a saved backup set named setname.SET to be loaded, ready to use at the start. All options established in the backup set are in effect.

The /? parameter displays a list of parameters and their effects.

Backup Selection Decisions

Before you can begin a backup, you have to make several decisions. Do you want to back up every file on your hard disk? Do you want to depend on the archive attribute to select files? Do you want to depend on another attribute or on a date range? Do you want to repeat the same general selections in later backups? You communicate your answers to these and many other questions through various settings on the **Options** menu.

Archive Attribute Methods

Some of the backup methods depend on the archive attribute, which is turned on by DOS whenever it writes to a file. Thus, when the file is originally created or copied to the disk, its archive attribute is turned on. Every time it is modified, its archive attribute is turned on. Thus, the presence of the archive attribute indicates that a file has been modified in some manner and is a candidate for backup. Some methods turn the attribute off after backing it up, indicating that the current version of the file has been backed up and is no longer in danger of being lost. Other methods leave the archive attribute alone.

A *full* backup means that you want all selected files on the selected drive and in the selected subdirectories to be backed up, regardless of whether or not a file has the archive attribute. For a full backup, you want the file backed up even if no changes have been made to some files. After a full backup, any archive attributes for backed up files are turned off.

If you want to do a full backup but leave the archive attribute alone, you want a *full copy* backup. The archive attributes won't be used in selecting files to be backed up, but they won't be turned off either.

You can use the *incremental* method if you want to back up only files that have been changed or created since the last backup and append them to a full backup. PC Backup will examine all the selected files, just as under a full backup, but it will back up only those that have the archive attribute turned on. After each file is backed up, its archive attribute is turned off. The history file is merged into the former one. You can use the *separate incremental* method instead if you prefer to keep the backups and history files separate. While the output is similar, you use a slightly different process in restoring these files. PC Backup prompts you in either case.

If you want the archive attribute to be used in selecting files but not turned off afterwards, use the *differential* method. This output from this method remains separate from other backups.

Limiting Files Selected for Backup

By default, all files in all directories are selected for backup, except those with the hidden or system attribute. However, you don't have to accept the default. You can limit the assortment of files in several ways. At one level, you might want a complete backup of all files on your hard disk. At another, you might want to back up all those changed this week, all files changed since the last backup, or all files with a particular extension. You can select or exclude files by directory, by generic filename, by attributes, or by specifying individual files. The general archive attribute method is applied to those files that are selected.

There are two general ways of selecting files. If you use one, then the other, the second overrides the first. The first method uses the **Choose directories** option from the **Backup** menu; you choose directories and files from the tree and file list windows. The other method uses the **Include/exclude files** option from the **Options** menu; you list the filespecs you want to include and exclude from the backup.

The **Choose directories** method is great for a one-time shot, since it is quick and easy to set up and use. But you have to redo it each time. You might use this the first time you do a complete backup, or to prepare a specialized backup diskette. It includes selecting the directories and files to be used; PC Backup then uses the selected files as a starting point, applying the archive attribute method currently in effect.

The **Include/exclude files** method lets you define special setups that you can reuse by loading when you are ready to do a backup. While it is more complex to establish, it can be reused very easily. With this method, you define files to be included and excluded by generic names. You'll see how to use both methods in detail a bit later.

PC Backup Options

Before you do a backup using PC Backup, you'll want to check the default options and make sure you know what to expect. Figure 14.5 shows the **Options** menu. The first group of options lets you create and use setup files; we'll deal with those later. The next group of options gives PC Backup instructions about the method and style of backup you want done. The third group of options can be used to select files for backup. While **Include/exclude files** sets the general type of file selection, **Subdirectory inclusion** applies to both types. The fourth group lets you specify how the backup process will interact with you. Changes on the **Options** menu become defaults if you choose **Save as default** on the **Configuration** menu before leaving PC Backup.

Backup Method

When you select the **Backup method** option, you see a dialog box like the one in Figure 14.6. You select the method you want depending on whether or not you want the archive attribute considered in selecting files and turned off after backup. **Full** and **Full Copy** ignore the archive attribute in selecting files. **Full Copy** and **Differential** do not turn it off. **Incremental** is not available for low speed backups. Pressing F1 while this dialog box is displayed results in a brief description of each method. When you select OK, you'll return to the **Options** menu to make more selections.

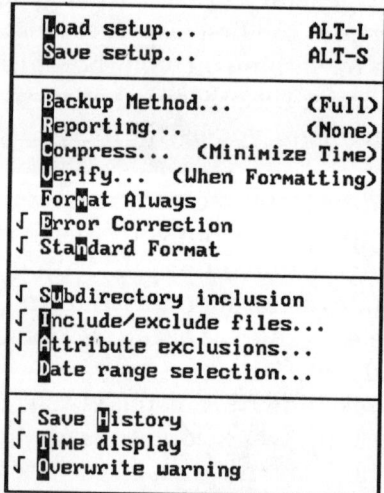

Figure 14.5   Options Menu

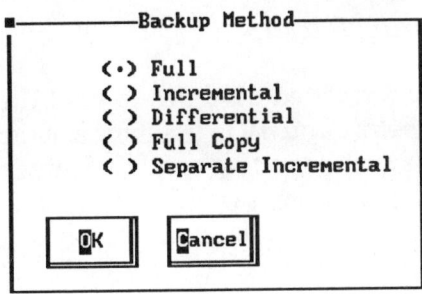

Figure 14.6   Backup Method Dialog Box

Compress Options

You can ask PC Backup to compress files during the backup process. Compression results in using fewer diskettes for the backup process. The process doesn't compress all files. For example, files with extensions PAK, ZAP, ARC, SQZ, and SEC won't be compressed, nor will any files smaller than 500 bytes.

If you select **Compress**, you'll see the dialog box shown in Figure 14.7. You can select **None** if you don't want the files compressed. If you select **Minimize Disks**, PC Backup compresses the data so it takes the minimum number of diskettes; you will have to do less disk swapping. In general, compression can reduce the number of diskettes from 10% to 60%. They will be decompressed automatically if you ever have to restore the files.

If you select **Minimize Time**, the amount of compression depends on the speed of your machine, the speed of your hard drive, and the type of output media. More compression is done with fast equipment, less with slow ones. It works only with the DMA backup type, however.

Once you start the actual backup, the maximum number of diskettes you need is shown on the screen. If any **Compress** option is on, you'll need fewer diskettes than are shown.

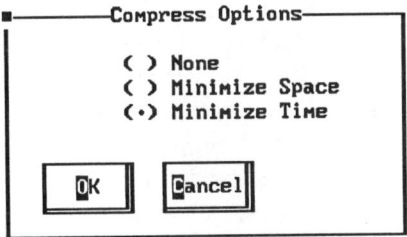

Figure 14.7   Compress Options Dialog Box

Formatting during Backup

Backups require formatted diskettes to hold the output. If a diskette hasn't been formatted before you try to use it for backup, you'll be notified and then PC Backup formats it. If you want all diskettes reformatted every time they are used, however, you can turn **Format Always** on. Then every diskette gets formatted automatically, whether or not it has been used before. This makes the backup process take longer, and it usually isn't necessary unless you have problems with your diskettes.

You'll generally want to use the standard format, which lets DOS read the diskette directory and enables you to identify where the diskette fits in a set. Nonstandard formatting lets PC Backup squeeze more data onto the diskette, however. Backup diskettes produced by PC Backup V5 and V5.5 used nonstandard formatting. If you want to reuse these diskettes without reformatting them and get the fastest possible backup, turn **Standard Format** off. Otherwise leave it on. The diskettes will be automatically reformatted for you into the standard DOS format.

Error Correction during Backup

PC Backup has an advanced error correction facility. You can ask PC Backup to correct any errors it encounters, even during the Restore process. If you are going to do this, you have to turn **Error Correction** on when you make the backup set. PC Backup then stores extra information on each diskette that it can use later if it has to correct any errors. Since this involves extra work, the process takes longer.

Verifying Data

You may want to verify the data placed on backup diskettes to make sure it is reliable and can be restored later if necessary. To do this, select **Verify** on the **Options** menu. You can specify that data be verified never, always, or only on diskettes that PC Backup formats. By far the most likely time that verification uncovers bad data is with a new or newly formatted diskette. Once the diskette is formatted, you can be reasonably sure it is in good shape. If you have any reason to worry, however, you'll want to verify always. Or you might want to consider getting new diskettes or having your diskette heads aligned. In the verification process, PC Backup checks that the data is readable, but it doesn't check that the dates, times, sizes, and contents of backed up files match those on the hard disk. You can do a more thorough comparison after the backup is complete.

Backup Reporting

If you wish, you can ask PC Backup to provide you with a report by selecting **Reporting** on the **Options** menu. In the resulting dialog box, you can ask that the report be printed or stored as a file in the directory from which you ran PC Backup. The filename takes the form *hyymmdda*.RPT, where *h* represents the hard disk, *yymmdd* gives the date with the year first, and *a* indicates which backup that day. C910412B.RPT is a report of the second backup of drive C on April 12, 1991.

The report includes information on the options in effect and lists all directories and files backed up. Figure 14.8 shows an abbreviated example. Notice that it doesn't include the options in effect.

Subdirectory Inclusion

By default, when a directory is selected for backup, its subdirectories are included as well. If you turn off the **Subdirectory inclusion** option from the **Options** menu, only files in the selected directories will be backed up. If you

```
PC Backup Directory Report 6.0
 (c) Copyright 1989,1990 Central Point Software, Inc. All Rights Reserved.
Backup Performed on 03/12/1991   07:31p

Total Directories:     2
Total Files:         104

     Name            Size      Date         Time    Atrib  Vol         Page 1
Directory: C:\WS5\TOOLS\
CHAP1.CAP              310 03/02/1990      03:31p   ----    1 Compressed
CHAP3.VGR              134 03/02/1990      03:46p   ----    1
CHAP1.CIF              128 03/02/1990      03:31p   ----    1
CHAP1.CHP             5886 03/02/1990      03:31p   ----    1 Compressed
...
CPS.LET                896 01/08/1990      03:18p   ----    1 Compressed
TRYIT.WRI              208 02/28/1990      03:28p   ----    1
BOOK.WS               4096 10/28/1989      04:48a   ----    1 Compressed
CHAP5.CAP              412 03/02/1990      05:50p   ----    1 Compressed
CHAP09.CHP            7715 03/08/1990      08:04p   ----    1 Compressed
UNTITLED               130 02/27/1990      12:18p   ----    1
...
CHAP09                32769 03/08/1990     08:04p   ----    2 Compressed
CHAP13                32042 03/12/1990     03:55p   ----    2 Compressed
COPYEDIT.BAK           3456 03/12/1990     09:22a   ----    2

Total Bytes:  1821791
```

Figure 14.8   PC Backup Report

want to select the directories for backup individually, turn this option off before you choose them.

Attribute Exclusion

You can ask PC Backup to include or exclude files by attribute. By default, it excludes files with the system or hidden attribute. If you select the **Attribute exclusions** option from the **Options** menu, you can choose whether or not to exclude hidden files, system files, or read only files in the resulting dialog box. The selections here affect only backups done through the **Include/exclude files** method.

Inclusion by Date Range

You can choose **Date Range selection** on the **Options** menu to cause PC Backup to select only files with dates before or after the ones you specify. It works in conjunction with subdirectory inclusion and attribute exclusion. You can include both earliest and latest dates in the dialog box as shown in Figure 14.9 to bracket the selected files. To limit it to a single day, use the same date in both the **From** and **To** fields. Date range selection works only if **Include/exclude files** is on. It has no effect when you use **Choose directories** to select files for backup.

Saving the History File

To cause PC Backup to put a history file in the PC Tools directory as well as on the last diskette of a backup set, turn **Save History** on before starting the backup. When time to compare or restore files comes, this option saves you a great deal of hassle. If it was off, you'll have to first insert the last diskette of

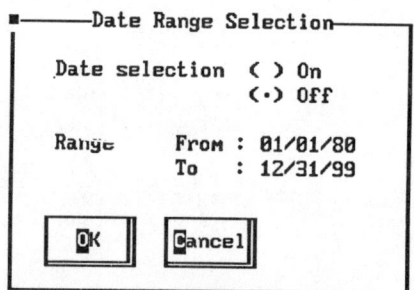

Figure 14.9   Date Range Selection Dialog Box

the set you want to compare or restore. If history files have been saved to the hard disk, you'll be able to select from among them by unique names you provided when they were created. If some history files are saved and some aren't, you can choose INSERT when PC Backup shows you history information, then insert the last diskette of the appropriate set. If PC Backup can get its preliminary information from the hard disk, you start inserting with the first diskette. This speeds up the compare or restore process.

When you start a compare or restore, you'll see a window listing information from all the history files on the hard disk. You select the one you want or choose INSERT if the history of the backup set you want wasn't saved. To simplify a later restore process, keep **Save History** turned on for all backup sets that you create.

Overwrite Warning

You can ask PC Backup to warn you when files will be overwritten during the backup or restore process. When **Overwrite warning** is turned on, you'll see a warning dialog box during backup if the target diskette was used in a previous backup. Overwriting may be normal for you if you recycle backup diskettes regularly; if so, just select this option to turn it off.

During a restore operation, the **Overwrite warning** option alerts you when the file being restored already exists on the hard disk. If you want this warning, leave the option on during a restore.

Time Display

When **Time display** is checked in the **Options** menu, you'll see the elapsed time continually updated in the status bar near the bottom of the screen. This function is really designed for use on networks. If you aren't on a network and haven't had any problems, you might as well leave it on. It gives you something to watch when you get bored.

✧ *Try It Out*

1. Start up PC Backup and examine the option settings.
2. Turn **Subdirectory inclusion** off; the highlighting in the tree changes. Turn it back on.
3. Check the **Attribute exclusion** settings.
4. Change any settings you want different.

The Backup Procedure

When you are ready to back up files on your default hard disk, minus any exclusions established on your **Options** menu, the status line shows the maximum number of diskettes you will need, without considering compression, and the estimated time it will take to complete the backup. To start the process, select **Start backup** on the **Backup** menu. A dialog box appears asking you to name the backup set. Enter up to 30 characters that you will recognize later to describe it. This name becomes a part of the history file. You can provide a password if you wish. The password must be used to restore the backups later.

You'll be prompted to insert the first diskette. As the process continues, you'll be prompted to insert additional diskettes. If you insert a previously used diskette, you'll be alerted. Choose OK to use it. Or you can change the diskette and choose RETRY. Each prompt provides the sequential number of the diskette; these numbers become important in the restore process, so you should attach them to the diskette labels. The red drive light stays on during the process, even while you change diskettes. You won't have to press Enter.

You can track the backup process by watching the percentage and time elapsed values in the status line or by watching the tree and file lists on the backup screen. The current file being backed up is highlighted, as is its directory. When the backup is complete, the history file is written to the backup diskette, as well as to the hard disk if **Save History** is on. You'll see a summary report on screen. If you selected the **Reporting** option, a report is written at this time.

Partial Backup

If you want to start the backup at a subtree or back up a nondefault hard disk, select **backup From entry** on the **Backup** menu. You'll see a dialog box asking for the path. The default path, generally C:\, appears; you type the path to the top of the subtree or disk you want backed up. When you select OK or press Enter, the procedure continues just as with the **Start backup** option. Previously set options control which files are selected from the path you specify.

Selecting Files

If you don't want to back up an entire hard disk or subtree, minus the exclusions, you can select files by directory or filename. If you are doing a one-time backup, use the **Backup** menu to select the directories and files you want to process. If you want to use the same set of files again, use the **Options** menu to specify what will be backed up.

Choosing Directories on the Screen

The **Choose directories** option on the **Backup** menu lets you select specific directories and files to back up. If **Subdirectory inclusion** is turned on, first unselect the root directory (by clicking or pressing Enter). Then select the directories you want backed up; PC Backup highlights the files as you select directories. All files in a selected directory are automatically selected, except for any with their attributes excluded. You can select or unselect any individual directory or file.

If the **Subdirectory inclusion** option from the **Options** menu is on, files in any subdirectories are selected as well. Just as in the standard PC Shell screen, you can use the right mouse button and dragging to select or unselect adjacent files in the list. Holding down the Enter key has the same effect. When you go to another directory and its files are displayed, any files selected before you changed remain selected.

Starting the Backup

Once you have specified the drive, directories, and files you want backed up, the message line shows you the estimated time and number of disks for the backup. Select the **Start backup** option, name the backup set, and insert diskettes as prompted.

Once the backup is complete, you'll see a report on the screen, much like the one shown in Figure 14.10. PC Backup then reverts to the default of selecting all except the files with excluded attributes on the default hard disk.

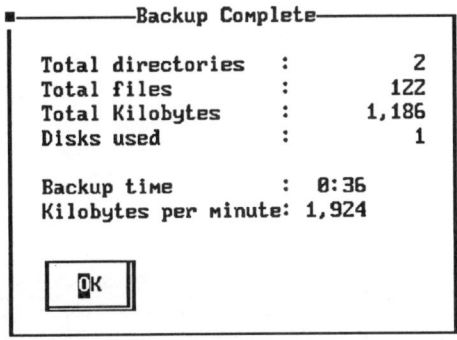

Figure 14.10   Backup Complete Dialog Box

Disk Management and Recovery

✧ Try It Out

1. Make sure **Reporting** and **Save History** are on. Send the report file to disk.
2. Insert a usable diskette of the type you specified into drive A:. Then use **Choose directories** to back up files in the subtree that starts with your PC Tools directory.
3. Respond to prompts as the backup proceeds. Notice how the highlights on the screen let you know what is being backed up.
4. When the backup is complete, check the directory of one of the diskettes. Examine the report file. Locate the history file on the hard disk.

Permanent File Selection

If you want to set up some generic processes so you can accomplish the same or a similar backup each time, use the **Include/exclude files** option from the **Options** menu. The dialog box shown in Figure 14.11 appears. The default description is *.*; this generic filename includes all filenames on the default hard disk with any extensions. Any attribute exclusion or defined date range is in effect, however. You can type up to 16 lines of filenames to include and exclude in the backup.

You can use the wildcard characters * and ? in filenames, as well as in

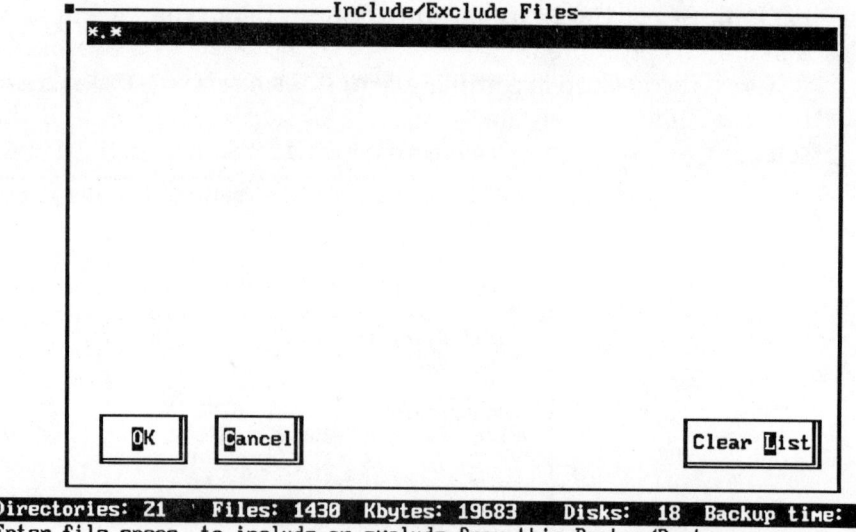

Figure 14.11   Include/Exclude Files Dialog Box

pathnames. If you precede a filename with a hyphen (–) matching files are excluded. If not, they are included. Table 14.2 lists several examples and their meanings. Except for the *.* or –*.* expressions, all include subdirectories only if the **Subdirectory inclusion** option is turned on. The entries you type on the screen are processed from top to bottom, so you can include all files, then exclude all COM files, then include GRABBER.COM if necessary.

Saving Your Backup Setup

Once the options are set as you want them and the screen shows the set of files you want to process, you can save it as a named setup. Then you can back up this same set of files again by loading the setup, then selecting **Start backup**. Alternatively, you can enter the PCBACKUP command, followed by the name of the setup file in angle brackets, to start the backup without going through the screen and menus. You can make changes in the setup while it is loaded if necessary.

To save the setup, select the **Save setup** option on the **Options** menu. You'll be shown a default name (starting with BACKUP1), which you can change if you wish. In most cases, you'll want to use a meaningful name, such as DAILY, DRIVED, or WEEKLY, so you can recognize it. PC Backup appends the extension SET to the filename you provide.

Using a Saved Setup

Once the setup is saved, you can load it from the dialog box that results when you select **Load setup** from the **Options** menu when you are ready to perform

Table 14.2   File Include/Exclude Entry Dialog Box

`*.*`	Include all files on disk (even if Subdirectory inclusion is off)
`-*.*`	Exclude (unselect) the entire disk
`\*.*`	Include all files in the root directory
`-\PCTOOLS\*.*`	Exclude all files in the \PCTOOLS directory
`\WS5\TOOLS\CH*.*`	Include all files in the \WS5\TOOLS directory in which the filename begins with CH
`-\HSG\*.EXE`	Exclude all files with extension EXE in the HSG directory
`-*.COM`	Exclude all files on the disk with extension COM
`*.SCR`	Include all files on the disk with extension SCR

that backup operation. All option settings are stored with the setup, so you should get the same effect each time.

Suppose you have saved a setup, such as DAILY. You can perform your backup operation at the DOS prompt by typing PCBACKUP DAILY. Or you can include the command PCBACKUP DAILY in a batch file. When DOS encounters the command, it starts PC Backup, loads the inclusions and exclusions from the setup saved as DAILY, and prompts you to insert a diskette. You can automate the process by using |PCBACKUP.EXE DAILY as an appointment with an alarm and leaving Desktop resident at that time. You could also define new applications to run from within PC Shell, using the PCBACKUP command and the saved setup name as a parameter.

✧ *Try It Out*

1. Define a setup that includes all files in two of your directories, except for any EXE or COM files.
2. Save the setup as PRAC1, then start the backup.
3. When the backup is complete, exit PC Backup. Then enter it again, reload PRAC1, and run it again. Use the same diskettes.

Comparing and Restoring Files

When you back up files, you hope never to have to restore them. But if you do, you want to be sure the backup disks are good. PC Backup lets you compare the backup disks to the files still on the hard disk. The **Restore** menu lets you compare files or restore them. You can do either a complete or a partial comparison or restoration. The methods correspond to backing up files.

Comparing Backed Up Files

The PC Backup comparison procedure lets you verify that the data on disk matches that in the backup set. You might also use a comparison to see if the files have the same dates and sizes in both locations. It's a good idea to compare files after you do your first backup to ensure that your chosen backup speed makes valid copies and to prove to yourself they are the same.

When you are ready to compare a backup set, pull down the **Restore** menu and select **Choose Directories** or **Start Compare**. If you have saved history files to your hard disk, you'll see a window like the one in Figure 14.12. The names reflect the names you provided when you started the backup itself.

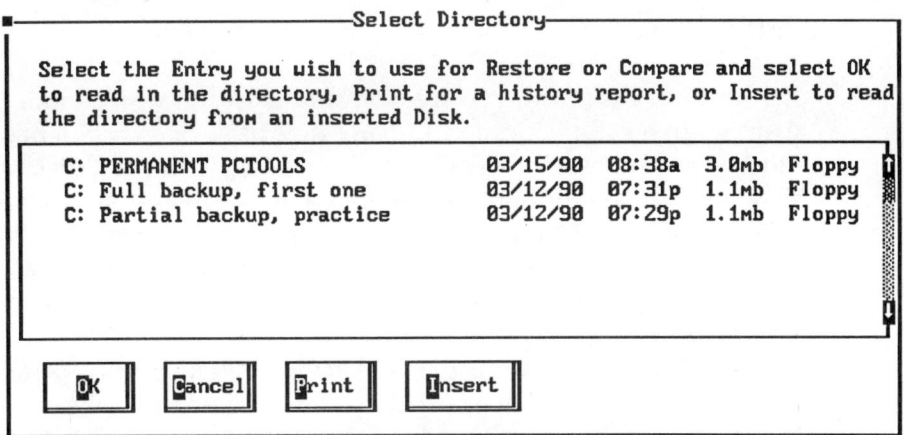

Figure 14.12 Select Directory Dialog Box

Highlight the name of the backup set you want to compare, then select OK. If it isn't shown, select INSERT and insert the last diskette of the appropriate backup set. Selecting PRINT gets a report of the information stored in the selected history file.

After you make your selection, PC Backup reads that history file and shows the tree and file list on the screen. All directories and files are selected, but you can modify it to compare a subset if you wish. When you select **Start Compare** again, PC Backup compares, decompressing if necessary. It notes differences in size, date, and content, but it doesn't pause. A symbol indicating the comparison results appears before each file name. The symbol = indicates that the files compare in all aspects. The symbols < and > indicate that the files compare but the backup file was older or newer than the hard disk file. The symbols << and >> indicate that the files didn't compare and the backup file was older or newer than the hard disk file. The symbol s indicates the size was different, – indicates the backup file was missing, and x means the date and time match but the files didn't compare. A dialog box like the one shown in Figure 14.13 summarizes the comparison. Once you remove the dialog box, all files that compared (those with symbols =, <, and >) are unselected, leaving those with differences selected and ready to be restored immediately if you wish to do so.

If reporting is turned on, COMPARE.RPT is sent to disk if any mismatches are detected. If you see many problems, especially directly after a backup, remove any TSRs that are running and try again. If there are still problems, use the next slower backup speed. Be sure you can get a clean backup before you rely on the backup system.

Full Restoration

If your hard disk fails, you may have to do a full restoration. You may also want to do a full restoration if many files have been accidentally deleted or otherwise destroyed. The first step is to fix up your hard disk, if necessary. It may have to be reformatted and have the DOS system installed; use your original DOS disks for these operations. Then reinstall PC Tools from the original diskettes. At this point, you can start PC Backup and restore the disk. If you are doing a full restoration without an intervening disk crash, you can start at any time.

If you want to restore the directories and files to a different drive or directory from the one in which they were backed up, you can use the **Restore to entry** option. The resulting dialog box lets you type a path, including a drive name if necessary, just as the **Backup from entry** option does. You'll be asked to insert the last diskette of the backup set so that PC Backup can get the necessary information from it.

Restoring the Files

To start the restore process, select **Choose Directories** or **Start restore** from the **Restore** menu. If the hard disk contains history files, you'll see the window shown in Figure 14.12. If not, you'll be prompted to insert the last, then the first diskette from the backup set. You'll be prompted to insert each diskette in turn.

If the process attempts to restore a file of the same complete file specification as one existing on the disk, you may see a dialog box like the one in Figure

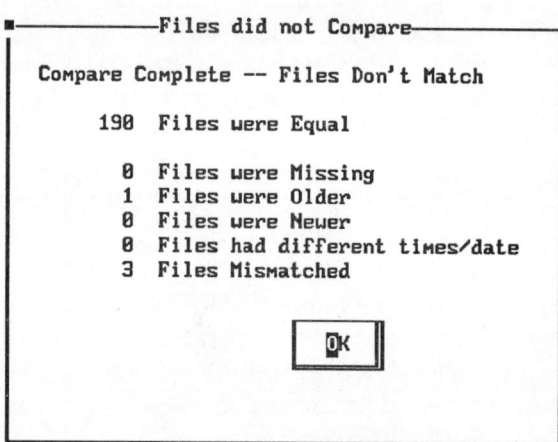

Figure 14.13   Comparison Summary Dialog Box

14.14. This happens only if the **Overwrite warning** option is selected. Otherwise, files are automatically overwritten.

If you want the identically named file on the hard disk replaced by the backup file in any event, select **Overwrite**. If you want it replaced only if the backup version is more recent, select **Overwrite with newer file only**. If you don't want the file replaced, select **Skip this file**. If you want your decision here to affect all the rest of the files, select **Repeat for all later files**; otherwise you'll see this dialog box for each restored file that matches a filename already on the hard disk.

You'll be notified when the restoration is complete.

Partial Restore

Sometimes you don't need a full restoration. You may have accidentally overlaid all data files in a particular directory, for example. You can restore based on what is currently on your backup diskettes, selecting the files from the backup set file list. If you choose to restore files in subdirectories that aren't present on the hard disk, PC Backup will create them in the restore process.

You can use the **Restore to entry** option to specify the top of a subtree or you can use **Choose directories** to select the specific directories and files you want restored. The tree and file information on the screen comes from the backup set's history file. You can use **Subdirectory inclusion, Include/exclude files, Attribute exclusions,** and **Date range selections** just as with backups, but now they apply to files for restoration.

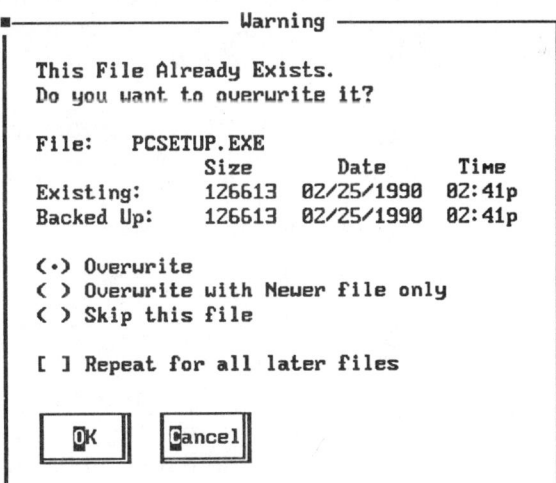

Figure 14.14 Restore Warning Dialog Box

When the desired options, directories, and files are chosen, select **Start restore**. You'll be prompted to insert diskettes by number if PC Backup has to look for files. You'll be notified when all specified files have been restored.

✧ *Try it Out*

1. Erase a few files you created from the directory you backed up last. Then restore the files from the backup set. Select any options you want.
2. When the restoration is complete, enter PC Shell and notice that the files you erased are back.

Restoration Problems

Various problems can occur when you restore files. You may have diskettes missing or damaged, for example. This section explains what to do in several situations.

No History Information. If you saved history files to the hard disk, and the disk hasn't been damaged, you have no problem. PC Backup always puts history information on the last diskette of a backup set. If that diskette is missing, PC Backup can use the hard disk file or regenerate the history information from the rest of the backup diskettes. When you select **Start restore**, you'll be prompted to insert the last diskette. If you don't have that diskette, insert the first one of the set. You'll be informed that your directory wasn't found and be offered the option of rebuilding it. If you select **Rebuild**, you'll be prompted for each diskette in turn while PC Backup rebuilds the directory. When you are finished, you can save your rebuilt directory on a new diskette or proceed immediately to restore files.

Another choice is **Retry**; use it if you inserted the wrong diskette by mistake. You can then remove the first diskette and insert the last one so that PC Backup can find the directory information.

Damaged or Lost Diskettes. If one or more diskettes in a backup set are damaged or missing, you can restore files from the remaining ones. When you are prompted to insert a disk you can't locate or that PC Backup can't recognize, just insert the next one in sequence. You'll be notified of the missing diskette, but you can choose to continue or retry. **Retry** lets you change diskettes in case you inserted the wrong one. **Continue** tells PC Backup to restore what files it can from the current diskette. If a particular file spans two disks, it won't be restored if either part is missing.

Unlabeled Diskettes. If you did not label your backup diskettes and don't know their order, you can figure out the sequence from file lists. Just examine the directory of each diskette. The sequential extension indicates the position of the diskette in the backup set. Diskettes produced using nonstandard format are not readable by DOS, so you can't check their files. But for either type of diskette, you can use a program called PCBDIR at the DOS prompt. Insert a diskette you want to check out in drive A: and type PCBDIR at the DOS prompt. You'll be prompted to type the drive name. The screen will show something like this:

```
PC Backup Directory Report
Copyright (c) 1990 Central Point Software.
   All rights reserved.
What drive:path contains the backup diskette?
a:
Disk is number 3 of a PCBACKUP set.
Disk was created with release 6.0 of PCBACKUP
BACKUP device was a 1.2MB drive, Media selected was 1.2MB.
Disk is formatted with 80 tracks of 15 sectors per side.
The directory starts on track 12 (ch) of this disk.
This disk is recorded in DOS standard format.
Advanced Error Correction was ON for this backup.
The compression setting for this backup is .
This disk was formatted by PCBACKUP.
The backup speed used was high.
```

If the diskette is the last and contains directory information, you can have a report of the files in the backup set sent to disk or to your printer through the **Print Directory** option of the **Restore** menu.

Tape Backup Considerations

If a tape drive is properly configured into your computer system, you can use tape as your primary backup medium. The tape must be formatted and certified before it can be used; you can perform these operations through PC Backup. If you insert a new tape during a procedure, PC Backup reminds you it needs formatting and follows your instructions. The tape drive will appear in the **Define Equipment** dialog box so that you can select it as the default. You select the tape capacity in the **Choose Drive and Media** dialog box.

Several options should be set before you back up to tape. Don't use **Format Always**, since that takes a great deal longer on tape and isn't necessary. You can set **Verify** to **Always**; this causes a complete comparison of files after backup to ensure that the backup is good. Since tapes are more susceptible to errors, turn **Error Correction** on. Make sure **Save History** is turned on, so you'll be able to locate backup sets more easily.

You select files for processing as usual. When you select **Start Backup**, you'll be prompted to insert a tape cartridge. Be sure never to remove a tape cartridge while the tape is moving or it will be damaged. You'll see a tape directory window, which looks much like the window in Figure 14.12. You can append the backup to that tape, erase the contents, or insert a new tape.

Comparing and restoring files from a tape backup is done much as with diskettes. You insert tapes when prompted. The results are displayed on screen just as with a diskette backup.

Now that you can back up and restore files, you can try the advanced features covered in the next chapters. PC Compress rearranges files on disk for better efficiency. PC Secure encrypts and compresses individual files for security. Both depend on you to have adequate backups in case anything goes wrong.

Chapter 15 | *Compressing Disks*

This chapter deals with disk and file access efficiency. The PC Tools package includes the COMPRESS program that helps you improve both. In this chapter, you'll learn to:

- Identify fragmentation
- Analyze disks and files
- Check for and mark bad clusters
- Analyze the disk surface
- Sort files in all directories
- Compress using several methods
- Order files on the disk

Efficiency of File Access

Various factors affect how efficiently your system can locate or access a file. The file itself may be fragmented into several nonadjacent clusters; this is referred to as being stored in non-contiguous areas. Or it may be stored in a distant location from the program that wants the file, requiring several movements of the read/write arm and perhaps searching through several levels of subdirectories. Subdirectories themselves and the files in them may be scattered all over the disk. You can make your applications more efficient by eliminating some of these problems.

Fragmentation

When you request a file, the shell or DOS looks for it on the disk. If the file is stored as one continuous set of data, the location is quick and easy. When a file is stored to disk, DOS uses the first free directory slot for the filename. Then it finds the first free cluster on the disk and starts writing the file. If the free space gets filled with data, DOS stops writing, finds the next available cluster, records its number for file access, and continues writing the file. This could happen repeatedly for a large file.

Suppose you have a newly formatted diskette and copy 30 files to it. The copy process handles one file at a time, so at this point each copied file is unfragmented, no matter how it was stored on the original disk. However, if a file is modified so that it runs over into another cluster, DOS finds a free cluster, probably not contiguous to the original set. If you delete half a dozen small files, you free up at least six clusters, which may not be adjacent. If you then copy a large file to the diskette, it will use some of those freed clusters, wherever they are, even if there is plenty of contiguous free space at the end of the disk.

Disks and diskettes you use frequently for word processing, spreadsheets, database processing, accounting, and many other applications very quickly develop many data files with non-contiguous areas. This can greatly slow down file access. It can also make undeletion of those files more difficult if Mirror has not been run recently. Since you won't be using Mirror on your diskettes, accidentally erasing a diskette can be a crisis. Even Rebuild isn't guaranteed to recover all your files.

The COMPRESS program lets you remove fragmentation from a disk and move all the free space to the end of a disk. This process speeds up disk access. It also lets you reorganize the disk. You can force all files in a subdirectory to be stored in the same area. This lets them be accessed from programs in the subdirectory with very little disk arm motion, resulting in quicker access. You can also force all the subdirectories to be placed in early FAT slots, so that processing path names is quicker.

Identifying Fragmentation Outside of Compress

You can identify fragmentation easily from within Compress, but you may also be informed of it if you use the **File Map** option of the **Special** menu under PC Shell. Figure 15.1 shows the result. Notice that the upper left shows the name of the file being mapped as well as the number of non-contiguous areas. The map itself shows where those areas are located, but it may not show the same number of areas, since each grid location represents several clusters, the number depending on the size disk being mapped. In the figure, you can see some of the fragmentation graphically. If you repeatedly select NEXT or PRIOR, you can page through similar displays for all files in a directory.

If you suspect your disk contains much fragmentation, you can check it out in detail from within the Compress application.

Running Compress

Compress does not make files smaller. (You can use PC Secure, covered in the next chapter, for that purpose.) It merely rearranges them on the disk so that less space is wasted and file access efficiency can be at its peak. It can also rearrange the directories in the process. One side effect of using Compress is that you can't undelete any files after it is finished. Both Delete Tracking and DOS Directory methods are invalid after a compression. You'll be able to undelete files deleted after that point, however.

Starting Compress

You can start Compress by selecting **Compress Disk** on the **Applications** menu or by typing COMPRESS at the DOS command prompt. While Compress supports various parameters at the command prompt, you can achieve the same effects by using pull down menus on the Compress screen, shown in Figure 15.2. As with PC Shell, the function keys displayed on the bottom

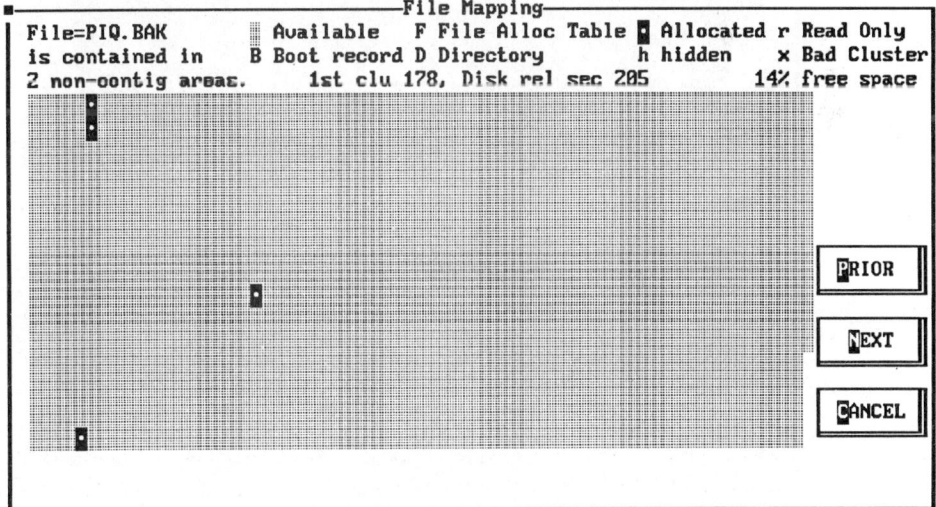

Figure 15.1   File Map Showing Non-Continguous Areas

line let you use various commands without selecting the menu options. F1 reaches context-sensitive help, while F2 reaches the help index. You can remove any dialog box or the entire Compress screen by pressing Esc or F3 or by clicking on the close box.

The Compress screen always comes up for the drive that contains the COMPRESS program. It displays a map of that disk, much like the disk map you get from the **Special** menu. You can select a different drive to display a map of any available disk, including diskettes as well as hard disks.

The Compress screen provides four menu names. Selecting **Help** on the menu bar brings up the help index. The **Sort** menu lets you specify the order in which filename entries are stored, which is reflected in directory or file listings. When the compression is done, the directory entries are rearranged as you request. The **Analysis** menu gives you more information about the current disk status and even locates bad clusters. The **Compress** menu lets you control the actual disk compression.

The Analysis Menu

The **Analysis** menu offers three options: **Disk analysis, File analysis,** and **Surface analysis.** These three selections give different levels of information

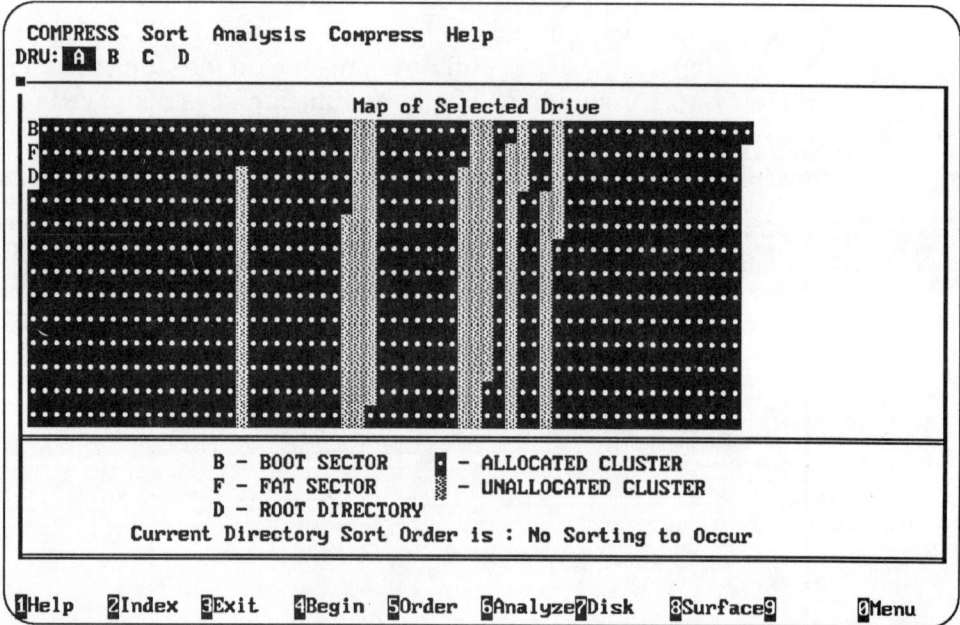

Figure 15.2   Compress Screen

about the disk in the selected drive. None of them performs any compression, but the surface analysis option can move data out of clusters that contain bad sectors.

Analyzing the Disk. The **Disk analysis** option provides technical information about the selected disk, as shown in Figure 15.3. In addition to general information about the clusters in use on the disk, it tells how much file fragmentation is present. A file chain refers to all the clusters allocated to a given file. The dialog box shown describes a diskette that contains 20 file chains, of which five are fragmented. The percent file fragmentation factor is calculated based on how many separate clusters make up the total number of files. If any significant amount of fragmentation appears on the disk, the message recommends that you use Compress. If there is no file fragmentation, the message recommends that you analyze the disk organization from the **Compress** menu.

The display also shows how many separate free space areas there are; ideally, all the free space is together so that a file can be allocated and stored in its entirety without being fragmented from the start.

The lower three lines of data should show 0; if any of the file chains have problems you'll see numbers here. Cross-linked file chains occur when the same cluster appears in more than one file. Unattached file clusters are clusters that are allocated but don't appear in any file chain. Bad clusters within file chains might make data unreadable. Any of these problems can occasionally result from mistakes in the directories or FAT, probably due to momentarily

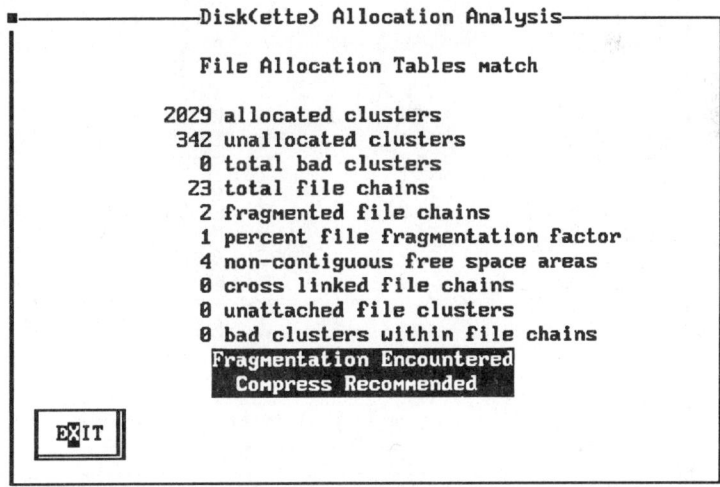

Figure 15.3   Disk Analysis Display

malfunctioning hardware or power fluctuations while writing to the disk. If any of these conditions are found, you will see a message telling you to run the PC Tools program called Diskfix.

Analyzing the Files. If you select the **File analysis** option, you'll see a listing of all the files in the root directory, including the first level subdirectories. You can page through all the files, seeing exactly which files are fragmented and into how many areas, along with the percentage of fragmentation in the file. Figure 15.4 shows the resulting screen.

You can move through the directories using the buttons on the screen. As you select NEXT DIR, you'll move through the first level subdirectories, then the lower level ones. You can't select directories by name on this screen.

You generally won't need to use this option unless you want specific information. If the **Disk analysis** screen recommends compression, you can go ahead and do it without knowing which files are fragmented.

Surface Analysis. The **Surface analysis** option does a more detailed analysis of the disk as a whole. Ignoring previously marked bad clusters, it checks all the remaining clusters and flags those that are even marginally bad, so they are identified long before DOS would catch them. Normally, if DOS has trouble reading a cluster, it tries several times before asking you to choose Abort, Retry, or Fail. A complete surface scan takes up to six minutes for a 1.2M diskette, or longer if many bad sectors requiring data movement are

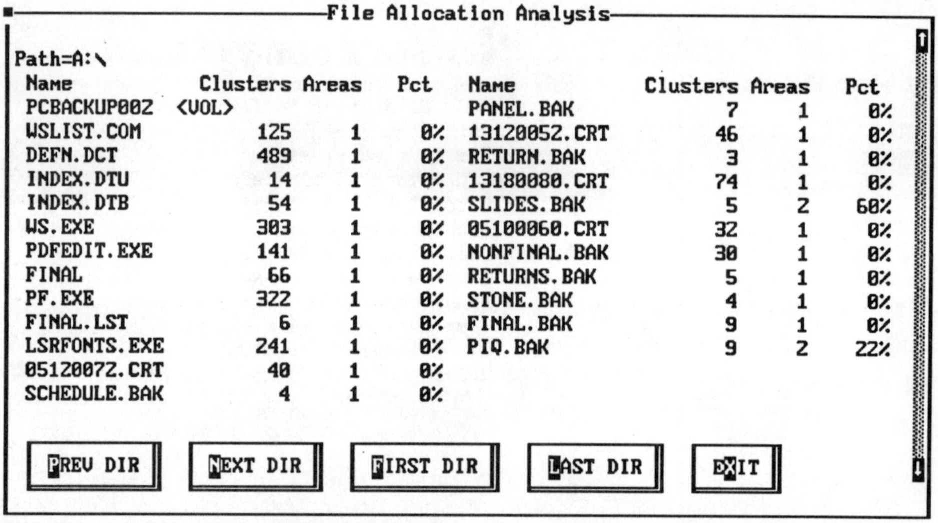

```
┌─────────────────────File Allocation Analysis─────────────────────┐
Path=A:\
Name          Clusters Areas  Pct    Name          Clusters Areas  Pct
PCBACKUP002   <VOL>                  PANEL.BAK        7       1     0%
WSLIST.COM      125      1     0%    13120052.CRT    46       1     0%
DEFN.DCT        489      1     0%    RETURN.BAK       3       1     0%
INDEX.DTU        14      1     0%    13180080.CRT    74       1     0%
INDEX.DTB        54      1     0%    SLIDES.BAK       5       2    60%
WS.EXE          303      1     0%    05100060.CRT    32       1     0%
PDFEDIT.EXE     141      1     0%    NONFINAL.BAK    30       1     0%
FINAL            66      1     0%    RETURNS.BAK      5       1     0%
PF.EXE          322      1     0%    STONE.BAK        4       1     0%
FINAL.LST         6      1     0%    FINAL.BAK        9       1     0%
LSRFONTS.EXE    241      1     0%    PIQ.BAK          9       2    22%
05120072.CRT     40      1     0%
SCHEDULE.BAK      4      1     0%

    [ PREV DIR ] [ NEXT DIR ] [ FIRST DIR ] [ LAST DIR ] [ EXIT ]
```

Figure 15.4   File Analysis Screen

found. It can take hours on a hard disk; surface scan is a good overnight job for a hard disk.

Before you do a surface scan, make current the diskette or hard disk you want scanned. When you select **Surface analysis**, Compress first asks you how many passes it should make; you can request one pass (the default), a larger number, or ask for a continuous scan until you interrupt the process.

You can also ask Compress to send a report to disk or the printer when it is finished. If you ask for the report to disk, you'll have to specify the drive, since it can't use the one being scanned; you can provide a path as well. A message tells you that the report will be stored in \SCANEXCP.RPT on the drive you choose. Here's the sort of report you get if errors are found:

```
Disk(ette) Surface Analysis
Exception Report

On Pass 01

Cluster 00255 is bad, Error in an unattached file chain.
Cluster 00255 moved to 00302.
Cluster 00255 is bad, marked bad in FAT.

Cluster 00291 is bad, marked bad in FAT.

Cluster 00339 is bad, marked bad in FAT.

On Pass 02

Surface scan completed.
```

In the example, two passes were requested. Three bad clusters were found on the first pass and none on the second. When each bad cluster is found, a message appears on the screen, but it generally doesn't stay there long enough for you to respond to it, much less read it.

When the print choice is made, Compress starts the scan using the displayed disk drive map. You can see which clusters are assigned to different functions and track the progress of the surface scan. As it continues, compress flags any bad clusters it encounters. If the cluster is allocated to a file, Compress transfers any readable data to another cluster and updates the FAT. As errors are encountered, messages similar to the ones in the report appear on the screen. Some serious errors may result in a message recommending that you run Diskfix, reboot, or solve some problem before trying the surface analysis again. Be sure to follow the instructions on the screen before continuing. When you enter Compress again, rerun the surface analysis for that disk to complete the process. If the scan doesn't complete, the report doesn't tell you what percentage of the disk was scanned or what the fatal problem was.

When the surface analysis is complete, you'll be prompted if any further action is necessary on your part. If you run surface scans regularly, you'll identify bad sectors before they cause any serious damage; this lessens the possibility of losing data in the future.

✧ Try It Out

1. Insert a diskette into drive A:; use an old, often used one if possible. Run a Disk Analysis. Notice whether or not compression is recommended. If not, check several other diskettes until you find one in which compression would be appropriate.
2. Run a File Analysis on the disk. Notice the name of a fragmented file and check the PC Shell file map for that file.
3. Do a surface scan of the diskette.
4. Do an analysis of your hard disk. If it has been backed up recently, do a surface scan.

The Sort Menu

The **Sort** menu lets you specify if and how the directories are sorted on the disk; this affects the order in which filenames appear in File Lists. The sort options here have no effect on where files are placed on the disk. Even though a sort option (or no sort) must be selected before doing the compression, Compress doesn't actually perform any directory rearranging until you start the compression.

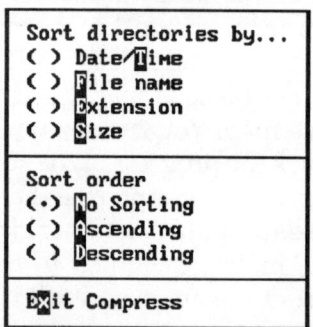

Figure 15.5   Compress Sort Menu

Figure 15.5 shows the options on the **Sort** menu. If you select a sort option other than **No Sorting,** all directories will be sorted in that way when you compress the disk. If you want a particular directory sorted differently, you can sort it within PC Shell after the compression is complete.

You can sort individual directories at any time from the **Directory sort** option of the **Special** menu. The Compress sort is much the same, but it does all the directories at once at the beginning of the compression process. The directories are all sorted in the same sequence, by **Date/Time, File name, Extension,** or **Size.** If you choose any option other than **File name,** the name is the secondary sort field. If you choose **File name,** the extension is the secondary sort field. When you select a sort option, **Ascending** is selected automatically; you can change it to **Descending** if you prefer. You can exit Compress from this menu as well.

The Compress Menu

Once you have analyzed the disk to determine that it would benefit from compression and selected any sort option, you are ready to start the process. The **Compress** menu is shown in Figure 15.6. The compression techniques are shown in the top portion of the menu. One and only one of these is always selected, as indicated by a check mark; if you select a different technique, the previously checked one is turned off. The operation won't be started until you select **Begin COMPRESS** when the menu is set up as you want it.

The **Unfragment only** option is the quickest. It rearranges the files on the disk so that each file is located in one contiguous area, but it will probably leave free space in unallocated clusters between files. Any new files you add may be highly fragmented because each will begin in the first free space; when that is filled, the next cluster allocated to the file comes from the next free space. If you use the **Unfragment only** option to save time, use it often. Your disk can get highly fragmented again very quickly.

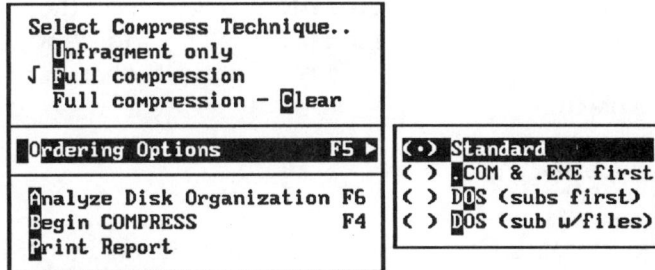

Figure 15.6   Compress Menu

Most of the time, you'll probably want to use **Full compression**. When this is executed, each file is placed so that it is stored in one contiguous area and all free space is moved to the end of the disk. When a new file is added, it starts at the beginning of the free space, so future fragmentation may not occur immediately.

The **Full compression - Clear** option includes the full compression effect, but then data in the free space is completely erased to remove all traces of data files there. This technique can also clear up traces of old subdirectories that may remain. It is useful for additional security so that nobody can find old data on the disk by searching it directly.

File Ordering Options. When you select **Ordering Options**, you can tell Compress how to arrange the actual order of files on the disk. You'll see the pop-up menu from Figure 15.6. It gives you four choices: **Standard, .COM and .EXE first, DOS (subs first),** and **DOS (subs w/files)**.

If you choose **Standard,** Compress can use any order as long as the files fit. Standard file order gets the compression accomplished more quickly than the other options. If you choose **.COM and .EXE first,** all files with extension COM or EXE will be placed first on the disk. This is useful if you have large program files that don't change. It means that later Compress runs will move much more quickly. If the programs do change, they are likely to become fragmented and later runs may take longer.

If you specify **DOS (subs first),** Compress moves all your subdirectories to the front of the disk, followed by all the files in directory sequence. This has the advantage of putting program files near the data files they use, so it can greatly improve performance. If you specify **DOS (subs w/files),** Compress puts each subdirectory just before its files. Whether this organization is more efficient depends on how you use directories.

Analyze Disk Organization

The **Analyze Disk Organization** option checks the fragmentation of free space and the physical arrangement of the directories and files on the disk compared to the selected options and recommends whether or not compression would be useful.

Print Report

You can ask Compress to summarize its actions after it is finished, but you must make the request before starting the compression. If you select **Print Report,** you'll be offered a choice of printing to your default printer or to disk.

If the report is sent to disk, it is named COMPRESS.RPT and stored in the PCTOOLS directory. A typical report might look like this:

```
PC Tools Compress Report

The elapsed time for compression of Drive A was 00:02:42.

Options used:
  Compression Technique : Full Compression
    Compression Order : Standard
  Directory Sort Order : None

Cluster statistics:
    Total clusters : 00354
  Allocated clusters : 00287
    Free clusters : 00063
    Bad clusters : 00004
```

No error information appears in this report. If the compression is interrupted, either at the keyboard or by the Compress program, that won't be noted in the report. The elapsed time shows how long the program ran, even if it was interrupted.

Begin Compress

When you select **Begin COMPRESS**, PC Shell uses your selections on the **Sort** and **Compress** menus and starts the process. First it displays a message box like the one in Figure 15.7. Notice that you are prompted to remove any memory resident programs except for PC Tools programs. It also suggests that

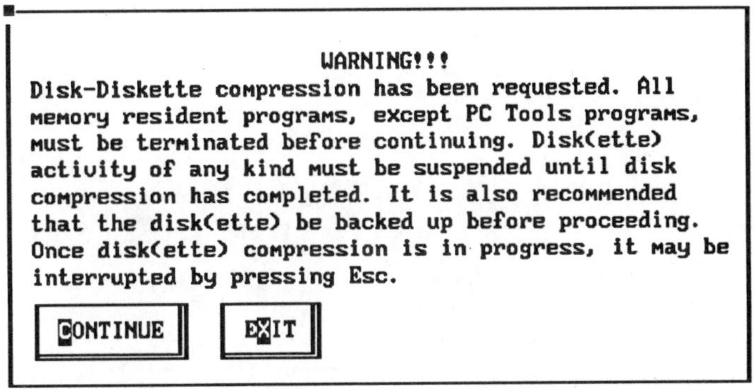

```
                    WARNING!!!
Disk-Diskette compression has been requested. All
memory resident programs, except PC Tools programs,
must be terminated before continuing. Disk(ette)
activity of any kind must be suspended until disk
compression has completed. It is also recommended
that the disk(ette) be backed up before proceeding.
Once disk(ette) compression is in progress, it may be
interrupted by pressing Esc.

    [CONTINUE]    [EXIT]
```

Figure 15.7   Disk Compress Warning

the disk be backed up in advance. If you neglected to do either of these preparatory steps, select EXIT, finish your preparation, and complete the compression later.

Normally, the Compress process updates the FAT after each write process to keep it up to date. It could happen that the process is interrupted by a power failure or other problem, however, leaving you with an unreadable disk. Although this is very rare, having a fairly recent backup is good for peace of mind. Remember that you won't be able to undelete any files or subdirectories that were deleted before compressing after the compression is complete.

The Compress process shows you a disk map in which each cluster is displayed. If you watch during the process, you can see what clusters are being read, where each is rewritten, and how Compress moves free space and files around. You'll also see messages specifying what file is being moved, how many clusters are involved, and when the FAT is rewritten. Depending on the amount of fragmentation and reorganization needed, the process can take a long time. When it is finished, you'll see a message box similar to the one in Figure 15.8. If you compressed a disk that is named in your MIRROR command, run Mirror immediately so you will be able to rebuild the disk in its compressed format; earlier Mirror files won't be valid.

After the process is finished, you'll get a message asking you to reboot. The compression process can make some DOS memory areas invalid, so you should reboot after using Compress, even if you compressed a diskette. First exit Compress normally to the DOS prompt, then reboot. Don't look at any files before you do this; if you're going to have a problem, examining files before rebooting may destroy data.

If the compression fails, you'll see a message giving the reason and telling you what to do next. You should still be able to access all the files after a failed compression, but a disk map won't show that it is compressed. Follow the suggested procedures, then try another compression to try for a clean compress. If the problem involved bad clusters, you should do another surface analysis just before repeating the compress.

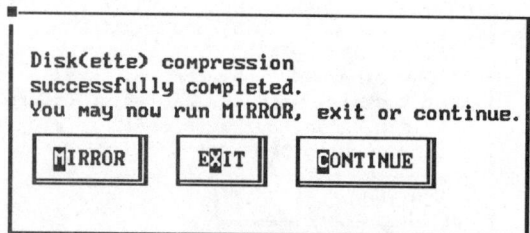

Figure 15.8   End of Compression Message

◆ Try It Out

1. Prepare to compress one of the fragmented diskettes you located. Set the directory sort option to alphabetical and use the standard order and full compression.
2. Analyze the disk organization.
3. Perform the compression, sending a report to disk or to the printer.
4. Reboot if so prompted, then examine the directories to check the order of filenames. Check the disk analysis report to see whether it still recommends compression.
5. If your hard disk is heavily fragmented and has been backed up recently, you might want to compress it at this time.

COMPRESS Command Parameters

The COMPRESS command normally brings up the screen and lets you use the pull down menus. You can use various parameters to modify how the screen comes up. Here is the command format:

```
COMPRESS [d:] [parameters]
```

While the drive name (*d:*) is optional, most people use it with the COMPRESS command to make sure they compress the desired disk. If it is omitted, the current disk is used.

Table 15.1 shows the parameters; you can use one from each group. If you include a compression parameter, the process will begin immediately, without first showing you the Compress screen. If you use only sort or ordering options, they will be set and you will see the screen; you can begin the compression from there.

If you have trouble reading the color display during Compress, you might want to start it with the /BW option, which suppresses colors during the program. If you use **Compress Disk** from the **Applications** menu, you can add /BW to the command by editing the menu entry. If you type COMPRESS at the command prompt, just add /BW to the command.

You can prevent Compress from running Mirror, including asking you to make a choice, with the /NM parameter. If you use the command COMPRESS A:/BW/NM, colors will be suppressed and Mirror will not be run at the end of the process.

You can also include parameters to specify the menu options directly from the command prompt. A different set of parameters applies to sorting the directory, organizing files on the disk, and specifying the type of compression.

There are no command parameters for analysis; this must be done through the menus.

The command COMPRESS C:/OD/SE/SD sets the ordering parameter to DOS with subdirectories first and the sort parameter to Extension and Descending. These values will be set when the Compress screen appears. The command COMPRESS C:/CF/SF/SA sorts the files by name in ascending sequence, then starts a full compression. If you omit a compression parameter, you get the Compress screen. If you omit an ordering parameter, the program assumes standard order. If you omit a sort parameter, the files won't be sorted. If you don't specify ascending or descending but do specify a sort order, they will be sorted in ascending sequence.

Table 15.1   COMPRESS Command Parameters

Program control:
- /BW   Suppress colors
- /NM   Suppress Mirror
- /350   Better resolution with VGA

Compression:
- /CU   Unfragment only
- /CF   Full compression
- /CC   Full compression - Clear

Ordering:
- /OS   Standard
- /OP   Programs (.EXE and .COM first)
- /OD   DOS, subdirectories with files
- /OO   DOS, subdirectories first

Sort:
- /SF   File name
- /ST   Time
- /SE   Extension
- /SS   Size

Direction:
- /SA   Ascending
- /SD   Descending

✧ *Try It Out*

1. If you expect to be using Compress at the DOS prompt, try it out on another fragmented diskette.
2. If you use the /BW parameter to run PC Shell, add it to the **Compress Disk** application.

The next chapter covers the major security features of PC Shell, one of which compresses files so they take less space on disk. If you want to make your files take less space, either to save storage or for some other reason, you'll be especially interested in some of the features of PC Secure.

Chapter 16 | *File Security*

PC Tools includes a program called PC Secure that lets you apply various security and compression features to files and directories. In this chapter you will learn to:

- Specify and use keys
- Encrypt files and directories
- Compress files and directories
- Decrypt files and directories
- Decompress files and directories
- Control what happens to files during security processing

PC Secure

If a file is in ASCII or near-ASCII form, anyone can read it from the disk. A file created by word processing or spreadsheet software can be read by anyone using the same package. Even if you have given a file the Hidden and Read-Only attributes, others can locate the file through PC Shell, change the attributes, and have their way with your data. Binary files can also be interpreted by those who know hex or have the appropriate software to help them make sense of the data.

You may have various reasons to want more security for your files. You may want to make sure no one can read certain information. Various government agencies, primarily the Department of Defense (DOD), have specific requirements about file security. Your company may have its own confidentiality policies. You may want to keep your own data files private until you are ready to share them. If you have to transfer data files to someone else via diskette or telecommunications, you may want to make sure the contents are not easily available to anyone except the chosen recipient.

By applying the features of PC Secure to your files, you can meet even the stringent requirements of the DOD. Others will not be able to get at your data unless they have access to a key you provided when the security was put in force. PC Secure can also compress individual files, so that more fits on a diskette or so that it can be transferred via modem more quickly.

Outside the United States

Federal regulations do not permit the encryption techniques of PC Secure to be included in PC Tools packages distributed outside the United States of America. PC Secure can be used for file compression but not for encryption in those packages. The terms "Encrypt" and "Decrypt" are replaced by "Compress" and "Decompress" in menus and messages if the encryption feature has been disabled.

Types of Security

PC Secure provides file security by using a key that you provide to encrypt a file so that it is unreadable on disk. In fact, the resulting encrypted output file resembles nothing so much as random bits. PC Secure requires the same key to decrypt the file.

Encryption is done by the DES method, which is one of the best pseudo-random-number generators known. The resulting encrypted file is virtually impossible to unscramble without the key, even if you know what was in the file before. Some of the details of how DES encryption is accomplished are included in the PC Tools documentation, but you don't have to know exactly how it works to use it.

The full DES encryption does 16 passes of encrypting, ensuring that the data is thoroughly randomized. This is in accord with Federal DOD standards for encrypted data. If you don't need quite that much security, you can use quick encryption, which does only two passes; this is also virtually impossible to decrypt without the key and PC Secure.

You can ask PC Secure to compress a file during the encryption process, or even to compress without encryption. The compression causes the file to take up less space on disk. The compression process by itself provides some security for a file. It is especially useful in allowing you to transmit files over modems in much less time. When you decrypt a file, PC Secure decompresses it as well if necessary.

A file can be encrypted repeatedly without intervening decryption; it will then have to be decrypted the same number of times. You can effectively compress a file only one time, however. If you compress a file that is already compressed by any method, it will most likely end up larger than it began.

General PC Secure Operation

Before you ask PC Secure to encrypt a file, you set various options telling it what process to use and how to handle the original and encrypted files. Then you ask it to encrypt. PC Secure lets you select the file(s) to be processed. You then supply a key for security. PC Secure copies the file, encrypts it, and compresses the copy according to the options you selected. If you requested that the original file be deleted, PC Secure deletes the original after the encryption is complete, then gives the encrypted file the name of the original. If you want to keep the original file, PC Secure gives the encrypted file the same basic filename with the SEC extension.

When you ask PC Secure to decrypt a file, it asks you to select the file and supply the key. Then it proceeds to decrypt and decompress the file. If the original file wasn't deleted or renamed, PC Secure will encounter a conflict when it tries to change filename.SEC to the original extension. You'll be notified if this happens. You can cancel the decryption process if necessary. If the original file hasn't been changed, you can let PC Secure overwrite it with the decrypted file. But if the original file has been modified since encryption, you would lose the modifications if you let PC Secure overwrite it.

Key Considerations

When you work with PC Secure, you have two different keys to keep in mind. The first time you (or someone at your installation) use PC Secure, a master key or password is requested. This master key can be used to decrypt any file encrypted with PC Secure on your system unless this feature is turned off for an individual file. It acts as a "backdoor" by providing another way into the file if the specific key is lost.

When you start up PC Secure and request the encryption process, you'll be asked for another key; this one is specific to the file you are about to encrypt. This key is the one you'll use most of the time to decrypt the file.

Both the master and file key can be alphanumeric or hexadecimal. An alphanumeric key can range from 5 to 32 alphanumeric characters in length; it is case sensitive. The strings *TROUTwalk*, *troutwalk*, and *TroutWalk* are all different. You must remember the exact position of each character in a key; they are not stored in any way that you will ever be able to locate them if you forget. When you enter an alphanumeric key, an asterisk appears in the dialog box for each character. Then you'll be prompted to enter it again for verification; if you don't enter it correctly the second time, you'll be notified and you have to start over.

If you prefer to use a hexadecimal key, press F9 as indicated on the screen, then type exactly eight hexadecimal bytes of two characters each (A through F and 0 through 9). Case doesn't matter in this string. Since hex strings are notoriously difficult to type, you are allowed to enter the characters in a single string, in two groups of eight characters, or four strings of four, separated by single spaces. The characters display on the screen as you type. Security is affected only if other people can see your screen while you type.

Don't use keys that are easily guessed; for example, don't use words from your name, your department, or your hobby. Select a few unrelated random words or nonsense syllables and join them. Or spell something backwards, transpose letters, or include mixed case letters. Don't be so esoteric you can't enter the key correctly. And keep track of your keys. If you use a different key for each file, you'll probably need a list, but don't attach it to your computer or store it in an accessible file. If your installation doesn't have security guidelines, you'll have to develop your own system for maintaining keys. If you know the master key, you can use it when you forget specific keys. But if you don't have access to it, keeping track of the file keys is even more essential. If you decide to routinely encrypt files on which maximum security is not required, develop a standard key. Then you'll have to keep track only when you use a different key for more security.

PC Secure lets you add even more security to a file when several people use the same copy of PC Secure and all have access to the master key. You can request that the master key be disabled for a given file encryption; then the specific file key must be used to decrypt it. If you do this, be absolutely certain to keep the file key or an unencrypted original, because there is no known way to decrypt a file without the key. If you forget the file key, try the master key. If that doesn't work, you're out of luck unless you have an unencrypted backup copy.

Using PC Secure

You can start PC Secure from the **Applications** menu or by typing PCSECURE at the command prompt. You can use any of three startup options in the command; you can add options through the **Modify Application List** dialog box so they apply to the menu selection or type them following PCSECURE at the command prompt.

The /BW option causes color display to be suppressed, so you see the screens in monochrome. You'll probably need to use this if you use /BW with your PCSHELL, PCBACKUP, or COMPRESS command. Applying the /BW option to PC Shell does not carry through to PC Secure.

If you have a VGA monitor, you may be able to get better resolution with the /350 option. If you use /350 in the PCSHELL command, you'll probably want to use it with PCSECURE as well. Applying /350 to PC Shell does not carry through to PC Secure.

If you need security according to DOD standards, you must use the /G option. This causes PC Secure to completely destroy the original file so there is no chance of recovery from the disk. The area is overwritten seven times, then verified. Using the /G option causes encryption to take longer than usual, of course, but it provides more security. If you are using /G so that your files meet DOD security standards, be sure you also request that the original file be erased. /G has no effect if the original file is left alone.

Start Up

Once you start up PC Secure, you'll see an empty screen with **File** and **Options** menus. If this is the first time PC Secure has been used, the screen includes a dialog box that prompts you to enter a master key or password. Give the master key some thought; remember it can help you decrypt files later on. You'll have to enter the key a second time to verify it. Press F9 if you prefer to enter a hex string. You can't change the master key later; you must use whatever you enter and verify the first time.

PC Secure works much like PC Shell. The function keys are displayed on the command line. You can exit the program by selecting **F3Exit** from the command line or by pressing Esc. In either case, you see the standard exit verification dialog box. The two pull-down menus, **File** and **Options**, work just as on other PC Tools screens.

Figure 16.1 shows the PC Secure **File** menu, which you'll use to start the encryption and decryption processes. Before you use the **File** menu to select and process files, however, check the **Options** menu to make sure all the options are set as you want them.

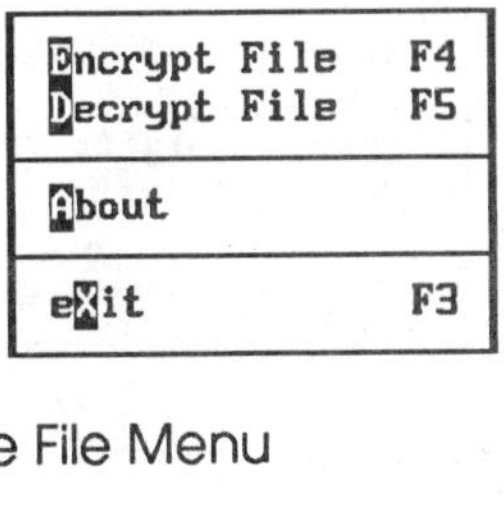

```
Encrypt File    F4
Decrypt File    F5
About
eXit            F3
```

Figure 16.1   PC Secure File Menu

Using the Options Menu

All the options you can set are in the **Options** menu, shown in Figure 16.2. Checks indicate the options that are turned on.

In the upper section you select the type of encryption and compression. Both encryption options cannot be selected at the same time. If you want only compression, turn off both **Full DES Encryption** and **Quick Encryption**. Compression is not appropriate for all files. For example, if the file being encrypted has been compressed by some other method, PC Secure's compression may actually result in a larger file. The extension ARC or PK usually indicates the file is compressed already, as do several others. Most data files benefit from compression, but if you are encrypting a file that has been encrypted before, don't try to compress it again.

The middle section includes options that affect the keys, the output file, and the original file. You can use any or all of the options. **One Key** specifies that the same file key will affect the entire session. Any files you try to decrypt during the session that use that key will be processed automatically. If you don't turn **One Key** on, you'll be prompted to enter a file key for each file you encrypt or decrypt.

Hidden and **Read-Only** specify attributes to be applied to the output file. Of course, you can change those attributes later using PC Shell.

Delete Original File specifies what happens to the original file after the copied file is encrypted. If this option is selected, the original file is deleted and the encrypted file is given the original filename. If **Delete Original File** is not selected, the original file isn't touched and the encrypted file is named *filename*.SEC. If a file with that name already exists, you can decide whether to overwrite the existing file or to abandon the encryption. If you started PC Secure with the /G option to meet government security standards, be sure **Delete Original File** is selected to achieve the required security level.

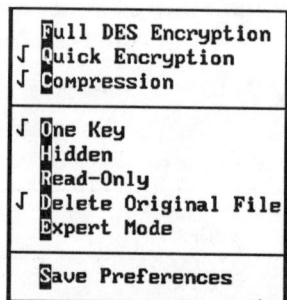

Figure 16.2   PC Secure Options Menu

Expert Mode determines whether or not the master key can be used to decrypt the file. If it is selected, the master key is disabled; it is even more important than usual to remember your file key.

The last option, **Save Preferences**, sets the defaults for PC Secure options to the current values in the **Options** menu. You can still change them for individual files.

✧ Try It Out

1. Bring up PC Secure and examine the screen.
2. Check the **Options** menu and see what defaults are established.
3. Turn on **Full DES Encryption** and **Compression**. Turn off **Delete Original File** and **One Key**.

Encrypting a File

You can encrypt a single file or all the files in a directory. First make sure all the options are set the way you need them. Then pull down the **File** menu, shown in Figure 16.1. It includes only four commands: **Encrypt File, Decrypt File, About,** and **Exit**. The **About** option provides information about the last file encrypted or decrypted during the current PC Secure session. The **Exit** option terminates PC Secure.

When you select **Encrypt File**, you'll see a **File Selection** dialog box for the current directory, like the one shown in Figure 16.3. You must press the Alt key to activate the buttons in this dialog box from the keyboard. To cancel the operation, press Alt-C, for example. You can use the Tab key to highlight the button you want, then press Enter if you prefer.

To encrypt a single file, select it so that its name appears in the text box, then select the ENCRYPT button. You'll see a dialog box asking for a file key,

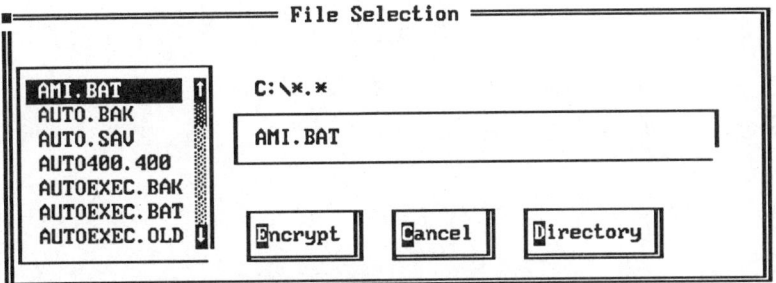

Figure 16.3 File Selection Dialog Box

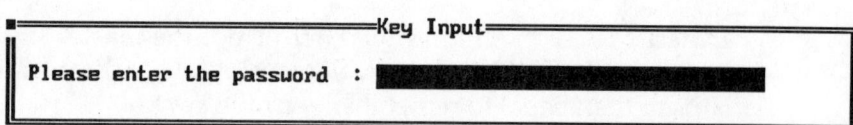

Figure 16.4   Key Input Dialog Box

as shown in Figure 16.4. Here you type a key specific to the file about to be encrypted; the key must be at least five characters long. You'll have to verify it before the encryption begins. This key will have to be entered later when the file is decrypted. If the **Expert Mode** option is turned off (not checked), the master key can be used instead for decryption.

If the **One Key** option is turned on, you will have to enter a key only for the first encryption done during the session. All the files encrypted with the same key can be decrypted with it as well. If you aren't prompted to enter a key for a file, the last key you entered earlier in the session will apply to this file as well.

When any required key has been entered and verified, you see a display like the one in Figure 16.5. This box shows you how the encryption and/or compression is progressing. As the process continues, you can see how many bytes were read and how many written; that represents the amount of space saved in the process. When the process is complete, the final file size appears in the box along with the **Completed** message.

At this point, the file is encrypted. If **Delete Original File** was turned on, the original file has been deleted and the encrypted and/or compressed file has the same name as the original. If the original file was not deleted, the output file has the same basic file name with the SEC extension. If a file already

```
======================= Progress =======================
Encrypting file : PCTRACKR.DEL

[▓▓▓▓▓▓▓                                              ]

Reading 425 K out of 2427 K total

Writing 294 K
```

Figure 16.5   Encryption in Progress Dialog Box

exists with named *filename*.SEC, you will see a message that the **File already exists**. If so, you can choose OK to replace the former file with that name or CANCEL to stop the process and abandon the encrypted file. You can then rename the existing SEC file or the file you are encrypting to eliminate the name conflict.

If you encrypt a file that is already encrypted, turn **Compression** off even if you aren't sure it was compressed earlier; compressing a file that is already compressed invariably results in a larger file. If the file is multiply encrypted, it must be multiply decrypted to restore the original file.

Encrypting a Subdirectory

Encrypting all the files in a subdirectory is similar to encrypting a single file, except that several files are encrypted. You'll be able to decrypt the files as a package or individually, depending on your needs. If the **One Key** option is turned on, you'll have to enter a password only at the beginning of the session. If not, you'll be prompted to enter a specific key for each file to be encrypted.

To start the process, select **Encrypt File** from the **File** menu and enter a key if requested. Select the appropriate subdirectory in the resulting **File Selection** dialog box as shown in Figure 16.3; they are enclosed in square brackets at the end of the file list. When you click or press Enter when a directory is highlighted, you see the files contained in it next. But if you select the DIRECTORY button instead, you can process the files in the directory as an entity.

You'll see a dialog box like the one in Figure 16.6, pointing out that the process will affect more than one file. If you want to affect all files in subdirectories of the selected directory as well, select **Include all subdirectories**. Then choose OK to continue. If some of the files have been encrypted before, they'll be scrambled again. If compression is requested, some of these files may end up being larger than before.

Next you'll see the **Enter Key** dialog box if PC Secure needs a password. After the key is verified, you'll see a standard Encryption **Progress** dialog box

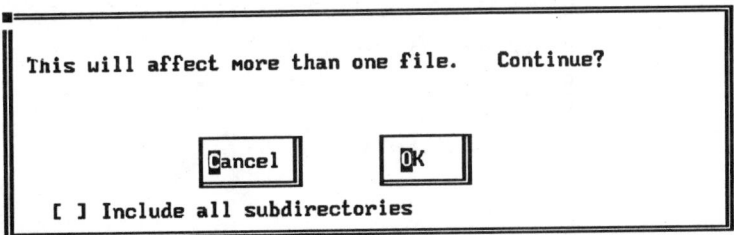

Figure 16.6   Directory Encryption Warning

for the first file. If the **One Key** option is not on, you'll be prompted to enter a password or key for the next file before it is encrypted. If **One Key** is turned on, PC Secure proceeds to encrypt all the files in sequence without your input. The screen keeps you informed about each file, just as during a single file encryption. Finally, you'll see summary information like that shown in Figure 16.7. You can tell how many files were encrypted and how many bytes were saved in the compression process.

Decrypting a File

It isn't necessary to set options before decrypting a file. PC Secure knows what options were in force when it was created. It knows what file key applies to the file and whether or not the master key will work to decrypt it. If compression was done when the file was encrypted, decompression takes place during decryption.

After you select **Decrypt File** from the **File** menu, you see the same **File Selection** dialog box as for encryption. You handle the box in the same way. When the text box contains the name of the file you want to decrypt, select DECRYPT. If necessary, you'll be asked for the password. If **One Key** is in effect and the key is the same as the current key you are using, you won't be asked for it. If the first key you type and the verification don't match, you'll be notified that the keys are not equivalent. If you type the wrong key twice, you'll be notified that you entered the wrong password.

If you select a file for decryption that hasn't been compressed or encrypted by PC Secure, you'll be notified that it is not a PC Secure file. You can then select a different file and try again.

Once decryption begins, you'll see a progress box much like the one for

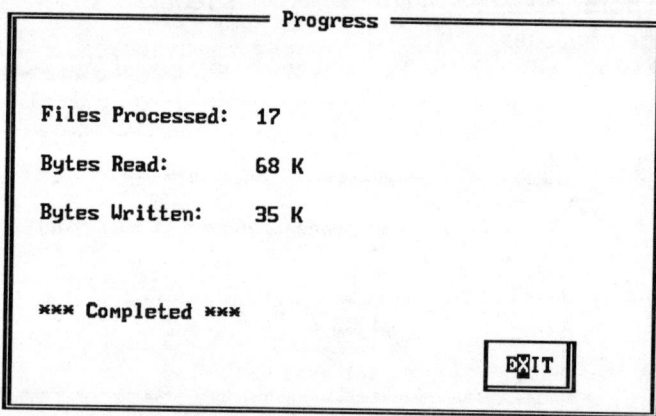

Figure 16.7   Directory Encryption Summary

encryption. You'll be able to see how much is read and how much written to the output file. When the process is complete, you'll see a box like the one shown in Figure 16.8.

Decrypting a Subdirectory

The process of decrypting a subdirectory is much like decrypting a file, except that after you select the subdirectory from the **File Selection** dialog box, you select the DIRECTORY button. You then see a box like the one you see for directory encryption, shown earlier in Figure 16.6. You can include subdirectories here whether or not you included them during encryption. PC Secure then begins decrypting the files, prompting for passwords, if necessary, and showing you its progress as it goes. Some of the files may have been decrypted earlier. That is no problem, since the directory decryption process ignores files that are not encrypted.

Additional Information

You can get information about the last file encrypted by selecting **About...** on the **File** menu. You'll see information like that shown in Figure 16.9. The amount of reduction is shown both in bytes and in percentage.

Security without the Menus

When you enter the PCSECURE command, you can include parameters and a file specification to encrypt or decrypt files without going through the

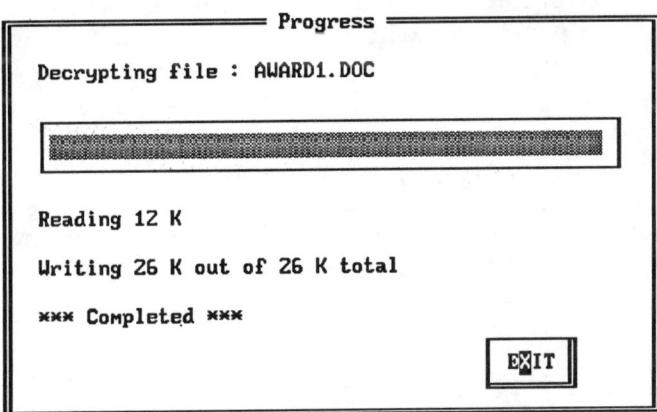

Figure 16.8   Decryption Complete

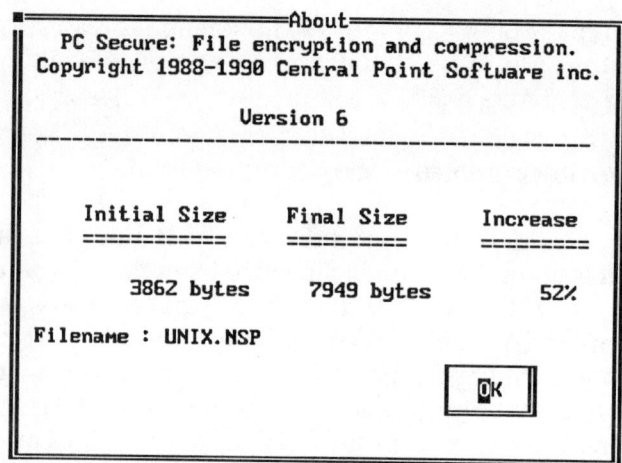

Figure 16.9   Encryption Information Display

menus. In this way, you can also include encryption and decryption in batch files. These are the permitted parameters:

/D   Decrypt the specified file(s)
/F   Fully encrypt the specified file(s)
/Q   Quickly encrypt the specified file(s)
/C   Turn off compression during the encryption process
/P   Prompt for a key
/K[xxx] Use xxx as the key, if provided; don't prompt

You can combine parameters as needed; use uppercase or lowercase and separate parameters with spaces if you wish. You must use /D, /F, or /Q in each command. You must also include either /P or /K. If you use /P, you'll see a prompt to "enter the key" on the screen. You can press Esc to cancel a partially entered password and start a new one. If you use /K with no key, no specific key is used to process the file; be sure not to insert a space between K and the key or PC Secure won't recognize the key next time.

When you work from the command line, no master key is supplied when the file is encrypted, so it can be decrypted only with the specific key. The command PCSECURE /Q /Kruth1 CLAIM.DM requests a quick encryption of the file CLAIM.DM using the key "ruth1". You can decrypt it with the command PCSECURE /D /Kruth1 CLAIM.DM. The command PCSECURE /F /C /Kpadre6 /PROC*.* performs a full encryption with no compression of all files that match the filespec; the same key is used for all the files.

If you use a PCSECURE command in a batch file, you can use the /K parameter to supply the key, since the batch file won't be able to run to completion unattended if it must wait for a key. If the key is to be supplied by the user at the time the batch is run, use the /P parameter instead so the user will be prompted at the appropriate time.

✧ *Try It Out*

1. Select README.TXT in the PC Tools directory and encrypt it using the current settings. Use your first name as the key.
2. Make a copy of README.TXT named NOCOMP. Then change the settings so that no compression is done and encrypt NOCOMP.
3. Check the information about NOCOMP.
4. Decrypt both files. If you have a name conflict, let PC Secure overwrite the original file. Erase README.SEC and NOCOMP.SEC.

You have now completed your study of PC Tools. You should be well prepared to make use of it to streamline your use of your computer.

Appendix: Installation Tips

Installing PC Tools is a straightforward procedure. The documentation instructs you how to get it started for your media and computer type. Then PC Setup takes over and you respond to questions presented on the screen. While the mechanics of entering the answers is explained on the screen, the implications of the choices you are asked to make are not. After you have answered all the questions, PC Setup prompts you to insert disks and performs the installation. In the process, PC Tools modifies your AUTOEXEC.BAT file. The former version is saved as AUTOEXEC.SAV. This appendix treats the various questions in sequence.

Type of Installation. You first have a choice of three types of installation. Choose 1 to copy selected PC Tools files if you are installing the software for the first time or reinstalling from scratch, as when upgrading from an earlier version. Choose 2 to modify an earlier installation of version 6. Choose 3 if you are installing PC Tools on a network.

Monitor Specification. You must select the type of monitor, whether color, monochrome, or LCD. EGA and VGA are included under the color option.

Parts of PC Tools. You choose whether you want to install the DOS shell (PC Shell), the data recovery utilities, the hard disk backup and restore system (PC Backup), and the desktop organizer (Desktop). As you select the parts on screen, a display shows you how much disk space is required if the currently selected parts are all installed. If you are short on space, be selective.

PC Tools Drive and Directory. PC Setup will create a new directory named PCTOOLS if you don't enter a different one. The directory you enter must not yet exist; it will be created automatically. The directory will be created on drive C: unless you name a different drive. The newly created path for PC Tools will be added to the PATH command in your AUTOEXEC.BAT file so that you can enter PC Tools programs from anywhere in the system. You can let PC Setup configure your system or do it yourself after installation.

PC Shell Specification. At this point, you must decide how certain components will operate. PC Shell can be on the disk but not installed; this is the default. If you want it made resident or just brought up automatically, PC Setup will put the appropriate command in the AUTOEXEC.BAT file. If you have changed your mind, you can remove PC Shell from the disk at this time. If you don't choose to remove PC Shell, the installation program renames the DOS utility program FORMAT.COM as FORMAT!.COM and creates a FORMAT.BAT file that will run its own PCFORMAT program.

LapLink Specification. If you transfer files between this system and a laptop computer, you may use LapLink® Quick Connect software. If you have the appropriate software and cable, you'll want to install this feature. If not, choose No.

Mirror Specification. The Mirror program creates special files containing the partitioning and structure of your hard disk. It can also maintain records of files you delete from the hard disk so they can be undeleted easily. You can make it resident or remove it. If you make Mirror resident, PC Setup will put the appropriate command in the AUTOEXEC.BAT file so it runs every time your computer is booted. You can also run it at other times.

PC Cache Specification. The PC Cache program uses a small part of expanded memory (EMS) for saving records of file and directory access. If you don't have expanded memory, it uses 64K of conventional RAM. If you have enough memory, PC Cache can speed up file access; it's most convenient when resident, in which case the command is placed in the AUTOEXEC.BAT file.

Desktop. The Desktop Manager can be included in your AUTOEXEC.BAT file as resident or not. If you just want it available, select No Change here.

Telecommunications Specification. If you don't have a modem or fax connection, you want this part of Desktop removed. If you do, you'll be prompted to configure your equipment at this time, including details about your modem port, whether it uses tones or pulses, and the baud rate. You can also enter your user ID and password for several services such as CompuServe and EasyLink. You can always bypass the configuration and do it through Desktop later. If you have a fax setup, you can specify details about it as well. If you'll be using modem telecommunications in the background while you perform other tasks at the computer, make BACKTALK resident.

Password Protection. At this point, you have answered almost all the questions. To control access to PC Shell, you can enter a password at this point. Then any users will have to enter the password to get into the shell. You can also set a default user level and define a password to protect it. Users will not be able to raise the user level without entering the correct password. You can password protect PC Backup as well. If your computer is used only by you, no password is necessary.

Inserting Diskettes. Now PC Install has all the information it needs. It will prompt you to insert diskettes. Follow the prompts and PC Setup does all the work and modifies your AUTOEXEC.BAT file. If you terminate the process at this point, none of your specifications take effect.

Index

A

Absolute sector, 114
Action macro, 237-239
Action script, 238
Activate macro file, 236
Active list switch, 60
Active memory option, PC Shell, 8
Active window,
  PC Shell, 11, 13
  Desktop, 131
Add
  application, 109-111
  directory, 37-38
  record, database, 180-182
  to-do entry, 163
Additional file information, 86
Alarm, 168
Algebraic calculator, 223-227
Allocation units, 22
Alt-B, background telecommunications, 210
Alt- +
Alt- –
Analysis,
  disk, 299
  file, 301
  in Compress, 298-301
  surface, 301
Analyze disk organization, 304
Append database records, 193-194
Application, controlling, 112
Application mode, 11
Application program parameters, 110
Applications, run, 106
Applications menu, 27
  modify, 108-112
Appointment, find, 170-171

Appointment schedule,
  daily, 161
  date/time, 162
  print, 175-176
Appointment scheduler, 159-176
  automatic display, 161
  customize, 173-175
  start, 160-161
Appointment settings, modify, 173-174
Archive attribute, 84, 276
Arrow keys, 13
ASCII file, 65
  print, 73-75
ASCII protocol, 208
ASCII table, 220-221
Associating files, 111-112
Attribute change, 84
Attribute exclusion, during backup, 282
Attributes, 83-86
  directory, 85-86
  file, 84-85
Auto indent,
  Notepads, 143-144
  Outlines,
Autodialer, 214-217
  configure, 215-216
AUTOEXEC.BAT, 5, 325, 327
AUTOEXEC.SAV, 325
Automatic actions, 168-169
Automatic macros, 245
Automatic undeletion, 41-44
Autosave, 137-138, 175

B

Backdoor to encrypted files, 313
Background mat, 50
Background telecommunications, 210

BACKTALK.EXE, 210, 326
Backup,
  archive attribute, 276
  attribute exclusion, 282
  choosing files, 285
  compression during, 279
  configuration,
    change, 273-274
    set, 271-272
  date range inclusion, 282
  equipment definition, 272
  error correction during, 280
  format during, 280
  history file, 282-283
  include/exclude files, 286-287
  limiting files, 277
  methods, 276-277, 278
  overwrite warning, 283
  procedure, 269-271, 284-288
  reporting, 281
  saved setup, 287-288
  select files for, 284
  speed, 272, 274
  subdirectory inclusion, 281
  tape, 293-294
  time display, 283
  to fixed disk, 271
  to removable device, 271
  user levels, 274
  verify during, 280
Bad clusters, 299
Baud rate, 199
BBS, 200
Begdef, 234
Binary viewer, 28, 51
Block,
  clipboard, 154
  editor, 70
Block operations, 70
Boot sector, 113
BOOTABLE, 253
Bootable disk parameter, 256
Bootable diskette, 253
Browse mode, Databases, 180
Buttons, mouse, 14

C

Calculator,
  algebraic, 223-227
  financial, 227-229
  programmer's, 229-231
  scientific, 231-233
Calendar display, 159, 161
Capture keystrokes, 238-239
Case sensitive, 139
CD command, 5
Central Point Software BBS, 204, 205, 206
Change colors, 132
Change current drive,
  keyboard, 13
  menu, 90
  mouse, 13
Change any hotkey, 220
Change user level, 52
Change window colors, 222
Character field, 178, 181
Check FAX log, 213
Check spelling, 140-142
Choose directories for backup, 277, 285
Clear file, 36
Clicking, 14
Clipboard, 153-157
  commands, 153
  Desktop applications, 153-154
  edit, 155
  non-Desktop applications, 156-157
  view, 155
Close box, 11, 14
Cluster, 113
Clusters,
  adjacent, 295-296
  block out, 266-267
  lost, 264
  undelete, 119-122
Colors, change, 222

Column format, database, 184-185
Command line, 50
Commands, script file, 206-208
Communications parameters, 198-199
Compare backed up files, 288-289
Compare diskettes, 94-95
Compare files, 82-83
COMPARE.RPT, 289
COMPRESS, 295
Compress,
   command line, 307-308
   disks, 295-309
   during backup, 279
   during encryption, 316, 319
   methods, 303-304
   parameters, 307-308
   process, 306
COMPRESS.RPT, 305
Confidence test, backup, 272
Configure Autodialer, 215-216
Configure fax telecommunications, 212
Configure PC Backup, 271-272, 273-274
Context-sensitive help, 16
Control character display, Notepads, 143
Copy,
   between lists, 61
   block, editor, 70
   Clipboard, 153-157
   diskette, 91-94
   editor, 69-70
   file, 31-34
   mouse drag, 34
Copy messages, 34
Copy records from active database, *see* Transfer records
Copy records into active database, *see* Append records
Copy to Clipboard, 154
Correction, during backup, 280
Cover page, fax, 212
COVER.TXT, 213
Create file, 66

Create outline, 149
Create through undelete, 121-122
Cross-linked files, 264, 299
Ctrl-Esc, 5
Ctrl-O, 216
Current date/time, 162
Current drive, change, 90
Cursor,
   Appointment Scheduler, 162
   Databases, 183
   editor, 68
   Notepads, 139
Cut and paste, editor, 69-70
Cut to Clipboard, 154

D
Daily appointment schedule, 161, 165-168
Data bits, 199
Data diskette, create, 251-253
Data recovery utilities, 4
Databases, 177-195
   compatibility with dBASE, 194
   create, 178-182
   cursor movements, 183
   delete record, 182-183
   field editor, 183-184
   field type, 178
   file, 179
   formats, 184-187
   in modem telecommunications, 201
   incompatibility with dBASE, 194
   print, 188-189
   search, 191-193
   sort, 193
   structure, 177-178
      modify, 183-184
   subset, 189-191
   undelete record, 182
   view modes, 180
   view record, 182
Date, in macro, 241
Date field, 179, 181-182

Date range inclusion, during backup, 282
Date/time, 53
dBASE interface, 194-195
Decrypt file, 320-321
Decrypt subdirectory, 321
Decryption, 312
Default hotkey, PC Shell, 5
Default record format, 184
Default viewer, 51-52
Define function keys, 51
Delete
  application, 108
  daily appointment, 168
  directory, 38-39
  file, 35-36
  original file, during encryption, 318
  record, 182-183
  to-do entry, 164
Delete tracking,
  establish, 259-260
  MIRROR, 40
  undeletion, 41-42
Deluxe Option Board, 275
Demote entries, 152
DES encryption, 312
Desktop,
  file selection, 133-134
  installation, 326
  introduction, 127-133
  menu, 130
  start, 129-131
  use through macro, 241
DESTROY format parameter, 258
Dialing
  through Autodialer, 214-217
  through Telecommunications, 202-203
Differential backup, 277
Directory,
  add, 37-38
  decrypt, 321
  delete, 38-39
  encrypt, 319-320
  graft, 87-88
  lost, 265
  maintenance, 37-39
  move, 87-88
  ordering during Compress, 304
  print, 76
  print, restore, 293
  prune, 87-88
  rename, 38
  sort, 57
    during Compress, 302-303
Directory entry, complete, 23
Directory list, rearrange, 56
Directory maintenance menu, 26, 37-38
Disable mouse, 10
Disk,
  analysis, 299
  compare, 94-95
  copy, 91-94
  edit, 118
  format, 249-258
  information, 90-91, 98
  initialization, 251
  map, 100
  menu, 26
  park, 97-98
  rename, 89-90
  search, 96-97, 118
  space, 22
  verify, 95-96
  view, 118
Disk capacity parameter, 256
Disk organization, analyze, 304
Diskfix, 263-267, 300
  drive analysis, 265
  media scan, 264, 266
  revitalize floppy, 266
DISKFIX.EXE, 263
Display format progress, 257
Display sort, 56
DMA controller, 274, 276
DOS command,
  enter, 13

line, 12, 50
  run programs, 106-107
DOS directory, undeletion, 42-44
DOS prompt, 12
DOS security standards, 315
DOS utilities, 4
Double border, 13
DOWNLOAD command, script, 207
Dragging, 14
Drive, change, 90
Drive analysis, Diskfix, 265
Duplex, 198

E

ECHO command, script, 206
Edit,
  application, 109-111
  daily appointment, 168
  disk, 118
  file, 65-70
  hexadecimal display, 115-117
  menu, Databases, 181
  mode, Databases, 180
  Outlines, 149-150
  toggles, Notepads, 143
  to-do entry, 164
Editor, PC Shell, 65-70
  copy, 69-70
  cut and paste, 69-70
Encryption, 312-320
  file, 317-319
  subdirectory, 319-320
Enddef, 234
Equipment for backup, 272
Error correction, backup, 280
Error dialog box, 263
Escape key, 14
EXIT, 14
Exit Notepads, 138
Exit PC Shell, 6, 15

F

F1, help, 13, 16-17

F10, menu bar, 13
F3, Exit, 13
Facsimile transmission, 211-214
FAT, 113
Fax directory, 211
Fax log, 211, 213-214
Fax telecommunications, 211-214
  configure, 212
Field, 177
  define, 178-179
  editor, Databases, 183-184
  length problem, 195
  macro, 242-243
  name, 178
  size, 179
File,
  analysis, 301
  attributes, 84-85
  clear, 36
  clusters, 56
  compare, 82-83
  copy, 31-34
  create, 66
  decrypt, 320-321
  delete, 35-36
  display options, 55-56
  edit, 65-70
  editor screen, 66-68
  encrypt, 317-319
  information, 55, 86
  key, 313
  list filter, 54-55
  list window, 11-12, 46
    run programs, 107
  lists, two, 59-61
  locate, 77-78
  locate menu, 79
  macro, 233
  map, 101, 296-297
  menu,
    Notepads, 136
    PC Shell, 26
  move, 34-35

File *continued*
  ordering during Compress, 304
  print, 73-75
  rename, 30-31
  security, 311-323
  select, 19-22, 54
    Desktop, 133-134
  size, 22, 56
  sort, 56-57
  undelete, 39-44
  unselect, 20, 22, 54
  verify, 81-82
File allocation table, 113
File allocation units, 113
Financial calculator, 227-229
Find, Notepads, 139-140
Find appointment, 170-171
Find free time, 171-172
Find text, 80-81
First character, supplying, 43-44
Fixed field, macro, 242-243
Fixing a disk, 263-267
Floppy disk, revitalize, 266
Footer, Notepads, 144
FOR files, 185
Force directory read, 48
Form letter, database, 186-187
Format,
  accidental, 261-262
  data diskette, 251
  Databases, 184-187
  disk, 249-258
  during backup, 280
  from Applications menu, 253-254
  from command prompt, 255-256
  from disk menu, 251-253
  from file list, 255
  full, 257
  hard disk, 258
  macro, 234-235
  parameters, 256-258
  quick, 257
  simulate, 258
  system disk, 256
  with DESTROY, 258
Formatted print, editor, 74-75
FORMAT!.COM, 250
FORMAT.BAT, 250, 255
FORMAT.COM, 250
Fragmentation, 296
Free space, 296
Free time, find, 171-172
Freeing memory, 49
Full backup, 276
Full compression, 304
Full copy backup, 276
Full format, 256, 257
Function key line, 13, 132
Function keys, redefine, 51

G
Global file rename, 31
Global filename, selecting, 20-21
Goto, viewer, 29
GOTO command, script, 207
Goto line, Notepads, 139
Grafting, 87-88

H
HANGUP command, script, 207
Hangup phone, 203
Hard disk, park, 97-98
Hard disk backup, 4
Hardware control options, Desktop, 131
Hayes-compatible modem, 198
Header, Notepads, 144
Headlines menu, 150
Help, 16-17
  dialog box, 16
  exit, 17
  index, 17
Hercules InColor card, 9
Hexadecimal,
  find, 80-81
  code, 114
  display, 114-115

edit, 115-117
key, 314
manipulation, 113-118
Hhyymmdda.DIR, 271
Hhyymmdda.RPT, 271, 281
Hidden attribute, 83
Hide windows, 46
Hiding database records, 189
History, in compare, 289
History file, 270
   saving copy, 282-283
Holiday settings, modify, 174-175
Home, 13
Hooked vectors, 103
Horizontal view, 46
Hotkey,
   Autodialer, 216
   change option, PC Shell, 9
   change utility, 220
   PC Shell, 4, 5, 15
   problems, 9
   selection, 220
HP-11C, 231-233
HP-12C, 227-229
HP-16C, 229-231

I
IF command, script, 207
Include/exclude files, 277, 286-287
InColor card, 9
Incremental backup, 277
Index, help, 17
Individual key, 313
Information,
   disk, 90-91, 98
   system, 98-99
INPUT command, script, 207
Installation, 325-327

K
Key,
   PC Secure, 313-314
Key names, in macro, 235

Keyboard,
   in editor, 69
   move window, 48
   scroll, 18
   selecting, 20
   shell screen, 13
   size window, 48
KILL, 6, 223

L
LapLink specification, 326
Launch option, 107
Launching files, 28-29
Launching programs, 105
LCD, 9, 275
Learn mode, macro, 238-239
LEARN.PRO, 239
Levels, user, 52
Limit backup files, 277
Limit file list, 54-55
Load format, database, 187
Load notepad automatically, 169
Locate
   across directories, 77-78
   files, 77-78, 96
   text, across directories, 78
   window, 78
Logical field, 179, 182
Lost clusters, 264, 299
Lost directories, 265

M
Macro, 233
   action, 237-239
   automatic, 245
   delay, 244
   editor, 233-246
   file, 233
      activate, 236
   format, 234-235
   functions, 241
   learn mode, 238-239
   nested, 246

Macro *continued*
  printer, 245-246
  script, 234-235
  text-only, 235-236
  use, 237
Main shell screen, 10
Make appointment, 166
Make system disk, 253
Manual dial, 203
Manual undelete, 119-121
Map
  disk, 100
  file, 101
  memory, 101-104
Mark block, 153
Master key, 313, 315
Media surface scan, Diskfix, 264
Memo field, 195
Memory, freeing, 49
Memory, map, 101-104
Memory blocks, 103
Menu bar, 11, 25
Menu entries, modify, 79-80
Menu selection, keyboard, 13
Menus, move window, 48
Menus, size window, 48
Message dialog box, 15
Message line, 13
MIRROR, 39, 258-260
Mirror, rebuild after, 261-262
Mirror installation, 326
MIRROR.FIL, 259
MI.COM, 103-104
Modem, 198
  background, 210
  recording session, 208
  script files, 205-208
  send and receive files, 208-209
  setup, 200
  switches, 215, 217
  telecommunications, 198-210
  using ASCII protocol, 208
  using XMODEM protocol, 209

Modify applications menu entries, 108-112
Modify display, 54-57, 59-61
Modify locate menu, 79-80
Modify PCFormat application, 255
Modify screen colors, 52
Monitor control options,
  Desktop, 131
  PC Shell, 8-9
Monitor specification, installation, 325
Monochrome monitor, 8
More file info, 86
Mouse,
  buttons, 14
  control options,
    Desktop, 131
    PC Shell, 9
  drag, 34-35
  move window, 47
  options, 275
  scroll, 18
  selecting, 20
  size window, 47
  switch buttons, 10
  usage, shell screen, 14
Move,
  application, 108
  appointment schedule, 161
  between lists, 61
  block, editor, 70
  directory, 87-88
  file, 34-35
  mouse drag, 35
  windows, 47-48, 132
Multiple file
  copy, 34
  delete, 36
  lists, 59-61
  rename, 31
Multiple list,
  copy, 61
  move, 61
Multiple phone directories, 202

Index

N
Nested macros, 246
Nondefault drive option, PC Shell, 8
Non-contiguous areas, 296
Note,
   daily appointment schedule, 168
   to-do entry, 164
Notepad window, 134-135
Notepads, 133-146
   edit toggles, 143-144
   exit, 138
   header and footer, 144
   page number, 144-145
   search and replace, 139-140
   setup, 145
   spell check, 140-142
   start, 133
   tabs, 145
Number criteria, Autodialer, 214-215
Numeric field, Databases, 179, 181, 195

O
Offset, 115
OLDPCT, 270
One key for security, 316
One-list display, 59
Options menu,
   PC Backup, 278
   PC Shell, 27, 45-61
Outlines, 147-152
   create, 149
   edit, 149-150
   manipulate, 150-152
Overtype, Notepads, 143
Overwrite warning, during backup, 283

P
Pack Databases records, 182-183
Page Down, 13
Page layout, database, 188
Page length, fax, 212
Page number, Notepads, 144-145
Page Up, 13
Parity, 199
Park disk, 97-98
Partial backup, 284
Partial restoration, 290-292
Partition area, preserve, 260
PARTNSAV.FIL, 260
Password, modem, 201
Password protection, 327
Paste, editor, 69-70
Paste from clipboard, 154
PATH command, 5
PAUSE command, script, 207
PC Backup,
   attribute exclusion, 282
   choosing files, 285
   compare files, 288-289
   compression during, 279
   configure, 271-272, 273-274
   date range inclusion, 282
   error correction during, 280
   format during, 280
   include/exclude files, 286-287
   overwrite warning, 283
   parameters, 275-276
   reporting, 281
   restore files, 290-293
   saved setup, 287-288
   select files for, 284
   subdirectory inclusion, 281
   tape, 293-294
   time display, 283
   user levels, 274
   verify during, 280
PC Cache installation, 326
PC Secure, 311-323
   backdoor, 313
   parameters, 322
   process, 313
   startup options, 315
PC Shell,
   exit, 6, 15
   files, 5
   menus, 25-27

ell *continued*
  dent, 4, 5
  nd-alone, 4
  artup options, 6-10
  BACKUP.000, 270
  BACKUP.CFG, 271
  CBACKUP.EXE, 270
PCBDIR, 293
PCFORMAT.COM, 250, 255
PCSECURE, 314, 321-322
PCSECURE, in batch file, 322-323
PCSHELL command, 5
PCSHELLC.TRE, 7
PCT00000.FIX, 265
PCTRACKR.DEL, 259
Permanent sort, 59
Phone directory, 199, 200
  edit, 201-202
PHONE.TEL, 200
Playback delay, macro, 244
Pointing, 14
Preserve partition data, 260
Preserve system area, 259
PRINT command, script, 207
Print
  daily schedule, 175-176
  database, 188-189
  directory, restore, 293
  directory list, 76
  field names, 188
  file, 73-75
  formatted, 74-75
  Notepads file, 136
Print layout, editor, 75
Print outline, 149
Print to disk, Notepads, 136
Printer macros, 245-246
Printing, Notepads, 135-136
Program launcher, 105
Program memory blocks, 103
Programmer's calculator, 229-231
Promote entries, 152
Pruning, 87-88

Q
Quick file view, 28
Quick format, 257
Quick run, 49
Quickload, 9
Qview, 28

R
Read-only attribute, 83
Rearrange files on disk, 297
REBUILD, 261-262
REBUILD parameters, 262
RECEIVE command, script, 207
Receive files via modem, 208-209
Record, Databases, 177
  delete, 182-183
  search, 191-193
  view, 182
Reformat, accidental, 261-262
Relative sector, 114
Remove screen component, 14
Rename directory, 38
Rename file, 30-31
Rename volume, 89-90, 252
Repair disk, 263-267
Replace,
  editor, 71
  Notepads, 139-140
Report, Compress, 304-305
Report on last encryption, 321
Reporting, after backup, 281
Resident memory
  Desktop, 129
  PC Shell, 7-8
Resident program, 4
Resize box, 11
Resolution, fax, 213
Restore,
  damaged diskette, 292
  disk, 261-262
  files, 290-293
  lost diskette, 292
  no history file, 292

unlabeled diskette, 293
   with exclusions, 291
Revitalize floppy, 266
Re-read directory, 7, 48
Row format, database, 186
Run, quick, 49
Run program automatically, 169
Run programs under PC Shell, 106-108

S
Save configuration file, 48, 112
Save edited file, 68
Save Notepads, 136-137
SCANEXCP.RPT, 301
Scientific calculator, 231-233
Screen colors, 52
Screen layout control, 50
Screen windows, 11
Script,
   macro, 234-235
   macro action, 238
   telecommunications, 205-208
Scroll, Notepads, 139
Scroll bar, 18
Search,
   disk, 96-97, 118
   editor, 71
   in viewer, 29
   Notepads, 139-140
   path, 5
   records, 191-193
Sector, 113, 114
   change, 116-117
   edit, 115-117
   print, 73-74
Security, PC Secure, 311-323
Select block, 69-70
Select file, 19-22
   dialog box, 134
   for backup, 284
   keyboard, 13
   menu, 54
Select records, Databases, 189-190

Select shortcut key, keyboard, 13
Send a fax, 211-214
SEND command, script, 207
Send files via modem, 208-209
Separate incremental backup, 277
Setup,
   save backup, 287
   use backup, 287-288
Setup configuration, 49-53
Shell screen, main, 10
Shortcut keys, 12, 50
Show time usage, 173
Show windows, 46
Size windows, 47- 48 132
Size/move window, 48
Snow suppression, 9
Sort,
   during Compress, 302-303
   multiple lists, 59
   options menu, 56-57
   permanent, 59
   Special menu, 57-59
Sort records, Databases, 193
Special menu, PC Shell, 27
Speed, backup, 272, 274
Spell check, 140-142
Standard mode, 11
Stand-alone,
   Desktop, 129
   PC Shell, 4
Startup options,
   Compress, 307-308
   Desktop, 130-131
   PC Backup, 275-276
   PC Secure, 315
   PC Shell, 6-10
Stop bits, 199
Structure, database, 177-178
Subdirectory,
   decrypt, 321
   encrypt, 319-320
   inclusion, during backup, 281
Subset, database, 189-191

Surface analysis, 301
Switch active window, 13, 47
Switch between lists, 60
Switch mouse buttons, 10
Symbols on appointments, 167
System area, preserve, 259
System attribute, 83
System date and time, 53, 162
System diskette, 253
System info, 98-99
System menu colors, 222

T
Tab, 13, 47
Tabs, Notepads, 143, 145
Tape backup, 293-294
Target directory, 33
Telecommunications installation, 326
Telephone directory, 199-202
Terminate modem connection, 203
TEST format parameter, 258
Text file, 65
Text search, 80-81, 96
Text viewer, 28, 46
Text-only macro, 235-236
Thorough format, 257
Time, in macro, 241
Time delay, macro, 244
Time display, during backup, 283
Time usage, display, 173
To-do
　entry, 163-165
　list, 161
　menu, 163
Tracks, 113
Transfer database records, 193-194
TRANSFER.LOG, 210
Tree window, 11-12, 46
Trigger, 234
Trouble, get out of, 14
TSR programs, 5
Two-drive backup, 271
Two-list display, 59-61

U
Unattached clusters, 299
Undelete,
　create, 121-122
　Databases records, 182
　delete tracking, 41-42
　DOS directory, 42-44
　file, 39-44
　manual, 119-121
　symbols, 41
　using clusters, 119-122
UNDELETE.EXE, 39
Unfragment, during Compress, 303
Unload PC Tools, 222-223
Unmark block, 15
Unselect files, 20, 22
　menu, 54
UPLOAD command, script, 207
User ID, 201
User levels, 52
　backup, 274
User mode display, 11
Utilities menu, 219-223

V
Variable, macro, 242-243
Variables, script, 207-208
Vectors, memory, 103
Verify,
　disk, 95-96
　during backup, 280
　file, 81-82
Vertical viewer, 51
VGA, 8, 9
View
　Clipboard, 155
　disk, 118
　record, 182
　window, 11-12, 46
View window, run programs, 108
Viewer,
　binary, 28, 51
　default, 28

horizontal, 46
　　　searching, 29
　　　specialized, 28, 29
　　　standard, 28
　　　text, 28, 46
　　　vertical, 51
Viewer configuration, 51
Volume, rename, 89-90
Volume label, 89-90 252
Volume label parameter, 257

W
Wait on DOS screen, 50
WAITFOR command, script, 207
Whole words only, 139
Wildcards, 20
Window, 46-47
　　colors, 132
　　move and size, 132
Wordwrap, Notepads, 143

X
XMODEM protocol, 209

Z
Zoom, viewer, 29
Zoom icon, 11
Zoom window, 47